P9-BXY-979

TEACHING the NEXT GENERATIONS

A COMPREHENSIVE GUIDE
FOR TEACHING CHRISTIAN FORMATION

EDITED BY **TERRY LINHART**

Baker Academic
a division of Baker Publishing Group
Grand Rapids, Michigan

© 2016 by Terence D. Linhart

Published by Baker Academic
a division of Baker Publishing Group
P.O. Box 6287, Grand Rapids, MI 49516-6287
www.bakeracademic.com

Printed in the United States of America

All rights reserved. No part of this publication may be reproduced, stored in a retrieval system, or transmitted in any form or by any means—for example, electronic, photocopy, recording—without the prior written permission of the publisher. The only exception is brief quotations in printed reviews.

ISBN: 978-0-8010-9761-4

Library of Congress Cataloging-in-Publication Data
Names: Linhart, Terry, 1964– editor.
Title: Teaching the next generations : a comprehensive guide for teaching Christian formation / edited by Terry Linhart.
Description: Grand Rapids : Baker Academic, 2016. | Includes bibliographical references and index.
Identifiers: LCCN 2016016461 | ISBN 9780801097614 (paper)
Subjects: LCSH: Spiritual formation. | Christian life—Study and teaching. | Christian education.
Classification: LCC BV4511 .T43 2016 | DDC 268—dc23
LC record available at https://lccn.loc.gov/2016016461

Unless otherwise indicated, Scripture quotations are from The Holy Bible, English Standard Version® (ESV®), copyright © 2001 by Crossway, a publishing ministry of Good News Publishers. Used by permission. All rights reserved. ESV Text Edition: 2011

Scripture quotations labeled NIV are from the Holy Bible, New International Version®. NIV®. Copyright © 1973, 1978, 1984, 2011 by Biblica, Inc.™ Used by permission of Zondervan. All rights reserved worldwide. www.zondervan.com

Scripture quotations labeled NLT are from the Holy Bible, New Living Translation, copyright © 1996, 2004, 2015 by Tyndale House Foundation. Used by permission of Tyndale House Publishers, Inc., Carol Stream, Illinois 60188. All rights reserved.

In keeping with biblical principles of creation stewardship, Baker Publishing Group advocates the responsible use of our natural resources. As a member of the Green Press Initiative, our company uses recycled paper when possible. The text paper of this book is composed in part of post-consumer waste.

16   17   18   19   20   21   22   7   6   5   4   3   2   1

In memory of Dr. Eugene Carpenter (1943–2012)
Old Testament scholar, mentor, colleague,
and dearly missed friend
—Terry Linhart

132366

Contents

Acknowledgments   vii

Introduction   ix

Section One   Core Concepts   1

1. The Contribution of Teaching to Discipleship   3
   Allen Jackson

2. Developing a Theology of Education   14
   Jeff Keuss

3. A Scriptural Basis for Teaching   25
   Ron Belsterling

4. The Essence of the Life of a Teacher   34
   Bob MacRae

5. Recognizing the Importance of Educational Philosophy   44
   Mark Cannister

6. The Shape of Human Knowledge and Christian Ministry   56
   Andrew Root

Section Two   Influences That Shape Learning   65

7. How People Develop Their Thinking   67
   Barrett McRay

8. Multiple Intelligences and Learning Styles   86
   Karen Jones

9. Faith Formation with Others   100
   Sharon Galgay Ketcham

10. Motivation and Ministry   112
    David Rahn

11. Why Culture and Diversity Matter   124
    Ginny Olson

Section Three   Curricular Implications for Teaching   135

12. Curriculum and Teaching   137
    Terry Linhart

13. Teaching Children   152
    Scottie May

14. Teaching Adults   164
    Amanda Drury

15. How Families Shape the Faith of Younger Generations   176
    Brenda A. Snailum

16. God's Equipping Pattern for Youth and Young Adult Ministry   187
    Ken Castor

17. Toward a Curriculum Theory of Educational Technology   199
    Mark Hayse

Section Four   Methods for Christian Teaching   209

18. Teaching the Bible So Young People Will Learn   211
    Duffy Robbins

19. The Value of Discussion   229
    Troy W. Temple

20. Teaching Large Groups   239
    Jason Lanker

21. Using Narrative to Invite Others into the Story of God   249
    James K. Hampton

22. Learning through Simulations   259
    Karen McKinney

23. Teaching to Change Lives, Outdoors   272
    Doug Gilmer

Section Five   Managing Teaching for Maximum Impact   285

24. The Importance of Evaluation   287
    Kerry Loescher

25. Equipping Others to Teach   301
    Robert Brandt

26. Technological Tools for Dynamic Christian Teaching   313
    Freddy Cardoza

Contributors   324
Scripture Index   329
Subject Index   332

Acknowledgments

This book is a credit to my colleagues who have given of their time and expertise to write its chapters. These scholars and leaders are model teachers, and their friendship and graciousness have made this a delightful process.

A very special thanks to Bob Hosack and the staff of Baker Academic, who have provided the very best advice and input, wrapped in patience and kindness, at every step along the way. Eric Salo provided flawless editorial oversight and wise counsel, while Rachel Klompmaker managed the project with grace. The Baker team has been delightful, and those of us who lead and teach in this field are grateful to Baker Publishing for its consistent leadership and support of Christian ministry and higher education.

I am especially indebted to Melisa Blok for her editorial assistance and advice throughout the entire project. Mahala Rethlake provided her usual proficiency in formatting and editing. These two have bright futures ahead of them in writing and publishing.

Thanks to Ginny Olson, Jon Swanson, Mark Cannister, Jim Hampton, David McCabe, Sharon Ketcham, and Cristian Mihut for their guidance and input. With each book project I complete, I am more amazed and thankful for Mark Root of Bethel College's Bowen Library for his reference expertise and his ability to obtain any book, dissertation, or journal article in record time. This project would not have been possible without the support of my fellow faculty members and the administration at Bethel College (Indiana), a vibrant, Christian learning community.

Finally, thanks to Jessica Baylis, Alissa Bremer, Crystal Cruz, Cole Farlow, Aaron Grosse, Tim Horton, Devin Hubbard, Ethan Klein, Calli McGrath, Phillip Parry, and Lindsay Ziegler for being the "pilot class" for this book.

This project would not be possible without the supportive communities of the Society of Professors in Christian Education (http://www.spceonline.org) and the Association of Youth Ministry Educators (http://www.aymeducators .org). Each of these organizations nurtures, supports, and champions Christian education, including youth and children's ministry, as a focus of study in Christian colleges and seminaries across North America.

Introduction

Any casual observation of young children reveals that people are naturally created by God to grow and learn. The world of the child is a natural place of inquisitiveness, discovery, and wonder, marked by questions of "why?" and "how?" and "why?" again . . . and again. Learning is at the forefront of each day's activity.

Somewhere along the way to adulthood, it seems that curiosity and a desire to learn take the backseat to other pursuits. Adolescents can describe school as "boring" or irrelevant, and newspaper headlines question the value of college education based on rising cost and potential earnings. Other critics suggest that consumerism and a media-saturated world full of bite-sized information and search engine expediency produce less-intelligent generations.[1] The most common question, "Is there Wi-Fi?" shows the role that technology now plays in how we all learn and interact with our world.

Perhaps we still are curious and really do want to learn.

It is into the dynamic and fluid context of young people that Christian teachers step, charged with ministering to the next generations and helping them grow in spiritual maturity and in wisdom and understanding of the Christian faith (Rom. 12:2; 2 Pet. 3:18). Rather than throwing up their hands in despair at changes and challenges, committed Christian workers strive toward greater understanding of the teaching dynamic and its role in Christian spiritual formation. Rather than settle for what is minimum

---

1. For instance, Mark Bauerlein, *The Dumbest Generation: How the Digital Age Stupefies Young Americans and Jeopardizes Our Future (Or, Don't Trust Anyone Under 30)* (New York: Tarcher, 2009).

or average, skilled teachers work to discover greater levels of effectiveness in engaging the next generations of learners.

The church needs good teachers more than ever, teachers who

- understand spiritual formation,
- know how learning takes place for all ages,
- can employ insights from important theologies and theories,
- possess a ready repertoire of creative methods,
- are committed to prayer, and
- have a history of seeing the Holy Spirit use their teaching for spiritual transformation.

The truth is that young people are still wired to learn. They do wonder about important questions, and they still engage in what is meaningful and relevant. Perhaps part of the problem today is not with the learners but is on the side of the teaching. It certainly feels like at no other time in recent history has it been as important for Christian teaching to be effective, engaging, and of excellent quality.

Teaching for Spiritual Growth

The Christian teacher works to see spiritual growth in the lives of those he or she teaches. He wants others to know Jesus (Phil. 3:10) through salvation (Rom. 10:9–10) and develop a love for God (Luke 10:27; John 14:15–23) and an understanding of his Word (Ps. 1:1–3; 1 John 2:5). She wants to see students translate trusting faith and belief into loving action toward others (Matt. 5:43–48; John 3:34) with mercy and grace that transcends and overcomes social divisions. Christian teaching participates in God's work by helping learners grow in wisdom, stature, and favor with God and with others.[2]

Perry Downs defines the goal of Christian teaching as "the ministry of bringing the believer to maturity in Jesus Christ."[3] This helpful definition is worth a closer look.

Maturity. The parallels between developmental and spiritual growth were obvious to the New Testament writers (1 Cor. 14:20; Eph. 4:11–14; Heb.

---

2. This is taken from Luke 2:52, a description of Jesus's growth between the ages of twelve and thirty. It has been used by Youth for Christ USA to form the "balanced life concept" for their Campus Life teaching curriculum.

3. Perry G. Downs, *Teaching for Spiritual Growth: An Introduction to Christian Education* (Grand Rapids: Zondervan, 1994), 16.

5:12–14). In the same way that a person grows physically, faith grows from greater experience, challenge, conviction, and understanding. In ministry settings, understanding gets less focus as a goal than the first three. Yet Paul knew of the role that it played: "We have not ceased to pray for you, asking that you may be filled with the knowledge of his will in all spiritual wisdom and understanding, so as to walk in a manner worthy of the Lord, fully pleasing to him, bearing fruit in every good work and increasing in the knowledge of God" (Col. 1:9–10). If understanding is important to maturity, then teaching is an important emphasis within Christian ministry.

In Christ. It is through Christ's presence that we are empowered to participate in a teaching ministry so that others may be transformed by his power. Believers participate in a new reality in Christ (2 Cor. 5:17) through the formation (nurture) of faith based on truth (knowledge) (Rom. 12:1–2), a truth centered on Jesus and his life, death, and resurrection (1 Cor. 15:14). The transformation through the Holy Spirit produces the virtues and fruit (Gal. 5:22–25) that reflect Christ's presence in our lives.[4]

The ministry of bringing. Christian teaching is not reduced to mere transfer of information; it plays a vital role in bringing to spiritual maturity. Christian teaching is part of the discipling process, an essential response to Christ's commission (Matt. 28:18–20). Teaching, then, is part of our ultimate purpose: to make disciples.

However, just because teaching is happening doesn't mean that learning, especially a "bringing to maturity," follows. The writer of Hebrews acknowledged as much, challenging readers to "move beyond the elementary teachings about Christ and be taken forward to maturity" (Heb. 6:1 NIV). It's a bit startling to think that we can be teaching, even about Christian topics, and not be serving our learners' growth at all. Teaching in a way so that we "bring" people to spiritual maturity in Christ seems to demand something from those who teach. This book intends to help readers faithfully fulfill those requirements and teach in ways where they regularly bring believers to maturity in Jesus Christ.

Our Challenge

We stand here in a new century with a significant challenge before us. Recent research suggests that the church is losing young adults, even those who "grew up" in the church. David Kinnaman says young adults leave in

---

4. There are quite a few lists of virtues in the New Testament: Rom. 12:9–21; 13:8–14; Eph. 4:25–5:10; Col. 3:1–17; 1 Thess. 5:12–22; 1 Tim. 3:13–4:4; and 2 Pet. 1:5–7.

part because the church has failed to help them think about and answer difficult questions.[5] Similarly, the largest study on the religiosity of youth in America showed that church teens were surprisingly inarticulate about their faith. When researchers posed questions about what they believed, young people said it was the first time that an adult had asked them about their beliefs, and they seemed unable to answer basic questions about the central doctrines of the Christian faith.[6] Though there is a lot of teaching in the church, could it be that there is not as much learning?

We need to revitalize the task of teaching the next generations, but not with default, "the way we've always done it" approaches or with an "anything goes" pragmatic recklessness that misses the mark in helping students grow in maturity. The next generation needs teachers—*engaging* teachers, *wise* teachers, *joyful* teachers, and *well-studied* teachers. Young people need to be engaged deeply in relevant ways beyond elementary teachings. They need a "thought-full" faith rooted in Scripture, empowered by the Spirit, and connected to everyday realities to face contemporary challenges, historical tensions, and the difficult questions.

This Book

This text champions the cause and goals of Christian teaching in ministry to young people and provides an introduction to teaching in all sorts of ministry contexts. The first section of the book explores core concepts that explain the focus and purpose of Christian teaching. The second section presents forces that give shape to teaching and learning contexts. It is critical for the Christian teacher to have a ready understanding of how developmental, social, mental, and cultural dynamics affect spiritual growth. The third section builds on the previous chapters and makes application to curricular theory as it relates to ministry across the earlier years of life. Given the current discussions and concerns, extra attention has been given to family and intergenerational ministry.

The fourth section helps readers grow in their methodological expertise and skills. Teaching the Bible, discussing in a group, and speaking in front of a large group are primary to most ministries. However, effective teaching and learning are not reserved to formal teaching times given the active and

---

5. David Kinnaman. *You Lost Me: Why Young Christians Are Leaving the Church . . . and Rethinking Faith* (Grand Rapids: Baker Books, 2011).

6. Christian Smith and Melina Lundquist Denton, *Soul Searching: The Religious and Spiritual Lives of Teenagers* (Oxford: Oxford University Press, 2005).

hyper-connected lives of today's young people. Trips, small groups, camps and retreats, and one-on-one conversations have been shown to be among the most effective forms of Christian ministry. This book uses simulation games and outdoor learning as just two examples of creative teaching methods.

The book concludes with three chapters on often-ignored topics that are essential to effectiveness. The first chapter in this section discusses evaluation—of our own teaching and of students' learning—as fundamental to our ongoing teaching success. The second chapter focuses on developing volunteers as teachers, a common task that often proves difficult. The final chapter provides teachers with numerous technological tools that offer enormous creative and dynamic opportunities for Christian teachers.[7]

I am thankful that you are joining us on the journey to be the best teacher you can be, one whom God uses to lead others to faith in Christ, to see them grow in spiritual maturity, and then to watch as they go out and do the same because they are well prepared in mind, heart, and practice. May God bless you as you read, study, learn, and grow. Let's get started!

Terry Linhart

---

7. In the coming years, perhaps someone will pioneer an effective and engaging, technologically aided learning environment.

SECTION ONE

CORE CONCEPTS

Anytime we teach, there is an implicit understanding at work about teaching's function and purpose. This first section highlights the theological, biblical, and philosophical purposes that undergird Christian teaching. The effective Christian teacher is conscious of the goals and strategies of teaching, and the reasons for them. In an information-driven age, regularly described as postmodern or pluralistic, the importance of clarity on these topics is as acute as ever. Christian teaching can otherwise lose its focus, misunderstand its purpose, and fail to serve the next generation's spiritual growth.

These six chapters are starting points toward a clear philosophy of Christian education, toward a biblical basis for our work as Christian teachers, and toward faithful participation in the mission that Christ has given to the church. Each chapter acts as an introduction to its given topic, with additional resources provided at the end of each chapter for those who want to go deeper.

The section concludes with a unique chapter about discovering a middle way between existing cultural and philosophical tensions that shape our teaching. The story contained in this chapter, meant to be read in full, uses two extreme examples to stimulate our critical thinking and to create greater clarity about our role and goal as Christian teachers.

1

The Contribution of Teaching
to Discipleship

ALLEN JACKSON

People come to faith in Christ through a wide range of means. One person can come to faith simply because a church bus picked him up as a child in his neighborhood, and another by listening to a person speaking on a sidewalk. Many come to faith because of the intentional conversation of a friend or family member, while others do so through a group program at a church, camp, or conference. The moment of salvation begins a new journey of spiritual growth, a pathway toward spiritual maturity that needs teachers along its way to help, inform, and guide.

This pathway (or process) is called discipleship, a "lifelong journey of obedience to Christ which transforms a person's values and behavior, and results in ministry to one's home, church, and in the world."[1] Dallas Willard says that discipleship is a form of spiritual formation, "the process of shaping our spirit and giving it definite character. It means the formation of our spirit is in conformity with the Spirit of Christ."[2] It is alongside this pathway and process that Christian teaching plays its role, a forming and shaping

1. Barry Sneed and Roy Edgemon, *Transformational Discipleship* (Nashville: LifeWay, 1999), 3.
2. Dallas Willard, *The Great Omission: Reclaiming Jesus' Essential Teachings on Discipleship* (New York: HarperCollins, 2006), 53.

Perhaps our greatest lessons of discipleship happen through informal interactions rather than a formal program. I remember learning to hang sheet rock on a mission trip with a youth group. The man who was supervising my team owned a drywall company, and he had agreed to try to mold a group of teenagers into expert hangers, floaters, and tapers. I am still okay at drywall, but I remember distinctly forming my theology of worship on that trip. I remember him talking about why he dressed up for church and how he paused before entering the worship space at our church to prepare for worship by clearing his mind and confessing his sins. I remember him telling me to think carefully about each lyric of each song that I would sing so that my words of worship would not be empty.

process focused on the nature and direction of a person's transformational journey with the Triune God.

Teaching is part of a collective discipleship process, a combination of relationships, formal events, intentional conversations, and personal disciplines (i.e., prayer, Bible study, and reflection). Perry Downs says that Christian education "begins where evangelism ends, helping believers grow in their faith."[3] Spiritual growth, though, requires more than a transfer of information; it is measured in development toward Christlikeness, a process where the formal and informal lessons intersect and fuel believers to keep moving toward maturity.[4]

Good teaching is rarely disconnected from a strong relationship between teacher and listener. This support of growth is a different educational focus than just teaching "stuff." The goal is the maturation of the students, and that requires diverse approaches to teaching methods and objectives. Most can recall very few of the specific lessons they heard in youth group, church, or similar programs. They were important lessons in the moment. Occasionally we may recall a key story or bullet point, but most teaching that contributes to maturity is tied to the relationships that surround it.

Before we discuss teaching, learning theories, and techniques, we have to establish the discipleship roots for the method and practice of Christian teaching. We cannot undervalue teaching's role in discipleship, as if spiritual growth requires no outside input or guidance. Neither can we overvalue

3. Perry G. Downs, *Teaching for Spiritual Growth: An Introduction to Christian Education* (Grand Rapids: Zondervan, 1994), 16.
4. Nick Taylor, "Spiritual Formation: Nurturing Spiritual Vitality," in *Christian Education: Foundations for the Twenty-First Century*, ed. Michael J. Anthony (Grand Rapids: Baker Academic, 2001), 91.

teaching, equating spiritual maturity with knowledge or something we create versus a work of God within. When we take a balanced approach to teaching's role in league with the work of the Holy Spirit, then we are able to better see how teaching plays a part in that maturation process.

As you read this chapter, reflect on these questions:

1. What part has teaching played in your spiritual growth over the last ten years?
2. If you were asked how discipleship and teaching worked together, what would your answer be?
3. What part did teaching play in Jesus's discipling ministry?
4. In the context of teaching and discipleship, what do you think is more important: good content or good process? What are the pros/cons of that position?

While it is a false distinction to try to identify which relational activities are teaching and which are discipling, *a discipler is a teacher, and a Christian teacher is a discipler*. Jesus's ministry exhibited the way teaching and discipleship are indistinguishable from each other. Jesus was often called teacher (John 13:13) or something similar.[5] Even the Jewish authorities viewed his ministry as that of a teacher (Matt. 8:19). Though teaching was a significant part of his ministry, the relationships he had with his followers provided the "living model" for his message. Formal moments of teaching, combined with the informal life together, produced a group of disciples who were "fully trained" (Luke 6:40–41) to carry on Christ's commission.

We often think of teaching taking place in a room that feels like a classroom, which makes us think about school. Imagine what a scene from the Bible may have looked like if that was taken to an extreme:

> Then Jesus took His disciples up to the mountain,
> and gathering them around Him, He taught them saying:
> "Blessed are the meek
> Blessed are they that mourn
> Blessed are the merciful
> Blessed are they who thirst for justice
> Blessed are you when persecuted
> Blessed are you when you suffer
> Be glad and rejoice, for your reward is great in Heaven!"

5. See, e.g., John the Baptist in Mark 9:38–39, Simon Peter in Luke 7:40–41, and Nicodemus in John 3:2.

Then Simon Peter said, "Do we have to write this down?"

And Andrew said, "Are we supposed to know this?"

And James said, "Will we have a test on this?"

And Philip said, "I don't have any paper."

And Bartholomew said, "Do we have to turn this in?"

And John said, "The other disciples didn't have to learn this!"

And Matthew said, "When do we get out of here?"

And Judas said, "What does this have to do with real life?"

Then one of the Pharisees present asked to see Jesus' lesson plans and inquired of Jesus, "Where are your terminal objectives in the cognitive domain?"

And Jesus wept.[6]

> "Equipping by its very nature is not just teaching skills but holistically growing people up in Christ's way of living and loving so that the whole body ends up increasing in maturity in him."
>
> —Julie A. Gorman, *Community That Is Christian*, 2nd ed. (Grand Rapids: Baker Books, 2002), 17.

The humor of the story is clear to us now; Jesus was trying to make disciples through teaching eternity-altering truth. The disciples in the story missed it because they had established patterns of just getting by with right answers or being fearful of a test, while Jesus was teaching to shape their lives and equip them for a mission.

A Holistic Discipleship

Author James Stewart identifies five principles from Jesus's ministry that can guide our own teaching.

1. Jesus's teaching was authoritative (Mark 1:27). His teaching was authenticated by his life and his words. His example and his content were not suspect or shallow but gave credibility to his message.

2. Jesus's teaching was not authoritarian (John 6:60–69). He did not impose or force his message on his hearers but plainly presented the costs of discipleship, encouraged those who listened to respond, and then allowed individuals to confront the truth.

3. Jesus's teaching encouraged people to think (Matt. 16:13–15). The use of parables and questions did not provide easy answers or require rote

6. "The *Other* Sermon on the Mount," http://webserv.jcu.edu/bible/Humor/MountSermon .htm. I first saw this in Peter L. Stenke's book, *How Your Church Family Works: Understanding Congregations as Emotional Systems* (Guilford, CT: Rowman & Littlefield, 2006). Most youth teachers will recognize some of their students somewhere in the parable!

responses. Jesus encouraged his followers to think for themselves and respond after carefully considering the truth.

4. Jesus lived what he taught (John 8:46). Jesus demonstrated how he wanted his disciplers to live, serve (John 13), and love (John 17) others. The "exampling" approach to Jesus's teaching supported his content in such a way that the disciples saw what he meant and could readily follow that example in their ministry.

> It is easy to read quickly over Stewart's five principles and assume that we understand them. If you look them over again and think about teachers who have struggled with them, it becomes clear that these are not automatic. In fact, if we are honest, one or two of them might be principles that we need to work on.

5. Jesus had a love for those he taught (John 15:12). This was made clear in his presence with the disciples and his relationship with them.[7]

When an educated young man (a lawyer or teacher of the law) approached Jesus and asked him about eternal life, Jesus referred to the law.

> And behold, a lawyer stood up to put him to the test, saying, "Teacher, what shall I do to inherit eternal life?" He said to him, "What is written in the Law? How do you read it?" And he answered, "You shall love the Lord your God with all your heart and with all your soul and with all your strength and with all your mind, and your neighbor as yourself." And he said to him, "You have answered correctly; do this, and you will live." (Luke 10:25–28)

Jesus's response reflects a holistic understanding of learning. You should love God in the cognitive domain (your mind), the affective domain (your heart and soul), and the psychomotor domain (your strength). A discipler is interested in learning of the head, the heart, and the hands, illustrating the three learning domains. So, for instance, when we memorize Scripture (cognitive), it can lead to a deeper appreciation for the richness of the text (affective), which then leads to a more confident willingness to obey (psychomotor) what the Scripture teaches. Whether these learning objectives were intentional or incidental, they still lead to a mature faith.[8]

If the goal of teaching for discipleship is to present some "mature in Christ" (Col. 1:28–29), then our teaching should shape a maturity that is reflected in what students think, feel, and do. We want our students to think and not just know. As we teach, we want them to move beyond words to discover the meaning behind the words. We want them to have more

---

7. James Stewart, *The Life and Teaching of Jesus Christ* (Nashville: Abingdon, 2000), 64–71.

8. There are other examples of Christian discipleship and teaching; this is just one. Some believers have disabilities that make memorizing Scripture difficult.

than a "bumper sticker" theology where they can say short catch phrases but can't explain what they mean with any structure or connection to the Christian faith.

To that end, Dr. Rick Yount says that teachers need to do the following.

- *Emphasize concepts more than words.* We often use words or phrases and assume that our students know what they mean, and many words in Scripture can have several meanings. Teaching for meaning helps students to think and study on their own, an important skill in discipleship.
- *Ask more questions and give fewer answers.* Students are invested when they have to answer a question, and they often develop some additional questions of their own.
- *Pose problems in our teaching versus giving reasons.* Problem-posing creates tension that leads to strength in thinking and conviction. It also inoculates against dependency.
- *Give examples versus facts.* There is no better way to connect deep truth to contemporary realities than by using examples, stories, and illustrations.[9]

Perhaps a helpful word instead of *teaching* is *preparing.* We often hear the word *equip,* but teaching to equip others sometimes looks no different from content-only approaches to teaching. And at the end of the process, the students aren't ready to do much of anything. Being prepared means that we're poised, ready, trained, and capable. So what is needed then for our students to be prepared as disciples? What does that require of how we teach?

Why Do We Teach?

Why do we teach the next generations? In ideal situations, a father or mother would answer that in various ways.[10] Parents teach their children to prepare them for the coming time when the children will be making decisions on their own. Parents teach because they are compelled by love for their sons and daughters, and they have a sense of urgency to share what they know about some task or challenge their children face. Most parents want to see

9. Adapted from William R. Yount, *The Teaching Ministry of the Church* (Nashville: B&H, 2008), 197–99.

10. Not all have loving parents who are present, and not all parents have children who heed their parents' instruction or example.

their children grow from an infant to a mature adult, a transformation that takes time, endurance, and intentionality.

With similar values, we teach the next generation. If we are living authentic lives as disciples of Jesus, then we have something we *must* share; and we do so because we love others. We share content (i.e., kingdom principles) through process (relationships combined with intentional conversation) in a (hopefully) natural way. Teaching is so natural in the disciple-making process that the intentionality of Jesus's interactions with the disciples (the Twelve and others) is overwhelming. For his curriculum, he utilized setting (have you caught any fish?), props (like a fig tree), local knowledge (will you give me a drink of water?), and traditions (you have heard it said). For Jesus as a teacher, *discipleship*—life in relationship with the Twelve and others—was the curriculum of the kingdom.

The apostle Paul was a teacher who understood the importance of presence, relationship, and example. Paul repeatedly invites believers to follow his example as he follows Christ (1 Cor. 4:16; Phil. 3:17; 4:9; 2 Thess. 3:7–9; Titus 2:7). He reminded the Thessalonians of his demeanor and example, not being vain or deceitful but rather taking a gentle and patient posture (1 Thess. 2). Perhaps Paul's encouragement to Timothy, "And the things you have heard me say in the presence of many witnesses entrust to reliable people who will also be qualified to teach others" (2 Tim. 2:2 NIV), serves as a strong example for how relationship and discipling are interwoven. There are four groups of disciples in this verse: Paul, Timothy, reliable people,[11] and others. Paul taught Timothy, who is asked to repeat and teach reliable people who will in turn do the same with others. Disciples are replicated through teaching and influence.

A caution might be in order when considering the discipleship relationship and such intentional teaching. According to theologian Andrew Root, if we are in relationship with students so that we might teach them or influence them, we are at risk of being disingenuous. Commenting on the ministry he had with neighborhood adolescents in Los Angeles, he says,

> I had to be honest with myself: I was trying to influence them. I was trying to get them to accept, know, trust, believe, or participate in something, believing it was best for them, believing it would fix them. But my desire to influence them was keeping me from really *being with them*—in a truly relational way. As my wife had reminded me, true relationships set their own terms for interaction (rather than being defined by one person's agenda).[12]

11. English translations vary here, but the Greek word *anthrōpoi* refers to both men and women.
12. Andrew Root, *Relationships Unfiltered* (Grand Rapids: Zondervan/Youth Specialties, 2009), 17.

As a discipler, Jesus was primarily in relationship with the Twelve. He poured his life into them, walked with them, and without a doubt influenced them. However, one of the Twelve was not on board with Jesus's kingdom vision at all. Yet during the last meal that the disciples shared before the crucifixion, Jesus washed Judas's feet. The relationship and ministry were not contingent on grasping the point of Jesus's teaching or even obeying it, though almost all did so eventually. The relationship was integral to the teaching and discipleship, and often whatever happened in the relationship was important to the teaching.

Discipleship Models

There is no shortage of materials and resources on the topic of discipleship, and yet there isn't clarity or consensus on what discipleship is. Each church or ministry operates with its own understanding of the biblical text. Author Michael Wilkins has identified five prominent models that shape how discipleship is understood today.[13]

Disciples are learners. The Greek word for "disciple," *mathētēs*, comes from the verb *to learn* and was used to describe "one who puts himself/herself under the teaching authority of a great teacher though it has no reference to whether or not the person is a Christian."[14] The use of the term in Scripture seems to mean more than a learner, though, and includes a posture of following and personal devotion (e.g., Acts 11:26).

Disciples are committed believers. This view sees discipleship as a step taken after salvation. This model looks at Jesus's challenge to "count the cost" and focuses on those who left all to follow Jesus in comparison to the crowds and "ordinary" believers.[15] This model is commonly used today but also has some problems. First, when Jesus invites others to count the cost, is it a call to salvation or to a deeper commitment (see Matt. 19:16–22 and Luke 14:25–33)? Second, assuming this model implies that there are less mature Christians and more committed Christians, it is difficult to give biblical support for a "two-class system" of Christians.[16]

Disciples are ministers. This model sees the disciples as those whom Jesus called to ministry, and so they are the ones called to serve others in

13. Michael Wilkins, *Following the Master: A Biblical Theology of Discipleship* (Grand Rapids: Zondervan, 1992), 26–33.
14. Ibid., 26.
15. Ibid., 28.
16. Ibid., 29.

ministry and missions. This model is prominent in church traditions that make a strong distinction between clergy (pastors) and laity and have a strong hierarchical structure. Wilkins says that this model has problems in that it too creates a two-tiered structure and is difficult to support with the use of "disciples" and other words in the New Testament.

Disciples are converts; discipleship comes later. This model separates salvation from discipleship. To "make disciples" means to make converts, and then discipleship is something that begins later. The problem is that the disciple-making commission also included "baptizing" and "teaching" in its command. Wilkins asks if it's even possible to be a disciple without being involved in discipleship.

Disciples are converts who are in the process of discipleship. This model sees discipleship not as an optional second step but as what it means to be a Christian. As Jesus called others to him, he also sent people out to make other disciples, meaning, "Growth in discipleship was the natural result of the new disciple's life."[17] This is a widely held view of discipleship, though the emphasis can vary among such things as a personal commitment, a disciple's impact on society, growth within the community of believers, or a focus on missional ministry.

> What model best characterizes the one you heard in church? Which one resonates with you as you understand discipleship? Why do you hold that view?

Perhaps the best way to start unpacking how we think about discipleship is to finish this sentence: *If someone is a true disciple of Jesus, then he or she . . .* How we respond to this prompt is telling about how we think of discipleship and how we present its essence to others. This is especially true when we teach young people. We are quick to reduce complexities into short phrases so that they can be understood. When we do that, we may inadvertently be presenting a form of discipleship that may not be faithful to Scripture or that offers only a partial view.

Wilkins defines a disciple as "one who has come to Jesus for eternal life, has claimed Jesus as Savior and God, and has embarked upon the life of following Jesus."[18] In the book of Acts, the word *disciple* is synonymous with those who are believers (Acts 4:32; 6:7; 9:26; 11:26). Wilkins adds that the form is usually plural, showing that individual believers are seen as linked to a community of disciples. Therefore, when we talk about Christian discipleship, it is about what it means to grow as a Christian in all areas of life: "Discipleship and discipling mean living a fully human

17. Ibid., 32.
18. Ibid., 40.

life in this world in union with Jesus Christ and growing in conformity to his image."[19]

There are at least two ways that teaching interacts with discipleship. First, teaching informs discipleship. During an unusually intense teaching time, Jesus apparently felt the urgency to teach about discipleship as he contemplated the difficult road ahead of him. Luke 9:51 tells us that Jesus focused on Jerusalem where crucifixion, burial, and ascension would take place. Luke tells three consecutive stories where Jesus taught about the requirements of discipleship. Each time the word *follow* is used to invite persons to become disciples of Jesus. In the first story, a man promised to follow Jesus wherever he went (Luke 9:57). In the second story, a man promised to become a disciple as soon as he said good-bye to his family (Luke 9:59). In the third story a man told Jesus, "Lord, I will follow you as soon as my father dies and I settle his estate." Jesus introduced this section with a lesson on discipleship and commitment: "And he said to all, 'If anyone would come after me, let him deny himself and take up his cross daily and follow me. For whoever would save his life will lose it, but whoever loses his life for my sake will save it'" (Luke 9:23–24).

These three stories demonstrate a few of the typical responses to teaching *about* discipleship. Jesus instructed about the commitment necessary to be a disciple. Teaching informs discipleship.

Teaching also organizes discipleship. The apostle Paul expected discipleship to be replicated from generation to generation. The process is described in 2 Timothy 3:14–17 (NIV):

> But as for you, continue in what you have learned and have become convinced of, because you know those from whom you learned it, and how from infancy you have known the Holy Scriptures, which are able to make you wise for salvation through faith in Christ Jesus. All Scripture is God-breathed and is useful for teaching, rebuking, correcting and training in righteousness, so that the servant of God may be thoroughly equipped for every good work.

When a disciple is taught in the context of a relationship that is not agenda driven but one that has a love motivation, like a parent to a son or daughter, the lessons move down from the head to the heart, from "learned" to "convinced of." The disciple is aware of his teachers—in Timothy's case, Paul referred to Timothy's mother, grandmother, and to himself. Teaching truths from Scripture gives the disciple wisdom that points to faith, and the text is trustworthy for the development of the disciple.

19. Ibid., 42.

Questions and Activities

1. What common misconception about teaching and Christian education is the author attempting to address?
2. Do a search for how a group or denomination you are familiar with defines or describes discipleship. How does its definition seem to affect its approach to teaching?
3. When you teach, do you emphasize thinking, feeling, or doing? How can you become more holistic in your teaching and support the other areas?
4. What was the content of Jesus's teaching? What role did theological content play in his discipleship and teaching?
5. Write three examples (from your life or from others you know) that show why teachers need to balance content and relationship with regard to discipleship.

Further Reading

Mulholland, Robert M. *Invitation to a Journey: A Roadmap for Spiritual Formation*. Downers Grove, IL: InterVarsity, 1993.

Packer, J. I. *Knowing God*. Downers Grove, IL: InterVarsity, 1993.

Wilkins, Michael. *Following the Master: A Biblical Theology of Discipleship*. Grand Rapids: Zondervan, 1992.

Willard, Dallas. *The Great Omission: Reclaiming Jesus' Essential Teachings on Discipleship*. New York: HarperCollins, 2006.

2

Developing a Theology of Education

JEFF KEUSS

One of the oldest statements of what it means to educate for faith is found in the Old Testament, after Moses has received the commands from God that will provide direction and care for the Israelites as they journey into both the land and the promise that the Lord has in store for them. Laying down the essentials by which they are to live into God's sustaining care and provision, Deuteronomy 6:4–7 says Israel is to "listen" deeply, focus intently on who the Lord is, and then teach this to the next generation. In these verses, we are given a grand call to educate for the sake of faith, requiring us to develop a theology of education if we are to answer that call:

> Hear, O Israel: The LORD our God, the LORD is one. You shall love the LORD your God with all your heart and with all your soul and with all your might. And these words that I command you today shall be on your heart. You shall teach them diligently to your children, and shall talk of them when you sit in your house, and when you walk by the way, and when you lie down, and when you rise.

As far back as the fourteenth century, William Langland mused, "Theology has always caused me a lot of trouble. The more I ponder and delve into it, the darker and mistier it seems to me to be. It is certainly no science for subtle invention, and without love, it would be no good at all. But I love it because it values love above all else; and grace is never lacking where love comes first."[1]

To be sure, theology causes many people trouble in that is does get rather "dark and misty" the more we plunge into the classic questions of God's sovereignty, the problem of evil, the nature of salvation, and the nature of the kingdom of God. Yet as educators of young people, we should not fear or avoid the difficult theological questions or topics. With sensitivity to our denominational traditions and with age-appropriate approaches, we can effectively help develop the theological thinking of young people today.

As noted by Old Testament scholar Walter Brueggemann,[2] the formation of faithful followers of God is framed by the sacred canon of Scripture through a people sharing and engaging a Holy God who is deeply mysterious yet available to us. The gathering together of the Old Testament into Torah, Prophets, and Writings was a framework around which the people of faith were to be centered in their collective understanding of what it means to grow deeper in their life journey with God (Jer. 18:18a).

A theology of education begins in part by acknowledging that we go through cycles in our faith journey. We have moments of crystal clarity of who we are before God and of what God desires for us. We also go through periods of wrestling with points of tension regarding new insights and differing views that need to be reconciled with our understanding of faith. At other times we rest in the mystery of God, who is always present, always healing, always drawing us closer in loving embraces. And at other times that embrace can feel elusive. Brueggemann sums up our call to education for the sake of faith drawn from the Scriptures as a call to teach the next generation certitude, disruption, and mystery. Another way to think of this is found in the titles of three traditional hymns: "How Firm a Foundation" (certitude), "It Is Well with My Soul" (disruption), and "O the Deep, Deep Love of Jesus" (mystery). These three are equal parts of the Christian life.

Creating a Space Where Theology Is Embodied in Community

There are many ways to define what one means by theology. Etymologically, "theology" simply means "God-talk" (*theos* [Greek] = "God"; *logos* [Greek] = "Word, speech, reasoned discourse"), underscoring the importance of dialogue

---

1. William Langland, *Vision of Piers Plowman* (New York: Everyman, 1995).
2. Walter Brueggemann, *The Creative Word: Canon as a Model for Biblical Education* (Philadelphia: Fortress, 1982).

between people. To engage in "God-talk" is to allow for space in which searching after God can come to fullness in wisdom and in truth. Stephen Pattison and James Woodward put forward a definition of theology as being "a place where religious belief, tradition and practice meets contemporary experiences, questions and actions and conducts a dialogue that is mutually enriching, intellectually critical, and practically transforming."[3] In this way the academic discipline of theology has broadened its scope beyond what Edward Farley once termed the "clerical paradigm," which saw that a theology of education was merely the occupational training of clergy. As the church has moved into the twenty-first century, it views a theology of education as a more comprehensive paradigm that, while keeping central its task of training and equipping people for the sake of ministry, now also calls all people of faith into a clear way of seeing and engaging God in all manner of life.

In *To Know as We Are Known*, Parker Palmer sees education as a spiritual journey in the truest sense of deep Christian faith. Drawing on his own faith tradition as a Quaker, Palmer believes education that is truly meaningful will be shaped by faith by *creating a space where embodied understanding is practiced through community*.[4] Let's examine each aspect of this phrase.

Creating a Space

To view the first task of a theology of education as "creating a space" is to allow for new ideas to arise and old ones to be given new voice. Students will come into an educational space with the clutter of past experiences and voices that can distract from or even silence the ability to hear anything new or revolutionary. Going back to the call in Deuteronomy 6 to love God with all our heart, with all our soul, and with all our strength will therefore require the educator to help make room in a student's heart, soul, and strength to receive what God wishes to say, challenge, redeem, and call forth into action.

If we as Christian leaders do not allow for space to be made for new voices and new ways of thinking and believing, then education can become merely the transfer of raw data or, even worse, the silencing of new insights from the students by which the teacher and other students can grow. In this regard theology can close off space for new insights to arise. As Henri Nouwen notes,

3. Stephen Pattison and James Woodward, "An Introduction to Pastoral and Practical Theology," in *The Blackwell Reader in Pastoral and Practical Theology*, ed. Stephen Pattison and James Woodward (Hoboken, NJ: Wiley-Blackwell, 2000), 9.
4. See Parker Palmer, *To Know as We Are Known: Education as Spiritual Journey* (New York: HarperSanFrancisco, 1993).

teaching can easily degenerate into a rabid consumerism of "getting just the facts"—mindlessly memorizing dogma, fixing sermons in three points, and so on—with teachers as the sellers and students as the consumers. He states, "As long as teaching takes place in [an enclosed] context it is doomed to be a violent process and evoke a vicious cycle of action and reaction. . . . The teacher who enters this arena is forced to enter into a process which by its nature is competitive, unilateral, and alienating. In short: violent."[5]

In contrast to this notion, to create a space as the first step toward a theology of education is to put aside the need to force the process of education toward some conclusion. To create a space is to expose our need to complete a topic—to race through a lesson, to give students merely the answer without taking time for learning deeply—as potentially being the need for control and mastery and an unwillingness to be transformed into new ways of thinking and being in the world.

Creating space in ministry involves an inherently *redemptive* process, which is suggestive of many voices finding new connections rather than of a competition in which one person must be right over and against others. In creating a space, we are to be reflective about real-life issues in order to bridge the call of God to the individual and the church with the deep needs of the world for which Jesus lived and died. It is therefore the goal of a theologically astute Christian teacher to nurture an inviting "space" that is welcoming and transforming for both teacher and student.

Embodied Understanding

As we move into a space that is hospitable and inviting, a theology of education must mirror the calling of Christ, an incarnational event that lives not merely in our brains but in our bodies, in active living and moving in the world. Going back to the foundations of educational theory found in Aristotle's writings, one sees that to be fully embodied humans with purpose is to live ethically in the world as people of character. Aristotle makes this point by distinguishing between *theōria* (contemplative thought) and *phronēsis* (practical reasoning). Regarding *phronēsis*, Aristotle held that the means of discerning right and wrong in lived experience is always dependent on the identity, social roles, beliefs, and traditions of individuals within a society that challenges them to live as moral agents themselves, prior to a theoretical and objectively certain moral principle for human action. Ethical decisions, therefore, are to be grounded in and through a way of life that is *embodied*

5. Henri J. M. Nouwen, *Creative Ministry* (New York: Doubleday, 1991), 6.

rather than merely an "idea in my brain." Christian theology needs, therefore, to be moving communities more and more toward "transformation models for truth"[6] where action as ethical people of character is the goal rather than agreeing to and memorizing good ideas that have no requirement for living out the call of Christ's gospel in the world. One theologian put it this way: "A theological system is supposed to satisfy two basic needs: the statement of the truth of the Christian message and the interpretation of this truth for every new generation. Theology moves back and forth between two poles, the eternal truth of its foundation and the temporal situation in which the eternal truth must be received."[7]

The challenge here for us is pretty profound: the truth of the gospel must always be interpreted as lived action in and with our world. It is not enough to believe the gospel of Jesus; we must become the hands and feet of Christ if our belief is to be true. In this way our theology of education must challenge our students toward a living, active participation in their world.

Practice

This leads to a third way a theology of education is to be engaged; it is not merely embodied but also practiced. Theologian Emil Brunner's oft-quoted statement on the church can be read in light of education for the sake of the church: "The Church exists by mission, just as a fire exists by burning. Where there is no mission, there is no Church; and where there is neither Church nor mission, there is no faith."[8] Just as Brunner called for mission as evidence for faith, Dietrich Bonhoeffer stated that the evidence of theological reflection was living in the world and "taking life in one's stride, with all its duties and problems, its successes and failures, its experiences and helplessness. It is in such a life that we throw ourselves utterly in the arms of God and *participate* in his sufferings in the world and watch with Christ in Gethsemane."[9]

This active participation in the "sufferings in the world" is akin to writer Frederick Buechner's statement that our call to mission is located in "the place where [our] deep gladness and the world's deep hunger meet."[10] Central to a theology of education is stirring this call to participation in the world through identifying areas of the world's deepest hungers and relating them to

6. David Tracy, *The Analogical Imagination* (New York: SCM, 1981), 71.
7. Paul Tillich, *Systematic Theology* (Chicago: University of Chicago Press, 1951), 1:3.
8. Emil Brunner, *The Word and the World* (London: SCM, 1931), 108.
9. Dietrich Bonhoeffer, *Prisoner for God* (New York: Macmillan, 1954), 169 (emphasis added).
10. Frederick Buechner, *Wishful Thinking* (New York: Harper & Row, 1973), 95.

students' respective gifts and talents. Through service learning, mission trips, internships, peer leadership, and other forms of living out our faith for others, students move into an arena for "experiments in truth"[11] that will show that any theology of education must take seriously the challenge and opportunity found in a call to reconciliation in the midst of the world's brokenness.

The challenge before students and teachers to participate in a theology of education mirrors Nouwen's commissioning

> to help people in very concrete situations—people with illnesses or in grief, people with physical or mental handicaps, people caught in the complex networks of secular or religious institutions—to see and experience their story as part of God's ongoing redemptive work in the world. These insights and experiences heal precisely because they restore the broken connection between the world and God and create a new unity in which memories that previously seemed only destructive are now reclaimed as part of a redemptive event.[12]

Ultimately, these concerns find themselves worked out in the space formed by and through community, which is a fourth pillar upon which to develop a theology of education.

Through Community

Theology at its core speaks in terms of community as the place where meaning and wholeness are located. Martin Luther states that "a Christian lives not in themselves, but in Christ and in their neighbor,"[13] and Bonhoeffer declares that in the end, the true location of meaning is a life lived for others, which is "a transformation of all human life around the understanding that Jesus is only there for others. . . . Christ exists as community."[14] Community more than a territorial locale needs to be recast as a space at the center of life allowing for the transcending of differences, changes in perspective, awareness for different realities, courage for choosing and changing, manifestation of spirit, and welcoming of new possibilities.

It is unfortunate that for some people the notion of community is seen as merely an overwhelming number of programs that only tire rather than

11. A phrase from the subtitle of Gandhi's autobiography.

12. Henri J. M. Nouwen, *The Living Reminder* (San Francisco: HarperSanFrancisco, 1988), 26–27.

13. Martin Luther, "The Freedom of a Christian," in *Martin Luther: Selections from His Writings*, ed. John Dillenberger (Garden City, NY: Anchor, 1961), 80.

14. Dietrich Bonhoeffer, *Letters and Papers from Prison*, ed. Eberhard Bethge, trans. Reginald Fuller et al. (New York: Macmillan, 1972), 381.

redeem and restore us. A theology of education draws us to the deep importance of community that is responsive to the cries of God's people for care, intimacy, and restoration. In one of his pastoral reflections, Eugene Peterson underscores this point:

> We [have] become avid for spirituality: we long to be in community, experiencing love and trust and joy with others. We are fed up with being evaluated by how much we can contribute, how much we can do. We hunger for communion with God, something beyond the satisfaction of self, the development of me. We are fed up with being told *about* God.
>
> We go to our leaders for help, and they don't seem to know what we are talking about. They sign us up for a program in stress management. They recruit us for a tour of the Holy Land. . . . When we don't seem interested, they talk faster and louder. When we drift somewhere else, they hire a public relations consultant to devise a campaign designed to attract us and our friends. . . . But they don't attract *us*. We are after what we came for in the first place: intimacy and transcendence, personal friends and a personal God, love and worship.[15]

Peterson's reminder to us is that a theology of education is a movement into community, but not a community that neglects "what we came for in the first place." Returning to the call on God's people found in Deuteronomy 6, the people of God should walk along the road together, talk with one another, write reminders of God's goodness on the walls and doorposts of their homes, train the next generation to ask questions, and dialogue in unity and intimacy. These movements and conversations happen in the context of deep relationships.

But community in the context of a theology of education is not merely a collection of individuals who remain neither unchanged nor unchallenged in their relationships. To be in community is to be transformed more and more into the image of God with others in deep unity. One of the Christian desert fathers of the fourth century, Abba Poemen, used the analogy of water dripping slowly on a hard rock to describe the process by which a disciple is transformed by the Word of God: "The nature of water is soft, that of stone is hard; but if a bottle is hung above the stone, allowing the water to fall drop by drop, it wears away the stone. So it is with the Word of God; it is soft and our heart is hard, but the [one] who hears the word of God often, opens his heart to the fear of God."[16]

15. Eugene Peterson, *Subversive Spirituality* (Grand Rapids: Eerdmans, 1997), 36–37.
16. Abba Poemen, *The Sayings of The Desert Fathers: The Alphabetical Collection*, trans. Benedicta Ward (New York: Macmillan, 1975), 183.

One of the essential aspects of a theology of education is the acknowledgment that transformation takes time and requires a wearing away of that which prevents us from experiencing the intimacy and call of God fully. It has been said numerous times that one of the qualities that unifies all those called by Jesus to "come and follow" is that everyone leaves something behind in order to journey with him.

Context: A Theology of Education Is Firmly Planted in the Here and Now

In order to teach effectively and prophetically in light of the ministry of Jesus, we must consider the place and people where we teach and where we are calling them to go. As Israel was called from their captivity into a new land, and as the apostle Paul shaped his missionary message of the gospel depending on whether he preached in Athens or wrote to Corinth from afar, so too our theology of education must attend to the context in which our teaching takes place.

Far too often education begins objectively, by diving into the doctrines and history of the church from a distance as if our current situation doesn't matter. As we have turned the page on the twentieth century and are well into the twenty-first century, we are faced with distinct contextual questions about race, gender, sexuality, poverty, cultural globalization, denominational fractures, and the rise of new church models and faith communities, to name but a few. Looking at the early churches of the New Testament, we see that each community was called to respond to the distinct needs of their place and their people. The churches cited in the New Testament Epistles—Corinth, Philippi, Ephesus, Rome—each have distinct spiritual callings as testified by the reality that they are included in our canon of Scripture and not considered to be repetitive. No one community is identical to another. This should give us pause in any attempt to reclaim a homogenous notion of the "first-century church."

The early churches that arose from the commissioning of the Holy Spirit at Pentecost had unique challenges, stories, and people speaking particular wisdom and prophesying to a particular context through a gospel of universal importance. This challenges us to remember that our theology of education

> New Testament scholar N. T. Wright argues that when teaching, we must first situate ourselves in our current context by asking five deceptively basic questions.
>
> 1. Who are we?
> 2. Where are we?
> 3. What's wrong?
> 4. What's the solution?
> 5. What time is it? (Where are we in the flow of God's saving work in the world?)
>
> —N. T. Wright, *Jesus and the Victory of God* (Minneapolis: Fortress, 1996), 138.

needs to be shaped by the questions and concerns of our local community and the people God brings to us in that place and time.

Canon and Community

A theology of education takes into account Scripture, dialogues with Scripture, and listens to interpreters of Scripture through the ages. Reading Hebrews 11 is like looking through a family photo album organized as a textbook for teaching faith. Name after name is underscored and textually hyperlinked in our canon of Scripture to tether the reader to how faith is to be understood and lived ("By faith . . . , By faith . . . , By faith . . ."). When God has something of vital importance to say, it is always wrapped in flesh; and Hebrews 11 testifies to the fact that we learn faith through the lives and stories of others, reaching into the past and pressing toward the future. No matter how we slice it, the theology of God's people is the story and life of God's people fully embodied and lived out in faithfulness. Walter Brueggemann summarizes the Old Testament call to biblical education: "The primal mode of education in the church, derived from the Torah, is *story*. There is a crucial match between the mode of story and the substance to be told. Trouble surfaces in the community of faith whenever we move from the idiom of story. As soon as we make this move, we create an incongruity between our convictions and the ways we speak our convictions."[17]

This is the heart of what it means to have a theology of education that is canonical in the fullest sense of the term: owning the story of faith as those before us owned the story. In addition to the authoritative Scriptures that the community of faith holds as true and right in giving us guidance for how we are to live and believe, it is vital that the community of faith interpret these Scriptures in the communion of God's people (both past and present) as a people "of the Book" who are bound together by the living and transformative Word of God. In this way, a theology of education begins with God's people and presses toward the gathering of God's people as a canonically formed people.

Do we somehow downgrade the centrality of Scripture by lifting up the canonical people of God? Not at all. Our culture has moved further and further away from the gathered people of God playing a role in discernment and discipline in favor of a more privatized and individualized faith. When a personal relationship with Jesus and a personal reading of Scripture supersede the communal interpretation and call to action, then we have lost

17. Brueggemann, *Creative Word*, 22.

the canonical spirit and truth of the very texts put before us through the movement of the Holy Spirit. As one theologian has put it, Christian education involves those tasks and expressions of ministry that enable people to (1) learn the Christian story, both ancient and present; (2) develop the skills they need to act out their faith; (3) reflect on that story in order to live in awareness of its truth; and (4) nurture the sensitivities they need to live together as a covenant community.[18]

Creation: A Theology of Education Generates New Insights through Sanctified Imagination

The reformer John Calvin speaks of the process by which God cultivates and perfects the faith in us, at once a corrective and a cure to our brokenness. But it is always a creative formation: "It behooves us to consider the sort of remedy by which divine grace corrects and cures the corruption of nature. . . . God begins his good work in us, therefore, by arousing love and desire and zeal for righteousness in our hearts; or, to speak more correctly, by bending, forming, and directing, our hearts to righteousness. He completes his work, moreover, by confirming us to perseverance."[19]

This "bending, forming, and directing" of our hearts is a continuously creative act of transformation that is essential to a robust theology of education. Perhaps this is the most challenging aspect of a deep theology of education: to be creative and imaginative, to think the new thought, to offer the new insight, to challenge the previous forms of thinking—this takes courage in every generation. But to educate for the sake of the gospel is to be imaginative. It involves awakening in students the faith, hope, and love just around the corner, which some might not yet see and which can only be accessed through imagination. To create a space where embodied truth can be practiced through community will take some imagination if the next generation is to awaken to the new story God desires for us.

Questions and Activities

1. What role do the "by faith" stories of others play in your own spiritual formation? What have they taught you?

18. Daniel Aleshire, "Finding Eagles in the Turkeys' Nest: Pastoral Theology and Christian Education," *Review and Expositor: An International Baptist Journal* 85 (December 1988): 695–709.
19. John Calvin, *The Institutes of the Christian Religion* 2.3.6, trans. Lord Lewis Battles (Grand Rapids: Eerdmans, 1986).

2. How does Scripture shape how your community talks about faith?

3. Who are the "saints" in your church, community, or denomination? How have their legacies shaped the theology of your faith community?

4. Think about how God has been "bending, forming, and directing" your heart since you were young. How has that shaped your imagination and produced new theological thought and insight?

5. Imagine you're being interviewed by a church board and asked why "teaching" has a place within the church. Write two paragraphs, with support from Scripture and theologians, that would serve as an answer to their question about your theology of education.

Further Reading

Estep, James R., Michael Anthony, and Greg Allison. *A Theology for Christian Education*. Nashville: B&H, 2008.

Oden, Thomas C. *Pastoral Theology: Essentials of Ministry*. New York: HarperOne, 1983.

Root, Andrew. *Bonhoeffer as Youth Worker: A Theological Vision for Discipleship and Life Together*. Grand Rapids: Baker Academic, 2014.

3

A Scriptural Basis for Teaching

RON BELSTERLING

Christians claim the Bible as a source of life and transformation. It plays a crucial role for all those who hunger to know God more deeply, regardless of their background or social status. King David, for example, articulates a deep love for the Bible and the crucial role it plays in his life. In Psalm 119, he writes, "I have stored up your word in my heart. . . . I will meditate on your precepts and fix my eyes on your ways. I will delight in your statutes; I will not forget your word. . . . Your word is a lamp to my feet and a light to my path" (vv. 11, 15–16, 105). Passing on the Word of God is important for the community of faith and to those who are called to the task of teaching, especially those assigned to teach the next generations of children and youth.

The Bible often speaks about learning and teaching. The early roots of Christian education are found with the family, the primary means by which God's Word is passed on to the next generation, "And these words . . . shall be on your heart. . . . Teach them diligently to your children. . . . Write them on the doorposts of your house and on your gates" (Deut. 6:6–9; see also Prov. 1:8; 4:1; Eph. 6).[1] Moses instituted public religious instruction for all Hebrews: "Assemble the people—men, women and children, and the foreigners residing in your towns—so they can listen and learn to fear the

1. Kevin E. Lawson, "Historical Foundations of Christian Education," in *Introducing Christian Education: Foundations for the Twenty-First Century*, ed. Michael J. Anthony (Grand Rapids: Baker Academic, 2001), 18.

LORD your God and follow carefully all the words of this law" (Deut. 31:12 NIV). The Hebrew word for learn, *lamad*, is the most common word used for learning in the Old Testament. It means "to stimulate, to exercise in" and denotes that learning requires a "readied" integration of knowledge into life that includes a change in action and commitment.[2]

The other Hebrew word for learning in the Old Testament, *hanak*, means "to educate" or "to dedicate." It is found in Proverbs 22:6: "Train up a child in the way he should go; even when he is old he will not depart from it." This form of teaching was usually communal and seen as an important collective value. Religious instruction and teaching were important values for God's people as a whole throughout the Old Testament.

Teaching in the Old Testament had the goal of *knowing* God, which resulted in obedience "ultimately to be found in the fear of the Lord."[3] Learning about and knowing God produce a healthy fear and an awareness of his goodness, that he is trustworthy, wise, and able to provide (Deut. 4:10; Prov. 1:7).

- Moses prayed, "Please show me now your ways, that I may know you in order to find favor in your sight" (Exod. 33:13).
- Hezekiah prayed for all of humanity, "Now, O LORD our God, save us, please, from his hand, that all the kingdoms of the earth may know that you, O LORD, are God alone" (2 Kings 19:19).
- King David declared, "Some trust in chariots and some in horses, but we trust in the name of the Lord our God" (Ps. 20:7).

David understood the role that learning and understanding Scripture had in his life: "Never take your word of truth from my mouth, for I have put my hope in your laws. I will always obey your law, for ever and ever" (Ps. 119:43–44 NIV). Teaching and learning mattered to the author of Proverbs: "Keep hold of instruction; do not let go. Guard her; for she is your life" (Prov. 4:13). Eventually teaching became so central for the Israelites that the synagogue became more a place of religious instruction than of public worship.[4] By the time we read of Jesus's early encounters with the synagogue, teaching had a clearly established prominence within the Israelite community (Luke 2:41–52; 4:16–22).

2. The word was used to describe soldiers trained for battle (1 Chron. 5:18).
3. Walter C. Kaiser, "1116 לָמַד," in *Wordbook of the Old Testament*, ed. R. Laird Harris, Gleason L. Archer Jr., and Bruce K. Waltke (Chicago: Moody, 1999), 480.
4. Edward L. Hayes, "Establishing Biblical Foundations," in *Christian Education: Foundations for the Future*, ed. Robert E. Clark, Lin Johnson, and Allyn K. Sloat (Chicago: Moody, 1991), 32.

The New Testament highlights God's redemption of humanity through Jesus Christ and demonstrates how God's previous Word (the Law and the Prophets) witnessed to Christ as well (Ps. 119:38; John 3:16; 1 John 1). Kenneth Gangel says, "The fact that Christian education must be biblical is precisely what makes it Christian. And to be entirely biblical, it must center on Christ."[5]

Early in Jesus's ministry he stated that he had come to fulfill the law, and in the process he elevated teaching's role in his new kingdom: "Therefore anyone who sets aside one of the least of these commands and teaches others accordingly will be called least in the kingdom of heaven, but whoever practices and teaches these commands will be called great in the kingdom of heaven" (Matt. 5:19 NIV).

The Teaching Mission

The oft-quoted "Great Commission" in Matthew 28 is a familiar passage, yet it is primarily used to support missional efforts. Two elements give impetus to seeing it as possessing an equal or greater teaching focus. First, the disciples were commissioned to teach, acknowledging that there will be an instructional component to the church. Second, the phrase "make disciples" actually means "to make or cultivate *learners*." The mission of the church was not focused on the quality of the teaching alone but centered on the learning (or maturation) of those who were being taught.[6]

The teaching ministry of the early church was empowered by the Holy Spirit. It is no different today. Through Christian teaching, the Holy Spirit convicts and guides Christians in various ways (Ps. 119:13, 42–43, 46; Luke 12:11–12; John 14:26). Central to a community of believers is a need for teaching that helps people uphold the ways of God written in the Word and on our hearts (Rom. 3:23; 1 John 1:9). Teaching brings to the individual and the community the wisdom found in God's Word that reflects the value Jesus placed on teaching in his ministry with his followers.[7]

Arguably, our best biblical examples for Christian teaching come from the writings of the apostle Paul. His ministry, and that of Timothy, was to be involved in teaching (Rom. 2:21; 12:7; 1 Cor. 11:14), a ministry that edified

5. Kenneth O. Gangel, "What Christian Education Is," in Clark, Johnson, and Sloat, *Christian Education*, 19.

6. Michael Lawson, "Biblical Foundations for a Philosophy of Teaching," in *The Christian Educator's Handbook on Teaching*, ed. Kenneth O. Gangel and Howard G. Hendricks (Grand Rapids: Baker, 1988), 62.

7. William Yount, *The Teaching Ministry of the Church*, 2nd ed. (Nashville: B&H, 2008). See chap. 2 especially.

the church (2 Thess. 2:15). Edward Hayes highlights five general themes from 1–2 Timothy that emphasize the importance of teaching:

1. Teaching is essential for proper handling of God's word (2 Tim. 2:14–15; 3:16–17).
2. Teaching is necessary for soundness of faith (1 Tim. 4:6, 11; 6:3–5; 2 Tim. 4:3).
3. Teaching is useful to establish harmonious households (1 Tim. 6:1–2).
4. Teaching ability is a requirement of spiritual leaders (1 Tim. 3:2; 2 Tim. 2:24).
5. Teaching is vital to the perpetuation of the faith (2 Tim. 2:2).[8]

Teaching Illuminates

Perhaps one of the best metaphors for the role of teaching is that of being light. There is an illuminating aspect to teaching and learning. Isaiah prophesied that when the light of Christ came, his people were to "rise and shine" as well (Isa. 60:1). Job, Daniel, David, Paul, and John all use the notions of being filled with the light of God and the knowledge of God interchangeably and discuss the responsibility of those whom God taught to shine as well (Dan. 12:3; Ps. 119:105, 130, 136; 2 Cor. 4:6; 1 John 1–2). Jesus told his disciples, "You are the light of the world" and commanded them to "let your light shine" (Matt. 5:14–16).

All of these passages indicate that those who receive the light of God will become reflectors of God's light.[9] Any light needs power, and for Christian teachers, that is the Holy Spirit.[10] Jesus indicated that Christians would be able to understand God's commands and love others with the self-giving love of God only under the guidance of the Holy Spirit (John 14:26). The Holy Spirit fosters the maturing of Jesus's disciples first by illuminating the truth of God's Word through disciplined hermeneutic effort,[11] and second by

8. Edward L. Hayes, "Establishing Biblical Foundations," in Clark, Johnson, and Sloat, *Christian Education*, 37–38.
9. Henry E. Dosker, "Shine," in *International Standard Bible Encyclopedia* (Grand Rapids: Eerdmans, 1939). There are eight Hebrew words in the Old Testament and four Greek words in the New Testament translated as "shine." Figuratively, the idea of God's people shining can be understood as reflecting God's light.
10. Roy B. Zuck, *Spirit-Filled Teaching* (Nashville: Thomas Nelson, 2003), 93–100.
11. John M. Koessler, *True Discipleship: The Art of Following Jesus* (Chicago: Moody, 2003), 83; Robert L. Thomas, *Evangelical Hermeneutics: The New Versus the Old* (Grand Rapids: Kregel Academic & Professional, 2003).

reproducing the character of Christ in his disciples. The Spirit empowers Christians to teach others competently through love, service, and challenging the world to consider the realities of Jesus's coming kingdom.[12]

The Word also acts as a mirror for Christians, allowing us to see ourselves clearly (James 1:23–25). Upon Spirit-led examination, Christians see intrapersonal areas of struggle (jealousy, bitterness, an argumentative spirit, etc.) and feel compelled to confess them as sinful (Pss. 51; 139:23; 1 Cor. 13:12; 2 Cor. 3:18). When those who make up the body of Christ personally admit their own weaknesses and failures, they are better able to both receive and provide corrective wisdom from and to their brothers and sisters in Christ (Matt. 7:3–5; Gal. 6:1; James 2:10). They are also able to see the structural sins within their communities and help individuals and communities mature in Christ.[13]

The only way for God's people to truly mature intrapersonally (as individuals) and interpersonally (as a community) is to learn and to help others learn God's intentionally communicated truth in grace and mercy (Pss. 25:4; 51:13; Isa. 28:9; Titus 1:2; Heb. 5:12). God clearly communicates requirements in exhorting us "to do justice, and to love kindness, and to walk humbly with [our] God" (Mic. 6:8). Jesus explains that this happens best when the people of God are rooted in his love: "I am the vine; you are the branches. Whoever abides in me and I in him, he it is that bears much fruit, for apart from me you can do nothing" (John 15:5). Christians and non-Christians alike will most clearly see God's true love when the community of Christ lives out of the love of Christ.

God Desires to Be Known

One of the primary reasons we are to teach is that God clearly desires that humanity come to know God "positionally," personally, and passionately.[14] God has been revealed through creation, conscience, historical deeds, the incarnation, the words of Scripture, and ultimately through Jesus Christ. God wants us to learn who he is and to be equipped to teach others who he is. Throughout Scripture, we see God's priority for us to know and understand

---

12. James M. Boice, *Foundations of the Christian Faith* (Downers Grove, IL: InterVarsity, 1986), 367–77.

13. Howard Hendricks and William Hendricks, *Living by the Book* (Chicago: Moody, 1991), 20.

14. In his Areopagus address in Acts 17:24–31, Paul confirms God's desire to be known by the world (see Gordon R. Lewis and Bruce A. Demarest, *Integrative Theology* [Grand Rapids: Zondervan, 2014], 1:69); this concept is further explored in W. R. Blackburn, *The God Who Makes Himself Known* (Downers Grove, IL: InterVarsity, 2012).

his love for us.[15] Many of the stories recorded in Scripture are accompanied by God's explanation that this happened so that humanity might know God and know of his care for people (Josh. 3:10).[16]

God is a God who places relational value on us as God's people and who desires for us to know him so that we might make him known.[17] Moses conveys this understanding: "Now this is the commandment—the statutes and the rules—that the LORD your God commanded me to teach you, that you may do them in the land to which you are going over, to possess it" (Deut. 6:1). God has especially communicated who he is and what he desires with his church; thus, God desires that his people would perpetuate his will to be known by teaching about him within and outside the people of God.[18]

> The transformation of a Christian's mind shows itself in the transformation of one's character and awareness of opportunities to love others.

This relationship with God is transformational, something that can happen by hearing God's Word.[19] Through teaching, God radically transforms the minds and lives of people. God's Word speaks truth, and knowing this truth calls those who want to be disciples to purposeful, peaceful, and joyful lives, no matter life's circumstances (Ps. 119:151, 160, 165, 174).[20] Empowered by the Holy Spirit, each member of the community of faith can learn to treasure God's Word in a way that takes hold of and transforms not only the mind but also his or her life toward maturity in Christ. The transformation of a Christian's mind shows itself in the transformation of one's character and awareness of opportunities to love others.

15. These are a few of the Old Testament references that acknowledge God's desire to be known: Gen. 22:12; Exod. 9:14; Lev. 23:43; Num. 16:28; Deut. 4:39; 12:11; Josh. 4:24; Judg. 6:10; 1 Sam. 17:46; 2 Sam. 7:20; 1 Kings 8:60; 2 Kings 17:26; 1 Chron. 28:9; 2 Chron. 13:5; Job 9:5; Ps. 46:10; Eccles. 3:14; Isa. 43:10; Jer. 2:19; Ezek. 20:20; Hosea 13:4; Joel 2:27; Amos 9:15; Zech. 6:15; Mic. 6:8; Zeph. 3:17; Mal. 2:16.

16. Wayne Grudem, C. John Collins, and Thomas R. Schreiner, *Understanding Scripture* (Wheaton: Crossway, 2012), 53–54.

17. Daryl Eldridge, "God as Teacher," in *The Teaching Ministry of the Church* (Nashville: Broadman & Holman, 1995), 3–20.

18. Acts tells the history of the early church doing exactly this; Galatians warns people to not abandon exhortations to learn and teach and to be discerning with truth against lies; and Galatians describes God's desires to see the church expand beyond the Jews and include gentiles. D. L. Turner, "Teach, Teacher," in *Evangelical Dictionary of Biblical Theology*, ed. Walter A. Elwell (Grand Rapids: Baker Books, 2001).

19. Barry Shafer, *Unleashing God's Word in Youth Ministry* (Grand Rapids: Zondervan, 2008), 58; Rom. 12.

20. Wayne A. Grudem, *Bible Doctrine: Essential Teachings of the Christian Faith*, ed. Jeff Purswell (Grand Rapids: Zondervan, 1999), chap. 2.

The Character of the Christian Teacher

Knowing why Christians need to teach offers clues as to what should be taught. Teaching must center on God's revelatory truth as it relates to the introduction of Jesus Christ, the incarnation of Jesus Christ, the teaching of Jesus Christ, the death and resurrection of Jesus Christ, the Holy Spirit's illumination of the written story of Jesus Christ, and the hoped-for second coming of Jesus Christ. The Bible, unlike any other source or resource, conveys the true story of God and Jesus Christ and the work of the Holy Spirit. Therefore, the biblical text and its message of redemption must be taught. One cannot understand or teach the valid message of Scripture apart from comprehending and acknowledging the reliable text of Scripture and the consistency of God.

How one defines "success" in life philosophically, the fundamental standards of life ethically, or the key components of a human being mentally makes large differences in the ways that one lives and communicates God's truth practically. One's metaphysical (grand reality) views concerning truth, beauty, death, morality, and appropriate relationships all depend on and reciprocally influence one's life goals and valued character traits.[21]

C. S. Lewis acknowledges that most people recognize certain character qualities (prudence, temperance, justice, and fortitude—the "Cardinal Virtues") as virtuous and worth pursuing.[22] He also suggests, however, that Christians identify virtues beyond the scope of the norm; theological virtues include faith, charity, and (God-focused) hope (Prov. 18:2; 19:3; 23:9). As Scripture advocates for selflessness, humility, generosity, and compassion toward others, the world advocates for self-centeredness, pride, consumption, and judgment. Maturity in Christ is evidenced in the fruit of the Spirit, growing in knowledge, becoming stronger in endurance and patience, and being thankful.[23]

Christian teaching guides people in crafting worldviews and dispositions consistent with God's kingdom, discerning the differences between true and false virtue, and utilizing methods likely to maximize success in conveying God's truth to others. The real transformation of the Christian's mind shows itself in the transformation of one's character and one's verbal and nonverbal witness. This encompasses many aspects of one's lifestyle, including developing visible compassion and practicing intentional dialogue.

21. William K. Frankena, *Three Historical Philosophies of Education: Aristotle, Kant, Dewey* (Glenview, IL: Scott Foresman, 1965).

22. C. S. Lewis, *Mere Christianity* (San Francisco: HarperOne, 2015).

23. Eleanor Daniel, *Introduction to Christian Education* (Cincinnati, OH: Standard, 1980), 93.

It becomes clear that the truth of God's Word has truly been "learned" when it is being lived out in the community of faith and in the world. Real learning is not just a cognitive process of absorbing information but also a process of discerning God's truth out of or relative to information (trends, biases, and comfortable cultural familiarity). It is the process of our entire lives being actively transformed.[24] It is a lack of transformation that prompted Lawrence Richards and Gary Bredfeldt to ask why Christian teaching, though common, seemed to have often failed to transform and "straighten out twisted lives."[25] They concluded, "The problem then in teaching does not lie in the authority of the Bible but it must lie in the teacher, the student, and the method of teaching, or some combination of the three."[26]

Implications for the Christian Teacher

Those who accept the responsibility to teach communally or professionally are held accountable to teaching accurately (James 3:1). God's teachers must walk a straight path with integrity, both in learning and in communicating God's will. "Christian teachers must have highly developed and thoroughly consecrated minds."[27] They must be so in tune with Christ as to hear his whispers (Matt. 10:27) amid a noisy world. They must be bold enough to share his longings amid an often disinterested world (2 Tim. 4:3).

Committed teachers will need to understand not only the content of Scripture but also its teachers' creative methods.[28] Scripture provides examples of one-on-one, small-group, and large-group teaching. Various forms of lecture, discussion, and question-and-answer methodologies are presented. Teaching in the Scriptures often takes place at meals, in boats, by lakes, in institutional settings, and at parties. Those who teach must be available with God's Word on their lips in all circumstances.

Effective teaching requires mastery of a subject area, skillful presentation abilities, relational concern, and passionate desire to see the fruit of the teaching beyond the classroom. The way to master God's lessons is to abide

24. Richard R. Melick and Shera Melick, *Teaching That Transforms: Facilitating Life Change through Adult Bible Teaching* (Nashville: B&H, 2010), 4.

25. Lawrence O. Richards and Gary J. Bredfeldt, *Creative Bible Teaching* (Chicago: Moody, 1998), 25.

26. Ibid., 35.

27. Kenneth O. Gangel and Howard G. Hendricks, eds., *The Christian Educator's Handbook on Teaching* (Grand Rapids: Baker, 1988), 74.

28. Richards and Bredfeldt, *Creative Bible Teaching*; Marlene LeFever, *Creative Teaching Methods: Be an Effective Christian Teacher* (Colorado Springs: David C. Cook, 1997).

gladly in Jesus as John did (John 15), to crave and meditate on the Bible day and night as David did (Pss. 67; 73; 119; 145), to humbly receive God's correction as Moses did (Deut. 32–33), and to follow Jesus closely enough to be covered in his blood, as Simon of Cyrene did (Luke 23). Relational motive reflects God's motive for those who teach on Christ's behalf. God desires to be known by his people, which can happen as those who are called to teach and empowered by the Holy Spirit hear God's Word, interpret it wisely, and live lives that are increasingly faithful to Jesus.

> "When the objective becomes changing students' lives, the focus and activities of the teacher will be influenced. Jesus was not obsessed with 'covering the content,' because that was not his objective. He could take the time to listen to students and interact with them because his agenda was their lives, not his content."
>
> —Perry G. Downs, *Teaching for Spiritual Growth: An Introduction to Christian Education* (Grand Rapids: Zondervan, 1994), 33.

Questions and Activities

1. Think of a ministry you're familiar with and reflect on the role that teaching plays in it. Would you say teaching is important? Why or why not?

2. Reflect and identify two moments in your spiritual life where a teaching time played an important role in illuminating a need, an area for growth, or a new direction. What role did the teacher play in that moment?

3. If you made a list of ten things that "had to be taught" to the next generation at your church, what ten things would you select? Are you currently teaching them through your life?

4. Perform a word search for the word *teach* using a Bible software program. Spend some time reading the verses and identify common themes.

5. Write a single paragraph about why Christian teaching is important in the ministry of the church and in the lives of individuals.

Further Reading

Parrett, Gary A., and S. Steve Kang. *Teaching the Faith, Forming the Faithful: A Biblical Vision for Education in the Church*. Downers Grove, IL: InterVarsity, 2009.

Wilhoit, Jim, and Leland Ryken. *Effective Bible Teaching*. 2nd ed. Grand Rapids: Baker Academic, 2012.

4

The Essence of the Life of a Teacher

BOB MACRAE

When we teach students the Bible and how to follow Jesus, we are doing more than dispensing information. We are involving ourselves in the discipleship process of our students. If we are doing it *right*, we are partnering with the Holy Spirit as his servant in this process called spiritual transformation; we must be ever aware of the goal. To be most effective in accomplishing that goal, the life of the teacher is used by God to help turn our students' hearts toward him.

It's a sobering thought to consider how powerfully our lives can enhance or thwart the work of the Holy Spirit in the lives of our students. Long gone are the days, if they ever existed, where simply what we said or taught was sufficient; students today look for the authenticity that affirms the message.

The following are six characteristics that we must embody in order to be effective Christian teachers: First, we must be *disciples*. We must also be *exemplary*, *loving*, *transparent*, *humble*, and *approachable*.

Disciples

The Great Commission commands us to "Go therefore and make disciples of all nations, baptizing them in the name of the Father and of the Son and of the Holy Spirit, teaching them to observe all that I have commanded you. And behold, I am with you always, to the end of the age" (Matt. 28:19–20). Turning students' hearts toward Christ means we ourselves must be disciples who are making disciples. If we are to be effective in answering Christ's commission, we need to be continually growing in our own faith journey (John 15:1–8) and faithful in following Jesus.

Disciples are students of the Word, the source from which our teaching must flow. To be committed as students of the Word, "we must prayerfully grow closer to the living incarnate Word, the incarnate Christ . . . we must diligently study God's written word, and . . . we must consciously guard against the temptation to redefine or reimagine the Word in our own image."[1]

> "The effective teacher always teaches from the overflow of a full life. . . . I, as a teacher, am primarily a learner, a student among students. . . . Kids aren't looking for a perfect teacher, just an honest one, and a growing one. Yet for so many of them, the pedestals are empty."
>
> —Howard Hendricks, *Teaching to Change Lives: Seven Proven Ways to Make Your Teaching Come Alive* (Colorado Springs: Multnomah, 1987), 17, 35.

Our commitment to proper study and use of God's Word cannot be minimized or overlooked. It is foundational. Our teaching must show that we have dug deeply into God's Word, teaching what it says and not just using it as a proof text for our own ideas. Our students must see that we love God's Word, respect it, honor it, and see it as our final source of authority.

A perfect example of consistency between study and behavior is Ezra, a teacher in the Old Testament. Ezra was committed to three things. He studied the law. And then he obeyed the law. And then he taught the law. He brought his behavior under the authority of God's direction before he taught other people what it said. And, the text says, God honored him (Ezra 7:9–10).[2]

Exemplary

We cannot minimize the importance of being an example to our students. Jesus said, "A disciple is not above his teacher, but everyone when he is fully trained will be like his teacher" (Luke 6:40). If we are to be disciples who are making disciples, we must be conscious of the fact that our students are

---

1. Walt Mueller, *Engaging the Soul of Youth Culture: Bridging Teen Worldviews and Christian Views* (Downers Grove, IL: InterVarsity, 2006), 176–77.
2. I am grateful to author and pastor Jon Swanson of Grabill Missionary Church for his help on this chapter. You can read his daily devotional thoughts on his blog, *300 Words a Day: Following Jesus*, at www.300wordsaday.com.

watching us for clues on how to live out what we teach. If our students will in some ways become like us, then what are they becoming?

This should be a sobering thought to every teacher. Will our students' hearts be turned toward God if they become like us? James Wilhoit and Leland Ryken state, "Students tend not to rise above the spiritual level of their teachers."[3] While it is true that some will grow or mature in spite of the spiritual immaturity of their leader, we can never count on that.

> You have probably heard the saying, "Character is what you do when no one is watching." If our students were to follow us for a day, unbeknownst to us, what would they see? If they were to secretly sit in the backseat of our car when we drove alone, what would they hear us say when the careless driver cuts us off? What would they see us watching on our TV or on our computer screen? Would any of their observations cause us embarrassment? It is a sobering question to ask, but one we should be mindful of consistently.

In his last letter to his apprentice Timothy, Paul reminds Timothy of their long relationship. "You, however, have followed my teaching, my conduct," Paul writes (2 Tim. 3:10). And indeed, Timothy did. They first connected in Lystra, Timothy's hometown. On his first visit to the town, Paul had been stoned and left for dead. On his second visit, Paul recruited Timothy as a companion. And now, near the end of his life, Paul is able to remind Timothy of all the things Timothy has learned about him. When Paul lists the places where he was persecuted and then says, "All who desire to live a godly life in Christ Jesus will be persecuted" (3:12), Timothy can nod in agreement. From the very beginning of their relationship, Paul provided evidence in his own life that following Jesus involved struggle, but that it was possible to remain faithful.

Those of us who lead through teaching must realize with humility that how we live our lives before students will undoubtedly have as much or more influence than our formal teaching. Each one who leads must consider and ask whether his or her life supports with full integrity that which is being taught verbally.

Loving

One of the first church songs children learn is "Jesus Loves Me." We say "God is love" so easily that we assume love is always part of the equation. However, too often love is absent in Christian settings, and mistrust takes its place. Jesus was clear about the importance of love: "A new

3. James Wilhoit and Leland Ryken, *Effective Bible Teaching*, 2nd ed. (Grand Rapids: Baker Academic, 2012), 46.

commandment I give to you, that you love one another: just as I have loved you, you also are to love one another. By this all people will know that you are my disciples, if you have love for one another" (John 13:34–35). How we love each other is actually the "proof" to the world that we are disciples or followers of Jesus.

We all have students who are easy to love, and we all have students who present a challenge for us. It is easy to love the students who are polite, grateful, expressive, and who think we are great. It is the rude, disinterested, calloused, and noncommunicative students who can present a challenge. Whether it is a student who is easy or difficult to love, how can we love our students effectively? We love our students by praying for them, learning their names, smiling, holding them to standards, and even pointing out areas for growth.

There are so many ways in which we can love our students. Some teachers love easily. For others it comes less easily and must be learned. In either case, we can often become so busy that we don't take the time to love our students, colleagues, and peers. We must be intentional about building loving moments into our lives. For those where loving is "less natural" and automatic, lists and specific goals can help in forming strong habits. After all, we are not only *doing* ministry but also teaching and demonstrating what *being* a Christ follower looks like.

Jesus demonstrated loving difficult people throughout his ministry. In fact, he emphasized that kind of love as a goal in an early sermon: "Love your enemies and pray for those who persecute you, that you may be children of your Father in heaven" (Matt. 5:44–45 NIV).

And then he set out to prove his capacity to love. The best illustration is his relationship with Judas. Jesus picked him as one of the Twelve. When Jesus sent the Twelve out on their first internship, Judas went on the trip, paired with another disciple. When Jesus fed the thousands, Judas was one of the disciples handing out food and getting his own basketful. He was allowed to carry the money, he was rescued from the storm with all of them, and he was included in every trip, in every lesson. Even down to the Last Supper, Jesus washed Judas's feet. Jesus knew that Judas didn't understand all the lessons and would fail the final exam. But he kept teaching him.

Reflection: Think back over the teachers you had at school, church, and other settings. List the ones you'd describe as "loving." List others who clearly didn't seem to care for students. What were the characteristics you used to describe who was loving? How did you determine who didn't seem to be loving? Do you think those are fair assessments of their care and concern? What would students say of you as a teacher? How would students determine if you loved them or not?

Transparent

It seems in recent years, in a desire to be authentic, we have been encouraged to be vulnerable and transparent in everything. Transparency can be good, but we are often unclear about what it means and what are its boundaries. Do we use the classroom or youth room as a confessional and expose all of our private stuff as a means of being authentically transparent? In our attempt to be transparent, must our students know about every time we lose our temper or respond inappropriately? No, but that doesn't mean we should try to make them believe we never struggle with being impatient or short in our answers. And, if our struggles are significant, perhaps we shouldn't be teaching, at least not for a while.

Sometimes there's a temptation to be vulnerable to provide an emotional connection or a shock to students. At other times, the microphone has a therapeutic allure, and too quickly the classroom or podium takes on a confessional role. And, before you know it, material has been shared that is inappropriate or unfiltered, and the damage has been done.

We must be wise in what we say, realizing that our words can never be unsaid and will most likely be shared, repeated, and retweeted. One helpful step is to honestly examine our motives. Ask yourself: Am I telling this to my students because it will help them and teach them or because I want them to feel sorry for me or to admire me? We must guard against teaching becoming something we do to meet our needs rather than something that serves the spiritual maturation of our students.

> **We must be wise in what we say, realizing that our words can never be unsaid and will most likely be shared, repeated, and retweeted.**

We must recognize that how we respond with transparency to our own sin and shortcomings will be a teachable moment for our students—and the lesson can be a good one or a bad one. Acknowledging a mistake or sin to our class or group, particularly one they have observed, will generally not diminish their respect. On the other hand, it's not good to share all of your emotions or problems when you're teaching or leading. For example, there may be times where you have an unresolved issue going on that doesn't have the ability to get resolved until after your teaching time is over. It serves no value to get up in front of your group or class and express that you're in the middle of an argument so "excuse me if I seem distracted." They don't need to know that, you don't need to tell them, and you need to pull it together for the sake of your students. In fact, you'll find that in leadership you are often involved in deeply personal matters, and even seasons of conflict or discouragement, of which your students need never know.

Larry Crabb describes the grief that Ezekiel was experiencing over the impending death of his wife, yet Ezekiel had to hold back on fully expressing his grief at the moment so that he could faithfully minister to the people.[4] Sometimes we do need to pull it together for the moment and then later deal with what is going on in our lives once we have a true grasp of the issues, our responses, our hurt, and our pain. Again, we must ask the question, what is the purpose behind our transparency? If it is to conjure up sympathy, we must resist. If it is to minister by teaching, we should feel the freedom. If it is to elicit prayer, we must be cautious and be sure to carefully analyze our motives to make sure we are not manipulating sympathy and support.

Paul wrote a long letter to the church in Corinth. At moments, the letter feels like a rant. Sometime later he wrote another letter, and in 2 Corinthians we get a glimpse of how he felt after writing such a direct letter in 1 Corinthians. Second Corinthians gives him the opportunity to show his fears and frustration and humanity. He talks about us being clay pots with cracks that allow the light to shine through. He talks about what other disciples get to do and how he doesn't. He talks about his struggles with their attitude toward him and his authority.

While he makes no apology for the content, he reveals the cost: "Even when we came into Macedonia, our bodies had no rest, but we were afflicted at every turn—fighting without and fear within. But God, who comforts the downcast, comforted us by the coming of Titus" (2 Cor. 7:5–6). Reading it feels uncomfortable, which is exactly how transparency can feel. Go too far, and we wonder why we are following you. Don't go far enough, and we think you are hiding something or are too good to be true.

Humble

As we mature in ministry (a fancy way of saying "getting old" in ministry), it's likely that we will have more and more success. For some, being in front of a group as a speaker or teacher can be a huge ego boost. We have a captive audience (many need to be there), and some of our students are sitting there poised to soak in our every word of wisdom. If we are not careful, such "power" and influence can go to our heads. In fact, there's an axiom that says you're never as vulnerable as you are when you're successful.

4. Larry Crabb, *The Marriage Builder* (Grand Rapids: Zondervan, 1992), 68.

Are you aware of the trappings that come with such a privilege of getting up in front of a group of students who may want to be like you someday as you pour out your gems of wisdom? We must acknowledge to our students when we don't know the answer, and as stated before, we need to deflate any inaccurate view our students may have of us.

With humility comes the ability and willingness to veer off course from what we may have planned and allow teaching to head in a different direction if necessary. This often comes through a thoughtful question, a relevant current event, or the simple prompting of the Holy Spirit. "Structure and flexibility are complementary parts of a whole. Well-planned class sessions are necessary but not sufficient for good teaching. Plans are lifeless, static, and cold in and of themselves. It is the dynamic of teacher, plan, and learners that brings life to teaching. Mature teachers balance structured planning with flexible execution."[5]

An important checkpoint question to ask is, "To whom are we drawing our students' attention?" When praise and admiration come because of teaching well, such responses can never become our goal. Our goal must always be to be used by God to help turn our students' hearts toward him.

While Paul was in prison, other people started preaching. As he says in Philippians 1, some of these people talked about Christ because Paul couldn't. They wanted to be helpful. Others, however, did it out of spite. "If Paul is locked up," they thought, "we can get ahead of him in the church planting competitions." Paul's response shows his humility. Paul says that it is more important that the gospel be shared than it is to tally the number of disciples anyone has: "the important thing is that in every way, whether from false motives or true, Christ is preached. And because of this I rejoice" (Phil. 1:18 NIV).

Approachable

While it is important to deliver depth in our teaching, it cannot be without a personal connection with our students if we are going to have maximum effectiveness. Our students need to sense that we are approachable and invite the conversations that come after a more formal lesson, where students can express questions, needs for clarification, heart issues, and real concerns. Wilhoit and Ryken comment, "The marks of effective teaching generally transcend specific teaching methods, teacher personalities, and

5. William R. Yount, *Called to Teach: An Introduction to the Ministry of Teaching* (Nashville: Broadman & Holman, 1999), 31.

instructional technologies. They cluster around two major dimensions of education: interpersonal rapport and intellectual substance."[6]

When teachers are approachable, they know and care for their students. Their demeanor should not be one of arrogance or making the learner feel foolish for trying to get clarification. We should be respectful when discussing the views of those with whom we disagree. Such respect will help students who may be concerned about raising an issue where they believe they may disagree with us. We will have eliminated their fear of public or private ridicule if we speak of others with respect.

When teachers are approachable, they use language students can understand. Many of us have sat through classes where we sensed the professor or teacher was trying to impress us with their wisdom more than helping us understand the subject. Such a demeanor intimidated more than welcomed us. Our goal should never be to have our students leave our class or group commenting on how smart we are, but rather our goal should be to hear them say, "I get it now."

Often teachers can take something simple and make it sound very complex, but Jesus was a master at taking the complex and making it sound simple. If our teaching is about pointing people to God, we need to remember it isn't about us. It isn't about trying to convince our students of our brilliance. A humble attitude will not only enhance the teaching setting but also result in an air of approachability, and our teaching and influence can be expanded through a conversation over lunch, a brief exchange while entering a room, or a response to an emailed question from a reflective student writing in the middle of the night.

Teaching is an investment in students' lives. When we are approachable, we are also making ourselves available to our students. Richard Dunn and Jana Sundene, in their book *Shaping the Journey of Emerging Adults*, describe our effectiveness in the disciple-making process this way: "Effective disciplemaking with emerging adults is not based on external factors such as age, marital status or career achievements. Rather, effectiveness is rooted primarily in a willingness to submit to Christ and an openness to invest intentionally and reflectively in an emerging adult's life."[7]

Our investment into our students' lives must be intentional. It will not just happen. We must be available. However, even if we are available, students will never take advantage of connecting with us if we don't come across as approachable.

6. Wilhoit and Ryken, *Effective Bible Teaching*, 47.
7. Richard R. Dunn and Jana Sundene, *Shaping the Journey of Emerging Adults* (Downers Grove, IL: InterVarsity, 2012), 18.

One way to tell whether someone is approachable is to look at the people who stay after class or who talk to students in the hallway. For Jesus, those people were the tax collectors and other sinners. In Luke 15 Jesus tells the story of a shepherd who goes looking for a lost sheep. He tells it to the religious leaders because they are complaining that tax collectors and sinners have been coming to Jesus and listening to his teaching. Jesus never compromised on his message of the kingdom of God. But he was so compassionate that the people who most needed hope were the ones who came to him and the ones he pursued.

What an incredible responsibility and privilege we have to disciple students through our teaching and play a role in the miracle of their spiritual transformation. While we will never be perfect this side of heaven, our character matters. Who you are as a person can enhance or thwart the work of the Holy Spirit in the lives of your students. The life of the teacher is certainly not disconnected from the goal of being used by God to help turn our students' hearts toward him.

Questions and Activities

1. Think of the most influential teacher you've had. How did or didn't this person's life play a role in their impact on your life?
2. Review the six characteristics of an effective Christian teacher, and for each one think of a time when you've observed that characteristic in a teacher.
3. Which one of the six characteristics is most natural for you?
4. Which two do you know you'll have to work on and nurture into stronger characteristics?
5. Read Jesus's woes to the teachers of the law in Matthew 23 in a variety of Bible translations. Grab a trusted commentary to learn more about the customs of the day to which Jesus referred. Imagine that Jesus would share seven woes for Christian teachers today, even for us: what woes might he choose to warn us about?

Further Reading

Hendricks, Howard. *Teaching to Change Lives: Seven Proven Ways to Make Your Teaching Come Alive*. Colorado Springs: Multnomah, 1987.

McDonald, Gordon. *Ordering Your Private World*. Nashville: Thomas Nelson, 2003.

Nouwen, Henri. *In the Name of Jesus: Reflections on Christian Leadership*. New York: Crossroad, 1992.

Sanders, J. Oswald. *Spiritual Leadership: Principles of Excellence for Every Believer*. Chicago: Moody, 2007.

5

Recognizing the Importance of Educational Philosophy

MARK CANNISTER

Every ministry has a philosophy of education. Often this is an embedded philosophy that goes unrecognized, yet it shapes the ethos and educational approach of our ministries. This philosophy is easily seen through examining the posters, flyers, e-blasts, announcements, and signage that promote the programs of Christian ministries.

Walking the hallways of a church, one might come across a poster promoting a six-week Bible study on the book of Romans with a bold header stating, "Know Your Bible!" Whether the planners of this program realize it or not, this Bible study is clearly based on a philosophy of education that promotes the transferring of knowledge from teachers to students with the aim of ensuring that students have learned the content correctly.

On the other hand, teenagers might receive an e-blast from the youth pastor promoting a small-group discussion series on the issue of sexuality and the church with a bold header declaring, "Discuss the Complexities of Sexuality in Today's Culture." This heading, intended or not, suggests a philosophy of education that values something more than simply passing along knowledge. It advocates for developing the cognitive processes of the mind to help students develop critical thinking skills through discussion. Such a philosophical approach recognizes that we live in the mystery of a world and a faith in which not everything is cut-and-dried and that students must learn to navigate multiple perspectives on complex issues.

Then there is a philosophy of education that focuses on social action and is often found underlying ministry programs that seek to identify social needs and provide solutions to those needs. This approach often supports mission trips and services activities in ministries. Another approach found in many ministry curricula is based on a philosophy of education that privileges the individual's development of personal meaning and life purpose. This is most often seen in programs where students are asked to choose topics or issues to explore that they find relevant and meaningful in their own lives.

As we will discover, each of these philosophical underpinnings to ministry curricula, programs, and activities has certain strengths and weaknesses. The goal is not to adopt the perfect philosophy; rather, we must first reflect on our own philosophy. Such reflection is helpful in identifying the limitations in our own experiences, which in turn provides the opportunity to broaden our approach and adopt the strengths of other philosophies into our own thinking. Equally important is keeping in mind that Christian ministry is always concerned with restoration and redemption. George Knight puts it this way:

> Fortunately, lost humanity is not left to its own helplessness. God has taken the initiative to help individuals out of their lostness and to renew and restore his image to its fullness in them (Col 3:10). This is the reason Christ came into the world. The first promise of this restoration and reconciliation may be glimpsed in Genesis 3:15, where Adam and Eve were granted the initial vision of the Redeemer.[1]

Therefore, the context of our teaching and the condition of our students should always provide the starting point of our educational philosophy as we strive for holistic reconciliation and restoration of the faith community.

Five Basic Philosophies of Education

Transmissive Education

Transmissive education[2] grew out of the philosophy of new scholasticism, which is a nonconstructive approach primarily concerned with proving existing knowledge through rationalism rather than creating new knowledge

---

1. George Knight, *Philosophy and Education: An Introduction in Christian Perspective* (Berrien Springs, MI: Andrews University Press, 2006), 195.
2. Also known as perennialism or essentialism. See ibid.

or new perspectives on current knowledge. The aim of this philosophy is transmitting "proven" knowledge from the teacher to the student. Transference of information is designed to foster intellectual growth through passing knowledge and skills from one generation to the next. In Christian ministries this approach is highly content centered, typically focusing on books of the Bible and doctrine. The educational aim is to pour knowledge into students in such a manner that they come to understand a Scripture passage or doctrine "correctly" as defined by the teacher.

The strength of this approach is transmitting objective facts for future recall, such as learning the names of the books of the Bible, the names of biblical characters, or key passages of Scripture. The weakness of this approach is that it fails to foster critical thinking because of the overdependence on the knowledge of the teacher. Students in this context often become passive as they wait on the teacher to offer the "correct" answer. Since this merely requires one-way communication from teacher to student without the need for discussion, debate, reflection, or significant questioning, this philosophy offers a high level of efficiency in education as the instructor can transmit large quantities of information to numerous people in a relatively short period of time, either in person or electronically.

Of course ministry is rarely as objective and efficient as other disciplines. Faith formation is always a messy process that involves doubt, questioning, and reflection, and is best fostered through discussion and debate involving multiple perspectives and interpretations of scriptural meaning and theological positions. While there is much historical, biblical, and theological information to be learned, Christian ministries must strive for more than simply transmitting knowledge if our aim is to foster a living faith among the community we serve.

Cognitivism

Cognitivism is a psychological theory that came to prominence in the late twentieth century and is concerned with studying how we think, understand, and know. The aim of this approach to education is to mature the intellectual processes of the student. This philosophy would argue that the transmissive focus on mere acquisition of knowledge is far too narrow and leaves students frozen in time while knowledge is constantly changing. Rather, in addition to passing on knowledge, it is essential to strengthen students' abilities to think critically and view issues from multiple perspectives. The development of such thinking processes equips people to discover new knowledge for themselves and integrate that knowledge into their lives. Paulo Freire argues that education is not a bank vault where students come to withdraw the knowledge they need for living, nor is knowledge a commodity to be passed from teachers to students.[3] Rather, students must construct knowledge from the knowledge, experiences, and skills they possess. In Christian ministries this approach would include developing the student's ability to use exegetical and hermeneutical tools so that they can begin to interpret the Scriptures for themselves.

Viewing knowledge and skills as tools that help people make sense of the world is very useful for focusing on the integration of complex and ambiguous biblical issues through deep reflection on the various contextual perspectives of an issue or a Bible passage. This approach values reflection on faith traditions, personal and communal experience, and one's own faith practices as well as the faith practices of others. "Learning is a process where knowledge is presented to us, then shaped through understanding, discussion and reflection."[4] Because this approach focuses heavily on the process of thinking rather than on content, there is the risk that students become so enamored with reflecting, questioning, and debating that such activities never lead to conclusions and the implementation of those conclusions.

As we strive to lead people to a point where they truly own their faith, a cognitive approach in our curriculum, programs, and activities becomes essential. Only after wrestling with ideas and discovering knowledge and insights for oneself in the context of a vital faith community do we truly come to possess a living faith. Knowledge can be transmitted, but faith must be discovered, and cognitivism is essential to fostering the faith discovery process.

Humanism

Humanism is a philosophical approach that emphasizes the student's development of personal meaning. This requires students to contribute to the construction of curriculum and the ministry programs in a manner that is meaningful and relevant to their lives. Educator John Holt describes humanism by stating "that children are by nature smart, energetic, curious, eager to learn, and good at learning; that they do not need to be bribed and bullied to learn; that they learn best when they are happy, active, involved, and interested in what they are doing; that they learn least, or not at all, when they are bored, threatened, humiliated, frightened."[5] This approach is observed when ministry leaders seek to discover those subjects, topics, or

3. Paulo Freire, *Teachers as Cultural Workers: Letters to Those Who Dare Teach* (Boulder, CO: Westview, 1998), 22.

4. Ibid., 31.

5. John Holt, *Freedom and Beyond* (Portsmouth, NH: Heinemann, 1995), 10.

activities that interest students. Once these issues are identified, curriculum and programs are developed to engage students.

This philosophy harkens back to Jean-Jacques Rousseau, the eighteenth-century philosopher who viewed the teacher as a gardener whose task is to nurture what is naturally springing forth from the students.[6] Teachers should not impose knowledge or thinking skills from the outside; rather, a student is seen as a growing plant to be given freedom to develop from within. The teacher guides the students as a gardener would cultivate a plant by providing a rich environment for growth. In this sense the student is given a significant amount of autonomy to strive for self-actualization.

Approaching education from this perspective is helpful in developing a warm, nurturing climate where students feel affirmed and valued. This builds self-esteem and confidence while meeting the felt needs of students. Students feel greater freedom to share their thoughts and feelings, hopes, and doubts in such an environment. In the extreme, when this is the only approach to education, humanism can foster an uncritical perspective on life, as only positive reinforcement is offered. When subject matter is chosen only by students, there are important areas of learning that are likely to be missed. When self-discovery is relied on disproportionately, students are robbed of the opportunity to understand multiple perspectives and consider a multitude of voices on topics.

Humanism is an important aspect of Christian ministries as we strive to create environments that are engaging for students and provide a safe place to question and explore issues of faith and life. Freire suggests, "There are no themes or values of which one cannot speak, no areas in which one must be silent. We can talk about everything and we can give testimony about everything."[7] May this be so in our Christian ministries as well! Humanism also offers a foundation for developing engaging, relevant, and age-appropriate curriculum and programs. This approach, while important, must be used in harmony with transmissive approaches and cognitivism. Engaging this approach alone will leave students with a patchwork faith that lacks breadth and continuity.

Developmentalism

Developmentalism understands knowledge as a tool that helps students make sense of the world. Therefore, developmentalism embraces transmissive education as a starting point but rejects the notion of accruing

6. See further Jean-Jacques Rousseau, *Emile* (New York: Basic Books, 1979).
7. Freire, *Teachers as Cultural Workers*, 58.

knowledge for the sake of mere knowledge acquisition itself. Developmentalism strives to apply the accumulated knowledge to real-life issues. "Developmentalists seek to promote an *instrumental* use of knowledge; that is, they want the student to be able to do something with the knowledge that has been learned."[8] In this sense it is not enough to know about the Scriptures or faith. Students must consider how that knowledge affects daily living. This often requires focusing on the integration of complex and ambiguous information in Scripture while developing a lifestyle of reflective thought and action. At its best, developmentalism strives to help students develop from reflection on tradition, experience, one's own practices, and the practices of others. "The developmentalist seeks to help Christians gain a more useful knowledge of the faith and to encourage them to work out an understanding of their beliefs that fit the world as they see it."[9]

When taken to an extreme, the grave danger of developmentalism, especially in Christian ministries, is the belief that knowledge is static and can be applied successfully to any particular situation. God's revelation to us will always be incomplete, and our understanding of Scripture will never be fully clear; we serve a living God and study the living Word of God. Hence, there is always danger in asking how we might "apply" the knowledge gained from a particular passage of Scripture, as if we have determined the full knowledge to be gleaned from the passage.

Reconstructionism

Reconstructionism is a philosophical approach that grew out of John Dewey's philosophy of progressive education, which challenged the traditional idea that the purpose of education was to passively transfer the cultural norms from one generation to the next. The progressives argued that education could and should be a primary agent of social reform. Reconstructionism assumes that the world is in crisis and that civilization will come to an end unless problems ranging from pollution to racism are not resolved. It also assumes that education is the major change agent in reforming society. Therefore, we must purposefully teach for social change.[10]

Such an approach, secular as it may be in popular culture, resonates with the passion of Christian ministries to be agents for reconciliation and restoration. Reconstructionism requires us to identify the needs of others

8. James Wilhoit, *Christian Education and the Search for Meaning* (Grand Rapids: Baker, 1991), 90 (emphasis original).
9. Ibid., 94.
10. Knight, *Philosophy and Education*, 119–21.

and strive to meet those needs. Proponents of this philosophy aim to take an eschatological approach to ministry that works to construct a better world that is more representative of the world to come, focusing as much on the reconciliation among people as the reconciliation between people and God.[11]

Taken to an extreme, the philosophy of reconstructionism can be akin to indoctrination, when teachers view students as vehicles through which to accomplish their own agendas. This robs students of the opportunity to develop skills in critical thinking and reflection. Yet working in harmony with other philosophies, reconstructionism brings an essential component to the work of the gospel that we strive for in Christian ministries.

Three Types of Curricula

What we teach is referred to as our curricula, and we approach curricula from certain philosophical perspectives intentionally or unintentionally. Curriculum broadly understood is far more than the booklet from which we teach a Bible study. The curriculum of our ministries includes everything that we teach and do not teach intentionally and unintentionally. This is very complex, as Dewey reminds us: "Perhaps the greatest of all pedagogical fallacies is the notion that a person learns only the particular thing he is studying at the time."[12]

Explicit

Explicit curricula are the content of learning that we have intentionally set out for our students to engage. This may include knowledge to be learned, critical thinking and reflection skills to be developed, or experiences that shape the heart and mind. Whatever the activity or content might be, it has been intentionally planned and designed to be educational.

Implicit

Implicit curricula are those things that students learn that we have not intentionally planned. This is often referred to as "the hidden curriculum" and typically is communicated through the socialization aspect of our ministries. When gathering for worship, we often set expectations unintentionally by modeling a certain level of reverence through our quiet and orderly participation. This teaches students to be compliant and respectful of God

11. See further Miroslav Volf, *Exclusion and Embrace: A Theology of Identity, Otherness, and Reconciliation* (Nashville: Abingdon, 1996).

12. John Dewey, *Experience and Education* (New York: Macmillan, 1938), 87.

and others, though it is unlikely that such learning was discussed in the worship-planning meeting.

We often teach implicit lessons to students through modeling certain behaviors that we may not even be aware others are noticing. The way we treat others, the compassion we show for suffering people, the manner in which we pray, the hope that we project, the love that we share, and the grace that we offer all contribute to the transformation process as students learn from our example. This is a powerful aspect of our ministry curriculum that should not be overlooked. It is often recognized only in hindsight by asking students what they have learned through our ministries over the years. The answers are at times surprising and humbling.

Null

Null curricula are the content and activities that are never taught. The reality is that we have a finite amount of time with students in ministry and must prioritize what is most important to communicate to our people. There are certain books of the Bible that often become part of our null curriculum as we prioritize certain Bible lessons over others. There are certain theological perspectives that reside in our null curriculum as we tend to favor the perspectives of our faith tradition. There are some spiritual disciplines that we teach rather than others because of our own faith journey experiences.

Concerning that which we do not teach, Elliot Eisner suggests, "Ignorance is not simply a neutral void; it has important effects on the kinds of options one is to consider."[13] Hence, it is important that we thoughtfully consider what we are placing in the null curriculum rather than allowing the null curriculum to develop by happenstance. What are the consequences of rarely teaching from the Old Testament, offering a limited number of spiritual disciplines, or never engaging in cross-cultural experiences?

Eisner offers a compelling summary of the importance of recognizing these three aspects of our curriculum.

> When we ask, therefore, about the means through which schools teach we can recognize that one of the major means is through the explicit curriculum that is offered to students. But that is not all. Schools also teach through the implicit curriculum, that pervasive and ubiquitous set of expectations and rules that defines schooling as a cultural system that itself teaches important lessons. And we can identify the null curriculum—the options students are not afforded,

13. Elliot Eisner, *The Educational Imagination* (Upper Saddle River, NJ: Pearson Education, 2002), 97.

the perspectives they may never know about, much less be able to use, the concepts and skills that are not part of their intellectual repertoire. Surely, in the deliberations that constitute the course of living, their absence will have important consequences on the kind of life that students can choose to lead.[14]

Three Types of Educational Objectives

Once we have a clear understanding of our educational philosophy as an overarching approach to ministry, it is important to define more specific objectives in terms of the outcomes that we hope students might achieve. Eisner offers three types of objectives that are extremely useful for achieving our goals in ministry.[15]

Behavioral

Behavioral objectives are the most common types of objectives and are also referred to as *instructional objectives* or *performance objectives*. The key to behavioral objectives is ensuring that they are specific, clear, measurable, and observable in terms of describing student performance.[16] That is, a student must be able to perform what is described in the objective and do so within a prescribed criterion. For example, students may be asked to name the Ten Commandments. This is an observable behavior. To be able to name the Ten Commandments is a fine objective; however, we rarely ask students to achieve perfection. Hence adding criteria to the objective by asking students to name at least eight of the Ten Commandments would be more reasonable. This provides students with an observable task to achieve and the criteria that will be considered acceptable.

Since we rarely test students in ministry the way they are tested in school, perhaps with the rare exception of a confirmation or baptism class exam in some traditions, naming the criteria is of less concern in a ministry context than naming the observable task. In the end it is the student's conscience that will determine if he or she has performed at an acceptable standard.

Behavioral objectives are very useful as we plan for the knowledge and skills that we hope students will acquire. There are certainly biblical contents, theological concepts, and study skills that we desire our students to obtain. Memorizing Scripture, retelling biblical stories such as the exodus and the

14. Ibid., 107.
15. Ibid., chap. 4.
16. See further Robert Mager, *Preparing Instructional Objectives* (Atlanta: Center for Effective Performance, 1997).

life of Jesus, describing theological concepts such as the Trinity and the atonement, and demonstrating the ability to use study tools such as commentaries, encyclopedias, dictionaries, and concordances that give greater biblical and theological insights may all be described in terms of behavioral objectives.

However, we would be less than satisfied in our ministries if our students memorized the entire Bible, mastered the biblical languages, and could debate every theological position yet not possess a meaningful faith. When it comes to acquiring knowledge and skills, behavioral objectives are quite useful, but when it comes to faith formation, we need additional objectives.

Problem Solving

Problem-solving objectives offer students the opportunity to develop critical thinking skills and individualized approaches to issues. With a problem-solving objective all students are given the same problem to solve, yet the solutions may vary from student to student or group to group as they work toward a solution. The answer is not as definite as with behavioral objectives, and this enhances cognitive learning and intellectual flexibility.

A classic example of this type of objective is the science class assignment to build a bridge of toothpicks across a two-foot span that will hold five pounds of weight for five minutes. Groups of students build bridges that look radically different from one another, but they all achieve the objective. In ministry settings such objectives can be extremely useful in faith formation, worship planning, and mentoring. For example, one might challenge students to grow in their faith through spiritual disciplines by introducing them to a dozen or more disciplines and then asking students to spend a month discovering the disciplines that most effectively connect them with God. At the end of the month as students report on the disciplines they find most effective, the group discovers that everyone has a different set of disciplines while also discovering significant ways to connect with God and grow in their faith. Several worship teams might be given an assignment to create an Easter worship service. Each team completes the assignment extremely well, yet every service is unique. A ministry that values relationships between leaders and students might charge the leaders to spend time with students outside of the regularly scheduled ministry programs. The leaders may brainstorm a list of creative possibilities for hanging out with students, but as leaders begin to build relationships with students, it becomes clear that no two leaders are doing the same things. As leaders report on how their relationship building or mentoring with students is unfolding, every story is different, yet everyone is accomplishing the objective that was set before them.

Expressive

Expressive objectives are useful when learning can be seen only once it has been achieved. Sometimes learning outcomes cannot be known in advance, and we cannot write behavioral or problem-solving objectives that define desired outcomes. However, given our experience and wisdom we know that certain activities have educational value even if we don't know the precise outcomes for the group or individuals. Expressive outcomes become the consequences of learning activities where we observe the learning with which we end up, intended or not, after some form of educational experience. This type of objective assumes that purpose need not precede activity. Rather, purpose can be formulated in the process of experience-oriented activities.

In schools this happens often on field trips, perhaps to a museum. The teacher knows that visiting a museum can be educational but does not know exactly how it will be educational for each student. Some students may be inspired by a certain piece of artwork, while others are inspired by a different piece. Some may focus on the magnitude of the museum, while others study one particular section in depth. At the end of the trip as the teacher debriefs the group asking various questions—"What did you learn today?"; "What would you like to learn more about?"; and "What remains a mystery to you?"—and each student responds with different answers to the same questions.

While this sounds similar to problem solving, the difference is that the teacher doesn't know what the learning outcomes will be until the students report on what they have learned following the experience. Mission trips are a good example of this type of objective in ministry. We know from experience that students grow in their faith through mission trips, but they do so in a variety of ways. All we can honestly say up front is that this mission trip will be formational to your faith. How that will happen or what that formation will look like cannot be predicted in advance. Only in hindsight, as people reveal how they have grown in their faith, are we able to recognize the faith formation that has taken place.

A Final Thought

Developing your philosophy of education for Christian ministries is neither done in isolation from the vast history of educational philosophy nor is it simply an adoption of one of the many historical approaches to education. Rather, your philosophy must be crafted thoughtfully and reflectively with your ministry team, giving careful consideration to a variety of perspectives on educational philosophy, your ministry context, and your faith tradition.

"We are programmed to learn, we live, or experience, or we find ourselves open to experience the relationship between what we inherit and what we acquire."[17] This constructive process will result in a philosophy of education that will keep your ministry grounded as you navigate the challenges of Christian ministry in the twenty-first century.

Questions and Activities

1. Read the announcements in church bulletins, e-blasts, flyers, newsletters, websites, and other promotional material. What educational philosophies are being promoted?

2. Thinking about transmissive education, what is the objective knowledge that is essential for your students to know and understand? Thinking about cognitivism, what are the cognitive skills and learning tools that are essential for your students to acquire? Thinking about humanism, what kind of environment would produce maximum engagement for your students? Thinking about developmentalism, what do your students need to learn how to do? Thinking about reconstructionism, how might your ministry be involved in the reconciling work of the gospel here on earth, as it is in heaven?

3. What are some implicit things you learned in school that were probably part of the implicit or hidden curriculum? What about in your church or ministry settings?

4. What are some things in your schooling that were probably part of the null curriculum? What about in your church or ministry settings?

5. Write three behavioral objectives for your current ministry. Write three problem-solving objectives for your current ministry. Write three expressive objectives for your current ministry.

Further Reading

Eisner, Elliot. *The Educational Imagination*. Upper Saddle River, NJ: Pearson Education, 2002.

Knight, George. *Philosophy and Education: An Introduction in Christian Perspective*. Berrien Springs, MI: Andrews University Press, 2006.

---

17. Freire, *Teachers as Cultural Workers*, 95.

The Shape of Human Knowledge and Christian Ministry

A Bad Walk in London: A Philosophical Story

ANDREW ROOT

I had already made so many bad decisions I shouldn't have been surprised to be right back where I started. But everything looked so different that I had persuaded myself I had never been here before, though I had started at this very point just an hour or so earlier. Nevertheless, I was convinced I was somewhere else. I had followed a trusted text; my map said I was across the park, but something wasn't right. And so here I was.

Just an hour earlier I had entered Hyde Park in London. Going through the Lancaster Gate, I took a minute to look at its flowers and fountains. I sat on a step and tried to notice it all, feeling a sense of gratitude for being there, enjoying the idea of having an afternoon to myself. It was an intro-vert's paradise—a beautiful crisp day, a new place to explore, a map to lead me, and only my own mind for company.

I suppose my goal was simply to soak in the scenic park and live in the thoughts of my head. But I had another stated objective; I wanted to walk across the park to the Churchill museum. The map had bold, numbered bubbles identifying important attractions throughout the city. I saw that the museum was number six, so I started walking toward it. Yet, after I found myself blocks away from the park and down a small street, I realized that I had a problem—this was no location for a museum. It was starting to feel like it was no place for a tourist at all.

At first, I thought I had a bad map. I wondered for a few minutes if I could trust it anymore; it was supposed to take me one place and instead had taken me to another. And this other place was no paradise. I supposed I could have quit and discarded the map, believing there was nothing authoritative or normative anymore to believe in, and go it alone.

Of course, if I had, I would have been stuck because I had no way back to the hotel. I would need to decide to move in and live in this seedy part of London, claiming that it was the only reality I could trust and believe in because all the other places in London that the map spoke of couldn't be trusted to exist at all. After all, the map had promised me the museum and failed, so how could I again trust that it had any correlation with reality? How could I even know there was a reality beyond my present experience? I suppose I could have discarded the map and settled for the local and cultural realities of the neighborhood.

I did finally locate the exact place the red bubble "6" indicated. And it was no museum but a rundown strip mall. I suppose I could have trusted the map more than my experience. Perhaps claiming that this strip of shops couldn't *be* a museum was to give too much authority to my subjective experience. I had an authoritative text that claimed that the Churchill museum was right here. This map, as I looked it over, was even stamped with the London tourist authority seal; clearly they know their stuff. Being that the map said this was *truly* the spot of the museum, I could have ignored my subjective experience, walked up to the curry restaurant, and asked to see the Churchill bunker. If they looked confused and said, pointing to the surroundings of the restaurant, "This is no museum, mate; this is a restaurant," I could have pulled out my map and said, "I know that is your experience, but I can't trust that because I have a map and it says that the museum is here."

A Face-Off between Two Teams

While perhaps sounding absurd, my incident in London illustrates a major debate that is going on that has a direct impact on our ministry. It frames how we understand people, the action of God, and the shape of reality itself. It raises questions about the shape of human knowledge and learning, the experience of God, and the practice of ministry.

We could think of this debate as being framed by two distinct ways of doing ministry, imagining two different teams claiming two different ways of seeing the world, young people, and the action of God. One of these teams could be called "Modernity's Man," the other "Society's Being."[1]

Team Modernity's Man

Modernity's Man believes that there are strong foundations in the world, that there are objective things that we can trust. And we can trust them because our human rationality can climb to a peak and see all of reality, knowing what is right, true, and good. The ability of Modernity's Man that allows him to think he can win the debate is the very power of human rationality itself. This team believes that there are foundations, truths that the human mind can uncover so completely that they can't be doubted. My map, Modernity's Man would assert, is a foundational truth. Out of the genius of rationality, people who had climbed to the peak of knowledge had seen the shape of London. Even if I couldn't perceive in my own mind that this was indeed the museum, my foundational map claimed it was true.

In the Enlightenment, with its emphasis on reason and individualism, philosophers and scientists believed that good, reasoned thinking could uncover the foundations of all things, leading them to climb to a peak and claim that they had mapped all of reality. And having this map, all we needed to do was follow it, and we'd find the good, the holy, and even God . . . if we needed God at all.

Team Modernity's Man plays its game convinced it knows all of reality; it knows just what it means to be a human being, just who God is, and just how every person should act and live. Rationality uncovers foundations, and these foundations are universally true! My map in London could be seen as a universal foundation discovered through rationality. My own subjective experience, because it doesn't correlate with the foundation, must then surrender to the rational foundation, which means the map is more real than my experience. I may see and feel that I'm nowhere near a museum, but the map is true; so my feelings and experience, because they are dangerously open to irrationality, must be ignored. Until my experience has walked each foundational step up to some objective peak, I simply can't trust it.

To do youth ministry for Modernity's Man is to get young people to confirm in their mind, and conform in action, to the foundations. A young person's

---

1. The two labels I use come from the work of Margaret Archer, *Being Human: The Problem of Agency* (Cambridge: Cambridge University Press, 2001).

doubts or experience of suffering are annoying or threatening because they strike against the foundations and can't be seen as a true expression of reality.

Of course, and please hear me, it is good and right to make God our foundation or core. However, on Team Modernity's Man, "God" can easily be turned into a foundation. But the problem with playing on Team Modernity's Man is that the offense we run is fully bound to rationality. Foundational rationality seeks to depersonalize; it seeks to find the unchanging, unmoving, static foundations. From this reductionist perspective God is not a living person who can actually encounter us in and through our experience but has been frozen into a map that we can use as an instrument.

Youth ministry, then, is about knowledge; it is driven by what philosophers call *epistemology*. Your goal is to help young people *know* the foundations, to assimilate the knowledge of the Bible. You do fun stuff to create enough trust or loyalty to convince young people of your knowledge, and you are a good youth worker if more and more kids *know* how to avoid sin and believe the Bible. You then need to spend a lot of time as a youth worker giving convincing, rational arguments for faith and the truth of the Bible to your young people.

Youth ministry, then, doesn't include imagining with young people how in and through their lived experience in the world they might encounter the living presence of the resurrected Jesus, who comes to them even today. Rather, youth ministry on Team Modernity's Man seeks to use techniques, programs, and events to make young people loyal to the foundations, to claim them as a cognitive rational actuality. Team Modernity's Man then stands tall on a foundation and with arrogance shouts that it knows all reality and has a map to prove it!

Team Society's Being

The adversary and great rival of Team Modernity's Man is Team Society's Being. While Modernity's Man believes it can get to a peak to see all that is true and real, Society's Being wants to see only the particular, local, and cultural. Team Society's Being believes that there are no foundations that can be called true or even real. Rather, we're all given certain maps of London, but these maps are always different; they're written through our own unique cultural and familial socialization, for instance. Every human is given a map, but this map is true only for the individual it is given to; everyone has his or her own map. And in the end when we really search, we discover that all maps don't take us anywhere anyhow, that there is actually no real museum; it was just in our minds.

Team Society's Being is *post*modern because it believes that the rational foundational project of Team Modernity's Man is a dream, asserting that all universal foundational maps are just written by those with power. Powerful people claim universal foundations that support their own position; they act as if they have ascended a peak to see all that is real, but this is just a ploy to justify their own position of power. Reality, then, is nothing more than stories and concepts our minds consent to; reality itself, the postmodernist hails, is mind-dependent. Anything that is true is not universally so; truth is just stories, thoughts, and perspectives that we adopt. There is no such thing as universal truth; there are just truths that we hold to for now because we have been convinced through our socialization to believe them. Team Society's Being believes that Team Modernity's Man is composed of stupid, overly muscular fools who can't see that their own position is given to them by nothing more than their socialization; they have confused social constructions for universal realities.

And the proof of this for Team Society's Being is in the incredible amount of plurality in our world. Team Society's Being points to this pluralism to claim that there simply can't be any foundational reality. As a matter of fact, Team Society's Being is so feisty and courageous that they are willing to claim that because there is such pluralism, there simply can't be anything real at all. All reality is nothing but socially constructed maps that we agree to believe are true.

Team Modernity's Man is triumphalist, beating its chest to say it knows, completely, the truth. Society's Being is defeatist, shrugging its shoulders, pointing to the plurality of our cultural worlds as proof that there is nothing real at all.

The funny thing is, to do youth ministry on Team Society's Being is to do it both radically different from and yet very similar to Team Modernity's Man. What is different is that youth ministry becomes about helping young people strip away the socializing layers of what they've been given by culture. The goal is to deconstruct the maps. Team Society's Being says that once we realize that no map correlates with reality, then we are free to discard the maps that are restrictive and oppressive. We ask young people to reflect deeply on why this or that map is here at all—that's the goal of youth ministry, to see how cultural narratives seek to cage youth, keeping them from acting in the world for God. Narratives like consumerism present maps of sexual beauty and money as one's ultimate purpose, but these are only social constructions that can be discarded. So youth ministry tries to deconstruct narratives regarding topics like consumerism and beauty, so that young people might be free from maps that capture and corrupt their action.

Team Modernity's Man believes young people are basically blank Lego pads, and our job is to take the blocks of biblical knowledge and snap them into their minds. Team Society's Being believes that young people are wrapped in the cocoon of many cultural narratives that must be stripped away so that they can find the freedom to act authentically in the world.

Some think Team Society's Being is at the advantage in this debate because Modernity's Man makes young people passive receivers of information to assimilate, while Society's Being seeks to free young people to be actors in the world. But Modernity's Man rebuts that Society's Being has used such a blunt instrument with such little precision that as it cuts out narratives, discarding them all in the bin labeled "social constructions," it also cuts out the reality of God. So afraid of foundations, Society's Being boldly, but nevertheless clumsily, cuts out the possibility that God could be a personal reality and not simply another socially constructed map. Those doing youth ministry from the antifoundational project of Society's Being will claim that there is still a place for God to be real. But it is hard to see how this is possible because all of reality has been made into a culturally bound map.

But oddly, where these two perspectives are the same is in their commitment to knowing. Team Modernity's Man says the goal of youth ministry is to get young people to *know* the foundations as unquestionably true. The goal of youth ministry from the perspective of Team Society's Being is for young people to *know* that they are free to act, that they can escape the narratives of consumerism, sexism, and all other cultural maps of -isms to freely act. What is ironic is that both perspectives seem to make *knowing* (epistemology) the goal of ministry.

A Way Between

Standing in the middle of the sidewalk, I continued to look down at the map and back again at the street, trying to figure out what had gone wrong. I was willing neither to discard the map nor to give it complete authority. I was willing to believe that it witnessed to something real. Finally, I realized my problem: there were two different colored bubbles; the red referred to restaurants and the green to museums. I had walked forty-five minutes in the wrong direction, not realizing I was following the restaurant listings. Exhausted but not deterred, I again entered Hyde Park, now following the map more attentively than ever. Yet, after another forty-five minutes I came to another gate that I believed would take me out of the park and to the museum. I was sure it was Queen Elizabeth Gate, but something wasn't right. Yet it had to be! I had followed the map and clearly I was at a real gate! This was where the map had told me to be.

It took me a whole five minutes to realize that though my mind was sure that I had walked across the park and was now at Queen Elizabeth Gate, the brute fact was that I wasn't there. After minutes staring at the gate, in the oddest way, it all of a sudden dawned on me; I was right back at Lancaster Gate, right where I had begun. I didn't recognize it because I was seeing it from another direction; coming upon it I was sure I was somewhere else. My mind had deceived me, hindering me from actually being able to embrace reality, but nevertheless I was really at Lancaster Gate; I was somewhere real beyond what my mind constructed.

This experience allows us to imagine a middle way in the battle of Team Modernity's Man and Team Society's Being. It reveals the strengths and weaknesses of each and gives us a deeper conception of ministry. Modernity's Man is right: there are objective, real things in the world and beyond. Society's Being is wrong to assume that there is no reality other than what is dependent on human minds and is therefore socially constructed. I couldn't deny that I was at a gate, and as much as I tried to imagine a different way of seeing both the text of the map and my own experience, I couldn't change that I was not at Queen Elizabeth Gate. I could even imagine what it was like to be at the other gate, but the brute fact was I was somewhere else.

Yet what was also clear was that my own experience was easily confused. I was at the gate where I had just been, but couldn't see it. It took me five whole minutes to recognize a gate I had walked through just hours earlier. Society's Being was right: there was no way for me to climb to some objective perch and stand on a foundation. I could only know the world from within it, and because that was the case, it was always possible that I could be confused or wrong. So there were no foundations—I agreed with Society's Being—but there was also something real, as Modernity's Man believed.

A way between in the debate is to claim that our experience is best understood in a third way, in what is called a *postfoundational critical realist* way. What this means is that we have minds for reality and real experiences of reality—even higher forms of reality that exist outside of our human minds. But this theory also claims that our own minds are always found somewhere in the middle of the layers of reality; therefore, our perceptions and perspectives are always open to error or confusion.

This allows for a major shift in how we think of teaching in ministry. In the standoff between Modernity's Man and Society's Being, we are fighting over *knowing*. For both teams, discussions of *real* experiences of God are hard to have, for God is bound and tied as either a frozen foundation or a relativized story. Both teams turn God into an object that can be controlled by human knowers.

Postfoundational critical realism actually makes it possible for us to claim that God is a subject that encounters our person. Ministry then becomes not about helping young people know stuff, asking how can we teach them stuff that will stick or that will lead them to act this or that way. Rather, the point of ministry is to invite young people to take on practices of ministry so that they might experience the very being of God. Ministry to the next generations, then, is obsessed by not knowledge (epistemology) but being (ontology); we want to know how it is that the beings of young people experience the being of God. We desire for our ministry to be formed in such a way that young people actually encounter the living being of Jesus Christ calling them to follow him. And this living Jesus cannot be imagined as a frozen foundation (as a bunch of information) but is rather a person who encounters our person, coming to minister to us.

Society's Being is right; we want young people to act not so that they can be free from social constructions but so that they might minister to their neighbor, finding the being of Jesus present as they do (Matt. 25). Our experience of the living Jesus will always be open to doubt and confusion because we cannot climb to some objective peak to know things completely. But this is good news; because if we could know things completely, we'd think that we could control God. The fact that our experience is always open to confusion and doubt only pushes us further to make our youth ministries about faith seeking understanding and not about assimilation of knowledge. And Modernity's Man is right that there is a trusted tradition that we must turn to, but this trusted tradition, from a postfoundational critical realist perspective, is used to give shape and interpretation to our experiences.

So we could say, in the end, ministry from a postfoundational critical realist perspective is nothing more than *testimony*. We ask young people to do mission, pray, and read their Bibles because these practices allow us to open ourselves to God. Youth ministry seeks not knowledge but transformational encounter with God. We want young people not simply to know about God but to encounter God's very presence. We can do this only if we move into a postfoundational understanding of ministry where we seek the experiences of God's coming to us in Jesus Christ. Youth ministry is a space where we continue to ask young people to receive, review, and reexamine their real (and at often times, confusing) call of the living Jesus to come and follow.

Maybe, then, at its most practical, ministry to the next generations is really just a space created by you, the Christian worker, for young people to hear the adults in the church tell their testimonies of their real experience with the presence and absence of God. And then you encourage them to do the same. It is in testifying that we avoid the hubris of Modernity's Man and defeatism of Society's Being and claim the real possibility that the living Jesus comes to us even today.

Questions and Activities

1. What is the critique of how Team Modernity's Man would lead a teaching ministry? What is the critique of Team Society's Being's approach?
2. What is the way between? How does it provide a solution to the two extremes?
3. What is the difference between perception and reason?
4. What role did trial and experience play in learning in the essay? What role did the map play in the essay?
5. Write down three or four implications from this essay on Christian teaching that seeks to lead people to a transformational encounter with God.

Further Reading

Archer, Margaret S., Andrew Collier, and Douglas V. Porpora. *Transcendence: Critical Realism and God*. London: Routledge, 2004.

Hart, David Bentley. *The Experience of God: Being, Consciousness, Bliss*. New Haven: Yale University Press, 2013.

Root, Andrew. *Christopraxis: A Practical Theology of the Cross*. Minneapolis: Fortress, 2014.

SECTION TWO

INFLUENCES THAT SHAPE LEARNING

No matter the effectiveness of the teacher or the depth of content, there are always influences beyond the teacher's control. For instance, the developmental process affects how people think and at what age their thinking changes. Students' past, their biological makeup, personality, and family of origin, all give shape to the way they learn. Their social environments, personal history with school and learning, and cultural upbringing and traditions influence their learning in dramatic ways. Wise Christian teachers understand these influences and shape their teaching and curriculum accordingly.

Dialogue between Christian theology and educational psychology is important. The chapters in this section provide an overview to important themes and concepts that are crucial for teachers to understand and to be conversant with. Readers will be well served to note the terms in this section and to make sure they understand their meaning and the resulting implications on Christian ministry.

Too often teaching takes a dominant and mechanistic approach, as if teaching can be designed to automatically produce learning. Therefore, this section includes chapters on the underlying factors at work, including the sociocultural and motivational contexts of learning. An appreciation for the power of community, an awareness of the gatekeeping role of motivation in learning, and a posture of humility with one another in our multicultural contexts can all benefit teaching. The underlying frameworks in these chapters help us to complete the teaching task to which we are called.

How People Develop Their Thinking

BARRETT MCRAY

> Every teacher, in order to edify all in the one virtue of char-
> ity, must touch the hearts of . . . hearers by using one and
> the same doctrine, but not by giving to all one and the same
> exhortation.
>
> —St. Gregory the Great, ca. 590 AD

Effective teaching, as Pope Gregory suggested almost fifteen hundred years
ago, depends on the ability of the teacher to understand how students learn
and to adjust teaching methods accordingly. In their book *Effective Bible
Teaching*, James Wilhoit and Leland Ryken suggest that effective teaching
ought to be measured by "how much . . . students learn and apply the Bible."[1]
The goal of our teaching, then, ought to be communicating the truths of the
Bible in such a way that students hear, understand, embrace, and begin to
embody them. True learning should lead to transformation in the students'
lives; and if our teaching does not lead to this kind of learning, then we may
do well to examine why this is so.

---

1. James Wilhoit and Leland Ryken, *Effective Bible Teaching*, 2nd ed. (Grand Rapids: Baker
Academic, 2012), 30.

Wilhoit and Ryken define learning as "educational experiences that engage students and prompt them to wrestle with information, test its validity, find ways of using what is learned, and relate or adapt it to previously learned material."[2] Robert Pazmiño puts it this way: "Learning in the biblical sense called for a complete response of the person to God's teaching."[3] For this type of learning to occur, the teacher must know the students, how they learn, and what barriers prevent their learning. Sounds simple enough, but people vary significantly in the ways that they learn, many factors affect learning, and some people face significant challenges in their capacity to learn.

During the past century, the field of psychology has emerged as a significant contributor to our understanding of such questions as:

- How does learning change over the course of a person's life as she grows and develops?
- How does learning occur across various dimensions of a person's life?
- What aspects of a person's physical, mental, or emotional well-being affect her learning?

And many more!

In this chapter, we will consider some of these questions and some of the significant contributions offered by the field of psychology.[4] Each new generation must engage the world in which they live, rediscovering Christianity in each new context.[5] To do this, we must be deeply rooted in historic Chris-

---

2. Ibid.

3. Robert Pazmiño, *Principles and Practices of Christian Education: An Evangelical Perspective* (Grand Rapids: Baker, 1992), 123.

4. It may be worthwhile for us to say a word about the relationship between psychology and the church. Some have argued that the developmental theories of educational psychology have undermined the integrity of the historic educational practices of the church. Some, on the other extreme, have even gone so far as to say that religious education must rely solely on contemporary educational theory, asserting that "no theological conceptualization" is adequate as a theoretical base for religious instruction. It is perhaps important to know that we are convinced that Christian educators need to dialogue with both theologians and educational theorists in forming the theoretical base for our teaching ministries. There is immense value in this dialogue for Christians and for the efficacy of their learning; this conversation is further valuable for those whose concerns regarding what helps and what hinders learning mirror ours but who may have different views about God and faith. Since barriers to student learning can arise from many factors in the context of the learning environment and relationships, including from within the students, we will also dialogue briefly with the field of clinical psychology to better understand a few challenges some of our students face. We will consider these in sidebars throughout the chapter.

5. Vincent Donovan, *Christianity Rediscovered* (Maryknoll, NY: Orbis, 2004).

tian faith and practice and fully engaged in "conversation with the cultural resources of our contemporary world through interdisciplinary dialogue."[6]

Dialoguing with Psychology

Researchers and theorists in the fields of psychology are in the business of seeking to understand why we humans behave in the ways that we do. To that end, they examine human experience and attempt to identify the constituent elements that make up an experience. As this relates to the human experience of learning, psychological theorists have sought to understand how we develop our thinking—by what processes we actually learn.

A Brief Overview of Learning Theories

During the past century several learning theories emerged, attempting to explain learning according to various ways in which learning was defined. Early theories defined learning as change in behavior and focused study on how people were conditioned by environmental factors to change. These are typically referred to as *conditioning theories*. Klaus Issler and Ronald Habermas described these theories as "learning by association."[7] We make associations between what we encounter (stimuli) and our reaction to these (responses), and these connections in turn shape our thoughts and behaviors. We are therefore conditioned by these associations to behave in certain ways. Issler and Habermas suggest that from the perspective of these theories, we learn primarily by one of two associations: "consequences" or "cues."

Consequences can be intentional or unintentional, but they form a powerful shaping force to change behavior. Consequences include feedback or events that *follow* student behavior, and these either encourage or discourage that behavior.

With cue associations, feedback or events *precede* student behavior to encourage or discourage the behavior. A cue is a stimulus most often targeting one or more of the five senses that becomes linked with a particular response (a thought, feeling, or action). This association increases the likelihood that the response will always follow the cue. For instance, a red light cues the driver to stop. The implications for our teaching, of course, are that we pay

6. Richard Osmer, *The Teaching Ministry of Congregations* (Louisville: Westminster John Knox, 2005), xiv.

7. Klaus Issler and Ronald Habermas, *How We Learn: A Christian Teacher's Guide to Educational Psychology* (Grand Rapids: Baker, 1994), chap. 4.

attention to the cues and consequences that we use to stimulate student learning. These associations are powerful shaping forces in the lives of students; however, we must be careful to not equate conditioned behavior with deep, transformative learning.

Evolving from these theories, others began to recognize that we learn not just by associations that condition us but also through observing others. These *social learning theories* focus on "learning by example."[8] They assert that we don't merely learn by experiencing the consequences or responding to the cues that are directed toward us. We also learn by observing the experiences of others and by evaluating the consequences that they experience. These theories acknowledge the power that role models have in our learning process.[9] As a young youth pastor, I remember stumbling onto the words of Paul to the church in Philippi: "Therefore, my brothers and sisters, you whom I love and long for, my joy and crown, stand firm in the Lord in this way, dear friends! . . . Whatever you have learned or received or heard from me, or seen in me—put it into practice. And the God of peace will be with you" (Phil. 4:1, 9 NIV). Paul writes of his deep love for those to whom he ministered and offered his life as an example for them to observe. Social learning theorists recognize the power of mentoring in our learning and encourage us to pay careful attention to how we model in structured ways (planned examples before students) and how we model spontaneously (living our lives before students) as part of our teaching.

About forty years ago, a major shift in learning theories occurred, changing the focus from behavior to cognitive processing. Commonly referred to as *information processing theories*, this group of theories suggests that we possess "a drive to make sense of the world by acquiring and organizing data, sensing problems, and generating solutions to them, and developing concepts and language for conveying them."[10] We could call these theories "learning by mental processing." These theories began to shift the focus of learning from how a student is shaped by external forces to how they learn through the active engagement of their intellect.

Teaching, according to these theories, primarily involves processes of identification and inquiry. Teachers work with students to identify what students currently know and what they don't know, building bridges from

8. Ibid., 81.

9. Albert Bandura, *Social Learning Theory* (Englewood Cliffs, NJ: Prentice-Hall, 1977); Albert Bandura, *Social Foundations of Thought and Action: A Social Cognitive Theory* (Englewood Cliffs, NJ: Prentice-Hall, 1986).

10. Bruce Joyce, Marsha Weil, and Beverly Showers, *Models of Teaching*, 4th ed. (Englewood Cliffs, NJ: Prentice-Hall, 1992), 71.

their present understanding to new concepts. Through the process of inquiry, teachers raise challenging questions and allow the students to wrestle with them, in what some call a "life to lesson" approach, seeking solutions for themselves and developing critical thinking skills.[11]

Throughout all of these shifts in the definition of learning, one thing remained constant—the view that learning was about the experience of the individual. Learning itself was conceived of as an internal change within a particular person as they acquired new information or a new skill. This view has given way in many circles to a more collective view of learning, known as the constructivist view that sees learning as a phenomenon created among people in collaboration. In the individualistic view of learning, knowledge is transferred from one person to another. Learning is about acquiring and re-producing either information or skills. In the constructivist view, conversely, knowledge is constructed in a creative process. This process draws on col-lective knowledge embedded within particular cultural contexts; however, each individual and generation must engage in the creative process of re-creating this collective knowledge. *Constructivist theories* focus on "learning through collaboration" and view learning as a meaning-making experience in which learning is not transmitted from one to another but created together. Constructivists tend to find traditional approaches inadequate for fostering authentic learning experiences: "Most constructivists would . . . agree that the traditional approach to teaching—the transmission model—promotes neither the interaction between prior and new knowledge nor the conver-sations that are necessary for internalization and deep understanding."[12]

Over the past decade, neurophysiological research has led to an explosion of literature on brain research and its contribution to our understanding of how we learn. Some are convinced that these new discoveries will have a dramatic impact on how we view the teaching-learning process. We might consider the focus of these emerging *neurophysiology theories* as "learning by brain change." However, not all are in agreement that brain research offers truly innovative contributions for how we should teach.[13] These skeptics would say that, thus far, brain research has merely confirmed known truths about learning.[14] *Neurotheology*, an interesting subfield of neurophysiology,

11. Issler and Habermas, *How We Learn*, chap. 3.

12. Virginia Richardson, *Constructivist Teacher: Building a World of New Understandings* (London: Falmer, 1997), 3.

13. Leonard Abbeduto and Frank Symons, *Taking Sides: Clashing Views in Educational Psychology*, 7th ed. (New York: McGraw-Hill, 2015).

14. William Yount, "Mind over Matter: Teaching Brains by Teaching People," in *Created to Learn: A Christian Teacher's Introduction to Educational Psychology* (Nashville: B&H, 2010), 509–64.

seeks to bridge the gap between the scientific study of the brain and the study of theology and spiritual experience.[15] Research studies are contributing helpful new insights for theologians to consider as they measure changes to the brain that accompany religious experience and result in changes to our thoughts, feelings, and behaviors.[16] The impact of these new areas of study on theories of learning has yet to be fully realized.

As we can see, many diverse perspectives exist on the *ways* in which people learn. This list of five theory groups (conditioning, social learning, information processing, constructivist, and neurophysiology) is not meant to be exhaustive but is merely representative of some of the contributions that research and educational theory offer to our understanding of how people develop their thinking. We shouldn't see these theories as mutually exclusive (even though some of the original theorists might have seen them this way). Rather, they offer diverse perspectives on the complexity of experiences that are involved in the development of our thinking, and they complement one another as we consider a more holistic way to view learning.

Integrating the contributions of diverse theories, Susan Ambrose and her colleagues define learning as "a process that leads to change, which occurs as a result of experience and increases the potential for improved performance and future learning."[17] They acknowledge that learning is a "process, not a product," and they also suggest that learning involves change—changes in "knowledge, beliefs, behaviors, or attitudes." They place responsibility for learning on the student, asserting that "learning is not something done to students, but rather something students themselves do."[18] These distinctions are critical, which will become evident as we consider how learning occurs in the various dimensions of a person's experience.

Dimensions of Learning

Over the past century, theorists in the field of educational psychology have typically identified three dimensions in which learning occurs (most commonly referred to as cognitive, affective, and behavioral). Christian educators

---

15. Andrew Newburg, *Principles of Neurotheology* (Burlington, VT: Ashgate, 2010).

16. For example, Paul Markham, *Rewired: Exploring Religious Conversion* (Eugene, OR: Pickwick, 2007); Michael Inzlicht et al., "Neural Markers of Religious Conviction," *Psychological Science* 20, no. 3 (2009): 385–92.

17. Susan A. Ambrose, Michael W. Bridges, Michael DiPietro, Marsha C. Lovett, and Marie K. Norman, *How Learning Works: Seven Research-Based Principles for Smart Teaching* (San Francisco: Jossey-Bass, 2010), 3.

18. Ibid.

and theologians have embraced this same way of thinking about learning. For example, Nicholas Wolterstorff identified three types of learning that are especially relevant to Christian education: (1) cognitive learning—attaining a true belief; (2) ability learning—gaining a capability, skill, or competence; and (3) tendency learning—developing a disposition to behave in particular ways depending on the situation.[19] Issler and Habermas added a fourth dimension, separating dispositional elements from affective ones:

- cognitive level—knowledge and intellectual skills;
- behavioral level—physical skills and habits;
- affective level—emotions and attitudes; and
- dispositional level—values and tendencies.[20]

We will briefly explore each of these four dimensions of learning (with slight modification) as a way to dialogue with some helpful concepts emerging from the field of psychology.[21]

Cognitive Dimension of Learning

The cognitive dimension of learning typically refers to the acquisition of knowledge and the ways we process information to form understanding. Jean Piaget, a Swiss biologist and philosopher by training, was captivated by questions such as: How do people come to know what they know? And how does that change over the course of life? His research led him to develop a four-stage view of the development of thinking from birth to adolescence (the point at which he believed that development reached maturity).

Some of the underlying assumptions of his theory are particularly relevant for how we think about teaching and learning in Christian ministry. Piaget believed that all humans possess an instinctual drive to learn and that this drive involves a natural tendency to try to make sense of our experiences by organizing them into categories we understand. Of course, these categories must expand and change as we grow and encounter new information that does not fit into our current categories. Piaget called this process *adaptation*. He proposed that learning is a process of constantly adapting our current understanding to the world that we encounter. When we are exposed to new information that we cannot "assimilate" into our current categories, it

---

19. Nicholas Wolterstorff, *Educating for Responsible Action* (Grand Rapids: Eerdmans, 1980).
20. Issler and Habermas, *How We Learn*, 1994.
21. It is important to note that these categories are not completely distinct. They bleed into one another, so it is best to consider them as intertwined rather than mutually exclusive.

is unsettling (what he called *disequilibrium*). Our natural instinct toward learning is to try to reestablish calm or balance in our minds—to equilibrate our cognitive categories or "schema."

In order to maintain this cognitive equilibrium, we must constantly adapt our thinking. Piaget asserted that we do this in one of two ways. Either we assimilate new information into the schema we already have or we *accommodate* our schema to the new information. In order to accommodate, we must change our categories and form new ones. This balance between assimilation and accommodation is the internal dialogue in which learning occurs as we continually adapt to the world we encounter. "We need both processes to create equilibrium between *what we know* and *what really is*."[22]

Another foundational assumption of Piaget was that our thinking develops from a primitive inability to perceive other perspectives than our own (egocentrism) toward a mature capacity to perceive and value the perspectives and experiences of others. The ability to see from another's perspective is essential for learning to progress to higher levels of understanding, and this ability is developed through social interaction. Piaget believed that this maturing process was in full bloom during the period of adolescence.

Lawrence Kohlberg believed that the process of moral decision making was a clear example of how we mature from primitive egocentrism. As a young man during World War II, Kohlberg witnessed injustices that led him to question the process by which people make moral decisions. He developed a theory rooted in some of the basic assumptions that guided Piaget.[23] Like Piaget, Kohlberg believed that the movement away from egocentrism was essential to mature moral decision making and that this was a significant part of the cognitive developmental work of adolescence. Also like Piaget, he believed that maturing cognitive development involved movement from concrete ideas to more abstract thought. You can see this progression across the six stages of Kohlberg's Stage theory:

Preconventional morality—decisions based on cost to self (egocentric)

1. concern for personal consequences
2. consideration of others' needs if benefits self

---

22. Yount, *Created to Learn*, 93.
23. Lawrence Kohlberg, "Moral Stages and Moralization: The Cognitive-Developmental Approach," in *Moral Development and Behavior: Theory, Research, and Social Issues*, ed. Thomas Lickona (New York: Holt, Rinehart and Winston, 1976), 31–53.

Conventional morality—decisions based on the approval of others

   3. concern about disapproval of authority figures
   4. concern about breaking societal rules

Postconventional morality—decisions based on abstract principles

   5. concern for the good as defined by society
   6. concern for good that transcends societal norms and definitions

The implications of these foundational assumptions are as follows. Learning is about discovery, about allowing the innate hunger people have to understand their world to fuel learning experiences. Learning is also about managing the balance between experiences of disequilibrium and equilibrium. At times, a student can become flooded by too much new information, which may overwhelm her capacity to adapt. At such times, she needs a teacher who can help her achieve equilibrium. At other times, she may become complacent, too comfortable within her perspectives on the world around her. At such times, she needs a teacher who can lovingly introduce disequilibrium. Piaget described the goals of this kind of teaching: "The principal goal of education is to create [people] who are capable of doing new things, not simply repeating what other generations have done—[people] who are creative, inventive, and discoverers. The second goal of education is to form minds which can be critical, can verify, and not accept everything they are offered."[24]

We don't need to teach young children to hunger to learn; they are eager to discover. Sadly, too often we teach them over time not to learn, because we provide educational environments in which the goal is not learning but content dissemination. In essence, we try to download the content knowledge of the teacher to the student, and in the process, we teach students to stop discovering.

"Our natural, unexamined model for teaching is telling," according to Donald Finkel in his book *Teaching with Your Mouth Shut*. It is as though we believe that the "fundamental act of teaching is to carefully and clearly tell students something they did not previously know. Knowledge is transmitted, we imagine, through this act of telling."[25] Even though research

24. This quote's source has been the topic of some discussion and it has been modified over time. The most reliable is the one used here, though the brackets are mine. It can be found in Eleanor Duckworth, "Piaget Rediscovered," *The Arithmetic Teacher* 11, no. 7 (November 1964): 499.
   25. Donald Finkel, *Teaching with Your Mouth Shut* (Portsmouth, NH: Boynton/Cook, 2000), 2.

Some students face significant challenges in their ability to learn. These challenges are typically grouped into four categories: sensory impairment (vision or hearing), intellectual disabilities (formerly known as mental retardation), autism spectrum disorders, and learning disabilities. The first three of these are often diagnosed early in childhood, as parents notice struggles these children experience. Learning disabilities, however, may go undiagnosed for a long time, and the symptoms that accompany them are often mistaken for laziness, poor intelligence, or emotional or behavioral disorders.

The most characteristic sign of a learning disability is a marked difference between the achievement you intuitively expect from a given student and his or her actual performance. Learning disabilities are actually neurological disorders (that is, problems in the way the brain functions), and they impact a student's ability to learn various academic and social skills (such as reading, writing, reasoning, planning, organizing, strategizing, remembering details, managing time and space, listening, and speaking).

Receiving the diagnosis of a learning disability can be a gift of grace to a student who is struggling and doesn't understand why. If you are concerned about a student, talk to her and her parents. Tell them about your observations. You also might suggest they seek advice from their school psychologist.

in education over the past twenty-five years has established clearly that lecturing alone simply does not lead to effective learning that is retained by students, we too often focus our efforts in teaching on what the teacher says. John Dewey, an American educational reformer wrote,

> No thought, no idea, can possibly be conveyed as an idea from one person to another. When it is told, it is, to the one to whom it is told, another given fact, not an idea. The communication may stimulate the other person to realize the question for himself and to think out a like idea, or it may smother his intellectual interest and suppress his dawning effort at thought. But what he *directly* gets cannot be an idea. Only by wrestling with the conditions of the problem at first hand, seeking and finding his own way out, does he think.[26]

According to Dewey and many others since, we learn by wrestling with ideas and reflecting on experience. Telling, or lecturing, too often assumes that students have already had an experience related to the topic being talked about. And too often, we who tell do the reflecting for the students. Teaching by telling can be effective only when the students actually have experiences

---

26. John Dewey, *Democracy and Education: An Introduction to the Philosophy of Education* (New York: Macmillan, 1916), 188 (emphasis original).

relevant to the topic we are teaching and we allow them to reflect on that experience themselves. "People learn only by thinking for themselves; the teacher's task is to set up conditions that provoke thinking."[27]

Piaget encourages those of us who teach to create learning environments in which students learn through discovery and where information, experience, and questioning exist in a dynamic balance, allowing the student's intrinsic motivation to explore and fuel the learning process.

Lev Vygotsky, a Russian psychologist, also believed that learning occurred in the context of discovery; however, he believed the driving force in that learning to be social interaction, not the biological drive within the individual student. Such social interaction within distinct cultural contexts forms the basis for learning, according to Vygotsky. While Piaget believed that cognitive development was essentially the same everywhere, Vygotsky believed that cognitive development was inextricably linked to the culture that provides the context for the social interactions that precede learning.[28]

Consequently, Vygotsky stressed the importance of the role of the "more knowledgeable other" in the learning relationship (in our case, the youth minister, small-group leader, etc.) who provides the context of a significant relationship within which learning and development occur. Utilizing the tools arising from the cultural context (the particular ways of communicating, the symbols representing cultural values, the perspectives by which the world is viewed, etc.) teacher and student engage in a social relationship out of which learning is co-constructed.

Vygotsky believed that people differ in their ability to learn a given task or concept and that effective teaching takes this into account. He proposed that a range exists between a person's ability to solve a problem or complete a task on their own without help and the upper limit of their ability to accomplish this even with the help of another. He called this the *zone of proximal development*.[29] He suggested that effective teaching involves providing learning experiences in that zone because the student would swiftly lose interest in learning tasks below the zone and would become frustrated with tasks above the zone. This structured assistance in the teacher-learner relationship functions like scaffolding on a building under construction— support that can be easily removed when no longer needed.

Both Piaget and Vygotsky inspire us with a vision for learning environments rich with discovery and meaningful dialogue between teacher and

27. Finkel, *Teaching with Your Mouth Shut*, 151.

28. Lev Vygotsky, *Mind in Society: The Development of the Higher Psychological Processes* (Cambridge, MA: Harvard University Press, 1978).

29. Ibid., 84.

Our goal in teaching is to help our students not just to know information but to understand the information and to be able to apply the information to their lives. Issler and Habermas show what that looks like for Christians:

1. *Awareness*: basic recognition of a concept
2. *Understanding*: in-depth perception of the meaning and significance of a concept
   a. Comprehension—demonstrated understanding of concepts
   b. Application—ability to solve new problems by use of concepts
   c. Analysis—ability to separate concepts into constituent parts
   d. Synthesis—ability to combine concepts to form new patterns
   e. Evaluation—ability to make judgments about work based on concepts
3. *Wisdom*: using the concept in an appropriate manner in making decisions according to a Christian worldview

—Adapted from Klaus Issler and Ronald Habermas, *How We Learn: A Christian Teacher's Guide to Educational Psychology* (Grand Rapids: Baker, 1994), 32.

student—environments in which the teacher knows the students well enough to know their zones and to engage them in learning tasks that awaken their hunger to explore and think creatively. If Piaget and Vygotsky could give us a few suggestions to guide our teaching of students, they might say:

- Teaching involves much more than merely talking to students.
- Know your students well enough to know how they learn.
- Create learning environments that involve discovery.
- Engage students in meaningful dialogue through questions that require them to think creatively and to think together with others.
- Let them wrestle with tough questions and learning tasks, but not ones that are completely beyond their zone; provide scaffolding for them in their learning.
- Teach students to use the tools of the community of faith.

Behavioral Dimension of Learning

The behavioral dimension refers to the engagement of the body in the process of learning. Too often, our efforts in teaching focus exclusively on the minds of our students. Engaging the whole person is vital for effective learning. To do this, teachers need to pay attention to two areas. First, we want our students to cultivate habits of behavior. Being followers of Christ involves acquiring physical skills that we develop into habits. The first

Some students find it very difficult to control their behavior and to conform it to what is expected (for example, focusing and paying attention). Various factors may contribute to such legitimate deficits in a student's ability to manage her behavior. One such factor is Attention Deficit Hyperactivity Disorder (ADHD), a condition increasingly diagnosed in children and adolescents.

ADHD used to be viewed primarily as a behavior problem caused by environmental factors; however, brain-imaging technology has indicated that significant differences in the structure and/or development of the brain exist for those with ADHD. For example, some with ADHD are delayed by an average of three years in the development of the part of their brain that involves the ability to control impulses, delay gratification, focus attention, remember momentary details, and plan ahead. For many of these same individuals, the part of the brain that controls movement seems to mature faster than those without ADHD. This discrepancy in brain development may explain some of the symptoms that make traditional learning environments difficult for those with ADHD.

As with learning disorders mentioned above, this condition can sometimes go undiagnosed until adolescence, by which time a student may have learned coping mechanisms and behavior patterns that are very difficult to change. Treatments are available that can be immensely beneficial to students with ADHD (both medications and therapy). Our task is to resist stereotypes and simplistic explanations and solutions and to come alongside families and students who are struggling to understand the reasons for the difficulties they experience. Our learning environments ought to set the standard for care and support for students who face challenges. Seek out those in the health and mental health field in your communities of faith who can help you understand and be more effective in teaching students with unique challenges like ADHD.

Christians were referred to as "followers of the Way" because their commitment was to following Jesus's way of life. James, the brother of Jesus, wrote, "I will show you my faith by my works" (2:18).

In our ministries, we need to teach our students to behave in the way of Jesus. Parker Palmer suggested that teaching is "creating a space in which obedience to truth is practiced."[30] On a practical level, this means our teaching should not be limited to the Sunday school room or youth room. We need to be living life together, bearing witness to what we are teaching by how we are living and dialoguing with our students about the ways that they behave in the world with family and friends.

30. Parker Palmer, *To Know as We Are Known: A Spirituality of Education* (San Francisco: Harper & Row, 1983), 69.

Second, when we are engaged in the more cognitive levels of learning in our classrooms, it is vital to recognize that students learn better when their entire bodies are engaged in the learning process. In her book *Learning to Listen, Learning to Teach*, Jane Vella suggests that effective learning must be active. It is "doing with built-in reflection. . . . [It] can be used in teaching knowledge, skills, and attitudes as learners do something with the new knowledge, practice the new skills and attitudes, and then reflect on what they have just done."[31] In short, "we learn through an active process, through doing something with what we are learning."[32]

Affective Dimension of Learning

In her classic book on the educational ministry of the church, *Education That Is Christian*, Lois LeBar states that students should be "alert and active intellectually, emotionally, and volitionally as they participate in group interaction."[33] We will consider what she refers to as the emotional and volitional form, the final two "dimensions" of learning. The emotional or affective dimension relates to the emotional state and well-being of students in the learning process. How we feel affects how we learn. The learning environment must feel safe for both the students and the teacher, and it ought to be a place of joy.

The psalmist wrote, "Blessed is the one . . . whose delight is in the law of the LORD" (Ps. 1:1–2 NIV). Learning ought to arise from delight. Just watch a small child as she explores her world, discovering new things, and you will see the powerful impact delight has on learning. It is heartbreaking when children come to experience a classroom as a place of boredom rather than joy, and it is tragic when they feel this way about the church or youth group. The feelings our students bring with them to the learning experiences we offer and the feelings that we evoke in those contexts have a significant impact on the learning they achieve.[34]

Researchers at the MIT Media Lab published a paper titled "Affective Learning—A Manifesto," in which they state,

31. Jane Vella, *Learning to Listen, Learning to Teach: The Power of Dialogue in Educating Adults* (San Francisco: Jossey-Bass, 2002), 14.
32. Jane Vella, *Taking Learning to Task: Creative Strategies for Teaching Adults* (San Francisco: Jossey-Bass, 2001), 51.
33. Lois LeBar, *Education That Is Christian* (Westwood, NJ: David C. Cook, 1998), 184.
34. Affective learning relates not only to the emotional experiences of students in the learning context but also to their learning about emotions themselves—how to recognize them, how to express them, how to manage them, and so on. For the purposes of our discussion, we will focus our attention on the impact student emotions have on their learning experience.

All students experience variations in their mood. We all know such feelings as happiness, sadness, fear, and anger and how difficult it can be at times to set our feelings aside in order to focus on a task like learning. Some students face chronic feelings that can make it overwhelmingly difficult to participate in and benefit from learning experiences. Feelings of hopelessness and helplessness can leave students desperately trying to find reasons to go on or lead them to injure themselves as a way to cope with the pain they feel inside. Feelings of fear and insecurity can lead students to withdraw from life, searching for relief from their distress.

Health and mental health professionals refer to these conditions as mood and anxiety disorders, and they can be enormous barriers to a student's desire to learn or be a part of a community of learners. As we have already mentioned, our job is to avoid simple answers and to come alongside students and families in pain. Reach out to resource people in your communities of faith to help you as you seek to understand the needs of these students and families.

On the most fundamental level, an accelerated flow of findings in neuroscience, psychology, and cognitive science itself present affect as complexly intertwined with thinking, and performing important functions with respect to guiding rational behavior, memory retrieval, decision-making, creativity, and more. While it has always been understood that too much emotion is bad for rational thinking, recent findings suggest that so too is too little emotion—when basic mechanisms of emotion are missing in the brain, then intelligent functioning is hindered. These findings point to new advances in understanding the human brain not as a purely cognitive information processing system, but as a system in which affective functions and cognitive ones are inextricably integrated with one another.[35]

The feelings we experience can either enhance our learning or hinder it, and paying attention to the "affective dimension" of student learning—the feelings and attitudes they bring to the learning environment and the affective atmosphere of the learning context—is an important part of being an effective teacher.

Dispositional Dimension of Learning

Most theoretical models of learning include only the first three dimensions we have discussed (cognitive, behavioral, and affective) because they fold what Issler and Habermas call the *dispositional dimension* into the affective.

35. Rosalind Picard et al., "Affective Learning—A Manifesto," *BT Technology Journal* 22, no. 4 (October 2004): 253.

"As it is currently conceived in educational literature, the affective domain is overly cumbersome. It seems to be a catchall collection of whatever does not fit in the more defined cognitive and psychomotor domains. It includes such diverse elements as feelings, emotions, moods, aesthetic appreciations, attitudes, values, and motivation."[36] They suggest that Christian educators give separate attention to the role of the will in the learning process, for it is the will that must be exercised to manage affect, motivate behavior, and focus cognition.

Dallas Willard, in his book *Renovation of the Heart*, suggests that the "heart" in biblical teaching is the manager of our dispositions. "We live from our heart. . . . [It] drives and organizes our life. . . . Those with a well-kept heart are persons who are prepared for and capable of responding to the situations of life in ways that are good and right. Their will functions as it should, to choose what is good and avoid what is evil, and the other components of their nature cooperate to that end."[37] As the writer of Proverbs states, "Keep your heart with all vigilance, for from it flow the springs of life" (4:23).

Spiritual formation, according to Willard, is the process of transforming and maturing the heart in its capacity to effectively organize all of human life (our thoughts, feelings, choices, actions, relationships) around God so that we love God with all of our being and love our neighbor. "Its aim is to bring every element in our being . . . into harmony with the will of God and the kingdom of God."[38] Our role as teachers is to help our students learn how to live their lives—their whole lives—in the way that Jesus Christ did, which includes the investments of their time and energy, the ways that they relate to others, the thought processes by which they make choices, the actions that they choose and the way they carry out those actions, the ways they manage and express their emotions, the thoughts they allow to occupy their minds, and on and on.[39]

The "dispositional dimension" of learning engages students in the quest to be willing followers of "the Way" of Jesus. David Krathwohl, Benjamin Bloom, and Bertram Masia offer a taxonomy for affective learning that seems more appropriate to our understanding of dispositional learning. Revised for our purposes, Krathwohl's taxonomy moves from a willingness to pay

36. Issler and Habermas, *How We Learn*, 30.
37. Dallas Willard, *Renovation of the Heart: Putting on the Character of Christ* (Colorado Springs: NavPress, 2002), 13, 29.
38. Ibid., 93.
39. Dallas Willard, *The Spirit of the Disciplines: Understanding How God Changes Lives* (New York: HarperCollins, 1988).

attention to new learning to a willingness to commit to a changed way of behaving based on the new learning:[40]

Receiving—willingness to listen

Responding—willingness to engage

Valuing—willingness to commit

Organization—willingness to evaluate and rearrange

Characterization—willingness to live out

So What?

At this point, if you are not feeling a bit overwhelmed by the prospect of teaching your students, then you haven't been paying attention. Teaching students so that they actually learn and begin to be transformed is a complex undertaking, and as James, the brother of Jesus, suggested, it's a high calling: "Not many of you should become teachers, my fellow believers, because you know that we who teach will be judged more strictly" (James 3:1 NIV).

The church is intended to be a community of people living as a witness of love for one another and for all people. We are to live in such a way that the values of the kingdom of God are evident on earth. Our teaching then must also bear witness to this. Vella writes, "Teaching . . . involves listening to learners at every level, respecting them as subjects or decision makers of their own learning, and evoking their innate power. We [do this] to prove that such a society is possible and to bring it into being."[41]

Teaching that ignores this truth, according to Henri Nouwen, is violent.[42] It treats students as files in which information is downloaded. Paulo Freire asserts that education either functions to subjugate through conformity or it "becomes the practice of freedom," the means by which people participate in the transformation of their world.[43]

Unless we are willing to invite our students into learning experiences within the church that engage them in all of the dimensions of their learning, we risk losing their interest in matters of faith and the mission of the church in the world. Engaging in dialogue with educators, researchers, and

40. David Krathwohl, Benjamin Bloom, and Bertram Masia, *Taxonomy of Educational Objectives, Handbook 2: Affective Domain* (New York: David McKay, 1964).

41. Jane Vella, *On Teaching and Learning: Putting the Principles and Practices of Dialogue Education into Action* (San Francisco: Jossey-Bass, 2008), xix.

42. Henri Nouwen, *Creative Ministry* (New York: Image, 1971).

43. Paulo Freire, *Pedagogy of the Oppressed* (New York: Continuum, 2003), 34.

theorists who study the human experience of learning helps us to see ways in which our teaching can be more effective and our students' joy in the discovery of learning can be rekindled.

In 2010, Ambrose and her colleagues wrote a book attempting to distill from all of the theories and research (which we have only scratched the surface of in this chapter) seven principles of learning to help teachers to teach better. They draw from their decades of teaching experience and study two foundational assumptions that undergird the seven principles: "(a) learning is a developmental process that intersects with other developmental processes in a student's life, and (b) students enter our classrooms not only with skills, knowledge, and abilities, but also with social and emotional experiences that influence what they value, how they perceive themselves and others, and how they will engage in the learning process."[44]

From these assumptions, Ambrose and her colleagues offer these seven principles rooted in the belief that we who teach truly "wish to inform [our] instructional decisions with research evidence and research-based theory":[45]

1. Students' prior knowledge can help or hinder learning.
2. How students organize knowledge influences how they learn and apply what they know.
3. Students' motivation determines, directs, and sustains what they do to learn.
4. To develop mastery, students must acquire component skills, practice integrating them, and know when to apply what they have learned.
5. Goal-directed practice coupled with targeted feedback enhances the quality of students' learning.
6. Students' current level of development interacts with the social, emotional, and intellectual climate of the [learning environment] to impact learning.
7. To become self-directed learners, students must learn to monitor and adjust their approaches to learning.

If we want to take our students' learning seriously, we must listen to the wisdom of teachers and researchers like these who invite us to a way of teaching that truly seeks to know how our students learn. We must engage our students in learning that is whole; attend to their cognitive, behavioral,

44. Ambrose et al., *How Learning Works*, 3–4.
45. Ibid., 4.

and affective growth; and invite them into the joy of discovering their faith and living it out.

Questions and Activities

1. Think of two examples from your own life for each of these theory sets: conditioning, social learning, and information processing. What have you learned via each?
2. To practice what this chapter teaches, review the main points and write down an example for each.
3. What parts of the chapter were the most confusing for you? Perform an online search for those major points and review.
4. In what ways might the Christian teacher who understands the principles in this chapter be a better teacher than the one who doesn't care about these ideas?
5. Take a common lesson plan you might use and review it for examples of various approaches to teaching found in this chapter.

Further Reading

Bloom, Benjamin, Max Englehart, Edward Furst, Walker Hill, and David Krathwohl. *Taxonomy of Educational Objectives, Handbook 1: Cognitive Domain*. New York: Longman, 1956.

Burgess, Harold. *Models of Religious Education: Theory and Practice in Historical and Contemporary Practice*. Nappanee, IN: Evangel, 2001.

St. Gregory the Great. *Pastoral Care*. Translated by Henry Davis. Mahwah, NJ: Paulist, 1978.

Hasse, Dan. "On Teaching and Learning" (website). https://sites.google.com/site/dhaase/.

Niebuhr, Reinhold. *The Purpose of the Church and Its Ministry*. New York: Harper & Row, 1956.

Multiple Intelligences and Learning Styles

KAREN JONES

> If all experienced God in the same way and returned Him
> an identical worship, the song of the Church triumphant
> would have no symphony, it would be like an orchestra in
> which all the instruments played the same note.
>
> —C. S. Lewis, *The Problem of Pain*

Being created in the image of God gives all persons a unique capacity to enjoy a relationship with him and with everyone they encounter. Bearing God's image doesn't mean we should all ultimately act, think, and respond in the same way, as if we all rolled off an assembly line. God's image allows for uniqueness and individuality in the way we relate, with different styles, and in our preferences, gifts, and abilities. Consider the very nature of God; God exists as three in one: Father, Son, and Holy Spirit. Yet, even in their perfect unity, each person in the Godhead reflects individuality, with unique tasks and ways of interacting with creation. It is only natural, then, that being made in God's image, we would also experience the world in unique ways. Our personalities and idiosyncrasies are part of the wonder of creation, the things that give excitement and joy to living in community. Our reaction to this reality should echo that of the psalmist:

"I praise you, for I am fearfully and wonderfully made. Wonderful are your works; my soul knows it very well. My frame was not hidden from you, when I was being made in secret, intricately woven in the depths of the earth. Your eyes saw my unformed substance; in your book were written, every one of them, the days that were formed for me, when as yet there was none of them" (Ps. 139:14–16).

Each of our students is an individual, wonderfully crafted by God, in his image, with a distinct manner of approaching the world. To fully appreciate this truth requires us to recognize that students also learn differently. The way they process information, how they are motivated, their interpersonal and self-awareness, their energy levels, and communication skills—all these meld into a distinctive approach to learning. Effective teachers focus on their students' learning preferences more than their own teaching "comfort zones." To do this, we must incorporate methods and structures that are most likely to intersect with our students' preferred styles of learning. Obviously, it wouldn't be practical to design individual learning experiences for each student in our ministries; neither would that be beneficial to them. All persons need to be challenged to grow beyond their comfort levels, and most people can learn even when they are being taught in a way that isn't in their "sweet spot." But if our ultimate goal in ministry is to help facilitate change in our students, to help them gain the knowledge, dispositions, values, and skills necessary for a life of Christlike commitment, then we will create the types of learning experiences that are most likely to facilitate that change.

It is only natural, then, that being made in God's image, we would also experience the world in unique ways. Our personalities and idiosyncrasies are part of the wonder of creation, the things that give excitement and joy to living in community.

Educators and psychologists have long been interested in researching these learning preferences, and a variety of theories and models have emerged over time. They each focus on a different aspect of learning; the learning theories we will look at in this chapter are: brain research, global and analytic learning, sensory learning (visual, auditory, and kinesthetic learning), the theory of multiple intelligences, emotional intelligence, the learning style inventory, and experiential learning. Familiarity with each of these theories will help you better understand the students in your ministry as you observe their behaviors and reactions and listen to them communicate with one another.

Brain Research and Learning Preferences

Recent discoveries in neuroscience have shed light on how the brain functions and have attracted much interest, especially in the field of education. Many of these developments address ideas about right- and left-brain learning. Traditional ways of teaching are said to neglect the more creative and artistic right hemisphere of the brain in favor of the more analytic and academic left hemisphere. Publishers and educational experts have argued that this neglect leaves students undereducated, so greater attempts have been made to focus on methods that engage the whole brain.[1]

Advances in technology have allowed us to actually glimpse the inner workings of the brain and gain insight into which portions appear most engaged when certain tasks are being performed. What is being discovered is that our categories of the analytic left brain and creative right brain aren't as clear as we once believed. Language, for instance, has commonly been associated with the left hemisphere. It is true that the left hemisphere of the brain is most strongly related to language for 95 percent of the people who are right-handed and 70 percent of those who are left-handed.[2] However, scientists are now discovering that actual language *performance* is not a function of just the left hemisphere of the brain but seems to stimulate the right hemisphere as well. Humor, metaphors, and analogies typically stimulate the right hemisphere of the brain as well as the left, even though they are also components of language.

What does this mean for the teacher? Put very simply, traditional teaching methods aren't predominately left- or right-brained, and we should be cautious about selecting curriculum resources that promote their "brain strategies" as a selling point. Despite the claims of some publishers, "there is no evidence to suggest . . . that people favor one side of the brain, or . . . that any educational tool or strategy can selectively activate one hemisphere."[3] Both sides of the brain perform different functions, but they are interdependent. The right side focuses more on larger chunks of information, and the left side analyzes and sorts those chunks of information.[4]

While recent neuroscience research is intriguing, many of the findings have been oversimplified and overgeneralized. The problem is that education

1. Annukka Lindell and Evan Kidd, "Why Right-Brain Teaching Is Half-Witted: A Critique of the Misapplication of Neuroscience to Education," *Mind, Brain, and Education* 5, no. 3 (September 2011): 121–27.

2. Tracey Tokuhama-Espinosa, *The New Science of Teaching and Learning: Using the Best of Mind, Brain, and Education Science* (New York: Teachers College Press, 2010).

3. Lindell and Kidd, "Right-Brain Teaching," 122.

4. Gayle H. Gregory and Terence Parry, *Designing Brain Compatible Learning*, 3rd ed. (Thousand Oaks, CA: Corwin, 2006), 7.

(teaching/learning) and neuroscience are two different fields and speak different languages. While an increased understanding of the brain and how it functions does hold potential for the future, there just isn't enough evidence at present to establish a specific relationship between neuroscience and teaching and learning, or to establish neuropsychological strengths and weaknesses.

Global and Analytic Learning

Brain research has largely debunked the right brain/left brain theory about how learners perceive the world, but the idea that people make sense of their world from one of two polarities is still a useful way of understanding learners. This idea was first promoted after studying the behaviors of naval fighter pilots in World War II. The psychologist Herman Witkin conducted tests to understand why some pilots flew out of a fog bank upside down and others were able to retain their upright orientation. He discovered that some of the pilots were more dependent on their field of vision to maintain an upright position. They were disoriented by being unable to see their surroundings and were labeled field dependent, or global, learners. Others were field independent, analytic learners and were able to maintain a correct orientation even when they couldn't see where they were.[5] This understanding was eventually applied to all learners; we all tend to encounter the world around us from one of two perspectives, global or analytic.

Your ministry will have students that learn best from one of these two perspectives. For example, if you were leading a study of John 6:1–15 on the feeding of the five thousand, some of the more analytic students might want to discuss the cost of feeding each person in the crowd, how Andrew was able to locate the one boy with the barley loaves and fish, or the strategy the disciples used to organize and feed so many people. Your global learners would probably be interested in why the crowd was there and needed to be fed. They might enjoy creating a visual representation of the grassy hillside or imagining the reaction of the disciples when they witnessed Jesus's miracle and collected all the extra food. To help both groups of students understand and fully appreciate the significance of this biblical account, it would be important to incorporate teaching methods that allow for both learning preferences.

5. Cynthia Ulrich Tobias, *The Way They Learn* (Colorado Springs: Focus on the Family, 1994), 104–5.

Which of the following examples best describes you?

1. A friend asks you about a movie you just saw.

   A. You tell your friend who was in the movie, you talk through the plot line, and maybe you even quote a few lines of the dialogue.

   B. You tell your friend how the movie made you feel and give a general idea of the theme, but you can't remember who the actors were, even though you do remember what they looked like.

2. Someone asks you how to get to the nearest fast food restaurant.

   A. You explain which direction to head, where to turn, names of streets, and an approximate distance.

   B. You confess that you aren't really sure which streets to take, but you are able to provide a general idea of where to head and you can describe the buildings and scenery they will pass on the way.

If you see yourself as more of an A, then you are probably more analytic, or field independent. If B sounds more like your style, then you might be more global, or field dependent.

The following chart provides an overview of some key characteristics of each of the two polarities.

Global	Analytic
Recognizes and remembers faces	Recognizes and remembers names
Interprets body language	Focuses on word meanings
Produces humorous thoughts	Produces logical thoughts
Focuses on the big idea	Emphasizes details
Subjective	Objective
Likes working with groups	Likes working individually
Makes emotional appeals	Makes logical appeals
Prefers demonstrational instructions	Prefers verbal instructions
Processes information randomly and with patterns	Processes information sequentially
Prefers fantasy, poetry, or myths	Prefers realistic stories
Prefers open-ended assignments	Likes well-structured assignments
Remembers pictures or images	Reads for details or facts
Paraphrases	Outlines
Prefers short answer or essay tests	Prefers true-false or multiple choice

While most of us don't always fit neatly into one polarity, we do tend to operate as either a global or analytic learner most of the time. As you look over these characteristics, think about ways in which a ministry might frustrate each type of learner. What methods or structures would be beneficial for either a global or analytic learner? What are some biblical examples of both analytic and global teaching/learning experiences?

Sensory Learning

Most of what we learn comes to us through our senses of vision, hearing, smelling, touching, or tasting. Unfortunately, traditional ways of teaching tend to rely mainly on auditory methods, even though auditory learners make up the smallest percentage of students in a typical classroom. It has been suggested that 87 percent of all learners must also see and experience their learning in a kinesthetic manner to be successful in learning.[6]

> Tell me and I forget, teach me and I may remember, involve me and I learn.
>
> —Benjamin Franklin

The three main modalities by which all of us perceive information are visual, auditory, and kinesthetic. Most of us have a preferred way of learning, and we are able to learn faster and better if we are taught in our preferred modality. This is especially important for students who have more difficulty learning in a traditional classroom setting. Even though we attempt to structure more informal learning situations in our ministries, much of our teaching still resembles a classroom. That doesn't have to be a negative, as long as we recognize that the students in our "classrooms" are visual, auditory, and kinesthetic learners.

Auditory learners benefit from hearing the sounds of the words, by listening and also speaking. In fact, it is most important that they hear themselves actually saying something in order to remember it. You may notice these students talking to themselves, reading aloud, repeating instructions, or even creating a song, rhyme, or rap based on their learning.[7] What they learn is often stored in the sequence in which they have perceived the information, and they may experience difficulty in remembering things if they are asked to recall facts out of order. They may even forget what they are taught unless they are given an opportunity to discuss it with others.

Visual learners benefit from pictures, charts, or diagrams. For instance, they may be able to visualize where to find a biblical passage in their own

6. Donna Walker Tileston, *What Every Teacher Should Know about Learning, Memory, and the Brain* (Thousand Oaks, CA: Corwin, 2004).
7. Tobias, *Way They Learn*, 91.

Bible, but have trouble remembering the exact chapter or verse. They would benefit more from reading a story themselves than from listening to someone else read or tell the story because this would allow them to see the words as they process them. They often write things down to remember them, and they sometimes give away their inner feelings through their facial expressions.[8]

Kinesthetic learners have a need to become physically involved with their learning, even if it is simply pacing back and forth or walking around while reading or studying. They don't often concentrate for long periods of time on their learning, but benefit from taking frequent breaks or shifting their attention or focus.[9] Kinesthetic learners remember what they have done more than what they have read or heard. To sit on the sidelines and observe is painful; they would much rather be involved. Watch their body language for a clue as to what they are feeling or thinking.

Multiple Intelligences

Intelligence testing has traditionally focused on exams that calculate one particular score for IQ (intelligence quotient). This number has placed students in categories used to predict future success and academic ability. Some researchers, such as developmental psychologist Howard Gardner, have questioned this system of labeling students. Gardner developed a different way of understanding intelligence and argued that evidence exists for a variety of intelligences or "frames of mind."[10]

Each of Gardner's eight intelligences involves a set of specific problem-solving skills useful for gaining knowledge. Other researchers have attempted to describe various types of knowledge, or ways of communicating, but Gardner focused on actual *ways of knowing*. For instance, someone who is not strong in spatial intelligence might use that as an excuse for not doing well in geometry, a field of study requiring spatial understanding. Areas of expertise, however, such as geometry or music, are content domains, or disciplines, and not *ways* of learning or knowing. The intelligences describe strengths in *how* students learn, not *what* they learn. Domains relate to specific occupations, but an intelligence can be used to gain knowledge in a variety of domains and is useful for more than one occupation.

8. Tileston, *What Every Teacher Should Know*.
9. Tobias, *Way They Learn*, 93.
10. Howard Gardner, *Frames of Mind: The Theory of Multiple Intelligences* (New York: Basic Books, 1983), 8.

Consider the geometry student who doesn't excel in spatial intelligence. He can still learn geometry, but the teacher will need to use strategies that allow him to use his preferred ways of learning.[11] In the same way, a student who is not strong in musical intelligence can still understand music theory and learn to play an instrument.

According to Gardner, intelligence is not static or genetically determined at birth, as many previously believed, but it can actually be taught and developed if multiple forms of intelligence are valued and nurtured.[12] Gardner's theory includes special abilities and preferences for knowing based on the following intelligences.

Verbal / linguistic—comprehending the spoken and written word; using language to convince, explain, and reflect on language itself; it is the most widely shared intellectual competence.

Logical / mathematical—using numerical symbols; putting information into sequences that allow for problem solving; understanding relationships; a strong ability to deal with abstract problems and convert them into rational ideas and solutions; being able to assess, analyze, and compute.

Visual / spatial—heightened ability to work in three dimensions and see various viewpoints; manipulation of mental images, as needed for playing chess well; a strong visual memory and imagination.

Bodily / kinesthetic—using the body to help learn and remember information, as in using manipulatives to learn math concepts; learning through movement, such as reaching, grasping, touching.

Musical / rhythmic—proficiencies with pitch, rhythm, and melody that inspire and help with memory and motivation; as an intelligence, musical composition is more doing than thinking.

Intrapersonal—strong self-awareness, including feelings, a sense of identity, and emotional reactions; using deep self-understanding and experience to guide behavior and make sense of the world; ability to learn in isolation.

Interpersonal—ability to communicate well with others, both verbally and nonverbally; deep understanding of others and their emotions; keen ability to empathize; excels in group learning.

Naturalist—unusual strength in reading signs and patterns in one's surroundings; understanding the environment to gain wisdom; street smart.

11. Ibid., 31–32.
12. Cited in Gregory and Parry, *Designing Brain Compatible Learning*, 97.

Emotional Intelligence

Building on Gardner's work, psychologists Peter Salovey and John Mayer developed the concept of emotional intelligence. They defined it in terms of understanding, identifying, and regulating one's emotions and using emotions to aid in critical thinking and problem solving.[13] Emotional intelligence advocates believe that students who are able to proficiently control their emotions are better able to make wise choices and to prevent outside circumstances from interfering with learning.[14]

Learning Style Inventory

The Learning Style Inventory (LSI) was first developed by Kenneth and Rita Dunn to assess student environmental learning preferences. Years of follow-up research has shown it to be perhaps the most widely used, valid, and reliable assessment of its kind for schoolchildren in the United States.[15] The LSI identifies a learning style as "a biologically and developmentally imposed set of characteristics that make the same teaching method wonderful for some and terrible for others."[16] The instrument takes into account preferences for the following learning factors:

- Environmental factors: sound, light, temperature, seating arrangements
- Emotional factors: motivation, conformity/responsibility, task persistence, learning/classroom structure
- Physiological factors: perceptual (auditory, visual, tactile/kinesthetic), intake needs of food/drink, time of day, mobility
- Psychological factors: analytic-global, impulsive-reflective
- Sociological factors: working alone, in a pair, with peers, in a group; relationship with authority; need for variety

Consider your own learning preferences. If you have an important exam coming up, how will you prepare if you want to make the best grade possible? How do you approach a major assignment?

13. Ibid., 91.
14. Ibid., 93.
15. Rita Dunn, "Rita Dunn Answers Questions on Learning Styles," *Educational Leadership* 48, no. 2 (October 1990): 15–19.
16. Rita Dunn and Shirley A. Griggs, *Learning Styles: Quiet Revolution in American Secondary Schools* (Reston, VA: National Association of Secondary School Principals, 1988), 3.

Bright lights or dark room with a study light?

Cool temperature or warm?

Snuggled onto your bed or sitting in a chair at your desk?

Music playing or absolute quiet?

Focused study session of multiple hours, or twenty minutes of concentrated time sandwiched between breaks?

Food and water/coffee/soft drink or total famine?

Alone, with one study buddy, or in a group?

Get up early to study or stay up late?

Big ideas or individual details? (Global or analytic?)

See and read the notes aloud? Listen to recordings of the lectures? Create notecards you can manipulate as you review? (Visual, auditory, or tactile/kinesthetic?)

What you need to remember when you teach is that your students have legitimate preferences that are strongly tied to learning outcomes. It is tempting to try and force everyone to adapt to the same learning environment; but if we want our students to experience genuine change, then we need to take the LSI research seriously. The importance of allowing students to access their learning preferences, as related to successful learning, has been clearly demonstrated. When we teach, we must make allowances for these individual preferences, as much as possible given our available resources.

Experiential Learning

David Kolb developed the Experiential Learning Model, which also utilizes a Learning Style Inventory (LSI), to assess students' strengths. Unlike the Dunns' instrument, Kolb's LSI focuses on individual differences in two distinct categories: the way information is perceived and the way information is processed. His theory is related to Carl Jung's personality types, and he believes learning strengths are fairly consistent throughout the life of the learner.[17] Individuals *perceive* the world primarily through concrete experience (feeling) or through abstract conceptualization (thinking). They *process* the information they have perceived through either reflective observation (watching) or active experimentation (doing). The LSI includes

17. David A. Kolb, *Experiential Learning: Experience as the Source of Learning and Development* (Englewood Cliffs, NJ: Prentice-Hall, 1984), 62–64.

several components designed to assess learners' responses in accordance to how they approach real-life learning situations, and the results are plotted on a two-axis graph, a two-dimensional learning style map.

Four learning types are identified, based on an interpretation of the learning style map. The *convergent* learning style describes the individual who relies on abstract conceptualization and active experimentation. They do best in situations where there is a single correct answer or solution to a problem, as would be expected on most traditional exams. Convergent learners prefer technical tasks more than dealing with interpersonal issues.[18] In ministry, these are probably the students who identify clear-cut solutions to problems, based on specific biblical precepts. They might have a difficult time interacting with others who talk about "gray areas."

The *divergent* learning style uses concrete experience and reflective observation to approach new learning situations. These learners perform best in situations that allow for multiple solutions, such as brainstorming, are more focused on people and possibilities, and are more feeling-oriented than convergent learners.[19] Using ministry case studies would be very beneficial to the divergent learner, allowing them to relate biblical concepts to real-life situations.

Kolb's third learning style is *assimilation*. The assimilator perceives information through abstract conceptualization and processes through reflective observation. This learning style focuses on inductive reasoning and theoretical models and is less interested in people than ideas, much like the convergent learning style. The key difference, however, is that the assimilator is more concerned with a theory that makes sense than one that has practical value.[20] Don't expect these learners to enjoy a quick question-and-answer review of a Bible study. They would much prefer time to process theoretical questions that require them to think about underlying biblical principles and how they might be applicable in today's world. Their ideas might not always be practical, but they will be logical.

The fourth and final learning style is the *accommodative*, which emphasizes concrete experience and active experimentation. These learners like to do things, to accomplish tasks, and to get involved in new experiences. They enjoy taking risks and learning through trial and error. While accommodators might appear pushy in their attempts to get things done, they enjoy working with other people as they learn.[21] As a minister, it is important

18. Ibid., 77.
19. Ibid., 77–78.
20. Ibid., 78.
21. Ibid.

Identify three specific things you would incorporate into a Bible study with teenagers for each of these learning styles: convergent, divergent, accommodative, and assimilation. Select a specific passage to use with all of your examples, such as Daniel 6.

to give these learners opportunities to learn in nontraditional settings or through service projects.

Bernice McCarthy developed the 4MAT learning style model,[22] which is very similar to Kolb's. A key difference in the theories is that McCarthy includes references to right brain/left brain theory in her model. A key value of her work is in the practical application she gives to actual classroom teaching strategies. The following chart shows the relationship between the two theories.

Kolb	McCarthy	Characteristics
Convergent	Common Sense (Type Three)	Integrate theory and practice; pragmatists; focus on practical application of ideas Favorite question: How does this work?
Divergent	Imaginative (Type One)	Integrate experience with self; value insight, thinking, and work for harmony Favorite question: Why?
Assimilation	Analytic (Type Two)	Learn by thinking through ideas; critique information and collect data Favorite question: What?
Accommodative	Dynamic (Type Four)	Integrate experience and application; reach accurate conclusions without logical justification Favorite question: What if?

The models summarized in this chapter represent the predominant ways in which educational specialists have attempted to understand individual learning preferences. It is not an exhaustive list, as revisions and new theories continue to be developed. As interest in neuroscience research expands and becomes an increasingly influential field of study, it will continue to inform our understanding of how change takes place in the life of the learner.

As teachers, one of our most important considerations is to realize that everyone is an individual, with unique ways of learning. If we take our

22. Bernice McCarthy, *The 4MAT System: Teaching to Learning Styles with Right/Left Mode Techniques* (Barrington, IL: EXCEL, 1987).

teaching role seriously, if we want to help our students experience transformation, then a mini-lecture followed by a small-group discussion can't be our normative practice. We have to focus on creating learning situations with the greatest likelihood of facilitating Christlike change for everyone in our ministries.

Questions and Activities

1. Consider the types of learners in a typical Bible study. How might you structure the learning situation to benefit visual, auditory, and kinesthetic learners?
2. What are the benefits to varying your approach to teaching?
3. How would you describe a "typical" teaching/learning environment in your ministry?

    Do you have music playing in the background during discussion times, or are voices the only sound?

    Are the lights kept low to create a warm and welcoming ambience, or is there bright overhead lighting?

    Is there a regular routine of having students form small discussion groups at some point in the evening, or do you allow opportunities for students to do some reflection or analysis on their own?

    Do you restrict eating or drinking in your "classroom," or do you always provide food and drink?

    Are there early morning or afternoon ministry opportunities, or does every Bible study take place at night?

4. Consider your own learning preferences, based on the brief descriptions in this chapter. How would you describe your preferred learning style in terms of how you perceive and process new information? As you observe teaching ministries, pay attention to what types of learners would thrive in that setting and what types of learners would struggle.
5. Review the nine intelligences (Gardner's eight intelligences and emotional intelligence). What teaching and learning strategies would benefit students whose strengths are in each of those intelligences?

Further Reading

Dunn, Rita. "Rita Dunn Answers Questions on Learning Styles." *Educational Leadership* 48, no. 2 (October 1990): 15–19.

Gardner, Howard. *Multiple Intelligences: New Horizons*. New York: Perseus, 2006.

Gregory, Gayle H., and Terence Parry. *Designing Brain Compatible Learning*. 3rd ed. Thousand Oaks, CA: Corwin, 2006.

Kolb, David A. *Experiential Learning: Experience as the Source of Learning and Development*. Englewood Cliffs, NJ: Prentice-Hall, 1984.

McCarthy, Bernice. *The 4MAT System: Teaching to Learning Styles with Right/Left Mode Techniques*. Barrington, IL: EXCEL, 1987.

Tileston, Donna Walker. *What Every Teacher Should Know about Learning, Memory, and the Brain*. Thousand Oaks, CA: Corwin, 2004.

Tobias, Cynthia Ulrich. *The Way They Learn*. Colorado Springs: Focus on the Family, 1994.

Faith Formation with Others

SHARON GALGAY KETCHAM

Two years ago, Faith Community Church hired Leah as a part-time youth minister. Right away, Leah began a high school summer Bible study that continues to this day. The group meets for an hour every Wednesday. Tonight, the room is filled with fifteen teenagers, two of whom just recently started coming. They spend the first few minutes lamenting the absence of Jason and Erin, who graduated last spring. José shares a story about the time Erin brought her pet anole to Bible study, and the whole group laughs as he folds his hands together to imitate the "praying lizard." Judging from the knowing smiles around the room, this story is part of the group's folklore. The group enthusiastically shares the backstory with the newcomers. Leah announces it is time to begin and offers a word of prayer. Many have their own Bibles, and others grab one from the well-used stack on the table. They are studying the Gospel of John.

After helping each locate the passage, they take turns reading aloud the story of Jesus changing water into wine. Leah helps navigate the discussion by asking questions and providing some background information to help the group understand the text. Jennifer, who grew up in Sunday school, tells everyone this is the first miracle Jesus ever did. Conversation about this "fact" ensues. Kyle wonders if, as a boy, Jesus ever changed his veggies into chocolate and, if he had, "Would that be a miracle?" Everyone laughs, and others imagine miracles performed by the boy Jesus.

Leah invites the group to look at each of the four Gospels and determine which miracle was recorded first. While they do this, Mike pulls out his phone and does a search for the first miracle of Jesus. One site says changing water to wine was the first *public* miracle. After looking through the other Gospels and rereading John's account, the group agrees this was likely Jesus's first public miracle. Jennifer is pleased, and Mike pokes fun at her saying, "You still hope to get on the honor role in Sunday school!"

Jenna tends to be the quiet one in the room, laughing at the jokes and taking it all in. But when Leah asks if they see miracles today, Jenna says she wishes so. "My dad has been sick for a while, and the doctors don't seem to help." Sonya grabs the group's prayer notebook and writes down, "Please help the doctors find the right medicine for Jenna's dad." They all agree to pray for him.

The discussion about miracles, water, and wine continues as people wonder about the text and its meaning in their lives. When it is almost time to go, they share other prayer requests, write them in the notebook, and review older requests to see how their prayers are being answered. Bibles are restacked, a couple of people hug Jenna, and all bid farewell until next week.

A Social Theory of Learning

What did the members of this Bible study learn? Did they only learn facts about miracles or benefit from the comparative Gospel study? Leah has led this study for two years. How might she describe its impact on the faith formation of these teenagers? Is faith formed when the group writes in the prayer notebook or deliberates over the Gospel writer's intent? Is faith formed when they joke about the praying lizard or Jesus turning veggies into chocolate? Reducing learning to the mere content of the Bible study and faith formation to tracking prayer requests misses the formative power in this scenario. This group of teenagers is not only participating in a Bible study but they are also practicing being Christian together.[1] They are experiencing transformation as they learn in the social realm.

Focusing on a social theory of learning invites those who teach the Christian faith to view formation through a social lens, to talk about learning as engagement with others, and to discover distinct ways to support a maturing faith in children, youth, and adults in a church or ministry setting. To accomplish this, this chapter will (1) explain the four components of Etienne

1. Adapted from Thomas Groome, *Christian Religious Education: Sharing Our Story and Vision* (San Francisco: Harper & Row, 1980).

Wenger's social theory of learning;[2] (2) in light of these, construct a definition of faith formation based on religious education theory and theological commitments; and (3) propose implications for a variety of ministry contexts. The opening Bible study scenario serves as an illustration throughout the chapter.

Learning as Doing

First, a social theory of learning inspires those who teach to view "doing" the faith as vital to faith formation.[3] Wenger resists traditional definitions in education that focus on individual process, cognition, and acquisition of information as the measurement of knowledge.[4] Learning in this realm separates the internal (experience with the content) from the external (the content) by wrongly assuming the individual can internalize a replica of the external information while ignoring what is done with the knowledge, what it becomes, or how it is used.[5]

Imagine if a Bible study focused on prayer. Adults might be taught about the structure of the Lord's Prayer, or children may memorize it. As valuable as this may be, Wenger argues that securing information is only part of learning. For example, those who understand the structure of the Lord's Prayer learn something different from what is learned while praying with a Christian community. Similarly, memorizing the Lord's Prayer does not guarantee it is meaningful when one says it.

In contrast, in Leah's Bible study scenario participants use a prayer notebook when Jenna raises the concern for her dad. Learning is taking place in the social realm as they "do" prayer together, and this is distinct from a lesson on the structure of the Lord's Prayer. It is not that one form of learning is more effective; rather, learning is generally measured by content

2. Etienne Wenger, "Learning in Doing: Social, Cognitive, and Computational Perspectives," in *Communities of Practice: Learning, Meaning, and Identity* (New York: Cambridge University Press, 1998). Jean Lave and Etienne Wenger, *Situated Learning: Legitimate Peripheral Participation* (Cambridge: Cambridge University Press, 1991).

3. Although it is necessary to describe what is distinct about each component of learning, such separation can result in minimizing the interdependence of the components. Hence, explanation of each component includes demonstrating how these are "interconnected and mutually defining." Wenger, "Learning in Doing," 5.

4. Ibid., 47–48. Some results of this overemphasis include teaching becoming the focus of learning, separation from the outside world, overuse of individual drills and testing, and teaching material out of context. In a ministry setting, the results may include focusing on facts about the Bible or memorization of a catechism without understanding. Primarily the concern is a focus on content while ignoring context.

5. Lave and Wenger, *Situated Learning*, 47.

rather than by what is done with the content. This is why Wenger proposes using the lens of the social realm to expand a definition of learning. It enables one to see the interaction between the external (content) and internal (experience with the content) by holding together knowing and doing, the objective and subjective.

Learning in the social realm involves being actively engaged in the practices of a community.[6] Practices are what people in the social realm gather around and what provides a source of coherence and meaning for a community.[7] Ministry settings are full of practices such as following a liturgy, serving on a leadership team, singing in a worship band, helping in a soup kitchen, or going on a retreat. People who are doing a practice together grow in both understanding (what one knows) and competence (what one is able to do).[8] Hence, the doing of a practice with others is an indispensable component of learning.

Similarly, faith formation should include growing in knowledge and competence by "doing" with others. In 1976, Christian educator John Westerhoff warned of an inherent danger of the dominant "schooling instruction-model" because of the primary emphasis on communicating information.[9] He argued that historically a church's focus on foundational knowledge worked. People lived in homogenous communities where they daily encountered lived expressions of the Christian faith through natural connections with friends and family members. A person's social realm included doing the faith with others in the community. Such communities still exist in many parts of the world. And yet, in America's increasingly pluralistic and multicultural contexts, Westerhoff's critique is valid. When doing the faith with others is removed from daily life, a disconnect will exist between the ideas of Christianity and the formative power of this story in people's lives.

Information-based teaching alone is insufficient for faith formation. People who know the faith do not necessarily morph into people who live the faith. Stanley Hauerwas affirms this, saying, "Like the early Christians, we must learn that understanding Jesus's life is inseparable from learning how to live our own."[10]

Others have also sought to expand perceptions of faith formation beyond information acquisition. For example, religious educator Thomas Groome

6. Wenger, "Learning in Doing," 4. Practice here should be understood broadly as what people engage in together over time.

7. Ibid., 72.

8. Ibid., 214.

9. John H. Westerhoff, *Will Our Children Have Faith?* (Minneapolis: Seabury, 1976), 2–12.

10. Stanley Hauerwas, *A Community of Character: Toward a Constructive Christian Social Ethic* (Notre Dame, IN: University of Notre Dame Press, 1981), 52.

emphasizes holistic formation, which includes three aspects of a person: the cognitive, affective, and volitional (relating to the will). These three aspects work together and result in a "lived Christian faith."[11] Similarly, theologian and philosopher Dallas Willard defines spiritual formation as transforming a person's "inner world," which includes thoughts, feelings, will, body, soul, and social world.[12] Craig Dykstra, a practical theologian, defines the "life of faith" as a new freedom, fresh seeing, and consecrated service. He emphasizes a new orientation to the world bound to a lived experience.[13]

Each of these describes faith formation as whole-person transformation. Yet even the helpful shift toward holistic transformation retains a focus on the person rather than the formative power of the social realm. Wenger's focus on the process between the person and the group while doing a practice is an additional insight for faith formation. Hence, supporting a maturing Christian faith includes growing in core knowledge, watching how other people live Christianly, and trying to live as a Christian with a group of people. *Faith formation occurs while "doing" the Christian faith with others.*

Learning as Experiencing

Second, faith formation includes learning as experiencing where people are making meaning. Experience here should not be reduced to hands-on or active learning, although it may include these methods. The focus is on the *process of learning* rather than solely the content (the facts in a Bible story) or method (acting out a Bible story). According to Wenger's theory, when a group of people gather around a practice, they have to explore what it means and decide what they need to know in order to carry out the practice. This involves working together to make it *meaningful*. The emphasis here is on the subjective (one's experience with the content) along with the objective (the content or information itself) and the affective (how one feels or responds) along with the cognitive (what one thinks).

In the Bible study scenario, how does the group make sense of the information Leah teaches about miracles? What do they do with it, what does it become, and why does it matter? Leah presents some information about the biblical text, but learning in the social realm occurs as the group experiences

11. Thomas H. Groome, *Sharing Faith: A Comprehensive Approach to Religious Education and Pastoral Ministry; The Way of Shared Praxis* (San Francisco: HarperSanFrancisco, 1991), 86–90.

12. Dallas Willard, *Renovation of the Heart: Putting on the Character of Christ* (Colorado Springs: NavPress, 2002).

13. Dykstra, *Growing in the Life of Faith: Education and Christian Practices* (Louisville: Westminster John Knox, 2005), 26–29.

the information. As they search to determine if Jennifer's insight about Jesus's first miracle is accurate or not, their quest is about more than right information. Jennifer's assertion about miracles, Mike's online search, and Kyle's musings about veggies and chocolate all make "miracles" meaningful for this group. And more, when Jenna speaks of her dad needing a miracle, this is learning as experiencing. They grab the prayer notebook and thus act as believers in miracles, which still has room for cognitive uncertainty. "Miracles" in the Bible study moves from a concept communicated by Leah to the group's meaning-filled idea to a real situation where the idea has value in Jenna's life.

This is learning as experiencing in the social realm. Meaning in this sense is produced through *active* engagement with a particular group of people. The backgrounds, knowledge bases, and life experiences of the people in the group shape the experience of learning.[14] Meaning is thus dynamic and dialogical. A different group of people at the Bible study or a different cultural setting would result in different meaning making. This does not say the content about miracles changes, but how people make sense of the content does change. Imagine the same study at an orphanage in Ghana or at a seminary in Nepal. These are all people having an experience of learning in their distinct social realm. Therefore, learning through experiences with others is inherent to learning any content as people "do" the faith together.

Faith formation does not only reside in the individual realm, a person's affective or existential moment,[15] but faith formation also occurs while with others. Learning as experiencing expands faith formation to include appropriation of the faith *with others*.[16] Christian educators have long recognized the importance of appropriation such as Groome's "Shared Praxis" approach to teaching.[17] Formation for Groome is not replicating information like asking the learner to repeat material back to the teacher or raising questions only for clarification. Groome suggests an approach of "critical appropriation" where people "judge and come to see for themselves."[18] Appropriation in this sense is a personal endeavor where people are in dialogue with a

14. Wenger, "Learning in Doing," 52.

15. Another common approach in Christian education is to begin with the person's experience and create an "avenue for learning" called "identification." See Klaus Issler and Ronald Habermas, *How We Learn: A Christian Teacher's Guide to Educational Psychology* (Eugene, OR: Wipf and Stock, 2002).

16. Appropriation involves taking in, forming, and constructing. This is different from assimilation, which involves absorbing or becoming.

17. Thomas H. Groome, *Christian Religious Education: Sharing Our Story and Vision* (San Francisco: HarperSanFrancisco, 1980); Groome, *Sharing Faith*.

18. Groome, *Sharing Faith*, 250.

community and then decide for themselves. The community provides helpful input, but appropriation ends in the person.[19]

Distinct from Groome, Wenger moves the locus of appropriation to the group. As they join a Bible study or worship team, they appropriate together how to carry out the practice in a meaningful way. Personal appropriation is not gone, but it is more intricately connected to the experience of making meaning with a group. Experience is bound to both a person's and the group's growing knowledge and competence in a practice. In this sense, *faith formation includes learning as experiencing where people are making meaning of the faith with one another*.

Learning as Belonging

To be a Christian is to belong to a story larger than oneself. As theologian Miroslav Volf poignantly says, "One cannot have a self-enclosed communion with the triune God—a 'foursome' as it were—for the Christian God is not a private deity."[20] Instead, God draws people into this common story. For example, the Pauline corpus is replete with adoption metaphors (Eph. 1:5) and kinship metaphors (Gal. 3:29). People of faith join with others who also belong to this community.

Learning in the social realm facilitates belonging. To belong is to be integral to the group. Neither a social connection based on proximity (all are from the same area of the city or in the same church) nor people having similar interests (a desire to serve the poor or a love of hymns) defines belonging. When, then, does someone belong? Belonging is established when a person contributes to the practice of a group, as this demonstrates a person's growing understanding (knowing) and competence (doing) of the group's practice.[21] Simultaneously, the group legitimizes this contribution by incorporating it into their practice, which results in a sense of belonging shared by the person and the group. Belonging evolves as the person actively engages in the community's practice.

When the teenagers in this Bible study pray, they are making sense of how and why to pray; and when they do, they experience belonging. When Sonya grabs a prayer notebook, she "belongs" because she knows how to use the prayer notebook as this group understands it. Even more, imagine if

19. Ibid. Groome does view the community as essential for input into the person's appropriation but does not pay attention to the process as the location for appropriation.

20. Miroslav Volf, *After Our Likeness: The Church as the Image of the Trinity* (Grand Rapids: Eerdmans, 1998), 173.

21. Wenger, "Learning in Doing," 5.

she interrupts the Bible study to write in the notebook, and someone from the group pulls her aside saying she should wait until the prayer time. Her experience of belonging would likely dissolve. On the other hand, suppose Mike suggests they take their prayer journal online to facilitate making requests during the week. Or maybe Jennifer creates a Facebook group where the "like" of a prayer request signals actively praying. When the group starts to "pray" in these ways, they say to Mike and Jennifer, "You belong." The person experiences belonging, and the group validates this by including his or her contribution. Belonging includes reciprocity between the person and the group.

Practical theologian Nancy Pineda-Madrid's definition of "traditioning" captures this idea of reciprocal contribution and resultant experience of belonging.[22] Pineda-Madrid asserts how the word *tradition* historically includes an "intrinsic relation of process and content."[23] By this she means tradition is both the teachings of the church and the lived faith of Christians. Hence, "a tradition is only a tradition to the extent that it has been received and internalized through some practice."[24]

Since the Christian faith is both an individual and a social event, it is the "process of interpretation that necessarily and invariably creates community."[25] When people interpret a tradition together, this facilitates the formation of community. This is parallel to Wenger's understanding of belonging. As people interpret the faith together by doing a practice and this group adopts a person's contribution, the result is a reciprocal affirmation of belonging—community is formed. *Traditioning* is exactly what the teenagers in this Bible study are doing. As they pray, they are interpreting prayer and acting as a community. Traditioning, reciprocal contribution, and belonging are essential to faith formation. *Faith formation occurs when contribution fosters belonging.*

Learning as Becoming

Becoming is the final component of learning in the social realm and is closely aligned with the idea of sanctification as described by John Wesley. After we are "born again, the gradual work of sanctification takes place . . .

22. Nancy Pineda-Madrid, "Traditioning: The Formation of Community, the Transmission of Faith," in *Futuring Our Past: Explorations in the Theology of Tradition*, ed. Orlando O. Espín and Gary Macy (Maryknoll, NY: Orbis, 2006), 204–26.

23. Ibid., 204.

24. Ibid., 205.

25. Ibid., 215.

enabled by the Spirit . . . as we are more and more dead to sin, we are more and more alive to God."[26] Christians are people in process; Christians are becoming. Wenger describes becoming as identity shaping, which is produced through lived experiences with others.[27] He is not implying pure socialization where the community is the only agent forming the person. Rather, through exchange and shared meaning making while doing a practice, the person and the community form each other. The focus is on their "mutual constitution."[28]

Identity in this sense is more than self-image (how one sees oneself) because becoming also involves seeing oneself in connection with others. To join a group's practice means encountering what is familiar (one's own areas of knowledge and competence) and what is unfamiliar (other people's knowledge and competence).[29] Self is understood as only a part, albeit a necessary part, of the whole. Such experiences shape a person's perspective and provide a lens for interpreting the world outside of the practice. Belonging to a group shapes the identity of the person just as the person shapes the group. For this reason, becoming is a key component of learning.

The teenagers in the Bible study are becoming people of faith, which is a lifelong journey of sanctification. Engaging in Bible study and prayer gives them an opportunity to do the faith, make faith meaningful, and experience belonging as he or she contributes. All of this shapes how they see themselves and the world outside the Bible study. Developing folklore about praying lizards, wondering about veggies and chocolate, and writing in the prayer notebook in response to Jenna's fear for her dad are formative for these people. They are *becoming* both as individual Christians and as a group of believers.

When recognizing the role learning plays in a person's becoming, those who teach recognize they influence identity, vision, and perceptions of self and others. Teachers help form people. Faith shapes who a person is becoming when "faith *functions* in persons, causing them to seek and understand God's will for the world and their responsibility to bring it about."[30] But this does not, and really cannot, happen in isolation. As social beings, it is one's engagement with others, and God as Other, that allows persons to become

---

26. John Wesley, "The Scripture Way of Salvation," in *The Works of John Wesley: Sermons II, 34–70*, ed. Albert C. Outler (Nashville: Abingdon, 1985), 153–69.

27. Wenger, "Learning in Doing," 151.

28. Ibid., 146.

29. Ibid., 153.

30. Carl Ellis Nelson, *How Faith Matures* (Louisville: Westminster John Knox, 1989), 145 (emphasis original).

and mature as followers of Christ. The person is becoming and the group is becoming as they do a practice together. This paradigm resists isolating the individual and welcomes an active encounter with others.

Implications for Ministry Contexts

Evaluate how learning and faith formation are understood in a ministry setting. Most of Western education emphasizes knowledge as the primary avenue for learning, and, subsequently, the church has a similar emphasis in teaching ministries. To determine if this is the case in a particular ministry setting, look at the programs, studies, and events in a calendar year(s). What do they say about the ministry's view of faith formation? Talk to those involved in the ministry. What are their hopes and aims for those involved? Make note of what is emphasized: knowledge, commitment, experience, relationships, groups, individuals, and so on. Determine what aspects of the ministry are best suited for introducing the value of doing the faith alongside knowing the faith.

Support practice in small groups (of all varieties). Small groups have a long history. In eighteenth-century England, John Wesley organized people into groups to facilitate their pursuit of holiness.[31] They gathered weekly and told one another about their progress and failure. These meetings were a catalyst for tremendous revival in the Anglican Church and demonstrate the great potential of small groups. Conversely, small groups can dissolve into spiritual self-help groups. Sociologist Robert Wuthnow writes about the rise of the small-group phenomena in America.[32] His research includes everything from Alcoholics Anonymous to youth groups to Bible studies to support groups. Wuthnow concludes that people participate in these groups primarily because they experience emotional support. Emotional support is important; however, if the group's value is measured by personal fulfillment, then the group is dispensable when one's needs are not met.

Envisioning learning in the social realm focuses a small group on the doing of faith with others (experiencing). A small group of young adults might talk about their desire for a fulfilling career or relationship, but these discussions come alongside practicing the faith (doing). For example, the group can study Ecclesiastes, provide rides to church for older adults,

31. Michael D. Henderson, *A Model for Making Disciples: John Wesley's Class Meeting* (Nappanee, IN: Francis Asbury, 1997).

32. Robert Wuthnow, "Small Groups Forge New Notions of Community and the Sacred," *Christian Century*, December 8, 1993, 1236–40.

or organize a prayer vigil. As they do these things, the group determines the why and how of the practice, thus making meaning and contributing (belonging). The group can see themselves as valuable (becoming) to the mission of the church.

Revise job descriptions. The role of a teacher (e.g., small-group leader, Sunday school teacher, Bible study leader) is twofold: to help a group of people grow in their *knowledge* of the faith and in their competence in the *practice* of faith. This is more than having a life application section at the end of a lesson. For example, how are children in a Sunday school class doing the faith? If an offering is collected, how are they becoming offer-ers alongside their growing knowledge about tithing? Maybe they decorate the offering box, take turns collecting, develop a ritual for collection, or raise money for a special mission project. To see themselves as offer-ers (becoming), they must contribute to how this class gives an offering (belonging). A teacher's job description includes both instruction of content and establishing ways people are doing the faith with others.

Create pathways for contribution. There is a considerable distinction between participation and contribution. Participation merely requires joining what is already being done such as attending the worship service or joining a class. In contrast, the root of contribution is causation. Valuing contribution asks people to cause a change by bringing, adding, creating, endeavoring, improving, and enhancing what is already being done. This is not a proposal for *ex nihilo*—creation out of nothing. Rather, teachers in ministry settings need to create pathways for appropriate contribution. Imagine a group of college students that express a passion for clean water in the two-thirds world while reading Jesus's water analogy in John 4. A teacher can create a pathway for this passionate contribution by providing a nuanced interpretation of John 4 or by helping students shape this passion toward the larger mission of their church or ministry. On a smaller scale, teachers create pathways for contribution by valuing differing opinions during a discussion or creatively engaging silent members of a group. The aim is to make space for people to be part of the ministry rather than to function only as receivers of ministry.

Conclusion

Wenger's components inform a more robust definition of faith formation because learning is seen through the social realm. This emphasizes doing the faith with others, experiencing individual and corporate appropriation, belonging through received contribution, and becoming a person of faith alongside a people of faith. Christ came to proclaim a message (knowledge) intended to transform a people called to join (doing) God's larger redemptive purposes in the world. To teach is to empower people in church and ministry settings to practice doing this faith with others and foster growth in both knowledge and competence.

Questions and Activities

1. Compare and contrast your understanding of learning with learning in the social realm.
2. How is faith formation expanded when seen through the lens of "doing the faith"?
3. How do the four components of learning overlap or depend on one another?
4. Define the role of a teacher when the social realm of learning is taken seriously.
5. Pick a ministry context you know well. If the teaching ministry in this setting sought to include the four components of learning (doing, experiencing, belonging, and becoming), what would change? What would remain the same?

Further Reading

Gorman, Julie A. *Community That Is Christian*. Grand Rapids: Baker Books, 2002.

Groome, Thomas. *Sharing Faith: A Comprehensive Approach to Religious Education and Pastoral Ministry; The Way of Shared Praxis*. San Francisco: HarperSanFrancisco, 1991.

Lave, Jean, and Etienne Wenger. *Situated Learning: Legitimate Peripheral Participation*. Cambridge: Cambridge University Press, 1991.

Myers, Joseph R. *Search to Belong: Rethinking Intimacy, Community, and Small Groups*. Grand Rapids: Zondervan, 2011.

10

Motivation and Ministry

DAVID RAHN

Brad was not a naturally gifted student. He had to put more time into his studies than his friends did to earn a B. On the other hand, things came pretty easy for Kevin. He wrote well, thought well, spoke well, and juggled lots of competing activities as he cruised to graduation with honors. Brad's drive to learn seemed deeper than Kevin's. It clung to the core of his character, inexorably attached to his calling from Jesus.

It's not that Kevin wasn't interested in his ministry preparation. On most college class days he was engaged enough that he could generate some enthusiasm for what the class was exploring. But he never gave the impression that he was "all in" for the learning at hand, in spite of his ability to routinely earn As for his work.

Brad and Kevin offer contrasting examples of student success stories. Each was motivated to learn. If the goal of our teaching were to showcase our brightest students, Kevin would be our poster child. But since our purposes are usually linked more directly to outcomes that advance the mission of God through graduates, Brad turned out to be the better example of the fruit for which we pray and work.

Some students come under our teaching influence already possessing a hunger to learn. Others are simply taking the next steps on the dutiful pathway assigned to them. It was Brad who clearly wanted to follow Jesus wherever he led. Brad regularly demonstrated he had "ears to hear" what the Holy Spirit was saying to him about what he should start doing and stop doing. The steeper growth trajectory belonged to Brad, maybe because he continually proved the sincerity of his dedication to Jesus by doggedly chewing on truth's morsels until he had captured every nutrient that might strengthen him for service. It turns out that Brad's type of motivation is transferable. It has equipped him well to lead a pioneering mission in Haiti where solving difficult problems is a way of life. The perseverance he cultivated as a twenty-year-old college student serves him well twenty years later.

While there has been abundant research done on classroom-based *achievement motivation*, the desire to learn, know, and grow is also a critical factor in nonformal ministry situations. My three-year-old grandson frequently peppers me with questions that reveal his appetite for discovery in spite of the fact that no schooling transcript will record his progress under my tutoring. The relevance of a learner's motivation to a teacher's strategic efforts transcends context. In fact, this single factor is so significant that—from a pure learning perspective—it should probably dictate any teacher's priorities. Teachers should keep in mind that

1. when students are not ready to learn, no teaching efforts make sense until their motivation is awakened; and
2. when students are clearly ready to learn, every teaching effort either nurtures or diminishes their existing motivation.

There's a lot at stake for those who teach the next generations. We need to understand how motivation affects learning. One proposition to consider at the outset is that our expertise in how people learn and grow informs our teaching effectiveness. There's a surprising dead end awaiting those who cultivate their teaching abilities but neglect their insights about how learning takes place. The outcomes we seek are never about what we do as teachers. Rather, they revolve around how someone else is changed. Author Scott Larson understands motivation's crucial place in the learning process: "There is no such thing as teaching. Only learning. Information cannot be pushed in from the outside. It has to be drawn in from the inside. So our job is to create an environment conducive to learning."[1]

It's worth our time to engage in deep reflection about both the skills and limitations we bring into any teaching-learning situation. Toward that end, a handy guide can help teachers evaluate their teaching plans and determine

---

1. Scott Larson and Daniel L. Tocchini, *Groundwork: Preparing the Soil for God's Transformation* (Loveland, CO: Group, 2015), 22.

how the four motivational factors may be at work in a given lesson. The following question acts as that guide while offering a framework for the rest of the chapter: *Why should (this person, these people) dive into (this learning experience) (with me) (right now)?*

As you consider the four important motivational factors embedded in this question, see if you can identify what value you might assign to each one (that is, the percentage of your effort spent on each factor) on the way to forming your own motivational teaching strategies. While you're at it, reflect on why most ministries today still adopt an "information-pushing" approach to teaching.

This Person/These People

It's not entirely clear from the Gospel record when Jesus first noticed Peter. But there's a transformational moment that takes place early in their relationship that reveals how savvy Jesus was in understanding Peter's preexisting motivations:

> On one occasion, while the crowd was pressing in on [Jesus] to hear the word of God, he was standing by the lake of Gennesaret, and he saw two boats by the lake, but the fishermen had gone out of them and were washing their nets. Getting into one of the boats, which was Simon's, he asked him to put out a little from the land. And he sat down and taught the people from the boat. And when he had finished speaking, he said to Simon, "Put out into the deep and let down your nets for a catch." And Simon answered, "Master, we toiled all night and took nothing! But at your word I will let down the nets." And when they had done this, they enclosed a large number of fish, and their nets were breaking. They signaled to their partners in the other boat to come and help them. And they came and filled both the boats, so that they began to sink. But when Simon Peter saw it, he fell down at Jesus' knees, saying, "Depart from me, for I am a sinful man, O Lord." For he and all who were with him were astonished at the catch of fish that they had taken, and so also were James and John, sons of Zebedee, who were partners with Simon. And Jesus said to Simon, "Do not be afraid; from now on you will be catching men." And when they had brought their boats to land, they left everything and followed him. (Luke 5:1–11)

It's not surprising that Jesus was able to engage Peter, moving him to begin a discipleship adventure that would define the rest of his life. He appealed to Peter's natural leadership gifts, his inclination to act boldly, and his desire to see awe-inspiring outcomes. Can we do the same with those we teach?

The mix of factors that influence an individual's readiness to learn makes for a combination of possibilities that can be intimidating. Some students have preferred learning styles (see chap. 8) that tilt in the direction of hands-on, trial-and-error experiences, while others are delighted to digest a well-chosen book and work out their own conceptual clarity of its meaning. Extroverts and introverts will respond to particular assignments differently. Sometimes a learner's family and socioeconomic backgrounds hold the key to solving our teaching challenges.

In 1968, Abraham Maslow asserted that there is a hierarchy of importance to persons' needs. His theory gave structure to the commonsense reality that someone who is desperately hungry might have trouble concentrating on a lecture that has to do with reaching her highest potential.[2] About the same time, Erik Erikson articulated how adolescents are commonly driven to work out their identity crises during their teen years; it's one of the eight stage-specific developmental tasks that learners must resolve over the course of their lifetime.[3] If Erikson, or any other theorist, is correct, teachers would be wise to expect students in a certain age range to be somewhat preoccupied by developmental impositions they are simultaneously experiencing and exploring. When Jesus invited young men like Peter to follow him, he may have tapped into their significant motivational quest to figure out their identity.

Peter O'Donnell, well-regarded ministry consultant and chief design architect for the DeVos Urban Leadership Initiative, offered the following question to guide our preparation and keep us from being paralyzed by the array of factors that teachers might consider: "What do I need to know and don't yet know about my target audience?"[4] It's safe to say that the more we can discover about those we seek to teach, the more likely we will be able to form-fit our instructional design toward what already motivates them.

Did you catch that? *Students are already motivated.* It's true that they may not yet be motivated to learn or do what we teachers would like them to. But rather than pretend that students' preexisting motivations aren't significant factors in the teaching-learning process, shrewd teachers will discover what makes their students tick in order to shape transformational learning experiences.

2. Abraham Maslow, "Self-Actualization and Beyond," in *Human Dynamics in Psychology and Education: Selected Readings*, ed. Don E. Hamacheck (Boston: Allyn and Bacon, 1968).

3. Erik Erikson, *Identity: Youth and Crisis* (New York: W. W. Norton, 1968).

4. Peter O'Donnell, "Different Strokes for Different Folks," lecture, Instructional Design Institute of the DeVos Urban Leadership Initiative, Grand Rapids, September 20, 2012.

This Learning Experience

Identifying a topic for teaching is a common but insufficient start in preparation. Recognizing the scope of the subject matter at least helps us to locate what portion of all the possibilities can be tackled during the upcoming learning opportunity. But too many of us feel powerless when it comes to shaping our particular teaching objective. *It is what it is*, we think, and our preparation should lead us to study well enough so that we become subject matter experts. Too often this leads us to conclude that a well-crafted presentation of what we've discovered will meet our teaching obligation. We subsequently work our tails off to make lessons interesting. Intuitively, at least, we recognize that students need to be engaged if they are going to learn.

> **Too often we conclude that a well-crafted presentation of what we've discovered will meet our teaching obligation.**

Why not include the learner engagement question (What is my audience already motivated by?) at the very start of the design process? Jesus's use of parables was a brilliant way to identify and engage those who were already motivated to learn. Consider the classic "good Samaritan" exchange he had with an expert in religious law whose motivations were not quite so pure: "But he [the expert], desiring to justify himself, said to Jesus, 'And who is my neighbor?' . . . [After telling the story, Jesus asked,] 'Which of these three, do you think, proved to be a neighbor to the man who fell among the robbers?' He said, 'The one who showed him mercy.' And Jesus said to him, 'You go, and do likewise'" (Luke 10:29, 36–37).

As profound as Jesus's lectures were, the evidence suggests that this was not his preferred teaching strategy. The Gospels record him asking nearly three hundred questions to engage followers, expose adversaries, and force curious fence-sitters to make a choice. Further study of these tactics reveals that Jesus's questions seldom came out of nowhere. His inquiries popped up out of the common experience of life and struggle he shared with the people. The motivational power of such a strategy is brilliant!

One of John Dewey's greatest educational contributions was to identify how important real-life experience is to the teaching-learning process.[5] Turn students loose to solve problems that matter to them, and watch their motivation to learn surge to new heights.

Ted Ward is widely credited with developing the split-rail fence model for theological education by extension. His respect for Dewey's observation about

---

5. John Dewey, *Experience and Education* (1938; repr., New York: Collier, 1979).

Years ago, I sought to develop a top-ten list that could summarize some design guidelines based on what had been discovered about the intersection of motivation and learning. The following list represents some of my most enduring best practices:

1. Because most student learning occurs outside of a room, where motivation has its natural, powerful influence, work to create interesting and meaningful assignments.
2. Because student choice is a critical element to their motivation, work to create processes that will allow them to pursue their own learning goals.
3. Because a major influence on what students learn is from what they read, work to choose the best readings and create activities that will require careful reading.
4. Because student-centered approaches to teaching are more effective at producing higher-level learning outcomes and discovering what we don't know about students, work to create purposeful discussions.
5. Because cooperative learning methods are more effective at producing positive student attitudes toward subject matter and other students, work to create opportunities for students to be interdependently linked in small groups or teams.
6. Because *specific* task feedback enhances student motivation and learning, work to make a specific response to students following learning activities.
7. Because student awareness of the purpose of learning tasks enhances learning, work to disclose the reasons and goals for your teaching.
8. Because student learning begins with student attention, work to be unpredictable in methodologies by using music, videos, films, role plays, case studies, simulation games, reflection papers, and debates.
9. Because student passivity is a barrier to learning, work to begin with student activators (such as meaningful problems plucked from their life context), especially when a lecture is scheduled.
10. Because accurate student feedback is needed to assess learning processes and outcomes, work to create an open atmosphere to hear and respond to student concerns and suggestions.

the power of real-life situations to leverage motivational forces is evident in this simple teaching-learning analogy. The fence's top rail represents God's truth, and the bottom rail represents life's experience. The posts connecting the two are what teachers must do to help students integrate and apply faith to life.[6] These are the strategies that build bridges of transformational meaning from that which is already important to students (their lives) to that which must become more important (God's truth).

There are few moments as discouraging for a teacher as to be in the middle of an instructional experience that is clearly not connecting with students. The disconnect can usually be traced to our failure to shape our preparation around the most significant motivational learning force at work in any situation: real-life experiences of students. It's a silent enemy when ignored and our best ally when it can be included with integrity in the agenda of the moment.

Nobody did this better than Jesus. Over and over again, those who heard him teach were *amazed*. Teaching that helps people connect the dots between what they learn and their daily lives doesn't have to be so rare.

With Me

Isn't it fascinating to realize that the Gospels never identify Jesus as an expert, though his knowledge clearly surpasses everyone else's? When he took on the limitations of becoming a human being, he willingly emptied himself of the legitimate claim he had to divine stature (Phil. 2:6–8). As he made it clear to his disciples, such a posture was necessary for anyone who wants to be great in his kingdom (Matt. 20:25–28).

Jesus's love for us moved him to make the ultimate sacrifice of giving his life for humankind. But it also led him into position to be near us, to know us, to let us spend real time with him. His call to the Twelve was first of all a call to be *with him* (Mark 3:14). All of this reinforces an amazing motivational consideration. When it comes to being an effective teacher, few factors are more important to consider than our relationships with students.

Sometimes an entire relational paradigm can be understood through the use of metaphors. Jim Plueddemann invited readers to consider which of the following best illustrates what they believe about the teacher's role in the learning process:

teacher as assembly line worker

teacher as farmer

teacher as medical doctor

teachers and students as pilgrims

6. Lois E. LeBar and James E. Plueddemann, *Education That Is Christian* (Wheaton: Scripture, 1989), 105–6.

teacher as salesperson

teacher as soccer coach

student as wild flower[7]

Clearly, these metaphors represent a variety of relational postures, exposing significantly different motivational connections. Teachers who see themselves as assembly line workers or farmers may think about what they do *to* their students, whereas teachers who see themselves as coaches or fellow pilgrims are more likely to think about what they do *with* their students.

There were quite a few moments during Jesus's ministry when the venue was too small for the crowd who wanted to hear this fascinating rabbi teach. One time his family sought to intervene on his behalf. Jesus's mother and brothers reasoned that if he and the disciples were in so much demand by so many people that they couldn't even find time eat, they were not in a healthy state of mind. So his family sent word from outside the venue that they wanted to talk with Jesus. His response must have been stunning to those packed tightly into the room: "And [Jesus] answered them, 'Who are my mother and my brothers?' And looking about at those who sat around him, he said, 'Here are my mother and my brothers! For whoever does the will of God, he is my brother and sister and mother'" (Mark 3:33–35).

By virtue of his profound teaching and miracle working, he had already been deemed amazing by his throngs of followers. His expertise was established. This is not insignificant when it comes to learner motivation. Credibility has long been identified as a critical factor for those who seek to have a persuasive influence on others,[8] and for nearly forty years a "go-to" resource for young professors has identified that one of the six roles critical to their success in higher education is being subject matter expert.[9]

So what happens when teachers, like Jesus, can offer both expertise and loving relationships to their students? Learning motivation soars!

Cooperative learning strategies offer teachers the opportunity to shift their posture and improve their relationships with students.[10] Inviting learners to join us in a cause that's important to us all positions us as *with* students under Jesus's common lordship. Our expertise as well-trained and

---

7. James E. Plueddemann, "Metaphors in Christian Education," *Christian Education Journal* 7, no. 1 (1986): 39–47.

8. Em Griffin, *The Mindchangers* (Wheaton: Tyndale House, 1976), 115–31.

9. Wilbert J. McKeachie, *Teaching Tips: A Guidebook for the Beginning College Teacher* (Lexington, MA: Heath, 1978).

10. David Rahn, "Cooperative Learning and Christian Education," *Christian Education Journal* 12, no. 3 (1992): 9–21.

Dave was one of my most favorite students ever, but he didn't always give himself as completely to my assignments as I would have wanted. Why not? Almost always it was because he had determined that there was a more important use of his time than the learning task I had designed. So he settled for learning what he could inside the time parameters he was willing to commit.

How could I argue with that? For a time, this question was a literal preoccupation of mine. I wanted to come up with a compelling reason for Dave to give more of his precious time to the learning journey I was leading. But as I began to discover what else Dave was doing, I became less certain that he would be more faithful to the Lord Jesus if he diverted more time my way.

Dave's response prompted me to examine my own theology of influence. I've concluded that Jesus is Lord, his Holy Spirit has been sent to guide people into all truth, and unless I'm willing to defer to his work in someone's life I may distract them from their particular journey of faithfulness.

I'm but a pawn in the big picture of what God wants to accomplish in someone's life. And the Lord works out his purposes by using some of the same minutes that my lesson plan might lay claim to. I want to cooperate with their motivation to be increasingly faithful to the Lord with their time, not compete with it.

experienced guides on the journey can give students the confidence they need to trust our educational mentorship.

But at the end of the day, no amount of impressive ministerial credentials overcomes a poor connection with students. And the relational threshold for Christians is equally accessible and demanding to all of us who aspire to teach: love is the standard God expects of us (1 Cor. 13:1–3).

Right Now

The universal gift of time comes to us from the Lord with an inherent limit. There are only so many minutes in any day, and our days are numbered. What we do with the time we've been allotted is the sort of life challenge that confronts us all. Followers of Jesus aspire to hear that they've been faithful with their moments, doing what the Lord has asked of us in a way that brings glory to him.

Paul urged young pastor Timothy to be patient and kind with those who were resistant and unresponsive to his instruction. He did so with the confidence that, even as teachers, we are called to submit to the Lord's timing. "Gently instruct those who oppose the truth. Perhaps God will change those people's hearts, and they will learn the truth" (2 Tim. 2:25 NLT).

Given the reality that anyone may be legitimately preoccupied precisely when we are trying to teach, what should we do? At the very least we should recognize how such unknown factors can hijack the motivation to learn in the moment. Is it possible for us to jump into the river that's already sweeping students in a particular direction, making nimble teaching adjustments so that we can use the existing current of their lives to our advantage? The immediacy of what else is going on in someone's experience is always a challenge affecting his or her motivation to learn.

Not surprisingly, Jesus was also a master at recognizing various driving forces that people brought to their encounters with him. Consider his interaction with the Samaritan woman he met during midday at a well. During their conversation Jesus managed to connect over a common thirst, break down social barriers, expose a secret shaming her into isolation, and offer her hope for spiritual reconciliation that had been all but extinguished from her heart. He was so attentive to what was going on in that exchange that he didn't take time for lunch. And she was so taken by Jesus that an entire village was evangelized (John 4:7–30).

So What? Who Cares?

We've heard these two questions a lot from young people, haven't we? They prompt even the most veteran leaders to be aware of the motivational factors at work in teaching. But I've found that if I can frame my teaching intentions to answer the questions "So what?" and "Who cares?" for those students I want to serve, my instructional design has a great chance to accommodate learner motivation. For example, look at the following description for what to expect from a college course titled Sociology of Families: "Analysis of the family as a social institution and as a social group, with emphasis on the impact of industrialization on traditional family functions, courtship, role expectations, child rearing, and family stability. The course will examine changes in work patterns, marriage, divorce, and cohabitation over time. Race, ethnicity, and gender differences will also be addressed." Could this description be modified to do a better job of whetting a student's appetite to learn by answering the questions "So what?" and "Who cares?" Consider adding this sentence to the beginning of the description: "Can the family of your future be better than your family of origin?"

By thinking carefully about the "So what?" and "Who cares?" questions, we may be able to come up with ways to appeal to existing learner motivations in our instructional design. This is true whether we are shaping a semester course, preaching a Sunday sermon, or leading a small group with middle school boys.

Finally, what weight should we give to each of the four motivational learning factors examined in this chapter? Motivation has a momentary dimension to it that makes this a dynamic and fluid challenge for teachers. *This person* may offer us a stable profile until we add *right now* to the mix. Nonetheless, I think teachers can put themselves into advantageous high ground by distributing their own motivational focus in the following way:

10 percent—this person/these people

30 percent—this learning experience

40 percent—with me

20 percent—right now

Take a few minutes to reflect on your own learning experiences, good and bad. Consider the four factors and distribute weighted values to each. Compare your responses with others who are trying to make sense of how motivation works in the teaching-learning process. Then revise the percentage distributions one more time for your future planning based on your conversations with those who, like you, are trying to teach others for the glory of God.

Questions and Activities

1. What was your response when you read this statement: "When students are not ready to learn, no teaching efforts make sense until their motivation is awakened"?
2. What are the implications of the fact that every teaching effort we do either nurtures or diminishes students' existing motivation?
3. Think through the benefits gained from, at the very start of your design process, reflecting on what will engage learners.
4. Review the list of ten best practices. Which one of those brought back a fond memory for you of a time where you were motivated to learn?
5. Review the last half of the chapter, and think about (and list) the implications for motivation's role in spiritual formation.

Further Reading

Barkley, Elizabeth F., K. Patricia Cross, and Claire Howell Major. *Collaborative Learning Techniques*. 2nd ed. San Francisco, CA: Jossey-Bass, 2014.

Cloud, Henry, and John Townsend. *How People Grow*. Grand Rapids: Zondervan, 2001.

Deci, E. L., and R. M. Ryan. "The Support of Autonomy and the Control of Behavior." *Journal of Personality and Social Psychology* 53 (1987): 1024–37.

Dewey, John. *Experience and Education*. New York: Macmillan, 1938.

Dweck, Carol. *Mindset: The Secret of Success*. New York: Ballantine, 2007.

Larson, Scott, and Daniel L. Tocchini. *Groundwork: Preparing the Soil for God's Transformation*. Loveland, CO: Group, 2015.

Nicholls, J. G. "Conceptions of Ability and Achievement Motivation." In *Research on Motivation in Education*, vol. 1, edited by Russell Ames and Carole Ames, 39–73. New York: Academic Press, 1984.

Pink, Daniel. *Drive: The Surprising Truth about What Motivates Us*. New York: Riverhead, 2011.

Weiner, B. "A Theory of Motivation for Some Classroom Experiences." *Journal of Educational Psychology* 71 (1979): 3–25.

11

Why Culture and Diversity Matter

GINNY OLSON

> It is time . . . to teach young people early on that in diversity there is beauty and there is strength. We all should know that diversity makes for a rich tapestry, and we must understand that all the threads of the tapestry are equal in value no matter their color; equal in importance no matter their texture.
>
> —Maya Angelou

> After this I looked, and behold, a great multitude that no one could number, from every nation, from all tribes and peoples and languages, standing before the throne and before the Lamb, clothed in white robes, with palm branches in their hands.
>
> —Revelation 7:9

The chapel speaker was telling a story about the time she took her youth group on a ski retreat to Tahoe. A seasoned presenter, she had honed this story in other settings. But the teaching point she was trying to make was lost on this group of urban students, who represented a broad range of ethnicities and socioeconomic classes. As a result, the audience was rapidly disconnecting from the speaker. You could see it in the subtle eye rolling and head shaking. Others crossed their arms and leaned far back in their seats. A few quietly but pointedly walked out. One student leaned over and summed up the scene in a whisper, "This one didn't do her homework on her audience, did she?"

The diversity of that chapel audience is the new norm among young people. Adolescents are the most racially and ethnically diverse generation in United States history, and many of them have a multicultural heritage of their own.[1] Growing migration patterns are resulting in changing neighborhoods, families,[2] and churches. Twenty-five percent of those who are under eighteen years of age in the United States live with at least one parent who's an immigrant.[3] Globally, the United Nations estimates that over twenty million people between the ages of ten and nineteen migrated in 2013.[4] Besides migration, students are connecting all over the world via social media as well as building friendships via the increasing number of exchange students.[5] For this generation, "diversity" and "multicultural" are words they learn at an early age.

As ministers and educators, we have to not only understand but also honor the mosaic of ethnicities and socioeconomic classes that are present in our communities and our ministries. This diversity needs to inform both what we teach and how we teach it. It's too easy to alienate teenagers and their families because we are unaware of how to minister in an increasingly diverse world. When we operate out of cultural ignorance, we become, in the words of Dr. Duane Elmer, "benevolent oppressors"[6]—compassionate people who are, in reality, harming people rather than helping. We must honor and understand the people and cultures that surround us in ministry.

1. Scott Keeter and Paul Taylor, "The Millennials," Pew Research Center, December 10, 2009, http://www.pewresearch.org/2009/12/10/the-millennials/.

2. "Language Spoken at Home: 2013 American Community Survey 1-Year Estimates," United States Census Bureau, http://factfinder.census.gov/faces/tableservices/jsf/pages/productview.xhtml?pid=ACS_13_1YR_S1601&prodType=table.

3. Jie Zong and Jeanne Batalova, "Frequently Requested Statistics on Immigrants and Immigration in the United States," Migration Policy Institute, February 26, 2015.

4. United Nations, Department of Economic and Social Affairs, "Trends in International Migrant Stock: The 2013 Revision—Migrants by Age and Sex," December 2013, http://www.un.org/en/development/desa/population/publications/pdf/migration/migrant-stock-age-2013.pdf.

5. Allie Bidwell, "U.S. Falls Short in Studying Abroad," *U.S. News & World Report*, November 17, 2014, http://www.usnews.com/news/blogs/data-mine/2014/11/17/how-studying-abroad-has-changed-in-the-last-decade.

6. Duane Elmer, *Cross-Cultural Servanthood: Serving the World in Christlike Humility* (Downers Grove, IL: InterVarsity, 2006), 20.

Cultural Awareness

The National Center for Cultural Competence defines culture as "an integrated pattern of human behavior, which includes but is not limited to—thought, communication, languages, beliefs, values, practices, customs, courtesies, rituals, manners of interacting, roles, relationships and expected behaviors of a racial, ethnic, religious, social or political group; the ability to transmit the above to succeeding generations; dynamic in nature."[7] Too often, one of the only times we lean into culture in ministry is when we're preparing for a mission trip. We teach participants the basics of the language and etiquette as well as a couple of worship songs. Some don't even do that. Jim Plueddemann, professor of mission and intercultural studies at Trinity Evangelical Divinity School, writes, "I've heard youth pastors tell their mission team, 'Just be yourself, and everyone will love you.' This is a formula for cross-cultural disaster."[8]

As teachers, in order to become culturally astute, we have to raise awareness of our own cultural norms. To better understand those in our own ministry we could visit another church . . . in another denomination . . . in another city. As a visitor, we can keenly see the patterns that are ingrained for regular attendees of a given ministry. Communion is a great example of this. A newcomer is asking all sorts of questions about this ancient ritual that seems different in every church. Do they pass a plate, or do they walk up front? Why is there only one cup? Do I eat the bread right away, or wait until everyone eats together? Add to that awkward visitor feeling a different ethnic expectation or socioeconomic awareness. Imagine the challenge of walking into a worship service where you know only fifty words of the host language. Or where everyone is dressed as if they're going to a barbeque and you have on your finest threads because you were taught to dress up for church as a sign of respect. If you're a student who already feels self-conscious, your radar is tuned to high alert for anything that will make that feeling more intense. And you're probably looking for a way to escape that situation as soon as possible.

Jesus was acutely aware of this, as we see in his conversation with the Samaritan woman at the well in John 4. He knew that, due to cultural norms,

7. C. Dunne, T. Goode, and S. Sockalingam, "Planning for Cultural and Linguistic Competence in State Title V Programs Serving Children and Youth with Special Health Care Needs and Their Families" (Washington, DC: National Center for Cultural Competence, Georgetown University Center for Child and Human Development, 2003), 5, available at http://nccc.georgetown.edu/documents/NCCC%20Title%20V%20Checklist%20(CSHCN).pdf.

8. James E. Plueddemann, *Leading across Cultures: Effective Ministry and Mission in the Global Church* (Downers Grove, IL: InterVarsity, 2009), 21.

having many Jewish men around might stifle crucial dialogue, so he sent his disciples to get lunch. He was also cognizant that this woman carried a lot of social stigma in that particular community. He used his knowledge of her culture and communicated in a way that broke through to her. Consequently, their conversation impacted a whole community. Throughout the Gospels, we see how Jesus respectfully honored people's diverse cultures when he interacted with them, and by doing so, honored them: Romans, females, outcasts, the poor, the rich, the ill, and the powerful. He applied cultural wisdom and strategic thinking for the sake of the gospel and the sake of his creation. He was moving the future church toward Acts 2, Galatians 3:28, and Revelation 7:9.

Astute ministry leaders are aware of how to enter another culture on a mission trip, but they sometimes overlook cross-cultural needs within their own ministries and communities. For example, a youth pastor wants to get neighborhood kids involved; but when the middle school students attempt to bring their younger siblings along with them, he doesn't allow them to do so. He fails to understand that in their culture they are expected to care for younger siblings while their parents are at work. Family is highly valued, and you don't hire someone else to watch your children. If they can't bring their siblings with them, they can't come to youth group.

> **"Good intentions are insufficient when entering another culture. We must also be equipped with the knowledge and competencies to function skillfully."**
> **—Duane Elmer**

In another instance, a children's pastor demands that students look her in the eye when speaking with her. She thinks their lack of eye contact is rude and that they're avoiding communicating with her when they look down or away. As a result, she sees it as her responsibility to help kids build their self-confidence when they address adults. What she doesn't know is that in this particular culture, looking an authority figure in the eye is seen as a sign of disrespect. And yet they want to honor her demand because she is a respected adult. They eventually quit coming because they don't know how to reconcile their internal conflict. The children's ministry, having become stressful and uncomfortable, is no longer a safe place.

Of course, one might argue that these leaders have good intentions. If they're awkward or insulting, well, that can be forgiven. After all, they mean well. However, in the words of Elmer, "Good intentions are insufficient when entering another culture. We must also be equipped with the knowledge and competencies to function skillfully."[9]

---

9. Elmer, *Cross-Cultural Servanthood*, 19.

Understanding the Iceberg

Think about the last time a student showed up late for an event, for the fifth time. What crossed your mind? Did you think the student was irresponsible? Overscheduled? That a ride fell through? When ministering in a diverse group with multiple ethnic and economic cultures, it's best to take a step back and first assess what you can observe (objective culture) before deliberating about the values (subjective culture). Patty Lane, a cross-cultural specialist, uses the metaphor of an iceberg to describe the two terms of objective and subjective culture.[10] Objective culture is the part of the iceberg that you can see above the water line, things like how students greet each other (a head nod, handshake, or a hug), how they dress (head covered, ripped jeans, visible underwear, or school uniform), their level of initiative (waiting to be told what to do or stepping in and taking control), and time consciousness (showing up before the event starts or "whenever").

Subjective culture, on the other hand, is the huge part of the iceberg beneath the sea—invisible but foundational. It signifies the worldview a community has toward things like values (is family or career a priority?), authority roles (do you obey authority, question it, or always be suspicious and on guard around it?), the concept of truth (is it absolute or fluid?), feelings (should they be suppressed or expressed?), motivations (is an event about the number of people who showed up or about the relationships built?), and beliefs about gender roles or sexuality. Christian workers often respond only to what they see (the objective culture) without diving below to understand the deeper, unseen subjective culture.

Reflection: Review the facets of subjective culture, and then think of three situations where these facets would affect teaching.

Name two observations about people in your current ministry. Describe the worldview or values that are beneath what you are observing. How will you adapt your teaching to affect both parts of the iceberg?

When we're working with multiple cultures, we must be gracious learners. That means that we suspend judgment. Why? Because once we move into a place of judgment, learning stops. We've made our decision about whether something is "good" or "bad," and so we no longer have to learn about the rationale or history behind it. Instead, we need to strive to discover why certain cultural practices, patterns, and rituals are in place. Ask questions, if that's culturally appropriate. (In some cultures, asking too many questions is viewed as prying.) Research the culture so that your questions come from a place of humble inquiry, not obnoxious ignorance

10. Patty Lane, *A Beginner's Guide to Crossing Cultures: Making Friends in a Multi-cultural World* (Downers Grove, IL: InterVarsity, 2002), 18–19.

(e.g., learn enough so that you know which terms can't be used by someone who's not of that ethnicity). Be willing to have your cultural biases challenged and changed. In modeling openness to both students and their families, Christian educators help students to feel safe, fostering trust. And building trust is one of the first steps toward an authentic and effective teaching ministry.

Serving via Systems

Once a leader gains trust, it's important to strengthen that trust by seeking to serve their people in a way that is meaningful to them. One way to do this is to educate people using the diverse systems that affect their daily lives.

The Economic System

Jesus was constantly dealing with economics as he ministered, whether it was taxes, debt, wealth, or giving. If you have a diverse community, the economic system is influencing both the students and their families. Prepare students by teaching them how to get and maintain an after-school job or by starting an employment resource center. Offer community education classes on how members can buy their own home or set up a college savings fund. Evaluate church programs and events to make sure they are affordable for all participants.

The Political System

Teaching about political issues raises challenges. In some churches, you're limited to a few hot-button issues. In others, the political system directly impacts the congregation, and ministry leaders feel obligated to become involved for the good of their people. Jesus didn't hesitate to confront corrupt political leaders. Consider how the political system impacts your students and their families. What is a key political issue that is affecting the least powerful of them? If your students feel strongly about an issue, like youth homelessness or poverty, help them learn to write policies and advocate for change. World Vision USA's Youth Empowerment program is an excellent example of how to educate youth to speak truth to power and change the political system.

The Justice System

If you're going to be in multicultural youth ministry, you need to be aware of how the juvenile justice system operates, both locally and nationally.

One simple thing Christian teachers can do is be careful about playing games with food. I used to be great at creating games by using all sorts of unusual food items. After one game, a student from a culture different from mine came up with tears in her eyes. It was extremely difficult for her to challenge an authority figure (not that I had that much credibility with squid juice all over me), but her deep concern gave her courage. Her deliberate eye contact informed me that this was serious. She quietly and forcefully said, "I live and work with many poor people back home. How can we play a game with food when so many in the world are going hungry?" It was not a question, and she was right. I had made a huge cultural (and ethical) gaffe. As I related this conversation later to other youth workers, I would hear similar stories of churches not just in impoverished communities but also in wealthy ones where the parents had been laid off, they were nearing foreclosure, and food was scarce. It was a hard lesson to learn: when the economic system is in jeopardy, we need to be careful with what we deem to be entertainment.

Hebrews 13:3 challenges us, "Continue to remember those in prison as if you were together with them in prison, and those who are mistreated as if you yourselves were suffering." There is a historical tension between communities of color and the justice system. What is the legacy in your community? When you're teaching, how will you incorporate stories about youth who stood up against injustice? The Old Testament is filled with those who challenged the justice system (Daniel and his peers and Esther) as well as those who supported the justice system (King David and Deborah). Consider offering these Bible studies at the local juvenile detention center.

The Educational System

Too often ministry leaders are only concerned about the educational system because they want access for outreach purposes: building relationships in order for students to come to ministry events. A ministry leader in a multicultural setting needs to look with a broader vision. They need to be thinking about the educational pathway of their students. ("Do all of my students have access to all the educational resources they need in order succeed as adults?") They also need to be thinking about whether the content and teaching style reflect the diversity in the group. In other words, are the students hearing stories that feature people from their culture as well as stories about the majority culture? Are the illustrations applicable to the different socioeconomic and ethnic groups? If the students come from a culture that values tests, achievement, and competition, think about how you can utilize those tendencies and also balance those with lessons about God's grace and unmerited love. If the students come from a culture that's highly verbal, seek to create scenarios where they can discuss and debate together. If art is highly valued, try to stay away from lectures and move toward visual expressions of the content. Find artists from the different cultures that express their faith in meaningful ways.

A multicultural ministry leader creates educational experiences that help students understand their own culture as well as the culture of others. danah boyd (who purposely doesn't capitalize her name) researched how adolescents behave online and discovered, "Birds of a feather flock together, and personal social networks tend to be homogenous, as people are more likely to befriend others like them."[11] This tendency toward connecting with people like us is one of the toughest challenges in leading a diverse group. Educational experiences like the Sankofa Experience organized by North Park University help break down barriers between students.[12] This four-day bus trip pairs students with someone from a different race, and together they process their experience. While they travel to key civil rights sites, students watch documentaries and discuss with their partner and the larger group what it's like to be a member of their race and what their struggles are. Hidden racism and prejudice come quickly to the surface in this environment. Experienced facilitators help guide the discussion, as students process experiences and emotions. The result can affect all those involved on a deep, life-altering level.

A multicultural ministry leader also advocates for her students when the local educational system breaks down. For example, First Covenant Church in St. Paul, Minnesota, stepped in to provide music education after it learned that local public school music budgets were cut. They believed that the arts were important to a child's education. The church had an excellent group of musicians and artists as well as other strong adult leaders. For the past several years, they have collaborated with two local schools in this multiethnic neighborhood for months at a time to produce musicals for students of all ages. By showing, not just saying, that they value education, they are building trust with both the faculty and the families of the kids who participate.

The Church System

Understanding external systems, like the economic system, the political system, the justice system, and the educational system, is important when

11. danah boyd, *It's Complicated: The Social Lives of Networked Teens* (New Haven: Yale University Press, 2014), 165–66.

12. *Sankofa* is a West African word that means roughly "in order to move forward, we have to remember the past."

doing student ministry, but what about the church system itself? Clearly, we're immersed in it. But is it geared to meet the needs of a multicultural youth ministry? There's a saying in the business world, "You are what you measure." Reflect on what you measure as a ministry and as a church. For example, when you evaluate a curriculum, what are the criteria you use? Do you think about how many kids of color are featured in the illustrations? Do you consider whether the language fits the students who are using it? Think about the teaching series you offer as a church. Do they reflect the issues that diverse families are facing, or do they only reflect the majority culture? How can you help the small-group leaders, Bible study leaders, and Sunday school teachers understand the different cultural forces at play in this diverse and changing church?

The Fivefold Test

If you're serious about growing a multicultural teaching ministry, consider what the Evangelical Covenant implemented a number of years ago. They were tired of talking about diversity and wanted to develop a plan so that they would be truly diverse in all areas of church life. They created a fivefold, multidimensional test to measure their progress. We have adapted it here for use in a ministry education environment.

1. Population: Are our classes or study groups diverse? Does the ministry reflect the different cultures present in the community? Do the students and teachers represent the different communities? How many from each culture is your goal? You may need to make some changes to reach your goal, like offering childcare during youth group.

2. Participation: Do our classes and study groups have a diverse group of people actively attending? If they're not participating in Bible study or classes, ask people why. It could be the content, the way it's being taught, or the time of day. Perhaps their parents have to work the night shift, and they can't get a ride to church. Do you have volunteer leaders from diverse cultures? How will you go about recruiting more?

3. Power: Do our classes and study groups have a diverse group of people actively leading and making decisions? Are there students and adults from diverse populations serving in teaching and leadership positions throughout the ministry and the church? Who decides on curriculum or teaching topics? What is our goal and our strategy in this area?

4. Pace-setting: How do we need to adjust our educational programs to make sure we're ministering well to a diverse group? After understanding both the objective and subjective culture at work in our ministry, what areas do we need to strengthen? What do we need to get rid of? And what do we need to create to better meet the needs of our people and our community?

5. Purposeful narrative: What do we need to do to create a more welcoming learning environment for those who are different from the original population? How do we weave together the stories of newcomers with those who have been here for a while? What inside jokes do we need to eradicate from our teaching? How do we create a new story that represents both who we are and who we want to become?

The Great Commission

With all the changing demographics around the world, ministry is poised to have a major impact on this generation of young people. But we must move ahead into this arena of multicultural ministry with wisdom and knowledge and well-honed skills. Efrem Smith, former youth pastor and current president and CEO of World Impact, puts it this way: "As the Gospel of Matthew comes to a conclusion, the resurrected Jesus set forth the Great Commission: he called his followers to go beyond just reaching their own Jewish people, to making disciples of all nations (Matt. 28:19). The homogenous church model narrows both the Great Commission and the gospel."[13] We can't narrow down either one anymore. The church must be a leader in modeling the richness that occurs when students from vastly different cultures come together to worship and serve Christ.

Questions and Activities

1. If racial diversity is the new norm, what are the implications for teaching and ministry?

2. What will it take for you to become culturally aware in your teaching?

3. Using the imagery of the iceberg, how do the underlying systems affect diversity in your current context?

13. Efrem Smith, *The Post-Black and Post-White Church: Becoming the Beloved Community in a Multi-ethnic World* (San Francisco, CA: Jossey-Bass, 2012).

4. Take a current ministry context that you lead or know and apply the Fivefold Test to it. What observations are you able to make?

5. Find three Christians who have a different ethnic heritage from you and interview them about their spiritual formation experiences. How did they grow? What were church and other ministries like for them? What were the significant experiences in their spiritual journeys? What is the Christian faith like for them today?

Further Reading

Chuang, DJ, ed. *Asian American Youth Ministry*. Raleigh, NC: L2 Foundation, 2006.

Deymaz, Mark, and Harry Li. *Ethnic Blends: Mixing Diversity into Your Local Church*. Grand Rapids: Zondervan, 2010.

Lane, Patty. *A Beginner's Guide to Crossing Cultures: Making Friends in a Multicultural World*. Downers Grove, IL: InterVarsity, 2002.

Livermore, David, and Terry Linhart. *What Can We Do? Practical Ways Your Youth Ministry Can Have a Global Conscience*. Grand Rapids: Zondervan/Youth Specialties, 2011.

Plueddemann, James. *Leading across Cultures: Effective Ministry and Mission in the Global Church*. Downers Grove, IL: InterVarsity, 2009.

Rah, Soong-Chan. *Many Colors: Cultural Intelligence for a Changing Church*. Chicago: Moody, 2010.

Smith, Efrem. *The Post-Black and Post-White Church: Becoming the Beloved Community in a Multi-ethnic World*. San Francisco: Jossey-Bass, 2012.

SECTION
THREE

CURRICULAR IMPLICATIONS FOR TEACHING

This section connects topics from the first two sections with the task of teaching. The role of teaching in faith formation, knowing how students learn, and the impact of physiological, social, and cognitive development all profoundly affect curriculum and teaching. Effective teachers have a clear and ever-growing understanding of curriculum and its intersection with other domains. They know how faith development and cognitive development intersect, and they design and lead learning events accordingly.

Every time we teach, there is an operant philosophy of curriculum at work. Our thinking about the role of the teacher, how to structure our methods and events, how to determine if we're effective, and even how to determine the content of our teaching all reflect our understanding of curriculum. This section ties all of the previous chapter topics together and helps the reader see the implications for Christian ministry. It is here that our effectiveness in Christian teaching is evidenced, and it is here where we need to make sure we have clear understanding.

One item of note: this section concludes with a discussion of technology and learning, an area changing so fast that it outpaces critical and theological reflection. These changes in technology outdate works on the topic before they're published. Therefore, this chapter focuses only on essential curricular issues that theorists have discussed regarding technology and learning. Readers can independently explore current research, connect those studies with these underlying curricular implications, and then make application to the local ministry context.

12

Curriculum and Teaching

TERRY LINHART

Imagine that you've been invited to observe one of the best teachers in your church. Lynn is known for her creativity, excellent preparation, and warmth with her students.[1] You want to observe the reasons for the glowing comments you've heard from the students who've had her as a teacher. You settle in the back of the room and watch Lynn as she begins teaching. As you imagine that, what do you think you would see? What do you expect teaching to look like from one who can get students excited about learning? What do you think the content would be like? How would the teaching be structured? What about the illustrations? Her relationship to the students?

Now, imagine that, as you make your observations, you start to think a bit deeper, taking in the entire scene and reflecting on what you're watching. What part of what you'd see there would be called the *curriculum* that the students are learning? Is the curriculum that material taught from a book? Is the curriculum something in the teacher's mind? Is it what the students "take away" from the lesson? Is it the environment itself? Or is it something else? How you answer this question reveals your theoretical thinking about curriculum.

When people hear the word *curriculum*, they likely envision worksheets in elementary school, a college syllabus, Sunday school word searches, or

---

1. I use Lynn to honor Lynn Ziegenfuss, who first fanned into flame the gift of teaching that I did not know I possessed.

(from high school days) a series of readings, papers, and tests. Though common, these teaching elements actually are only part of the larger definition for curriculum. The word *curriculum* comes from the Latin word *currere*, which means a "race track" or "course to be run," and it encompasses all that is involved in a teaching setting . . . and beyond. For the Christian teacher, the curriculum is the total sum of the parts of a teaching initiative that contributes to the maturing of a believer.[2]

Any time a person teaches, there is an implicit curricular philosophy at work (see chap. 5). Even a line-by-line approach to teaching the Bible has an embedded understanding of what is appropriate for teaching Scripture and how people learn. The moment one begins to teach, one reflects a curricular philosophy built on foundations and principles that have been learned over time and are reflected in the structure of the lesson and in interactions with students.

Let's go back to the imaginary scene with Lynn's group of students to help us understand more about curriculum. Every component of that scene is part of the curriculum, what is being taught. It is more than a lesson; it is a holistic understanding of how we learn. As you look around the room to watch student learning, you'd see that there are different elements that are part of the learning process, such as the teacher herself, the content of the books, engagement activities, the setting, the church or school, and the students. Let's look at learning from the perspective of each of these elements. If isolated, each one of these elements represents an overarching theoretical perspective on what is curriculum.

The teacher. The curriculum is the teacher. Her example and her reservoir of knowledge and wisdom are what matter. She transfers what she has studied to her students, and she exemplifies to her students how to think and live. She is central to the lesson, and effectiveness is measured by how well the material is presented. This is often the default method for Christian teaching for both men and women.

The books. The content of the lesson serves as the curriculum. The role and interpretations of the teacher and students are secondary to the course content. Effective teaching and learning, then, is to "have covered" and "to know" the content. This theory assumes that the knowing of content is sufficient for effective practice.

The activities. The activities of the class define the curriculum. Students "learn by engaging" so the teacher coordinates the process of engagement.

2. R. Habermas and K. Issler, *Teaching for Reconciliation: Foundations and Practice of Christian Educational Ministry* (Grand Rapids: Baker, 1992), 135.

A short-term mission trip often uses this approach, relying on a "if you send them, they will learn" confidence in the method.[3]

The setting. This broad focus on curriculum is inclusive of the environment, community, and setting that creates the learning culture. Though context is often overlooked when discussing curriculum, it has a dramatic shaping role in learning and on the desired outcomes. Christian educator Karen Lynn Estep says that Christ's commission and message of reconciliation provides a context for why we teach: "Context is essential to the identity and uniqueness of Christian education, which seeks to reach the world with its purpose."[4]

The church or school. Context is more than cultural and social, and whether we like it or not, teaching and learning are shaped by the institution and tradition in most if not all situations. The platform represents those shaping authorities in our lives. Teachers and learners are rarely independent of powerful currents that shape what is taught, how it's presented, what isn't taught, and ultimately what constitutes effective teaching. Even as you're reading this book, you're filtering the material through embedded theories you have learned over time via your tradition and the institutions (i.e., churches and schools) where you've been.

The students. This perspective is less focused on what is taught or studied, though those still matter, but is concerned with the outcomes (what students think, feel, and do with the teaching) that the curriculum produces. This view evaluates effectiveness by what students have learned. Curriculum that is designed using this theory determines the "product" for the teaching experiences and then works via a "backward design" to determine the methods and content necessary to achieve that end.

> Which of these elements has been the way you've defined *curriculum*? Which one seems like the best way to think about curriculum? What role does content play in each of these?

The purpose of thinking in terms of curriculum is to answer the fundamental question, "How do we know that learning has taken place?" In chapter 5, Mark Cannister covered the philosophical approaches to answering this question. In this chapter, we will examine the practical implications of those curricular theories, how to create curriculum, how to select and evaluate curriculum, and how to coordinate student learning over an extended period.

3. I detailed this in Kara Powell et al., "If You Send Them, They Will Grow . . . Maybe," *Journal of Student Ministries* 1, no. 6 (2007): 24–28.

4. Karen L. Estep, "Charting the Course: Curriculum Design," in *Mapping Out Curriculum in Your Church: Cartography for Pilgrims*, ed. James R. Estep et al. (Nashville: B&H, 2012), 181–200.

Curricular Theories and Practice

There are two dominant curricular theories employed today. The current philosophy for American schools is a technical one; identify the desired outcomes, teach in systematic ways so that you produce them, and then test to make sure students can recall those outcomes. The other theory seems like a reaction to this, and it emphasizes personal experience: create a context or experience for students and then let them determine what they learn. Montessori education, as an example, allows students to construct their own learning.[5] You can see this philosophy at work at times in ministry to young people where leaders create experiences and then give participants freedom to discover and learn on their own.

One of the problems with each extreme is that neither automatically fosters critical thinking. Students can gain knowledge, or have amazing experiences, and yet understand little more and remain unable to use the learning in everyday contexts as they face challenges. Despite getting good grades in school or having meaningful experiences at church, students can be underserved by these approaches without careful attention to the curriculum. This reality has surfaced in recent studies on young people.

Recent research suggests that the church is producing high school graduates who have shaky foundations for their faith and are likely to fall away from attending church.[6] There seems to be a disconnect between students' church experience and an ability to have a conversation about their Christian faith. In their research, Christian Smith and Melinda Denton found that teens had difficulty articulating their faith with others when asked. The conclusions from their two-year national study provide an impetus for this chapter.

> Curricular understanding possesses
>
> - basic worldview assumptions and a vision for teaching/learning;
> - a view of knowledge and of the person, and how these affect curriculum and how we go about planning; and
> - the general aims of the curriculum.
>
> —Modified from H. Van Brummelen, *Steppingstones to Curriculum: A Biblical Path* (Colorado Springs: Purposeful Design Publications, 2002), 25.

> It appears to us, in other words, that . . . leaders concerned with youth need simply to better engage and challenge the youth already at their disposal, to work better to help make faith a more active and important part of their lives. . . . Adults often seem to want to do little more than "expose" teens to religion. . . . However, we believe that *most teens are teachable*—even if they themselves

5. Maria Montessori, *The Montessori Method* (Seattle, WA: CreateSpace, 2012).
6. The research comes from Lifeway, Pew Research Center, and Barna Group.

do not really know that or let on that they are interested. . . . More important in the effective religious teaching of teens than, say, new pedagogical techniques will be the building of sustained, meaningful, personal adult relationships with the teens they teach. This will require investments of time, attention, and readiness to be open and vulnerable with teens.[7]

We seem to more easily understand curricular planning in schools, but when it comes to spiritual growth and the work of God, it can seem less urgent because of the transformational work of God in our lives. We must understand the biblical principle that we are co-working with God (1 Cor. 3:9) in our teaching ministry. Perhaps Jesus's parable of the talents helps us further. The master in the story is pleased with the two who were "faithful" with what they were given by "making" more talents (Matt. 25:14–30). The ones given talents and opportunity were asked to work them both to their best ability.

For some reason, God has chosen to use men and women to teach and pass on the faith to the next generations. It is our opportunity to make the most of it, to "press on" for the purposes of the church (Phil. 3:14; Eph. 4:11–13). The old Proverb is true, "The horse is made ready for the day of battle, but victory belongs to the LORD" (Prov. 21:31). Curriculum makes us ask, "What kind of learning and experiences do we desire for our students? What is the best way to guide their spiritual formation? And how will we know when they are spiritually mature?" Curricular understanding helps us prepare the horses.

How Curriculum "Works"

Curricular theory helps us connect the dots about content, learning, and growth. We don't just pick up a lesson and start teaching without some "translation." The teachings of Jesus and Paul illustrate how theological truth is presented, using various methods and lived examples, so that learners of a particular culture can learn and grow. Figure 12.1 illustrates how curriculum builds toward spiritual growth.

The foundation for the Christian educator is the revelation of God. The focus is on the Creator who revealed himself through creation, who has given us his living Word, who pitched his tent among us, who redeems our

7. Christian Smith, "Implications of National Study of Youth and Religion Findings for Religious Leaders, Faith Communities, and Youth Workers," 2005 Princeton Lectures on Youth, Church, and Culture, http://www.ptsem.edu/lectures/?action=pdf&id=youth-2005-06 (emphasis original).

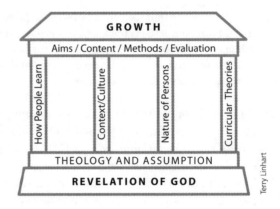

Figure 12.1 The Curricular Supports to Spiritual Growth

lives, and who sent the Spirit to purify and empower us. Our thinking and speaking about God's revelation is shaped by the church and leaders who have helped us to develop theological understanding. Our hermeneutic is shaped by a particular perspective and culture, with language and theological heritage that give focus and form to our work. In many discussions about God's revelation, the focus is on the hermeneutic of how we interpret God's revelation. This is why a Christian teacher needs to be committed to biblical and theological study, to strive for the most faithful interpretation. These theological and hermeneutical influences shape our actions and give emphasis and language to our teaching.

On those underlying realities stand four columns that inform teaching practices: how people learn, context and culture, nature of persons, and curricular learning theories. No teaching aim, content choice, creative method, or evaluation exists independent of the influence and support of these four columns. Every time we write an aim or select a lesson plan, we operate on the basis of what we think about people, how they learn, and where they come from. The pinnacle of our efforts, as stated throughout this book, is spiritual maturity, which is evidence that learning has taken place. Through a transformational work of the Holy Spirit, God has called us to teach "with all wisdom, so that we may present everyone fully mature in Christ" (Col. 1:28 NIV).

Creating Curriculum

Regardless of your teaching philosophy, there are some useful and necessary components to curriculum. The first is to have a stated target for your teaching, what is often called an *organizing principle*. And, despite the fact that this seems obvious, it's too common that there's not a stated aim for a learning event or lesson.

There are many ways to write an aim, but the most basic one is:

"As a result of this _____ (lesson, name of event), *students will* _____ (a cognitive, affective, or action verb) _____ (phrase that defines the subject)."

Here are a few examples of lesson aims:

As a result of this study, students will understand what Jesus meant when he said we are to "abide" in him.

As a result of the Wednesday evening service, students will appreciate the role of prayer in the life of a believer.

As a result of this small-group training, students will implement basic responding skills when helping others in need.

A somewhat technical model for writing these uses AIM as an acronym: state what you want students to *achieve* (their level of learning), what *indicates* that they have learned or *investigated*, and what is the *main subject being taught*.[8] A version of this would be, "The student shall demonstrate a(n) _____ (*achievement level*) of the _____ (*main subject*) by _____ (*indicator*)."[9] The achievement and the main subject are the easiest to determine, but the indicator takes more time. In schools, indicators of learning are often determined by tests, written papers, or presentations. In drivers' training school, we evidence learning by, well, *driving*. In Christian ministry, we may confuse students sitting quietly while listening, or "being good," as indicators that learning has taken place. A well-developed aim helps us to think more completely about the desired outcomes for our teaching.

Grab a scrap piece of paper and write two *different* aims in the two formats described above. Becoming proficient in writing a good teaching AIM is the first step toward better teaching and will help you make decisions about what is included and excluded from your teaching. You'll find that writing teaching AIMs isn't always easy to do, but that's the point: though we will rarely if ever state these AIMs in front of students, the honing work they make us do up front helps us clarify our goals and purposes.

8. Habermas and Issler, *Teaching for Reconciliation*, 137.
9. Ibid., 138.

Hook, Book, Look, Took

After the purpose is clarified, structuring the lesson is the next step. One of the most prominent curricular formats in Christian ministry was developed by Lawrence Richards and Gary Bredfeldt.[10] They point to Paul's Mars Hill discourse (Acts 17) as a model to structure curriculum. Paul starts his "lesson" in the world of his listeners (*hook*) and stimulates curiosity before exploring truth (*book*). He then leads his listeners through the implications (*look*) and concludes with a call to respond in repentance (*took*).[11]

Hook. Learning happens best when learners are actively and cognitively ready and can give their full attention to what they're about to learn. A good hook begins a "melting" process that gains the students' attention while overcoming natural barriers to learning (i.e., distraction, indifference). Novice teachers may fail to spend enough time and energy in this section, choosing instead to get to the "meat" of the lesson. But when we go out to eat at a restaurant, we don't just want the food handed to us in a cardboard box; rather, we enjoy a greeting from the host, a chance to look over the menu, and maybe even an appetizer as we anticipate the main course, which is later presented to us in a pleasing way. In the same way, a teacher should prepare a student for the main course of the lesson.

To make a strong "hook," not just any fun element will do. The measurement of a strong hook is if you have people's attention and if they're focused and eager to learn. Of course, humor and laughter is a critical element in that process, but just showing a video clip of funny cat tricks is going to fall short. The hook involves the students, surfacing a need to the point where students "own" the topic themselves, giving them a reason to take the next step with you in the lesson.

Book. In this section, "the teacher seeks to clarify the meaning of the passage being studied."[12] The goal is to help the learner understand, not just hear, the information, so the methods can be varied. This section of the lesson helps clarify what students are about to study and why. Most purchased curriculum from publishing houses do this well.[13]

Look. Once the biblical material is presented and understood, this section of the lesson begins the application portions where students should

10. Lawrence O. Richards and Gary J. Bredfeldt, *Creative Bible Teaching* (Chicago: Moody, 1998).
11. Ibid., 153–54.
12. Ibid., 156.
13. E.g., see Terry Linhart, *Talksheets: Life of Christ (High School)* (Grand Rapids: Zondervan/Youth Specialties, 2009).

discover the implications. This is typically the longest part of the lesson as it takes time for students to make connections and know the relationship between the material and real life. It is not just simply a discussion or more information, but the look should have students actively involved in making life applications.

Took. This section answers the question "So what?" that learners are asking. Thus, this may be the most important part of the lesson, yet is often the most underserved (often because we've run out of time!). A response is required, a specific understanding of how change will happen. For younger children and adolescents, it's often best to have them do something right away since the next day's worries will overshadow anything you ask them to remember. Don't leave students with something vague. If the goal for our teaching is transformation, then that requires change; and change demands responsiveness.

As is discussed throughout this text, the default teaching method is "information transmission." But if transformation is the teaching goal of Christian teachers, then the *took* requires our best effort. Too often we think that if we have students sharing about the implications, it's the took. It's not. That's the look. The took section demands action for long-term learning transfer so that we answer students' "So what?" questions.

4MAT Curriculum[14]

Howard Gardner developed a theory of learning that showed people were intelligent in various ways. His "multiple intelligences" theory provided the foundation for an approach to curriculum, developed by Bernice McCarthy. Karen Jones highlighted this approach in chapter 8 on learning styles. Jones noted that the theory highlights four types of learning in how we perceive and process information.

This curricular model for writing lessons identifies four dominant learning styles displayed as four quadrants separated by two axes. One axis represents how people perceive information (sensing and feeling versus thinking) while the other axis represents how people process (doing versus watching). Christian workers must have a working knowledge of how people learn in different ways and how to incorporate that into their teaching. Taking an approach to our methods that circles through the four main learning quadrants will broaden effectiveness, keep us fresh and creative, and deepen our understanding. Better still, students will love it and grow. We will help them

14. Bernie McCarthy, *The 4MAT System: Teaching to Learning Styles with Right / Left Mode Techniques* (Barrington, IL: EXCEL, 1987).

know the meaning (why?), understand the key concepts (what?), have the skills (how?), and be able to make the adaptations or think critically (what if?) about the topic at hand.[15]

Backward Design

Have you ever taken a course in school, even received good grades, and a year later were unable to use or recall much from the course? The reasons for this are varied, but this issue prompted Grant Wiggins and Jay McTighe to develop their popular "backward design" approach to creating curriculum.[16] Simply put, they propose starting with the final goal for students, then designing the curriculum backward.[17] Traditional approaches to teaching have involved the acquisition of knowledge, or "knowing stuff," without concern whether students can understand or utilize the material. This approach is similar to teaching a kid to swim by telling them about swimming without getting them into the pool.

The backward design begins with determining the established goals with a particular focus on the big ideas of the topic or discipline. The next step involves identifying how students will be able to use their learning and writing that out. What should students understand, know, and be skilled at (the "head, heart, and hands" goals)? Once you have determined the desired results, then what evidence will you want to see that shows students have learned? How will you determine if they've learned? This is where many fall short because they determine success by how well the material was presented. The backward design puts the focus on what is learned and then creates the learning plan from those evidences.[18]

Modifying Curriculum

Most Christian teachers do not write lessons from scratch but rather use ingredients or full lessons from published materials and then modify them. This is advantageous but also presents the Christian educator with the need

---

15. For more about 4MAT, visit the *About Learning* website, http://www.aboutlearning.com/what-is-4mat.

16. Grant Wiggins and Jay McTighe, *Understanding by Design*, 2nd ed. (Alexandria, VA: Association for Supervision and Curriculum Development, 2005).

17. Grant Wiggins and Jay McTighe, "Put Understanding First," *Educational Leadership* 65, no. 8 (2008): 36–41.

18. You can find resources for the backward design model at McTighe and Associates, http://jaymctighe.com/resources/downloads/.

for careful evaluation of curriculum. It is not enough to just find something in a "grab and go" fashion and then hope it works. Christian publishers usually expect lessons to be adapted to local contexts, and some even provide additional options for adaptations.

Historically most published curriculum was produced by well-trained Christian educators who worked in groups to provide denominations and ministries with regular and sequenced lessons, primarily designed for use in Sunday schools. As the publishing world changed, so did the production of available curriculum. Today, there are curricular materials from countless sources, though the authors are not always known. Additionally, there is no guarantee that the materials have been edited or vetted beyond that the author tried it once and it "worked." With the abundance of downloadable resources, it is as important as ever to give careful review to the biblical, theological, and educational foundations.[19]

There are three primary concerns that you will need to examine, and together they form an integrated way to evaluate Christian education curriculum.

Theological basis. The first area to examine is the biblical and theological basis of the curriculum. More than looking to see if Scripture is used, examine the nature and role of its use. Is it appropriate, and how will students engage it in study? Take an additional step to look at the implied theology of the lesson and if it's truly Christian. That may seem strange, but some curriculum can be moralistic (or political) in emphasis and teach little about Jesus Christ, the Holy Spirit, God the Father, salvation, the church, or other prominent theological themes. Finally, is the theology appropriate to your denominational or theological tradition, and does the lesson fit within the purposes, framework, and philosophies of your church, organization, or group? If you don't know the answer to the last two questions, it is important to check with others for help. If you have volunteers selecting curriculum, you will need to give that process gracious supervision to ensure quality and consistency.

Pedagogical objectives and methods. The second area builds from the biblical and theological basis and examines the objectives and their intention in helping students grow in maturity (Col. 1:28–29). A focus on the teaching process incorporates methods for teaching the lesson. Does the lesson aid the teaching/learning process in worthwhile ways? What methods are included in the lesson? What response does the lesson ask for? Is it appropriate to the biblical passages used, your students, your context, and to the Christian faith?

19. Dan Lambert, *Teaching That Makes a Difference: How to Teach for Holistic Impact* (Grand Rapids: Zondervan/Youth Specialties Academic, 2004), 107.

The learners' perspective. It's imperative that we have mastered an understanding of where our students are and how they interact with the world. Examine the curriculum via a student-centered approach. Is it appropriate to the developmental levels of your audience? Focus on the teaching objective and then look at the outcomes in the lesson. Do they make sense for your group? Are they substantive enough? Do they fit what you want in your overall teaching program?

Evaluation is more crucial than ever for those who want to be good teachers who are used by God to facilitate spiritual maturity in and among students. There is a pragmatism today that assumes whatever works and functions well in the moment *works*. However, this does not guarantee that it will develop wisdom, grow hearts of deeper commitment to Christ, and produce people who serve and care for others. Functionality doesn't automatically cultivate the deeper purposes of your ministry. You will need to stay vigilant to pragmatism's temptations and stay faithful to focusing on your students' thinking and faith development. You don't want to get to the end of a season of teaching and realize that, despite the cool lessons you've taught, your students do not understand or believe more deeply than they did when you began.[20]

Managing Curriculum: Scope and Sequence

When thinking in terms of curriculum, the focus isn't only on each lesson but on what is being taught over a particular time period, like a semester or year. This framework, called the "scope and sequence," shows what you are going to teach and in what order it will be taught. The scope determines the range of content that the lessons will cover over time. It allows larger content to be broken down into particular topics (with lesson aims) and also determines what topics won't be covered. Like looking through a telescope, the scope helps teachers to zero in and focus their teaching efforts. Sequence determines the best order for the topics, building from one lesson to the next where appropriate. What do you intend to teach and in what order? How will you sequence from one lesson to the other, and how will your lesson build on previous lessons? Topics may fit well at a particular time, or they may need to be repeated. Students need not engage every relevant topic but just the most important ones. Therefore spending time on your overall teaching plan is a necessary and fruitful exercise.

20. There are two helpful charts for evaluating curriculum in Richards and Bredfeldt, *Creative Bible Teaching*, 205–6.

Once the scope and sequence is set, it provides a useful tool to examine five qualities of the curriculum that aren't readily noticed. First, it identifies what is the "core curriculum," the set of topics that show up often, intentionally or unintentionally, over time. Second, the scope illuminates the null curriculum, the topics and Bible passages that are not being taught.[21] Third, the sequence allows leaders to consider the context for teaching, matching themes and objectives against special holidays, seasons, and other contextual factors. This also prompts a fourth benefit: teachers can look for places where repetition might be helpful, thinking holistically and developmentally about the learners. For instance, it may be helpful to do a salvation-oriented topic at equal intervals or to talk about identity more than just once. Finally, a scope and sequence can be compared to ones from other years to look for patterns, gaps, and repetitions. Based on these, necessary changes can be made as desired to maintain a balance in teaching. When there is overall curricular "map," it provides a depth of focus and purpose beyond teaching from a list of cool topics.

Provided at the end of this chapter is a checklist to use for evaluating a published lesson. Feel free to modify this checklist for your own use.

Questions and Activities

1. What are the essential questions you want your students to be able to answer?

2. Too often curriculum is seen as "traditional" thinking. How do the principles in this chapter apply to nontraditional ministries? How might these principles help leaders of drop-in centers? How does curricular thinking inform church planting?

3. Think about a ministry you know well, and list out five or more events or different teaching times you remember. For each, identify the operant philosophy at work for how teaching and learning take place.

4. Practice using the checklist above by selecting a published lesson that you have never seen before, and work through the questions. What did you learn about the lesson? How easy was it for you to answer the questions?

5. If you modified the checklist for your own use, what question(s) would you add?

21. It's usually not appropriate to teach every topic in a given time period. The scope allows you to know what isn't being taught in case a crucial subject is missing.

Checklist for Evaluating a Lesson

Group name:

Age range:

Content	
Is it age appropriate? Will it connect well with the audience? Is it appropriate to the cultural context of the students?	
What is the nature and role of the use of Scripture? What translation is used? What hermeneutics are used?	
Is the content balanced well between Bible study and life application?	
Is there a christological focus? Is it appropriate for Christian teaching?	
Does the content fit within your theological tradition? Are the activities and examples appropriate for your group?	
Do students have to study Scripture as part of the lesson?	
Process	
Is the teaching objective clear? Does the lesson plan and final section align with that objective?	
How does the lesson engage ("hook") students? Why will they want to participate in this? Will they be engaged throughout, or are there lulls?	
Is the learning comprehensive and balanced? Does the lesson yield great depth and breadth of insight into the topic?	
Does the lesson teach to the head, heart, and/or hands of students?	
Do the methods possess sound educational principles for fostering spiritual maturity?	
Audience	
Are the teaching examples current?	
Is there time for student reflection and application?	
Does the response the lesson desires fulfill my goals for its aim?	
Can the students respond to be "doers of the word, and not hearers only"?	
Are the materials and graphics appropriate for the age group?	
If other adults will be teaching, will the lesson be easy for them to use?	

Further Reading

Ferguson, Nancy. *Christian Educators' Guide to Evaluating and Developing Curriculum*. Valley Forge, PA: Judson, 2008.

Lambert, Dan. *Teaching That Makes a Difference: How to Teach for Holistic Impact*. Grand Rapids: Zondervan/Youth Specialties Academic, 2004.

McCarthy, Bernie. *The 4MAT System: Teaching to Learning Styles with Right/Left Mode Techniques*. Barrington, IL: EXCEL, 1987.

Wiggins, Grant, and Jay McTighe. *Understanding by Design*. 2nd ed. Alexandria, VA: Association for Supervision and Curriculum Development, 2005.

13

Teaching Children

SCOTTIE MAY

There are few things as captivating as watching children learn and discover. We can learn so much from them as we make the time and space to listen to them. It's important that a book on teaching the next generation includes a chapter on teaching children. There are six overarching principles, taken and adapted from a couple of sources, that serve as the scaffolding for the core of this chapter:[1]

- Make purpose a priority.
- Provide experiential learning and active involvement.
- Develop meaningful, authentic learning tasks.
- Ensure moments for awe, wonder, and reflection.
- Allow social participation and collaborative work.
- Encourage connections through research and transfer to life.

These six concepts are interconnected in ways that make it difficult to discuss and implement each separately. All six need to flow together for effective teaching, especially in a children's ministry context. When all six are

1. These principles are adapted from Stella Vosniadou, "How Children Learn," International Academy of Education, Educational Practical Series 7, http://unesdoc.unesco.org/images /0012/001254/125456e.pdf; and Scottie May et al., *Children Matter: Celebrating Their Place in the Church, Family, and Community* (Grand Rapids: Eerdmans, 2005), 256–57.

in place and available for the children, an atmosphere of engagement can be palpable. To think about implementing these six factors when teaching may feel like an overwhelming task. Admittedly, it is a paradigm shift from how people usually envision teaching children. Simply stated, employing these principles makes the teaching of children more like life and less like traditional schooling. These principles are also evident in the teaching ministry of the Lord Jesus himself.

Jesus had a purpose for what he did: it was to glorify his Father (John 17:1), and we are to do the same (Matt. 5:15; Rom. 15:6; 1 Pet. 2:12). A significant part of Jesus's ministry while here on earth, in addition to preaching and healing, was to teach. When looking at Jesus as teacher, the Gospels reveal that Jesus taught through experiences (Luke 5:1–11), through authentic tasks (Mark 12:13–17), and even by facilitating moments of awe and wonder (Matt. 6:27–29). Additionally Jesus called for "social participation" when he instructed the eleven disciples to bring Good News to the world (Matt. 28:16–20; Mark 16:15–18). And he connected his teaching to life, even when the learning was hard, as it was for the rich, young ruler (Mark 10:17–22).

Have you ever wondered if Jesus used a passage tucked into the middle of Isaiah 41 as a guide to his teaching? Isaiah 41:20 says, "So that people may *see* and *know*, may *consider* and *understand*, that the hand of the Lord has done this, that the Holy One of Israel has created it." We don't know if the prophet Isaiah ever taught children, but the sequence of the verbs in this passage is so important for teaching, especially teaching children. The verb "see" requires a sensory experience with what is to be learned so that the child may "know"—have a kind of a relationship with the subject. Then the child is able to "consider" it—to reflect on it in order that "understanding" can happen. This understanding must come from within rather than be imposed from outside the child, although the teacher has a key role as a guide in this process.

By now you are probably wondering how this process actually looks. That is coming, but first the purpose of the teaching must be considered.

The Purpose of Purpose

Too often churches have programs in their ministries that actually conflict with the mission statement of the church. The appropriateness of a certain ministry within the church may be ignored because the church has always had this program, or because the leaders just wanted to try something different; or, even more concerning, because a church across town was drawing scores of kids using that same program. Thus, there is a disconnect between purpose and program. Scholar and educator Jim Wilhoit explains it like this: "Christian education is in crisis. It is not healthy and vital; as a discipline, it is bankrupt. . . . The current crisis stems, in large measure, from a lack of clear purpose at the grassroots level. The people most directly involved in Christian education—Sunday school teachers, youth counselors, and Bible-study leaders—often have no idea of the ultimate purpose of their educational endeavors."[2]

All too often, leaders fail to take time to consider if what a ministry is accomplishing is actually what was intended. The intended outcome and the actual outcome may be in disharmony. It is too easy, especially in ministry with children, to look for games or craft ideas and plug that into a lesson plan just because it seems fun. For example, in an online lesson about the kindness that David showed to Mephibosheth, children are instructed to squirt cheese from a can onto a soft tortilla and wrap it around a pretzel rod while they talk about being kind. The only response is, *Huh?*

For many people the ability to think through to a logical conclusion the purpose of a ministry or of a specific lesson is an acquired skill. One of Paul's companions was Titus, a young worker for the gospel. Paul writes to him about instructing slaves, whose partial duties were to be pedagogues of their master's children. Titus 2:10 says, "So that in every way they will make the teaching about God our Savior attractive" (NIV). Titus was being told to teach these children about God attractively. In order to do this, the slaves needed to have godly character, know the truths about God, and know the personalities of the children they were teaching. For sure, it did not mean beautifully decorated walls, snazzy handouts, or the latest in technological communication—though there is nothing inherently wrong with those things in the right context; they simply do not help accomplish the core purpose of teaching.

A helpful resource for the process of developing an appropriate purpose that enables attractive teaching is the work of the late William K. Frankena, a Christian philosopher and ethicist at the University of Michigan. He developed a series of five questions that a teacher or leader can ask in order to create a cohesive lesson or ministry.[3] His questions have been adapted for teaching children: (1) What is the purpose of this teaching session? (2) What are the children and the context like; also, what are the theological realities?

2. Jim Wilhoit, *Christian Education and the Search for Meaning* (Grand Rapids: Baker, 1991), 9.
3. William Frankena, *Philosophy of Education* (New York: Macmillan, 1965).

(3) What character qualities, virtues, or skills (aims) are to be developed in the children? (4) What is known about how to develop those qualities? (5) What learning activities will help accomplish the purpose and aims of this session or ministry, given the realities noted?[4] (Although applied here to children's ministry, these five questions are useful in any teaching or ministry setting.)

The important thing about these five questions is that they are all interrelated. Each response must feed into the rest; none should be an outlier. Every question is important. These questions address the What, Why, and How factors of any teaching setting. When planning a new lesson or ministry, it is helpful to begin with question 1 and work through to question 5. If critiquing an existing setting, begin with question 5 (what is actually happening), then identify the learning theories or strategies in place, moving backward through the five questions. Does what is happening in the ministry lead directly to the responses to questions 3 and 1? If not, determine where adjustments should be made.

Question 2 is very important and needs to be considered carefully and thoroughly. These additional questions can be helpful when thinking about the empirical data and the realities of the context: Who are the children attending this lesson? What are the families like? The economics? Racial and ethnic factors? The type of schools attended? Are the children churched or nonchurched? What is their view of God?

The whole process of developing the purpose in a specific ministry needs to be bathed in prayer—prayer for wisdom in identifying the needs of the children, for the desired outcomes, and for the processes that should be used to achieve them.

Once the purpose of a ministry, event, or specific lesson and who will be attending has been determined, consider what is known about how learning best happens (question 4). This is where the other five principles come in.

Principles That Guide

Children of all ages—even adults—learn by doing. A few years ago in a college class on teaching in the church, a student made this profound statement: "If people remember what they *do*, why don't we have them *do* what we want them to remember?" This provocative thought should be pondered by everyone who teaches, especially teachers of children. The saying that

4. For a more complete explanation of the Frankena model, see May et al., *Children Matter*, 285–88.

"teachers talk and learners listen" is popular but may be helpful to very few children. Even less helpful is the age-old directive: "Sit still with your hands in your lap and your mouth shut." The focus needs to be on *learning* more than on teaching and on controlling children's behavior.

What Helps Learning Happen?

Studies show that learning happens best when children are engaged in meaningful, authentic tasks. Educator and author John Holt writes, "It is a serious mistake to say that, in order to learn, children must first be able to 'delay gratification,' . . . to learn useless and meaningless things on the faint chance that later they may be able to make use of them. It is their desire and determination to do real things, not in the future but right now, that gives children the curiosity, energy, determination, and patience to learn all they learn."[5]

Because the Bible is about real people and places, there are many aspects of the biblical narrative that can be experienced in ways that are meaningful and authentic. The stories can come to life through simulations and "field trips," even if they take place inside the church building. Imagine creating an exile experience for the children, or simulating captivity, or going outdoors to walk off the actual size of the ark, or building a full-size model of Goliath out of scrap lumber and stuff you gather, such as a salad bowl for a helmet and work gloves that become hands.

Children love and need to be active but not always in the ways adults think they do. There is a place for high-energy games and songs with wacky motions, but they are not helpful in a context that intends to engage children in the biblical story. But it is helpful to provide multiple learning activities so that children can choose the task that most interests them. If the group is large, one activity for every eight to ten children is a good rule of thumb; you might have multiples of some activities. For one-third of the teaching hour, consider having activities that make the biblical setting of the lesson come to life.

The various ways children learn need to be recognized and accommodated. Children have not had as much life experience as adults in which to learn how to adjust if the style of the teacher or the type of activity is incompatible with the way a particular child learns best. The different learning styles among children are another reason why it is helpful to provide a variety

5. John Holt, *How Children Learn*, rev. ed. (New York: Perseus, 1995).

of activities related to the time period of the biblical lesson being taught. Ongoing projects can be offered to the children, which are meaningful and authentic and also reflect life in that day. With careful planning, projects can appeal to every type of learner just as activities do in life today. For example, there can be contextualized projects that require children's artistic abilities, writing skills, building or construction aptitudes, ability to research details about that time period, or make foods and clothing of that day. Authentic Bible-time projects can become the impetus for a completely different approach to teaching children about the Bible.

But there is more to the effective teaching of children. A sense of awe and wonder plays a significant role.

The Power of Awe and Wonder

Few things warm a teacher's heart more than to watch a child's eyes widen and see that child engage deeply. That's the child silently saying, "Wow!" It's not the same as when a kid gets a high score on a video game and says, "Awesome!" Awe and wonder happen when a child reflects on, contemplates, and meditates on the character and actions of God through a Bible story (special revelation) or when the child marvels at what God has made (general revelation).

More than sixty times the Bible states that awe and wonder were the responses of God's people when they encountered the power and majesty of God. The words *reflect*, *contemplate*, *think about*, or *meditate* occur about one hundred times in Scripture. Clearly, these are biblical processes.

To guide a child to do this requires a shift in the usual way teachers interact with children. The teacher must model this; it requires a slowing down of actions and thoughts as well as external and internal quietness. No matter where the teacher and child are—whether in a classroom, at home, or in nature—that space becomes sacred space when filled with awareness of God's presence.

Though some children may need time to adjust to experiences like this, what children say they *want* is very different from what they *yearn for*. Quietness and slowness are what many children in North America yearn for because there is so much in the culture that prevents their ability to wonder. Even children who are reportedly in constant motion yearn for this. When teachers have these kinds of experiences for themselves, the insights and transformation that take place increase their willingness to try repeatedly, through trial and error, to help children receive these same benefits.

Collaboration and Connections

Helping children learn to work together is an important life skill. It feels very different from the instruction children frequently receive: "Keep your hands to yourself and your eyes on your own work." Helping children learn to work together is also a way to help them begin to understand the many "one another" commands given to the churches by the apostle Paul in his Epistles. Collaborative learning can be especially helpful when it comes to memorizing Scripture. Have children learn blocks of text, such as Psalm 1 or 23 or 1 Corinthians 13, in addition to individual verses. They may rehearse the passage regularly as a group, but they can also help one another memorize as partners. When the whole group can recite the passage, celebrate with a pizza party or by making a giant banana split.

Providing opportunities to do acts of service for the faith community and the community at large is another way to collaborate. Maybe one Sunday each quarter could be devoted to serving—weeding the church flower beds, picking up litter in the neighborhood, making treats for a homeless shelter or nursing home, or any group tasks appropriate for the setting. For collegial learning to be effective, the environment must be safe, especially emotionally safe. That means no put-downs, respect for every person, and attentive listening to each person's comments.

All this being said, children still need opportunities to reflect and debrief individually so that they can own their own learning.

How Teaching with Children Might Look (Not Your Mother's Sunday School)

Imagine it is Sunday morning and time for children to learn about the Bible (call it Sunday school, Bible hour, or any other term).[6] You, as the leader of children's ministry, have designed a ten- to twelve-week series of lessons for elementary-age children about the Israelites' captivity, exodus, and wanderings in the wilderness under the leadership that God gave to Moses. (This is just one example of many series of Bible lessons that can be experienced in ways I am describing.) You have three parts to this sixty- to ninety-minute time: *Entering In*, *God's Work in Bible Events*, and *God's Work Today*. Each section is twenty to thirty minutes long.

6. For additional information on different approaches to Bible learning with children, see May et al., *Children Matter*, 246–81.

During *Entering In*, you help the children experience the context of that biblical period—what life was like when Moses was the leader of the Hebrew people. So, you provide materials to help that happen: rolls of butcher paper for the children to paint simple backdrops as the story unfolds; cardboard boxes to build pyramids; old drapes, sheets, and bargain roll-ends of fabric to make garments worn then; supplies for cooking with grains and breads from that era; materials to make musical instruments such as drums, tambourines, cymbals, and flutes; and resources for older children to write story scripts. The learning happens in the doing, so the adult helpers need to be comfortable guiding the children without trying to make the finished product look professional. The adults' roles during this time are to aid children to understand how the various projects help them learn about life in that day. By the way, letting children choose a learning task that is engaging to them helps manage behavior concerns: children cooperate when doing what interests them.

As the series unfolds, children can create a new backdrop mural depicting the bleakness of the Sinai wilderness. At least one story might depict the routine life of the Israelites during that time. At the same time, groups of children might begin creating the tabernacle: the various pieces of furniture, garments for the priests and high priest, and a script for a Day of Atonement celebration, which could be the culmination of this series.

As children arrive, they choose a project that interests them—something they will enjoy doing.[7] After children create various aspects of life in that day, the lesson transitions to *God's Work in Bible Events*. It is time for the lesson, time for them to hear about God's work while Moses was leading God's people. This teaching can be done by people who don't consider themselves teachers but enjoy drama and are good storytellers. Their responsibility is to tell a twelve- to fifteen-minute story based on the text. The story will be engaging for the children if told by a costumed character telling it as if she or he were actually there. Here are possible characters who might tell the stories for this series: Moses, Moses's wife, Aaron, a Hebrew teenager, or maybe Pharaoh himself or his daughter.

The third part of the time, *God's Work Today*, in many ways is the most important time. This is when the children make connections between the God of the biblical story and the same God who works in their lives today. It is helpful, even essential, to have the same person each week facilitate this process with a small group (eight to ten) of children. These adults can

---

7. Brainstorm with a team about the logistics of this three-part model. The details of how it is organized and how it might flow are beyond the space allotted for this chapter.

I work regularly with girls in grades 5–7 in a casual, relational setting at my house. We don't call it Bible study or discipleship, but that's what it is. We begin every time by informally talking about life—catching up with what's been fun, hard, and special. Then we light a Christ candle (an oil lamp that we use to remind us that Jesus is the light of the world, and his presence is with us) and sing a prayer song to begin our "God time."

After we spend time in Scripture, there is time for the girls to respond to the text. Sometimes they create a skit to retell the story, or they might be asked to draw what they think happened the next day, or retell the passage in a contemporary setting, or imagine where they might be in the story had they been there.

Last spring, after spending time in the Gospel of John on the Upper Room Discourse, I provided the girls with an eight-foot length of butcher paper, markers, and colored tissue paper. I asked them to represent the emotions that may have been felt by the people there (as described in chapters 13 and 14) without using words. That was all I said. They went to work, looking at those chapters, talking about what they might do. Then they began tearing tissue paper into tiny pieces in order to create a mosaic of emotions. It took a couple of meetings to complete their work; the girls were very engaged as they worked together talking about the possible dynamics and feelings the disciples may have had.

In addition to a few content-based (closed) questions, I try to ask lots of open-ended questions—questions that have no specific answers—with the intent of stretching their thinking and helping them to imagine the situation because imagination plays a key role in spiritual growth.

We also memorize Scripture as a group. I try to focus on helping them understand the passage more than simply reciting it. Yes, knowing it from memory is an important spiritual discipline, but to be most effective, it must also be understood and internalized.

be called something other than teachers because they don't actually teach. Rather, they guide or facilitate connections the children make. These people may be called shepherds. Consider mixing ages in these small groups; maybe divide the groups into lower and upper elementary groups. The dynamic between older and younger children can enhance learning and cooperation among groups. It is also often helpful to mix genders with these ages; doing so can help moderate some of the stereotypical gender-specific behaviors that may occur. Since children always meet with the same small group, even though they may choose different tasks to do at the beginning, they are able to build relationships, share concerns, and pray for one another.

Bottom line: *It is important to create experiences that help children see the reality of the biblical story: that the biblical characters were real people, in a real place, at a real point in time, and that their issues, challenges, and joys are similar to what God allows us to experience today though the circumstances may be different.*

The kinds of experiences that are created are more important than trying to gear a task for a specific age of children. Older children will naturally gravitate to research, writing opportunities, and sophisticated tasks, but any age child can build, create, cook, or paint. The difference comes in what children take away from the learning tasks and how they connect the biblical stories with their own lives. That happens in the small groups, which become twenty-minute discipleship groups.

Discipleship with Children

What does discipleship with children look like? It is intentional, planned conversations about God and life and the growth of spiritual developments. Sometimes the plan may be developed by the adult, such as a study on the names of God or the "I am" statements of Jesus. Other times the plan may be shaped from the questions about which the children are curious, questions such as: What is heaven like? Will pets be there? Why do kids bully? What is it like to die? and, Why is there so much sickness in the world? Of course, discipleship can include book studies or be based around core doctrines of the Christian faith, but many times questions of doctrine are covered because they flow out of issues the children raise.

Curricular Choices

First of all, it must be said that there is no perfect curriculum! Every lesson plan must be adapted for the context and for the learners. When selecting materials to use to teach children, consider the scope and sequence—what content is being covered and in what order (see chap. 12). If that accomplishes your purposes, you can then make adjustments, drawing on the principles given earlier, for other areas of the lesson that may be less satisfactory.

Here is what to look for:

- How is the Scripture passage treated and presented?
- Is it "dumbed down" or age appropriate?
- What is the role of the teacher?
- What is the view of the learner—is the child viewed as capable and creative or seen as just a puppet who will follow directions?

Many ministries choose the challenging task of writing their own curriculum. If you lead one of these ministries, here is a structure that may be helpful, a five-step process called the Five "-ates" to Educ-ate: (1) locate, (2) elaborate, (3) illuminate, (4) integrate, (5) activate:[8]

> Locate—Locate a felt need or problem from life or from Scripture. What situations are the children in that relates to the aim or the text?
>
> Elaborate—Elaborate or draw out the problem to its logical conclusion. Help the children realize what might be the implications if the problem is not resolved. Explore why the problem exists and what are its implications.
>
> Illuminate—Illuminate the problem with the truth of God's Word. How is this problem evident in the text being used? In what ways did God intervene? What did the people in the biblical story do? How did they respond to God's actions?
>
> Integrate—Integrate the truth of the passage through the help of the Holy Spirit. Do this in a way that shows the children how to apply the truth to their own situation. What does this truth mean for their lives?
>
> Activate—Activate a plan under God's direction that will bring change to their lives. Let the children determine this for themselves. How can they specifically be different with God's help? To whom can they be accountable to follow through on the desired change?

Admittedly, it takes time to get comfortable with such a process. Note how it starts with the life of the children, next takes them into the truths of Scripture, and then back to their own lives. It is flowing movement between life today and life then. God has not changed, but our concrete lives certainly are different from those in Bible times even though our problems are often quite similar.

When developing a lesson plan, start with the biblical passage, a problem, or an event that has affected the children. Prayerfully let the Holy Spirit lead you to ways the passage is relevant for the children, and then proceed to construct the process, including as many experiential ways as possible. Creative experiences are especially helpful in steps 2 and 4.

A Final Word

It is a joy and privilege to teach children about God and for the Spirit to help us do it attractively. We need to remember to put the child in the

---

8. I developed this when writing my own lesson plans. The word *educate* does not mean either simply "to teach" or "to learn" but means to "lead out."

middle as Jesus did—not our teaching or my methods, but the child—and for us to become like children, blessing them each time we are together as Jesus also did.

Questions and Activities

1. Do you remember a particular Bible story lesson from your childhood? What did your teacher do that made it so memorable? What role did awe and wonder play?
2. What do you think are the main differences between teaching children and teaching teenagers?
3. As you review this chapter, what are the most important guidelines that you notice for the effective teaching of children? What do you notice that may be particular to the teaching of children?
4. Find a local church's children's ministry that will let you have their materials for explaining their purpose, organizing their volunteers, and training their people. Review the stated purpose(s) of the ministry, examine the resources they provide for teachers, and make note of the principles that are guiding their work. If you were to describe their ministry to another person, what would you say?
5. Look over the section of how teaching with children might look. Take a favorite Bible story and create a first draft of an original lesson using the three parts and their principles.

Further Reading

May, Scottie, Beth Posterski, Catherine Stonehouse, and Linda Cannell. *Children Matter: Celebrating Their Place in the Church, Family, and Community*. Grand Rapids: Eerdmans, 2005.

Stonehouse, Catherine. *Joining Children on the Spiritual Journey: Nurturing a Life of Faith*. Grand Rapids: Baker, 1998.

14

Teaching Adults

AMANDA DRURY

At twenty-three years old, I returned from the nursing home heavyhearted. I had been interning under the chaplain for a number of months and had just witnessed the death of a resident. I walked through the door and shared with my husband the difficulty of watching a resident die. I ended my sharing by blurting out, "And she was so young—only seventy-two!"

John gave me a puzzled look, "Seventy-two is young?"

Had I not spent so much time at this nursing facility, I would have found this an odd statement as well. Seventy-two is young? But after months of interacting with residents in various stages, it was clear there was a big difference between seventy-two and eighty-two. From my perspective, yes, seventy-two seemed young to die.

There is a tendency for those who are just entering into adulthood to lump people in a large category labeled simply "adults." We have a number of categories for those under the age of twenty—newborn, baby, toddler, preschooler, elementary schooler, pre-teenager, middle schooler, high schooler, teenager—and our conversations are starting to branch out to include those in the emerging adult category. We have multiple categories for the first two decades of life, but very few categories when we move beyond the mid-twenties. It is strange to have such a limited vocabulary when describing the span in which one spends the majority of his or her life.

Just as we have multiple terms for people under twenty, so too the church tends to offer multiple options for spiritual formation for the young. Depending on the size of the church, children are normally divided into classes geared toward their own age bracket, the Sunday school teachers gear their lessons toward a particular age group, and, while we separate two-year-olds from eight-year-olds, we often consolidate the thirty-year-olds and the seventy-year-olds into one big category: "adults."

To be clear, this is *not* a chapter advocating for the segregation of adults based on age; it is, however, a call for church leaders to deepen their understanding of what it means to minister to those in their adult years. It should also be noted that the differences that emerge between adults are not limited to age. Many other factors come into play when we consider race, class, ethnicity, education, and the like. And then within each of these categories one must take into account differences concerning one's family status. Married or single; divorced or widowed? Do the adults have children? If so, are the children young or grown? As you can see, there is no such thing as a "typical adult."

What's more, even if we did have a room full of homogenized people—men and women of the same age, race, socioeconomic level, and with identical family commitments—we *still* would not be able to teach with a one-size-fits-all mind-set. Though we may have striking similarities with those around us, the Holy Spirit speaks to each one of us with both content and timing that is different from person to person. When we take all of these differences into account, one is left wondering how it is even possible to effectively teach a room full of diverse adults.

In an effort to combat the above assertion of a one-size-fits-all adult, many in the field of adult education have attempted to identify stage theories in order to categorize their differences.[1] While these stage theories are a standard way to talk about adult development, they are certainly not the authoritative word on adult experience. Indeed, some may critique these various theories for being too limiting, as will be explained shortly. While stage theories may have limitations, they may be helpful when used in a nonrigid way in order to become attuned to differences within an adult classroom. Therefore we will engage in a brief discussion on stage theory and then allow it to become part of the background scenery of what it means to teach adults.

1. For example, Erik Erikson (1902–1994) developed an eight-step theory on identity development from infancy to adulthood. Lawrence Kohlberg (1927–1987) studied moral reasoning and created six developmental stages outlining the process.

While people like Erik Erikson and Lawrence Kohlberg offer categorizations of the psychological development of children and adults, James Fowler developed a six-step theory called Stages of Faith, which combines the psychological with the spiritual. His abbreviated theory is as follows:

Stage 0: Primal or Undifferentiated faith (birth to two years)—"The infant is forming a basic sense of trust, . . . forming what I call pre-images of God or the Holy, and of the kind of world we live in. On this foundation of basic trust or mistrust is built all that comes later in terms of faith."

Stage 1: "Intuitive-Projective" faith (ages three to seven)—"It's marked by the rise of imagination. The child doesn't have the kind of logic that makes possible or necessary the questioning of perceptions or fantasies. Therefore the child's mind is 'religiously pregnant,' one might say."

Stage 2: Mythic-Literal faith (mostly in schoolchildren)—"The child develops a way of dealing with the world and making meaning that now criticizes and evaluates the previous stage of imagination and fantasy. The gift of this stage is narrative. The child now can really form and re-tell powerful stories that grasp his or her experiences of meaning."

Stage 3: Synthetic-Conventional faith (arising in adolescence; aged twelve to adulthood)—"It's marked by the beginning of what Piaget calls formal operational thinking. That simply means that we now can think about our own thinking. It's a time when a person is typically concerned about forming an identity, and is deeply concerned about the evaluations and feedback from significant other people in his or her life. . . . At any of the stages from two on you can find adults who are best described by these stages."

Stage 4: Individuative-Reflective faith (usually mid-twenties to late thirties)—"Stage Four, for those who develop it, is a time in which the person is pushed out of, or steps out of, the circle of interpersonal relationships that have sustained his life to that point. Now comes the burden of reflecting upon the self as separate from the groups and the shared world that defines one's life."

Stage 5: Conjunctive faith (mid-life crisis)—"One begins to recognize that the conscious self is not all there is of me. I have an unconscious. Much of my behavior and response to things is shaped by dimensions of self that I'm not fully aware of. There is a deepened readiness for a relationship to God that includes God's mystery and unavailability and strangeness as well as God's closeness and clarity. . . . Stage Five is a period when one is alive to paradox."

Stage 6: Universalizing faith (various ages)—"Few persons we find move into Stage Six, which we call universalizing faith. . . . These are persons who in a sense have negated the self for the sake of affirming God. And yet in affirming God they became vibrant and powerful selves in our experience. They have a quality of what I call relevant irrelevance. Their 'subversiveness' makes our compromises show up as what they are."[2]

While Fowler's Stages of Faith theory can be a helpful tool in initial conversations, stage theory in general ultimately has drawbacks. Aside from the fact that most people bristle at the idea of their faith or psychological development being put in a box, categorizing people into various stages does not take into account the richness of the human experience, which is seldom sequential and never neat.

Consider Ruby Bridges, who at six years old, flanked by federal marshals, was regularly seen praying for those who protested her attendance at a previously all-white school. Her age would land her in Fowler's first stage ("'intuitive-projective' faith"). Her acts of compassion and grace toward those threatening her, however, more closely resemble the "universalizing faith" of stage six. Stage theory can be a helpful starting point, but it has major limitations. Perhaps more helpful than stage theory is the concept of andragogy, the theory and practice related to adult learning.[3] If there were a patron saint of teaching adults, it would most likely be educational theorist Malcolm Knowles (1913–1997), who is best known for his writing on andragogy:

Adults have the need to know why they are learning something.

Adults learn through doing.

Adults are problem solvers.

Adults learn best when the subject is of immediate use.

As the adult matures, the motivation to learn becomes more internal than external.[4]

---

2. James Fowler, quoted in Harold Kent Straughn, "My Interview with James W. Fowler on the Stages of Faith," John Mark Ministries, October 13, 2006, http://www.jmm.org.au/articles/18316 .htm. A full formulation of Fowler's theory can be found in his book *Stages of Faith: The Psychology of Human Development and the Quest for Meaning* (San Francisco: Harper & Row, 1981).

3. This term originated with German educator Alexander Kapp and developed into a theory by Eugen Rosenstock-Huessy. *Andragogy* is Greek for "man-leading" (though of course in this context it extends to men and women), meaning the adult learner has elements of self-direction. This is contrasted with *pedagogy*, which is Greek for "child-leading."

4. Malcolm Knowles, *Andragogy in Action* (San Francisco: Jossey-Bass, 1984), 12.

The remainder of this chapter will focus on five guidelines for teaching adults that are grounded in Knowles's understanding of andragogy and are appropriated for the church.

Teaching as Co-learning

So just how *does* one go about teaching adults? How do we teach to such a broad and diverse audience? Some of the most basic guidelines of teaching are true whether our subjects are three years old or eighty-three years old. These most basic guidelines focus less on *what* we teach or *how* we teach than on *who we are*. Regardless of one's audience, the most effective teaching begins with the person of the teacher. Educator Parker Palmer writes, "Good teaching cannot be reduced to technique; good teaching comes from identity and integrity of the teacher."[5]

At the heart of effective teaching is a knowledge and groundedness of one's identity, particularly as it relates to being a beloved child of God. Obviously, this kind of self-knowledge takes a lifetime and cannot be reduced to a mere book, much less a chapter. Nevertheless, it is the cornerstone of teaching regardless of one's subject or subject matter.

What does it mean to be an intentional and mindful teacher of adults? Before we even step foot inside a classroom, there is a good chance a battle is already raging in our minds. "Have I prepared enough?" "Will these people like me?" "What if no one talks?" Oftentimes, good teaching begins with acknowledging these places where we experience discomfort or anxiety.

You don't have to be the smartest person in the room in order to be a good teacher. It's easy for recent college graduates in their first call to find themselves in one of two extremes. First, there are those who fear they don't have anything to offer to congregants who are ten, twenty, or thirty-plus years older than them. "I'm too young to have anything worthwhile to say." "No one is going to listen to me."

Then there are those on the other extreme who believe their education and experience make them experts on all things spiritual. They've read the commentaries. They know the theories. They won the preaching award, and no doubt the congregation will be on the edge of their seats, eager to learn.

Most teachers probably find themselves oscillating between the two extremes—sometimes within the same class period. Those who struggle with feeling inadequate may find encouragement in the Scriptures where

5. Parker Palmer, *The Courage to Teach: Exploring the Inner Landscape of a Teacher's Life* (San Francisco: Jossey-Bass, 1998), 13.

the boy Samuel is chosen to hear the voice of God. Where the stutterer Moses is told, "Who has made man's mouth? Who makes him mute, or deaf, or seeing, or blind? Is it not I, the Lord? Now therefore go, and I will be with your mouth and teach you what you shall speak" (Exod. 4:11–12). And the young Timothy is told to "let no one despise you for your youth, but set the believers an example in speech, in conduct, in love, in faith, in purity" (1 Tim. 4:12). We have scriptural precedence for God using the young to teach the old. Those whom God has called are not imposters within the church; they are anointed children set apart and emboldened for ministry.

> Think back to your favorite teachers from the past. What about them appealed to you? Chances are your response was not that their intelligence most appealed to you; most likely, your answer had something to do with the way they related to their students.

Ultimately, we must remember our goal is not to create disciples of ourselves; rather, we continually strive to make room for the Holy Spirit to transform us all into the image of Christ. When we see ourselves as co-learners seeking to be transformed into the image of Christ, as opposed to experts on the material, we ask ourselves questions like, "How is this material changing *me*?" It means we ask questions of our fellow learners to which we do not already have pat answers prepared. Being a co-learner as opposed to an expert is difficult in that it requires we relinquish a certain amount of control in the classroom. Furthermore, it means we take seriously the idea of a "priesthood of all believers." We acknowledge that God might speak through us as well as other members of the congregation.

This role as co-learner leads us feeling both relieved and terrified. We experience relief knowing that we are not the experts. We are not the ultimate agents of change. We cannot earn our own salvation, much less the salvation of those in our ministries. Our job is to be open to the Spirit. However, it's the openness to the Holy Spirit that is also terrifying. We teach with a specific lesson plan in place knowing that, like the wind, the Spirit "blows wherever it pleases. You can hear its sound, but you cannot tell where it comes from or where it is going" (John 3:8 NIV).

Teaching to "Scratch an Itch"

Have you ever gotten a gift that you just didn't need? Such a gift may be snow boots when you live in Hawaii, shampoo when you don't have hair, or a new pair of socks when you already have a drawer full. Now apply the same concept to ideas—have you ever been given an idea that you just didn't need? For example, did you know that "almost" is the longest word in the English language that has its entire letters in alphabetical order? Or that it's possible for a cockroach to live several weeks with its head cut off? Did you know camels have a total of three eyelids in order to protect their eyes from sand?

Chances are the above statements have nothing to do with questions you are currently asking. You might find some of these facts moderately interesting, but they most likely will not be integrated into your understanding of life. Since these are ideas that you don't need, these factoids run the risk of slipping our minds. They are irrelevant.

Now imagine the complete opposite: an offer of an umbrella in the pouring rain, a slice of pizza when you are famished, the results of an eagerly anticipated football game, or even the punch line of a joke. The main difference between information about camel's eyelids and the result of a football game is based entirely on the interest of the listener. Some information is wanted, while other information is not. Some information is sought after, and other information is an afterthought. Some information is satisfying, and other information is redundant.

Some of the best teaching occurs when the teacher can "scratch an itch." We listen best when we anticipate the information we are about to receive as somehow relevant or important. If we have a felt need for the subject at hand, we are more likely to pay attention and retain information.

Effective teaching addresses questions we are already pondering. Effective teaching also prompts us to consider worthwhile questions to begin with. Too often teachers settle for teaching for content over teaching for transformation. Teaching for transformation requires attention to a felt need.

Consider the difference between these two teachings:

1. Jesus told Peter to drop his net and follow him. Fishing was a strenuous task for first-century fishermen. One can only wonder how fishing for fish prepared the disciples for Jesus's task of fishing for people. Are you living your life in such a way that you are fishing for people?

2. Jesus told Peter to drop his net and follow him. Can you imagine what would have happened to Peter had he tried to follow Jesus while still clutching his net? He'd be tripping over his own feet and becoming considerably slowed down by the added weight. When Jesus calls us, he calls us to drop our nets—those things that would slow us down from following after him. What kinds of things are you tempted to clutch that may hold you back in your spiritual journey?

There is nothing false about the first statement. This is accurate information, and there is a vague question at the end. The second teaching, however, raises a question that plays to the imagination. *What if Peter hadn't let go?* This teaching leaves room for wonder and nudges the listener to a more personal response. One teaching provides information; the other piques interest.

Malcolm Knowles stresses the importance of adults believing that what they are being taught is worth their time. The best teaching speaks toward a felt need—it seeks to scratch an itch. What we teach does not always have to be immediately relevant or applicable, but it should engage our minds in such a way that we are caught up in some element of beauty or wonder. This kind of teaching requires the teacher to engage contradictions, mystery, and untidy endings without having all the answers. Again, this kind of teaching might be frightening for the teacher since it requires the ability to sit with tension and unresolved questions.

Teaching for Change

Perhaps one of the biggest challenges in teaching in general and especially when teaching adults is to strike the right balance between comfort and discomfort. We want people to feel comfortable and safe enough to engage as their authentic selves, but we also want to provide enough stimulating challenges that they are compelled to pursue something deeper. We want adults to be comfortable, but not bored; challenged, but not terrified. The Russian psychologist Lev Vygotsky (1896–1934) described this task with what he called the "Zone of Proximal Development" (ZPD; see fig. 14.1).[6]

The smallest zone consists of those actions that I can do by myself. The largest zone represents things I can*not* do. The middle zone consists of actions that I can do with proper guidance from someone else. It is the middle zone that is considered the ideal spot for teachers. Here the student is stretched outside of her comfort zone, but there is enough support in place that she will not succumb to failure.

If everything that we teach falls within the smallest perimeter, our teaching is redundant. To take this to the extreme, most adults would not benefit from a large class session on how to tie their shoes. They will feel bored, as if we are wasting their time. Just as it's important to not teach that which adults have already mastered, it's also critical that we avoid teaching that which is beyond the adults' abilities. A technical lecture on quantum physics

6. Lev S. Vygotsky, *Mind in Society: Development of Higher Psychological Processes* (Cambridge, MA: Harvard University Press, 1978), 86.

Figure 14.1 Zone of Proximal Development (ZPD)

would be way over most adults' heads. Here our adult learners are left frustrated, perhaps even anxious about their own mental capacities.

The middle zone, however, is full of potential. It is here where growth occurs when the proper amount of support and assistance is given. Here we teach toward things an individual might not be able to reach on her own but is able to explore with the help and guidance of another. For example, the call to "love your enemies and pray for those who persecute you" may sound impossible for some. The hope is that with the proper guidance/questions/exploration, the concept of forgiving one's enemy, though still difficult, has moved from the impossible to the possible.

Teaching toward Intimacy

Consider the life of a forty-five-year-old woman. Let's imagine she spends fifty hours a week working as an executive director at a marketing firm. Her days are filled with meetings, pressing decisions, and the need to create appealing designs. Following a full day of work, she joins her husband for their son's JV basketball game. They run through a drive-thru for a quick dinner and then head home, where she unloads the dishwasher while mentally running through the next day's agenda. Although much of her day has been spent in the presence of other people, there is a good chance she is nevertheless feeling lonely and in need of intimacy or some other kind of

How do we as teachers help facilitate loving one's neighbor? Consider these tips:

1. *Allow for more silence than you think necessary.* When you ask a question—particularly if it's a question of a personal nature—be prepared to sit in silence. Many teachers are uncomfortable with silence and will intervene too quickly. Give space for people to form deeper answers or muster the courage to speak. The temptation is to berate either yourself or the participants in the silence: "Maybe I asked a dumb question." "Why won't anybody talk? Aren't they paying attention?"

2. *Listen without trying to fix.* When someone shares something of a sensitive nature, listen and respond with empathy. Don't respond with advice or proof-texting from the Bible; simply receive what is shared with grace and empathy. You might find yourself saying things like: "I really appreciate your sharing." "I cannot imagine how difficult that must have been for you." After a particularly intense round of sharing, you might even invite the class to honor the sharer by simply sitting in silence for two minutes or by offering a prayer.

3. *Record any prayer requests given.* If you provide space for adults to share prayer concerns, write the requests down on a piece of paper in order to provide follow-up (always ask permission before sharing any of the requests with others). Referring to past prayer requests also creates natural space for people to share where and how certain prayers have been answered.

meaningful connection. Whether we spend our days in an office or with our young children, many adults are craving some kind of intimacy. The desire to be known can be overwhelming (perhaps only second to needing a good nap).

There can be great benefit in allowing time for personal interaction and sharing within a class setting. It could be that spending time sharing prayer requests and praying for one another provides a much-needed addition to one's spiritual formation. Allowing for this kind of space within a class setting, and having a spirit of flexibility in terms of your planned lesson, is one of the ways in which we attempt to make ourselves open to the prompting of the Holy Spirit.

Finding the proper balance of intimacy is important. Too little intimacy and you are left with unsatisfying small talk. Then again, too much intimacy may result in deathbed-confessional-like dialogue that leads to anxiety. However, our goal in teaching adults is not to pump information into heads, it's to teach toward transformation into the image of Christ. We live out our faith in the ways in which we interact with one another. The two greatest commands are to love God and love our neighbor. Just as we seek to be intentional about growing in our love for God, so too we need to be intentional about growing in our love for our neighbors.

If we want those in our care to be able to grasp even on a small level what it means to be the body of Christ, we must provide space for the community to practice toward that end.

Teaching toward Fun

Finally, don't underestimate the need for fun with adult learners. "Fun" does not necessarily mean humorous. Someone might describe an action movie as "fun" because it kept him on the edge of his seat—it held his interest. Most educators know our lessons have to be interesting if we want to hold younger listeners' attention. But something strange happens when we shift from teenagers to adults. Being interesting, engaging, or "fun" seems less important when we are dealing with adults than it does when we are with children. This observation prompts the final thesis: don't underestimate the adult need for fun. Just because an individual is middle-aged does not mean she now wants to sit still and soak in a thirty-minute lecture on the Synoptic Gospels. Adults get bored too and perhaps just as quickly as teenagers do. The main difference is they tend to be more polite about their boredom than the younger members of our church.

As you are preparing your lessons, continually ask, "Do I find this interesting? Is this engaging my attention? Am I compelled to hear more?" It is almost a guarantee that if *you* are bored with your material and preparation, then your audience will be as well.

Conclusion

While there are many theories concerning adult education, our task is somewhat different in that we are not interested in merely educating adults; we want to see adults transformed into the image of Christ. The world does not need more of what John Westerhoff calls "educated atheists" (people who know a lot about the Bible but don't believe in or love God).[7] What we need are women and men who are fully alive to God. While this kind of transformation is first and foremost a product of the Holy Spirit, as John Wesley says, "God, not man, is the physician of souls. . . . But it is generally his pleasure to work by his creatures: to help man by man."[8] Teaching adults

7. John H. Westerhoff, *Will Our Children Have Faith?* (Harrisburg, PA: Morehouse, 2000), 18.
8. John Wesley, "On the Education of Children," in *The Works of John Wesley*, vol. 7, ed. Thomas Jackson (Grand Rapids: Baker, 1979), 88.

may seem to be a daunting, nebulous task, particularly for those who are just starting off in ministry. Rest assured, the Father has given us the Son, and Christ himself gave the apostles, the prophets, the evangelists, and the pastors and teachers to equip his people for works of service, so that the body of Christ may be built up until we all reach unity in the faith and in the knowledge of the Son of God and become mature, attaining to the whole measure of the fullness of Christ (Eph. 4:11–13).

Questions and Activities

1. What three or four points in this chapter helped you to deepen your understanding of what it means to minister to adults?
2. As you reflect on Fowler's faith development theory, how does it help you understand your own spiritual development?
3. "Effective teaching addresses questions we are already pondering." How does that statement intersect with what we read in chapter 10 on motivation? What are the implications for Christian ministry? How, then, do we teach toward change?
4. How does teaching toward intimacy give new life to adult ministry? Where might many adult ministries improve their work by understanding this guideline?
5. For each of the five guidelines for teaching adults, write one example of when you've best seen it in action: teaching as co-learning, teaching to "scratch an itch," teaching for change, teaching toward intimacy, and teaching toward fun.

Further Reading

Drury, Amanda. *Saying Is Believing: The Necessity of Testimony in Adolescent Spiritual Development*. Downers Grove, IL: InterVarsity, 2015.

Fowler, James. *Stages of Faith: The Psychology of Human Development and the Quest for Meaning*. San Francisco: Harper & Row, 1981.

15

How Families Shape the Faith of Younger Generations

BRENDA A. SNAILUM

After a presentation on family ministry, a youth worker raised his hand and confidently declared, "God called me to minister to teenagers. I don't want to have to minister to their parents and little brothers and sisters, too!" It is hard enough to lead in youth ministry, let alone adding any additional obligations. However, in order to minister to young people well, we have to consider one very important thing—*family influences everyone, in every way, all the time*. This chapter surveys how families influence the way we learn and grow in faith, explores biblical and cultural ideas of family, and evaluates several family ministry strategies so that we can better understand how to minister to youth in a way that honors and supports family influence.

Almost everything we learn as children is learned in our family context, which influences us directly and indirectly, explicitly and implicitly, for better or worse. Family is commonly defined in two ways. The *structural* view of family is like the structure of a family tree that can include extended and stepfamily relationships. Family can also be defined by the roles or organization of relationships that connect people who live together—they behave like a family. This *functional* view of family includes those who may not be related by legal or genetic means, but they function in family roles with one another.[1]

Whether you define family structurally or functionally, it is one of the most powerful forces in human development, affecting us at the genetic and environmental levels, what is more commonly called *nature* and *nurture*. It is in the context of the family that children develop their identity as a person—they learn *who* and *whose* they are at the core of their being. "For good or for ill the family environment serves as a mirror which through its action reflects our being back to us, and in so doing determines it."[2] A child's identity is partially determined genetically—it is *who* they are in flesh and bone. Children are inextricably bound to their parents and siblings through shared DNA with a specific set of physical, psychological, and behavioral traits. This biological reality creates an imprint on the person that works its way out in daily living.

We are more than our genetics, though; our identity is also socially constructed. Family is best understood as a complex interrelated system, and the whole is greater than the sum of the parts. Within the family system, children learn *whose* they are—they learn their unique contribution and identity in the community of family. Indeed, the family itself has its own schema, or fingerprint, that dynamically influences every member as it shapes character, morality, values, behavior, and faith.[3] The institution of the family claims authority over the individual, and children do not have the ability for self-reflection to critically examine their reality—they just live in it.[4]

It is within the family system that children develop what Jason Santos refers to as "anchor identity," or the core foundational sense of who they are.[5] This reality forms the anchor for navigating the intense period of identity development and individuation in adolescence and emerging adulthood.[6] As adolescents broaden their social circles, they interpret and apply what is learned from "secondary" relationships to their developing identity. Parental and familial influence does not necessarily weaken but rather shares the stage as peers, nonfamilial adult relationships, and the broader culture

1. Diana Garland, *Family Ministry: A Comprehensive Guide* (Downers Grove, IL: InterVarsity, 2012), 53–56.

2. Andrew Root, *The Children of Divorce* (Grand Rapids: Baker Academic, 2010), 39.

3. Diana Garland, *Inside Out Families: Living the Faith Together* (Waco, TX: Baylor University Press, 2010), 18.

4. Peter Berger and Thomas Luckmann, *The Social Construction of Reality: A Treatise in the Sociology of Knowledge* (New York: Anchor, 1966), 69.

5. Tim Baker interviewing Jason Santos, "Adolescent Ontology: YWJ Roundtable," *Youth-Worker Journal*, July/August 2014, 31.

6. Berger and Luckmann, *Social Construction*, 59.

become influential in the "secondary socialization" of the young person.[7] These secondary relationships can be critical in helping the young person by providing a place of belonging, particularly when compensating for difficult family situations. However, it is important to keep in mind that individual agency (free will) and many other relational and environmental factors combine with family influence in a complex matrix that influences identity development.

How Do Families Influence Learning?

Learning happens experientially within the family system, and children, especially infants and toddlers, learn affectively and intuitively. Children learn how to learn and how to value education from their family. Few parents have formal curriculum for education or have articulated their learning goals and strategies for teaching their children. Yet families often share a common set of educational values that are implicitly transmitted to children and teens through informal conversations and by their modeling of those values in their everyday life.

Whether intentionally or not, families greatly influence the values, content, and quality of institutional education. The US Department of Education asserts, "When families are involved in their children's education, children earn higher grades, attend school more regularly, complete more homework, demonstrate more positive attitudes and behaviors, graduate from high school at higher rates, and are more likely to enroll in higher education."[8] Not only do families influence their child's formal education,[9] but families also greatly influence learning motivation and desire for achievement.[10] Low levels of family support promote poor school performance and increased dropout rates, while high levels of support can provide a buffer that promotes stability and fosters academic motivation and achievement in spite of negative environmental circumstances.[11]

7. Ibid., 140.

8. Janie E. Funkhouser, Miriam R. Gonzales, and Oliver C. Moles, "Executive Summary," in *Family Involvement in Children's Education: Successful Local Approaches—An Idea Book* (US Department of Education, Office of Educational Research and Improvement, October 1997), 2. Accessed at http://www2.ed.gov/pubs/FamInvolve/execsumm.html.

9. Tim Urdan, Monica Solek, and Erin Schoenfelder, "Students' Perceptions of Family Influences on Their Academic Motivation: A Qualitative Analysis," *European Journal of Psychology of Education* 22, no. 1 (March 2007): 9.

10. Glen H. Elder and Avshalom Caspi, "Economic Stress in Lives: Developmental Perspectives," *Journal of Social Issues* 44 (1988): 25–45.

11. Damiya Whitaker et al., "Neighborhood and Family Effects on Learning Motivation among Urban African American Middle School Youth," *Journal of Children and Family Studies* 21 (2012): 131–38.

What Is the Role of Families in Faith Formation?

One of the most important things we learn from our families is who God is and who we are in relation to God and others. A common theme throughout Scripture is that every generation is responsible for teaching their children matters of faith in every aspect of life. As Deuteronomy exhorts, "And these words that I command you today shall be on your heart. You shall teach them diligently to your children, and shall talk of them when you sit in your house, and when you walk by the way, and when you lie down, and when you rise" (Deut. 6:6–7). So it is no surprise that recent research studies assert that one of the "best social predictors of what the religious and spiritual lives of youth will look like is what the religious and spiritual lives of their parents look like."[12]

Parents shape our concept of who God is through their parenting style, modeling, shared action, and faith dialogue. A child's perception of the nature of God is strongly influenced by their parent's presence or absence, their responses to mistakes, and their ability to forgive. If the parent is overly punitive, absent, or distant, the child may view God the same way. But when parents are generally loving, gracious, and accepting, children will likely view God that way as well.[13]

Parents can have a key influence in promoting autonomous or "owned" faith as teens move through adolescent identity development and individuation.[14] This is a critical period when parental support is needed through transitions and milestones along the way toward an adult faith that is grounded in their identity in Christ. In this stage of life, teens are seeking supported autonomy—wanting to grow up while needing to know that they will be all right on their own. It is important for parents to delicately balance holding on and letting go. Parents can also be influential in helping their teen discover and develop their unique God-given gifts and talents, and in so doing, the young person can find their own place in the faith community and the greater mission of God.[15]

Through the overall family schema, children and teens learn religious norms, values, and traditions; they learn how faith is expressed and shared, and how it influences daily life and attitudes. There is *bidirectional reciprocity*

12. Christian Smith, *Soul Searching: The Religious and Spiritual Lives of American Teenagers* (New York: Oxford University Press, 2005), 261.

13. Roger L. Dudley, "The Relationship of Parenting Styles to Commitment to the Church among Young Adults," *Religious Education* 95 (2000): 39–50.

14. Mark Cannister, *Teenagers Matter: Making Student Ministry a Priority in the Church* (Grand Rapids: Baker Academic, 2013), 88.

15. Ibid., 196–99.

as all family members interact to influence and shape one another's faith.[16] Family rituals, devotions, and worship greatly influence religious practices, and family church attendance influences their teen's church attendance, which can last throughout their adult years.[17]

Where Does the Church Fit in This Picture?

Throughout Scripture the most commonly used image of the church is that of "family."[18] In the Old Testament, a person's identity was situated within one's household, clan, and tribe, and each successive unit generally meant a larger and more diverse sense of family. The smallest unit, the *household* or "father's house," was a collection of families that often represented three or more generations, and included widows, orphans, proselytes, servants and their families, and, in some instances, Levites or craftsmen (Deut. 16:11, 14). The *clan* was a collection of households that imparted territorial identity, or a geographical address, that was rarely smaller than a town.[19] The *tribe* was the largest family unit, denoting a genealogical line, such as the "line of David," but included those belonging to households and clans whether or not they were genetically or legally bound. Even at the tribe level there was a strong sense of familial relatedness.

When Jesus established his church, he established an entirely new family—his family. Because of the blood of Christ, Christians are blood siblings, and natural familial bonds are subordinated.[20] This new family paradigm deeply influenced how early believers perceived themselves in relationship with God as their Father and other believers as brothers and sisters. It was understood that the *church is family* and includes all of whom Jesus claims as brothers and sisters, regardless of their age, or whether they have spouses, parents, or siblings, or whether they are orphans or widows. Given the strong natural familial bond in Jewish culture, this was a radical reordering of how they related to one another as family.

16. Chris J. Boyatzis and Denise L. Janicki, "Parent-Child Communication about Religion: Survey and Diary Data on Unilateral Transmission and Bi-directional Reciprocity Styles," *Review of Religious Research* 44, no. 3 (2003): 252–70.

17. Wes Black, "Stopping the Dropouts: Guiding Adolescents toward a Lasting Faith Following High School Graduation," *Christian Education Journal* 5, no. 1 (2008): 28–46.

18. Joseph Hellerman, *When the Church Was a Family: Recapturing Jesus' Vision for Authentic Community* (Nashville: B&H, 2009).

19. T. Wills, "Family," in *The New Interpreter's Dictionary of the Bible*, ed. D. N. Freedman (Nashville: Abingdon, 2006), 2:429.

20. For a thorough discussion on this topic, see Hellerman, *When the Church Was a Family*, 74–75, 205–206.

A collectivist understanding of family continued through the mid-nineteenth century in Western civilization, when individualism, increased family affluence, and mobility normalized the smallest form of family in history—the nuclear family. Concurrently, industrialization, economic crises, and the rise in divorce contributed to an increase in frazzled and fragmented families and often stigmatized those families that did not fit the "norm"—not only in the culture but also in the church. The proliferation of mandatory secularized public education in the mid-twentieth century made it easy for parents to relinquish education to schools, further separating children from familial influence, especially in matters of faith. The iconic "rebellious teenager" of the 1950s and the "generation gap" in the 1960s cultivated greater isolation of teens and further division within families and churches. In response to this fragmentation, many Christian leaders developed contextualized, age-stratified ministries in order to more effectively reach and teach each generation and to provide a place for people to belong with friends their own age.[21]

As Western culture became more divided, families and children were often casualties. Currently, concepts of family are fluid and open to self-definition and reform, and children can be considered a liability rather than an asset.[22] Consequently, we have a burgeoning number of teens and young adults without a strong anchor to family or church that provides a place to belong. They are abandoned to develop their own individual identity, and they lack a reciprocal sense of committed connections to the church community that are forged through family and intergenerational experiences.

While youth and children's ministries have greatly contributed to shaping the faith of young people,[23] we are experiencing some ramifications of the church/family division. All too often the spiritual development of children is a low priority for parents and adult congregations, and concurrently families are seldom a priority for youth ministry programs. Families and churches often function autonomously from each other, and youth and children's workers have been caught in the tension between the two. Clearly that division needs to be addressed. We are challenged to take steps toward more inclusive ministry strategies that bring healing to hurting families and unite the generations in order for the church to become the unified family of Christ depicted in the New Testament.

21. Mark H. Senter, *When God Shows Up: A History of Protestant Youth Ministry in America* (Grand Rapids: Baker Academic, 2010).
22. Root, *Children of Divorce*, 20–22.
23. Brenda Snailum, "Integrating Intergenerational Ministry Strategies into Existing Youth Ministries: What Can a Hybrid Approach Be Expected to Accomplish?," *Journal of Youth Ministry* 11, no. 2 (Spring 2013): 7–28.

How Can We Structure Ministry to Families?

Given the profound influence families have on every aspect of our lives, how can we develop Christian ministry strategies that honor and support that influence and mend the church/family gap? There are scores of family ministry resources that attempt to answer that question. To help us make sense of the various ministry approaches, Timothy Paul Jones organized them into three general categories: *family-integrated*, *family-equipping*, and *family-based* ministry.[24]

Family-Integrated Approach

A movement of *family-integrated* churches, led by Scott Brown and others,[25] aggressively seeks to restore the authority of parents, particularly fathers, as the primary spiritual influence of their children. Family-integrated proponents strongly assert that age-segregated programming in churches and schools is responsible for the division in churches and the abdication of parental responsibility in the spiritual formation of their children.[26] Therefore, they eliminate age-specific ministries so that families attend all church programs together, with the exception of a few small groups that are focused on training Christian fathers to be spiritual heads of their households. The family-integrated church model honors fathers as the primary spiritual leaders of their families, and women serve in complementarian roles under their headship. Renfro admits that this may be difficult as "some men have no desire to fulfill God's expectation. If so, the family-integrated church is not for them."[27] Nevertheless, family-integrated churches are to be commended for taking an assertive approach to honoring families and leveraging parental influence in the everyday faith formation of their children. This approach can be successful for strong Christian families who share the same views of child discipline and women's roles in leadership.

One problem is that family-integrated church proponents condemn contemporary youth ministry, claiming there is no biblical basis for age-segregated ministry. However, a critical examination of first-century Hebrew

24. Timothy Paul Jones, ed., *Perspectives on Family Ministry: Three Views* (Nashville: B&H, 2009), 42–43.

25. Scott Brown, *A Weed in the Church: How a Culture of Age Segregation Is Destroying the Younger Generation, Fragmenting the Family, and Dividing the Church* (Wake Forest, NC: The National Center for Family-Integrated Churches, 2011); Paul Renfro, "Family-Integrated Ministry: Family-Driven Faith," in Jones, *Perspectives on Family Ministry*, 54–78.

26. Brown, *Weed in the Church*, 19; Renfro, "Family-Integrated Ministry," 55.

27. Renfro, "Family-Integrated Ministry," 74.

culture reveals that their educational model was age-graded, and Jesus was presumably functioning within that model when he called his group of young men (likely fifteen to twenty years old) to leave their families to follow him.[28] It is possible that Jesus and his disciples more closely resembled a youth group than a family-integrated church. Further, age-graded education was utilized very effectively by the church throughout history.[29]

Another difficulty with the family-integrated approach is that it undervalues peers as an important developmental influence. There is sufficient biblical evidence that faith is formed in friendship and mentoring relationships with people of similar age. There is also a large body of research indicating youth groups and same-age peers play a significant and unique role that complements and in some cases mediates family influence in adolescent spiritual formation.[30] By eliminating youth and children's ministry entirely, family-integrated churches have no clear mechanism for realistically engaging the broader culture with the mission of God or evangelizing youth and children in unchurched families.[31]

Family-Equipping Approach

The *family-equipping* ministry approach emphasizes that church and family are equal partners in faith formation and should work together in a naturally integrated manner.[32] Churches should intentionally focus on family programming and scale back on age-segregated programs. The principal focus is on empowering families while maintaining a commitment to adolescent spiritual development primarily through accessing and supporting parental influence.

This approach elevates the role of family influence in spiritual formation and empowers parents to assume the responsibility for their children's faith while acknowledging some benefits of same-age ministry. This approach could be particularly beneficial for churches that have a good number of strong families that desire more family worship opportunities and need support as primary disciple makers in their homes. A family-equipping approach may

---

28. Michael J. Wilkins, *Following the Master: A Biblical Theology of Discipleship* (Grand Rapids: Zondervan, 1992), 70–94; see also Brenda Snailum, "Integrating Intergenerational Ministry and Age-Specific Youth Ministry in Evangelical Churches: Maximizing Influence for Adolescent Spiritual Development" (PhD diss., Biola University, 2012), 217–21.

29. See Senter, *When God Shows Up*, for how God ministered to and through youth throughout church history.

30. Snailum, "Integrating Intergenerational Ministry Strategies," 9.

31. Brandon Shields, "Responses to Paul Renfro," in Jones, *Perspectives on Family Ministry*, 81.

32. Jay Strother, "Family-Equipping Ministry: Church and Home as Cochampions," in Jones, *Perspectives on Family Ministry*, 140–67.

be somewhat difficult for churches to implement since many people are accustomed to having youth and children's ministry programs in churches and schools. This approach may not be as effective at ministering to alternative forms of family and those who have unbelieving family members.

Family-Based Approach

Family-based youth ministry equips families and congregations to better facilitate faith formation among teens and children by leveraging existing youth and children's programs to empower parents to fulfill their responsibility for facilitating mature faith in their children, as well as establishing some new programs that cultivate an intergenerational ethos throughout the church.[33] This approach honors the powerful roles that families *and* youth ministries play in adolescent spiritual formation and offers a strategy for age-stratified churches to transition to a more intergenerational community. This approach would be useful for churches that have strong youth and children's programs but desire to make deeper connections with parents and families in order to maximize effectiveness. A risk of this model is that family ministry becomes just another program if it is not valued by all church leaders and parents, and consequently, the church will remain an age-segregated congregation that does not leverage family or intergenerational influence effectively.

The previous ministry approaches challenge us to expand our understanding of church and family. One problem they all have in common is that they view the church as a composite of nuclear families rather than the church *as* the family. Using this narrow definition of family may miss ministry opportunities to single-parent families, those whose spouses or parents do not attend church for various reasons, or those who have another form of family. It also overlooks the value of nonfamily adults and the broader faith community for faith formation.

Research shows that nonfamily adults are an important stream of influence, as are peers and youth groups. Each stream of influence—parents, peers, and nonfamily adults—makes a unique contribution to faith formation but also interacts synergistically with the others, making the total greater than the sum of the parts. Any model of ministry that constricts one or more streams of influence risks truncating the spiritual development of everyone involved.[34] We need to minister in ways that honor all streams of influence within the

33. Mark DeVries, *Family-Based Youth Ministry* (Downers Grove, IL: InterVarsity, 2004).
34. Snailum, "Integrating Intergenerational Ministry Strategies," 15–16.

larger context of an intergenerational church family. In this way, churches *are* family, not merely comprising nuclear families or family programs.

Perhaps the best approach is an *intergenerational ministry* strategy that shares the responsibility for faith formation with the entire church and is characterized by mutual love, unity, loyalty, and interdependence among all of its members regardless of age or natural family status. We should cultivate a communal and inclusive mind-set and develop ways of relating to one another that truly values every generation and honors one another as siblings in the family of Christ. This radical reordering of relational priorities flies in the face of the generation gap and the cultural forces of ageism, individualism, and the idolization of nuclear family at work in many churches. We are challenged to expand our ecclesiology and understand how God ministers to and through *his* family. How differently would we behave if we truly saw members of different generations as siblings instead of operating from a paradigm characterized by a superior/inferior way of relating to one another? What should we do in a youth ministry context?

By understanding the influence families have, we can better minister to children and youth in ways that honor and support their families while strengthening the church family. There are a few important concepts that can guide us in this process:

1. Do not do this alone! This is a *whole church effort* that requires the leadership of the church to work together to cast vision, teach, and support one another over the long haul. Teamwork is essential.

2. Take seriously the idea of the church as Jesus's family. Honoring family influence does not necessarily mean transitioning to a "family ministry" program as much as it means creating an environment where everyone is included in Christ's family.

3. Have a humble vision for your ministry role. Youth ministry is one integral part of a complex system of faith formation. Honor and work together with parents and the rest of the church family to maximize effectiveness.

4. Be intentional about connecting to other ministries. Unity does not come easily. We must be diligent in identifying ways we can work with other ministry leaders and programs to create a more intergenerational ethos.

5. Honor and equip parents and families. It is important to view youth as part of their family system. Youth workers need to realize that parents are a primary influence and will be so for decades after their children are no longer in our programs. Can we honestly say we value the parents and families of the youth in our sphere of influence?

6. Understand your context. How you go about leveraging family influence and creating intergenerational community depends greatly on your context, culture, and situation in your church. Work with your leadership team to help your faith community develop as a strong spiritual *family* that welcomes everyone as a true family member and thus compensates for any lack of natural family support.

Questions and Activities

1. Write down ten characteristics about who you are. Look over your list of characteristics and put a percentage next to each one for how much nature (genetics) and nurture (environmental/social) played roles in developing them.

2. How can you enlist others who are willing to work toward building a team with an intergenerational vision? How can you promote new ways of relating to one another as brothers and sisters? How can you view your role as a youth worker within the larger church family with true humility?

3. How can all the ministries in your church work together to provide significant places for children, youth, and young adults to belong, serve, and grow?

4. Which of the various family ministry approaches was most familiar to you? Which was new? What are the strengths and weaknesses of the various approaches?

5. Perform a search for articles on family ministry and make a note of what principles are emphasized and what the author is working to address and correct.

Further Reading

Garland, Diana. *Family Ministry: A Comprehensive Guide*. Downers Grove, IL: InterVarsity, 2012.

Joiner, Reggie. *Think Orange: Imagine the Impact When Church and Family Collide*. Colorado Springs: David C. Cook, 2009.

Nel, Malan. "The Inclusive-Congregational Approach to Youth Ministry." In *Four Views on Youth Ministry and the Church*, edited by Mark Senter, 1–38. Grand Rapids: Zondervan, 2001.

16

God's Equipping Pattern for Youth and Young Adult Ministry

KEN CASTOR

> Every church struggles with the challenge of passing on the
> meaning of faith to each succeeding generation.
>
> —George Hunter III, *The Celtic Way of Evangelism*

Samuel dismissed him: "Surely he is too young." His brother criticized him:
"What are you doing here? You should be at home!" King Saul wanted him to
wear his suit of armor: "This is how we are supposed to do it. We've always
done it this way." With that, David picked up five smooth stones and slew a
giant misconception about generational leadership.

Each generation is tempted to resort to familiar customs rather than
take a posture that allows younger generations to embrace a life-changing,
world-shaking vitality of faith. Yet the story of David reveals a remarkable
truth about countless other youth and young adults: God intends to equip
the younger generations to lead.[1]

Older generations have historically struggled to treat younger people as
equal partners in ministry. While not maliciously intended, many congregations

---

1. See 1 Sam. 16–17: God had proven this during David's defense of the flock, his administration of the family business, and certainly his remarkable stand against Goliath.

inadvertently create scenarios where youth never feel as if they are an integral part of the family. Their traditional behaviors unintentionally omit young people from the table. As has been observed, "We are far more likely to consider youth as objects of ministry rather than agents of ministry; people to be ministered to rather than people Jesus has called into ministry in their own right."[2] The resulting perception is that we have a next-generation exodus.[3]

It might be a misdirected question to ask why young people are leaving the church. Perhaps we need to answer a deeper question of whether those young people were ever actually a part of the church in the first place. Just as David was not invited to the battle (1 Sam. 17:15, 20), those young people who appeared to be so active in our programs may never actually have been invited to be full participants in mission.[4] While they may have attended age-specific ministry programs, many of them were not invited to be active, contributing, and *significant* parts of the body. Many young people have unwittingly been separated from the multigenerational community during their most spiritually formative years.

The scope of this chapter is not to add debris to the perceived demise of young adult involvement in established churches in North America. Instead, the aim of this chapter is to provide a constructive framework for operative ministry with youth and young adults that results in the generational perpetuation of faith in Jesus Christ. This constructive perspective stems from the unremitting plan that God initiated: the sharing of faith to successive generations. In that hopeful and confident tone, this chapter seeks to propose the basic pattern that enables youth and young adults to receive the baton of the church's mission from older generations. Like a relay race, God's blueprint for discipleship and evangelism historically has been the generational handoff of faith and leadership.[5]

The pattern looks like this: People who have been equipped in faith and equipped to lead in the practice of faith inevitably pass those two factors on to the generation that follows them. Led by God's Spirit, this catalytic formula repeats itself throughout history:

$$eq(f) + eq(l) \rightarrow g(e)$$

2. Kenda Dean, *Starting Right: Thinking Theologically about Youth Ministry* (Grand Rapids: Zondervan, 2001), 30.

3. Robert Wuthnow, *After the Baby Boom: How Twenty- and Thirty-Somethings Are Shaping the Future of American Religion* (Princeton: Princeton University Press, 2007), 214.

4. David Setran, *Spiritual Formation in Emerging Adulthood: A Practical Theology for College and Young Adult Ministry* (Grand Rapids: Baker Academic, 2013), 16–17.

5. Ken Castor, "Enabling Generational Transference of Ministry Leadership in the Local Congregation" (PhD diss., Trinity Western University, 2010).

Equipping (eq) the next generation in faith (f) in Jesus Christ plus equipping (eq) them in the leadership (l) of that faith translates into generative (g) empowerment (e) of faith and leadership. Both in principle and practice, this simple blueprint is God's recurring pattern throughout Scripture. As Francis Chan has noted, "From the start, God's design has been for every single disciple of Jesus to make disciples who make disciples who make disciples until the gospel spreads to all peoples."[6] So while contemporary leaders may toil to decipher and implement the latest, elaborate, age-targeted models, there is need to remember that God has already been proactively addressing generational issues for quite some time.

Equipping Generative Faith and Leadership: In Scripture

Youth and young adult ministry might seem to be a relatively new phenomenon, but God has been intentionally pursuing young people since the events of Genesis 3. Once the need for salvific ministry arose, *next* generations have been both the focus of God's mission and the means by which God has chosen to accomplish it (Gen. 3:15). This process has been repeated perpetually throughout history, from the great *shema* to the Great Commission.

In both the Old and New Testaments, God ordains his followers with an inherent mission of equipping the next generations to embrace and spread the good news of Jesus. As God worked to solidify the identity and mission of his people, God conveyed a generational vision: that God's principles and character be passed on to children and grandchildren so that future people would come to know God.[7] In this scope, God's people covenanted to keep the next generations at the forefront of their entire practice of ministry. For example, the writer of Psalm 78 declares determinedly, "We will not hide these truths from our children but will tell the next generation the glorious deeds of the Lord . . . even the children not yet born—that they in turn might teach their children." The psalmist's vision reflects a transmitted pattern:

Our ancestors → us → our children → their children → their children

Whether it was Abraham steadfastly believing in God's plans for Isaac, Moses transferring public authority to Joshua, Samuel anointing David, or Elijah deliberately giving his mantle to Elisha, biblical leaders who were

6. Francis Chan, *Multiply: Disciples Making Disciples* (Colorado Springs: David C. Cook, 2012), 7.

7. E.g., Gen. 17:7; Exod. 3:15; Deut. 6:4–9; 7:9; Isa. 53:10–12.

faithful to God regularly searched for next-generation leaders whom they could trust with God's calling.[8] A typical framework for the generational handoff of faith and leadership emerges throughout the Old Testament:[9]

- Effective generational leaders exhibited genuine relationship with God.
- The next generation was intentionally given high-level opportunity to lead.
- Younger-generation leaders humbly partnered in mission with the older-generation leaders.
- Transfer of leadership authority and vision involved a trusting relational core.
- Sharing leadership was altruistic—for the sake of the community.

The Psalms overflow with these concepts. "One generation shall commend your works to another, and shall declare your mighty acts," one psalmist appeals (145:4). The writer of Psalm 71, who has become old and gray, begs God to allow him to equip a new generation. Psalm 102 is written specifically so that older generations will hand over the responsibility of praising the Lord. Other psalms, like Psalm 22, keep future generations in their sights.[10]

Admittedly, there were times when the transfer of ministry leadership was haphazard at best. In the book of Judges, for instance, it seems a miracle that a lineage of faith survived, as one generation after another failed to follow God. But scattered throughout the Old Testament, from Genesis 9 to Proverbs 2 to Joel 1, the theme of generative empowerment is recurrent. No matter the geography, the cultural climate, or the administrative structures, the generational equipping of ministry has always been an integral aspect to God's redemptive mission.[11]

Equipping generative faith and leadership was central to Jesus's approach with his disciples, many of whom were young adults. Jesus commissioned them with his authority and empowered them with his Spirit so that they could make disciples of others (Matt. 28:19–20; John 13:34–35; Acts 1:8). Through this group of young followers, Jesus drafted the world-changing blueprint of disciples who were to make disciples.[12]

---

8. E.g., Gen. 22; Deut. 1:38; 3:28; 5:1–3; 31:4; 32:44; 34:9; 1 Sam. 16:13; 1 Kings 19:19.

9. Castor, "Enabling Generational Transference," 80–81.

10. E.g., Pss. 22:30–31; 45:17; 71:18; 79:13; 89:1; 102:18; 145:3–7.

11. See Castor, "Enabling Generational Transference," 76–77.

12. See Rick Lawrence, *Jesus-Centered Youth Ministry: Moving from Jesus-Plus to Jesus-Only* (Colorado Springs: Group, 2014), 115–19.

In the first Christian communities, older men and women were instructed to mentor and encourage young people (Titus 2:1–6).[13] Barnabas, Peter, John, Priscilla and Aquila, and hosts of others actively equipped younger leaders. And Paul, perhaps more personally than anyone else, understood the need to resolutely hand off faith and leadership to emerging leaders. He learned this truth directly from Barnabas, who had received opportunity to lead from the disciples—who had been equipped by Jesus. This enabled Paul to see next-generation leaders like Timothy and Titus as essential to the spread of the gospel for generations to come. Paul apprenticed young adults, called them to a high-capacity commitment to Christ, and gave them extensive leadership opportunities (1 Tim. 4:12).[14] He commissioned many young adults to raise up other emerging leaders who would then perpetuate the generative process themselves.[15]

Jesus → disciples → Barnabas → Paul → Timothy → leaders → others

Throughout Scripture, the generational pattern of faith and leadership was shaped not by scripted programs but on the truth of disciple making.[16] Paul wrote, "Follow my example, as I follow the example of Christ" (1 Cor. 11:1 NIV), and "Whatever you have learned or received or heard from me, or seen in me—put it into practice" (Phil. 4:9 NIV). Like the passing of a baton, the early church believed that older and younger persons alike had an obligation to serve Christ as partners. Passages like Romans 16 or Colossians 4 serve as a generational testament to the intergenerational cooperation and shared leadership of the early church.[17]

This leads us to some practical considerations about ministry today:

- A local church should keep next-generation mission as its focus—it could be said that the next generation is always the most important generation in the church.
- A local church should embrace contextualized, adaptive methods that give youth and young adults opportunity to lead as central partners in the development of vision, strategy, and oversight of ministry endeavors.

13. See Castor, "Enabling Generational Transference," 76.
14. See ibid., 92.
15. See J. Oswald Sanders, *Paul the Leader* (Colorado Springs: NavPress, 1984), 181.
16. "Making disciples is far more than a program. It is the mission of our lives. It defines us. A disciple is a disciple maker." Chan, *Multiply*, 31.
17. E.g., Acts 2:41–47; Eph. 4:1–12; Titus 2:1–8; 1 John 2:7–14.

- A local church should emphasize a daily lifestyle of faith that intentionally encourages and champions young people.

Utilizing these scriptural foundations, a series of interviews examined leaders of churches across North America that exhibited effective empowerment of next-generation leaders.[18] While each of these churches had unique leadership structures, ministry models, target communities, and historical backgrounds, several collective generative empowerment principles (GEPs) emerged.

Three Essentials for Generative Empowerment

Each church in the research project strongly emphasized three principles they believed were indispensable to generative faith and leadership. In other words, these were the "essentials" they believed had to exist in order to pass faith on to the next generation.

Essential #1: Jesus-Centered Character

Both older and younger generations must center their lives on Jesus. Each congregation in the study highlighted this singular posture as the most essential aspect for the empowerment of future generations. Every other aspect that encourages effective youth and young adult ministry stems from those who are passionately formed by Jesus.

> Though your job description may give you oversight only over the youth or young adult programming, your calling actually involves shepherding both the younger and older generations in your local community to grow closer to Jesus so that the next several generations might possess a Jesus-centered faith.

In the interviews, one pastor suggested that older people who are being shaped by Jesus naturally foster a desire to invest in younger people. He also suggested that younger people who are being shaped by Jesus develop an inner longing to be cultivated by older leaders. Jesus, by his very personal work through his Spirit, burdens people with a desire to see the next generations grow closer to him.[19]

In his book *Jesus-Centered Youth Ministry*, Rick Lawrence has suggested that a next-generation ministry "of brilliant tips and techniques must now take a back seat to a youth ministry that is inexorably centered around Jesus."[20] With

18. See Castor, "Enabling Generational Transference."
19. Ibid., 126–29.
20. Lawrence, *Jesus-Centered Youth Ministry*, xvii.

this in mind, every generation, whether old or young, is on the same journey of growing closer to Jesus. If one generation does not reflect this heart, it becomes very difficult to transfer faith and leadership to the next generation.

Essential #2: Intentionality

Older generations must become extremely intentional about equipping younger people. A local church, even one with substantial resources, can't expect to hand off faith by merely creating an age-specific ministry group. The best-case scenario for enabling young people to embrace Jesus and take ownership of disciple-making leadership requires a full, strategic reorientation around the faith and leadership development of the next generations. This, said several of the interviewees, was God's instruction to the people of Israel. It involves shifting the focus of congregants from a "what do I get out of it" attitude toward a "how can we equip the next generation" attitude.

One pastor cited his own history in this regard. Veteran church leaders intentionally selected him as a leader while he was a teenager, provided him opportunity to grow as an intern, and then entrusted him with significant ministry leadership. Another church encouraged its older participants to prioritize investment in younger-generation leaders in order to leave a legacy of faith. Students in another church were strategically paired with older and younger people from the congregation so that they would have someone "ahead who is guiding them and someone behind them who they're guiding."[21] Another community urged people over fifty years of age to seek out younger-generation leaders to succeed their roles of influence in the community because "that is the biblical pattern."[22]

Intentional personal investment from older generations is essential for equipping young people with a long-term faith commitment. In their intense juncture of life, David Setran has suggested, young adults need older followers of Jesus to shape them through deliberate mentoring. "Mentors," he wrote, "help emerging adults open their eyes to God's work in their lives and in the world through attentiveness to the past, present, and future."[23]

Many churches might be well intentioned, but they may not be intentional. Your high calling as an architect of local ministry involves enabling older-generation followers of Jesus to deliberately reframe the expression

21. Castor, "Enabling Generational Transference," 130–32.
22. The pastor of this congregation shared that he needed to embolden many older members who were afraid of change. See ibid., 133.
23. Setran, *Spiritual Formation in Emerging Adulthood*, 206.

and practice of their faith in such a way that younger-generation people are equipped.

Essential #3: Environment of Encouragement

Young people must be embraced in church communities that exhibit an environment of encouragement. Lawrence has suggested, "Life is draining out of the Western church, and most youth ministries, because we're not setting the kind of growth environment that is conducive for disciples."[24] Older generations, by putting the needs and concerns of younger generations above their own, successfully encourage next generations to follow Jesus and effectively empower them to lead in faith.

One young pastor noted that people in his church "genuinely cared and loved" him and "wanted the best for him." He credited his congregation as having "a great spirit of affirmation" as part of their DNA. A church, he said, should be an "environment and hothouse where a leader can flourish and be developed."[25]

The youth pastor of another church spoke about "culture" and not "program." Traditions and structures are temporary, he argued, but a community of spiritual formation is the permanent practice. The "guts" of his church, he said, was to provide every person a place to belong and to serve. "And so," described the youth pastor, "we develop as a culture that you seek people out that are down the road [generationally] from you . . . that you can hand the baton to."[26]

Another interviewee said that his church "tries to create an atmosphere" where people receive "a lot of support, a lot encouragement." He explained, "I think that leadership is a place not to restrict people but to guide biblically . . . in order to encourage and empower. . . . Everybody, whether it's a six-year-old in my church . . . needs to learn how to lead [and] how to live out the gospel and flesh it out."[27]

Two Strategies

Each church in the GEP project demonstrated two key strategies in their pursuit of generative empowerment. These strategies were diverse in their

24. Lawrence, *Jesus-Centered Youth Ministry*, 17.
25. "We bring a lot of young [people] in," he stated, "and we encourage them, we put structures around them so they can succeed." Castor, "Enabling Generational Transference," 135–37.
26. Ibid., 137.
27. Ibid., 138–39.

methodologies but pervasive throughout the ministry approaches of each congregation.

Strategy #1: Training

The older generation should provide learner-based training for younger followers of Jesus. This involves relevant biblical and practical theological education, room for critical thinking, and provision for extensive on-the-job learning activities (such as apprenticeships, participations, missions practice, etc.).[28]

Strategy #2: Opportunity

The older generation should "step under" the younger generation by giving youth opportunity to lead. Just as there is a moment when a parent must give the car keys to their sixteen-year-old or a moment when the first runner must hand the baton to the second runner, so older leaders must provide younger leaders with a chance to practice significant ministry.[29]

Three Traits of Generative Empowerment

How do you know if your church is effectively equipping young people in faith and leadership? The interviews yielded several measureable traits.[30]

Trait #1: Generational Interaction

Congregations that are centered on Jesus and intentional about developing and encouraging the next generations observe an abundance of interaction between older and younger generations. Many of the generational segmentation issues that plague much of the North American church culture today are overcome naturally, not forcibly, by the fruit of the GEP Essentials and Strategies.

Trait #2: Missional Mind-Set

The foundations for generative empowerment are also demonstrated in the partnership of younger people with older generations in the mission of a church. As one interviewee stated, "We're not here to do the same thing every week. . . . We're here to accomplish a purpose."

28. Ibid., 139–40.
29. Ibid., 140–42.
30. Ibid., 142–44.

Trait #3: Recognition of Gifting

Finally, generative faith and leadership will recognize the emerging giftedness of younger followers of Jesus.[31] Upon the foundation of a Jesus-centered character, the talent of individuals called into leadership can be identified and harnessed through effective training and opportunity. Setran notes, "A growing awareness of spiritual and natural gifts represents a means by which emerging adults can see how God, in his providence, has wired them for fruitful service in church and world (1 Cor. 12:11)."[32]

Two Generative Empowerment Obstacles

The churches studied in this GEP project were not immune from facing obstacles that, if allowed to fester, could inhibit younger generations from following Jesus. Two significant obstacles emerged from the project interviews.

Obstacle #1: Possessive Leadership

The GEP project leaders frequently lamented older-generation leaders who failed to release youth and young adults to shape directions and initiatives in ministry.[33] The temptation to hold onto power, rather than handing off leadership, can be overwhelming.

- Control: For some older leaders, the desire for control darkens their willingness to let younger leaders take the reins.
- Judgmental attitudes: Judgmental attitudes create scenarios where the generations don't trust one another and are therefore tempted to turn inward.
- Ecclesial ceilings: Many older leaders fail to intentionally step aside (or "under") so that younger leaders receive opportunity to partner in mission and exercise their gifting. As a result, young adults "hit their head" on the feet of older adults.

Obstacle #2: Paradigmatic Challenge

Generations operate from different paradigmatic lenses, filters by which the world is understood. Paradigmatic challenges can wreak havoc within

31. Setran, *Spiritual Formation in Emerging Adulthood*, 130.
32. Castor, "Enabling Generational Transference," 142–44.
33. Ibid., 146–52.

congregations that fail to focus on Jesus, fail to intentionally reorient ministry toward younger-generation paradigms, and fail to be environments where encouragement is a prevailing value.

To combat this, a congregation should remember to adapt their own inclinations toward a "learner-based" approach for younger people. Younger generations process information differently than their parents and grandparents. Therefore, instead of trying in vain to get young people to agree with them, the priority of older influencers should be to enable the next generations to grow deeply in a relationship with Jesus. This simple but profound posture trusts Jesus to filter and shape a younger person's practice within their unique contextual perspective.

Equipping Generative Faith and Leadership in Your Community

As indicated above, the generative empowerment of faith and leadership does not result from the application of latest ministry trends or methods. With this in mind, the following list is intended to be not a "how to" formula but merely a simple set of ideas. These are tools that, when used by leaders and young adults who have a Jesus-centered character, could serve to equip generative faith and leadership.

- Evaluate via a GEP filter. The question has often been posed: "Will the next generation follow in our steps?" But this isn't a fair question. Instead, the question should be reframed: "Will the next generation follow in the steps of Jesus?"
- Create encouragement. Become the community that is known for embracing and equipping youth and young adults. Invite students over for lunch, raise money to pay for their college costs, and enjoy lots of laughter together. For a twist, try a "games" day where the youth or young adults invite the older generation to teach their long-loved board or card games.
- Study 1 Samuel 17 via a generational lens. With multiple generations, study "David in Saul's armor." What relevant generational leadership issues do you see in this story?
- Remember what it was like. In a small-group setting, ask older followers of Jesus to recall what it was like as a teenager (1) when an adult gave them an opportunity to lead and (2) when an adult wouldn't let them do something, but they chose to do it instead.

- GEP self-reflection: Ask leaders what GEPs are already exhibited in your ministry. Brainstorm how could you strengthen/enhance/capitalize on these GEPs.
- Self-reflection about obstacles: What obstacles are currently (or could in the future be) rearing their ugly head? What might your ministry be inadvertently doing that could hinder youth or young adults from personally embracing faith and leadership? Brainstorm some ways that your ministry team could address these obstacles.

Questions and Activities

1. What is one thing you'd like the younger generation of your church to know about the older generation and vice versa?
2. In what ways are youth and young adults inspired by older generations? How could you be a catalyst for inspirational activities in your church?
3. How could the younger generations show thankfulness to the older generations?
4. If you grew up in church, what did that church do well with regard to generative empowerment? If you were to implement some of the principles in this chapter, which one(s) would it be?
5. We can learn a great deal from older generations. Find five older adults from various age groups and interview them about their own faith development and the role of the church in their lives.

Further Reading

Castor, Ken. *Grow Down: How to Build a Jesus-Centered Faith*. Loveland, CO: Group, 2014.

Chan, Francis. *Multiply: Disciples Making Disciples*. Colorado Springs: David C. Cook, 2012.

Myers, Jeff. *Grow Together: The Forgotten Story of How Uniting the Generations Unleashes Epic Spiritual Potential*. Manitou Springs, CO: Summit Ministries, 2014.

Powell, Kara, Brad Griffin, and Cheryl Crawford. *Sticky Faith: Youth Worker Edition; Practical Ideas to Nurture Long-Term Faith in Teenagers*. Grand Rapids: Zondervan, 2011.

Rainer, Thom S., and Sam S. Rainer III. *Essential Church? Reclaiming a Generation of Dropouts*. Nashville: B&H, 2008.

17

Toward a Curriculum Theory of Educational Technology

MARK HAYSE

Educational technology arguably began with the invention of the first alphabet—tools that empowered the symbolic aspects of teaching and learning. Likewise, books and paper are educational technologies, as are printing presses and pencils, slates, blackboards, dry erase boards, copy machines, and overhead projectors—each, in its turn, brought new energy to teaching and learning, even while threatening to overturn so-called traditional educational methods.

Digital tools now occupy the space that old analog tools, such as audio recordings and filmstrips, once held. Yesterday's innovations become tomorrow's "old school." Online learning management systems (i.e., Blackboard or Moodle) have captured educational imaginations at high schools, colleges, and seminaries, and educators turn mainstream technologies (i.e., social media) toward teaching and learning. New educational technologies and platforms proliferate faster than any teacher or student can navigate, much less master. And churches and ministries quickly put new technology to use without much consideration to its role in learning and spiritual formation.

The educational technology discussion is a complex, *curricular* discussion. For example, consider the conversation about explicit, implicit, and null curriculum (see chap. 5). The explicit curriculum publicly identifies the topic under consideration "out loud and on purpose." In contrast, the implicit curriculum operates as a "hidden" curriculum "beneath the surface and behind the scenes." The null curriculum teaches by "silence, censorship, and omission."[1] Now, consider this discussion about explicit, implicit, and null curriculum in terms of educational technology. Often, educators in schools say things to parents and kids such as: "Keep up with the newest technologies, or you'll get left behind in the global marketplace! Everyone needs to use technology in order to succeed!" These words constitute the explicit curriculum of educational technology, and ministries feel similar pressure to keep up and adopt the latest technology to stay connected.

The implicit curriculum of educational technology is subtler and harder to identify, however: "Using technology is 'normal.' It's 'just what we do now.' Faster and more efficient technology is always better." Typically, teachers send these messages subtly rather than overtly, by attitude rather than with words. These messages constitute the implicit curriculum of educational technology. The null curriculum of educational technology is the hardest of all to identify because it is taught by silence and omission. Hard questions about technology's use in ministry settings typically remain unasked, such as: "Should we question technology—even as we use it? Is technology 'neutral'? When we use it, what do we lose, and what do we gain? Is that tradeoff worth it?"

This chapter aims to ask hard questions about educational technology, the use of technology for teaching. These questions can equip readers to think deeper about learning, faith formation, and educational technology. Many proponents of educational technology tend to think of it in terms of a *tabula rasa* (blank slate). However, critics recognize that educational technology is anything but a blank slate. To these persons, the medium matters as much as the message—perhaps more so. Furthermore, these critics often speak with a historical perspective that transcends twenty-first-century digital developments. Their arguments are old arguments, yet they can speak persuasively to the teachers and students of today.[2]

It may seem strange to critique the use of technology in education in this digitally saturated world. The rise of technology as an integral part of life has outpaced research on how it is shaping our thinking and values. We've embraced Google and GPS without considering the conditioning effects they have on memory, spatial thinking, and other ways we interact.[2]

1. Elliot W. Eisner, *The Educational Imagination: On the Design and Evaluation of School Programs*, 3rd ed. (Upper Saddle River, NJ: Prentice Hall, 2002).
2. Four studies done in 2011 suggest that people who have access to search engines tend to remember fewer facts and less information overall because they know they can find the answer easily using the internet. See Betsy Sparrow, Jenny Liu, and Daniel M. Wegner, "Google Effects

Digging Deeper into the Implicit Curriculum

In the midst of modern education in the United States, John Dewey wrote that students often pick up a form of "collateral learning" in their educational experiences.[3] There is the lesson *taught to* students, and then there is the lesson *caught by* students. In other words, students learn much, much more than that which the explicit curriculum intends to teach. From Dewey's perspective, the educational environment teaches "enduring attitudes . . . likes and dislikes" in a way that lesson plans do not. Dewey argues that these collateral attitudes about learning are "fundamentally what count in the future" for student success.

> Intuitively, every teacher knows this about "collateral learning." Think about a classroom or education experience you had that fostered a love for learning in you. Identify similar moments in your spiritual life. What teacher or group fostered an excitement for learning more about Jesus, the Bible, and growing spiritually? What was the long-term effect of that excitement in your spiritual life?

Other curriculum theorists pick up Dewey's discussion about collateral learning, reframing it in terms of the implicit curriculum. For example, Philip Jackson argues that the collateral learning of students tends to follow the subtleties of educational "crowds, praise, and power."[4] Thus, students will tend to accept the priority of educational technology in direct proportion to how many use it, sing its praises, and require its use. Teachers are not much different; just as they may take for granted straight rows of chairs facing the front as part of a classroom, they may also imagine that the use of classroom technology is necessary and inevitable. Those who minister to the next generation may take for granted that such a program will quickly embrace and use the coolest technology and software.

Maxine Greene once dramatically warned that the implicit curriculum compels students to embrace "an unthinking, nonreflective acceptance of what is presented as a social destiny."[5] These strong words resonate today when one considers the current state of affairs concerning educational technology as integral to our social destiny. The economic pressure regarding school funding, tuition, and getting a job has created a climate where few now stop to think critically about their use of technology. Instead, they tend to unquestioningly accept its use as the status quo for daily living and learning.

---

on Memory: Cognitive Consequences of Having Information at Our Fingertips," *Science* 333 (August 5, 2011), 776–78, http://scholar.harvard.edu/files/dwegner/files/sparrow_et_al._2011.pdf.

3. John Dewey, *Experience and Education* (New York: Touchstone, 1938), 48–49.

4. Philip W. Jackson, *Life in Classrooms* (New York: Holt, Rinehart and Winston, 1968), 33–36.

5. Maxine Greene, introduction to *The Hidden Curriculum and Moral Education: Deception or Discovery?*, ed. Henry Giroux and David Purpel (Berkeley: McCutchan, 1983), 1–5.

Historical Views on Educational Technology

In the 1960s, B. F. Skinner described a "technological" approach to teaching that today strongly influences educational efforts to create measurable outcomes and high accountability.[6] To Skinner, effective education stems from the scientific understanding of behavioral reinforcement. Any so-called art of teaching is reducible to a teacher's expertise in shaping student behavior because that is what brings about learning. In short, Skinner views education as a technical process.

In this, Skinner is not alone—far from it. Before Skinner, Ralph Tyler famously argued that curriculum should focus on behavioral objectives in order to produce measurable student outcomes.[7] Across the industrial and technological revolutions of the nineteenth and twentieth centuries, educators like Skinner and Tyler viewed education through technical lenses. In this way, the computer serves as a contemporary emblem of their commitment. Skinner foresaw a day when technical approaches would dominate education.[8] One need only review the recent No Child Left Behind Act in order to see that public education in the United States places its hope in digital technology for virtual salvation.[9]

You can see the parallels to our current context. Almost all conversations about the value of a college education center on "getting a job" in the future. Schools evaluate their teaching effectiveness by a systematic analysis of how well schools met their predetermined and measurable objectives. In what ways is there a similar technological approach to learning in Christian ministry settings?

On the other hand, historical critics argue that educational technology undermines certain educational aims, even as it supports others. For example, educational technology promises to simplify teaching and learning—but does it deliver? To some critics, computer technology is "oversold and underused" in the classroom.[10] Schools clamor to update their classrooms with the latest technology even as they struggle to implement its effective use. Never-ending technological upgrades trap teachers and students on a treadmill of time-heavy distraction from nobler educational pursuits.

6. B. F. Skinner, "Review Lecture: The Technology of Teaching," *Proceedings of the Royal Society of London, Series B, Biological Sciences* 162, no. 989 (1965): 427–43.

7. Ralph W. Tyler, *Basic Principles of Curriculum and Instruction* (Chicago: University of Chicago Press, 1949).

8. Skinner, "Review Lecture," 443.

9. US Department of Education, "No Child Left Behind," 2001, http://www.ed.gov/nclb/landing.jhtml.

10. Larry Cuban, *Oversold and Underused: Computers in the Classroom* (Cambridge, MA: Harvard University Press, 2001).

Some theorists lament that the constraints of educational technology tend to limit the creativity and imagination of its users.[11] Steve Jobs, former CEO of Apple, was a "low-tech parent," limiting his children's use and dependency on iPads and computers.[12] Teachers and students often spend more time learning how to operate technology and less time trying to accomplish things that the technology fails to address. The same can happen in ministry settings.

Educational technology implicitly supports a curricular agenda that values efficiency, predictability, transmission, measurement, and control above all.[13] As a machine is, so a machine does. In the final analysis, critics all ask the same question: "What is *lost* by the use of educational technology?" That's a helpful question for Christian workers to ask as well.

To be fair, other experts see great promise in the use of educational technology. Some say technology can increase the use of imagination and creative expression.[14] Early critics in the 1990s believed that technology could enrich the breadth and depth of human spirit rather than reducing users to robotic computer users.[15] They envisioned an era in which educational technology facilitated the safe exchange of ideas, the sharing of personal experience and perspectives, a sense of familiarity with others, and the cultivation of a collaborative spirit.[16] The recent developments of social media and teaching apps on smartphones and tablets have taken this promise to its highest heights—so far.

Widespread access to broadband internet now allows those once isolated from one another to move closer to a vision of global community. Anyone

11. Michael W. Apple, "Teaching and Technology: The Hidden Effects of Computers on Teachers and Students," in *The Curriculum: Problems, Politics, and Possibilities*, ed. Landon E. Beyer and Michael W. Apple (Albany, NY: State University of New York Press, 1988), 289–311.

12. Nick Bilton, "Steve Jobs Was a Low-Tech Parent," *New York Times*, September 10, 2014, http://www.nytimes.com/2014/09/11/fashion/steve-jobs-apple-was-a-low-tech-parent.html.

13. Ted T. Aoki, "Interests, Knowledge and Evaluation: Alternative Approaches to Curriculum Evaluation," in *Paradigms Regained: The Uses of Illuminative, Semiotic, and Post-modern Criticism as Modes of Inquiry in Educational Technology*, ed. Denis Hlynka and John C. Belland (Englewood Cliffs, NJ: Educational Technology, 1991), 65–81.

14. Elliot W. Eisner, "What Can Education Learn from the Arts about the Practice of Education?," in *Reimagining Schools: The Selected Works of Elliot W. Eisner*, ed. Elliot W. Eisner (New York: Routledge, 2005), 205–14.

15. John W. Murphy and John T. Pardeck, "The Technological World-View and the Responsible Use of Computers in the Classroom," in Hlynka and Belland, *Paradigms Regained*, 385–99.

16. Gary M. Boyd, "Emancipative Educational Technology," in Hlynka and Belland, *Paradigms Regained*, 83–92. Also Joshua Meyrowitz, "Taking McLuhan and 'Medium Theory' Seriously: Technological Change and the Evolution of Education," in *Technology and the Future of Schooling: Ninety-Fifth Yearbook of the National Society for the Study of Education, Part II*, ed. Stephen T. Kerr (Chicago: University of Chicago Press, 1996), 73–110.

who uses current social media tools in order to exchange thoughts, images, and videos can see how these hopes have come to fruition. In contrast to others, these historic supporters ask: "What is *gained* by the use of educational technology?"

Questioning Educational Technology: Then and Now

Hard questions must be asked of the "techno-utopianism" that we are currently in. To that end, theorists such as Marshall McLuhan pose questions that probe the advantages and disadvantages of using technology. Shane Hipps has drawn heavily from McLuhan's theory in the book *The Hidden Power of Electronic Culture: How Media Shapes Faith, the Gospel, and Church*.[17] McLuhan's now-classic "tetrad" (four perspectives) proves very useful for this discussion:[18]

- When using educational technology, what does it *enhance*? What aspect of a student's experience does it intensify?
- What does educational technology *render obsolete*? What "old ways" of teaching and learning are displaced by "new ways"?
- What does educational technology *retrieve*? What educational experience does it recover or reintroduce to students?
- What does educational technology *reverse*? How does it change when pushed to an extreme?

McLuhan applies his tetrad to computer technologies, but it's also useful to think about the purposes of Christian ministries. In what way does technology enhance, render obsolete, retrieve, or reverse important elements of spiritual faith and understanding?

McLuhan argues that the computer (and by extension, the internet) *enhances* the retrieval of data.[19] At the same time, the computer/internet renders physical library storage facilities and systems *obsolete*, at least in some sense. The computer/internet *retrieves* the individual's ability to work encyclopedically in a new way, even though it threatens to *reverse* the computer/

17. Shane Hipps, *The Hidden Power of Electronic Culture: How Media Shapes Faith, the Gospel, and Church* (Grand Rapids: Zondervan/Youth Specialties, 2006).

18. Marshall McLuhan and Eric McLuhan, *Laws of Media: The New Science* (Toronto: University of Toronto Press, 1988).

19. Marshall McLuhan, *Understanding Media: The Extensions of Man* (1964; repr., Cambridge, MA: MIT Press, 1994).

internet into a closed source of "data for sale" instead of an "open access repository" that is free of charge to all. Many regard McLuhan as a media and technology prophet. His questions prove helpful and broadly applicable for all kinds of evaluative processes for those involved in ministry.

Don Ihde asked only two questions of computer technology:

1. What kind of thinking does technology *amplify*?
2. What kind of thinking does technology *reduce*?[20]

In response to his own questions, Ihde argues that computer technology facilitates a type of thinking about truth in analytical ways—as data, bits, and categories—rather than as an integrated whole.

This argument parallels Nicholas Carr's more recent work in *The Shallows: What the Internet Is Doing to Our Brains*.[21] Using a neurological argument, Carr asserts that rapid browsing between text, image, and video on computer and smartphone screens seems to inhibit one's ability to think deeply with sustained contemplation. Whether one agrees with these theorists or not, their questions deserve careful consideration.

Ruben R. Puentedura's SAMR (Substitution, Augmentation, Modification, Redefinition) model adopts a more practical posture toward educational technology.[22] He asks four questions about when to use educational technology, and for what purpose:

Substitution: How can educational technology substitute for another educational tool, with *no* change in function?

Augmentation: How can educational technology substitute for another educational tool, with an *improvement* in function?

Modification: How can educational technology allow for the *redesign* of a learning task?

Redefinition: How can educational technology allow for the *creation* of new learning tasks that were previously inconceivable?

In Puentedura's model, the first two questions target the *enhancement* of teaching and learning through using educational technology. They modify something that already exists. The last two questions target the

---

20. Don Ihde, *Technics and Praxis* (Dordrecht, Netherlands: D. Reidel, 1979).

21. Nicholas Carr, *The Shallows: What the Internet Is Doing to Our Brains* (New York: W. W. Norton, 2010).

22. Ruben R. Puentedura, "Transformation, Technology, and Education," 2006, http://hippasus .com/resources/tte/.

transformation of teaching and learning through using educational technology. They add something new to that which already exists. Puentedura contends that educators should understand why and how they will use educational technology, rather than using it simply "because they can."

> Puentedura's model is helpful for Christian workers when considering using technology-based methods. If you use technology, are you changing the teaching and learning functions in any way? Is there an improvement in instruction? In what ways does it redesign the method? Does it offer something creative and new for learning or spiritual growth? Does it connect with students and their lives in helpful or deeper ways?

In contrast, Audrey Watters raises an alarm about the potential repercussions of educational technology.[23] Watters speaks with a sharp and irreverent voice—but it cannot be easily dismissed. Even though she believes in the value of educational technology, she also believes that the corporate-industrial element to technology creates as many problems as it solves.

Innovation. When companies create new technologies, do their products create new ways of teaching and learning, or merely new ways of making money? Do their products help students to find and express their own unique voices, or do their products mute differences by reducing avenues for self-expression?

Open source. Contemporary technologies promise to provide students with equal access to the tools of success. In many cases, however, this access is not open, public, or free. Thus, a "digital divide" between affluent and poor students threatens to push them further apart instead of bringing them closer together.

Gender. Watters notes that men dominate STEM (Science, Technology, Engineering, and Math) fields.[24] Watters contends that men end up "explaining" (read: controlling) the internet disproportionally to women. In this way, a digital divide threatens to intensify the disempowerment of female students.

Some may read Watters and say, "What's the big deal? That's just the way it is." However, Watters demonstrates the power of asking hard questions about what is taken for granted. The culture that surrounds technology threatens to remake students in its own image.

Nancy K. Baym argues that technology is much more complicated than most folks realize. She says that although "machines do have effects," those effects do not determine how technology is used.[25] For example, Baym argues

23. Audrey Watters, *The Monsters of Education Technology*, 2014, http://monsters.hackedu cation.com.

24. See also Claire Cain Miller, "Technology's Man Problem," *The New York Times*, April 5, 2014, http://www.nytimes.com/2014/04/06/technology/technologys-man-problem.html.

25. Nancy K. Baym, *Personal Connections in the Digital Age* (Cambridge: Polity, 2010), 152.

that computers can help people to find and deepen the social connection that they crave, even though computers can create distance between people too. Baym asks questions like these:

How does technology both support and strain the practices of communication and community building?

How do people adapt technology for uses beyond its original purpose (such as the invention of text messaging shorthand for the quick communication of emotional experience)?

As Baym questions technology, she explores its impact on society—and by extension, on teaching and learning in a digital age.

In contrast to Baym's optimistic tone, Sherry Turkle adopts a more pessimistic stance toward technology, communication, and community building. Turkle analyzes the ways in which technology strains human intimacy, arguing that "in text, messaging, and e-mail, you hide as much as you show."[26] She also expresses concern that digital communication may dull or displace a person's taste for face-to-face intimacy. Turkle's questions raise concern for a vision of education that requires the presence of an embodied community:

Connection: "Does virtual intimacy degrade our experience of the other kind, and indeed, of all encounters, of any kind?"[27]

Communication: Do digital social networks flatten communication, conditioning us for superficial friendships that are "so often predicated on rapid response rather than reflection?"[28]

In the spirit of McLuhan, Turkle cites Winston Churchill, who said not once but twice, "We shape our buildings, and afterwards our buildings shape us."[29] Turkle could have said just as easily, "We design our technology, and afterward our technology redesigns us." The title of Turkle's book tellingly broadcasts her convictions—*Alone Together: Why We Expect More from Technology and Less from Each Other.*

A chapter on educational technology should teach readers how to question their own assumption, rather than providing a top-ten list of "hottest educational apps." Digital technologies possess notoriously short shelf lives.

---

26. Sherry Turkle, *Alone Together: Why We Expect More from Technology and Less from Each Other* (New York: Basic Books, 2011), 207.

27. Ibid., 12.

28. Ibid., 17.

29. Ibid., 310n.

One's ability to navigate the waters of educational technology depends first on the ability to think critically, not on the ability to upgrade your system.

Questions and Activities

1. What have you heard teachers say about the value of educational technology in ministry settings? Based on this chapter, what important issues do educators fail to discuss about educational technology?
2. What attitudes do you hold toward the use of technology in your personal life? Positive, negative, or a mixture of both?
3. How does technology help or inhibit your learning? Can you give some examples from this past week? How can the use of educational technology strengthen or weaken your own disciple-forming work in ministry?
4. What does educational technology do well? Do poorly?
5. Does technology tend to increase or decrease the quality of your friendships? Your compassion for others? Your sense of right and wrong? Your desire to know Jesus better?

Further Reading

Detweiler, Craig. *iGods: How Technology Shapes Our Spiritual and Social Lives*. Grand Rapids: Brazos, 2013.

Dyer, John. *From the Garden to the City: The Redeeming and Corrupting Power of Technology*. Grand Rapids: Kregel, 2011.

Hipps, Shane. *The Hidden Power of Electronic Culture: How Media Shapes Faith, the Gospel, and Church*. Grand Rapids: Zondervan/Youth Specialties, 2006.

Schultze, Quentin J. *High-Tech Worship? Using Presentational Technologies Wisely*. Grand Rapids: Baker Books, 2004.

SECTION FOUR

METHODS FOR CHRISTIAN TEACHING

The most visible aspect of teaching is at the point of contact between teacher and student, commonly called *methods*. Effective Christian teachers possess and use a wide array of methods to better teach the full range of learners and to better integrate application and learning transfer beyond the lesson. In recent years, the emphasis has been on lecture as the almost exclusive method for teaching young people. However, the interactive and visual social media world and a critique about youth ministry's outcomes are forcing Christian leaders to seek various methods that immediately connect with the lives and interests of students.

This section covers the most prominent methods for teaching the next generation and gives particular attention to simulations and outdoor learning, which have a long history of effectiveness but are often underutilized. Teaching the Bible, discussing, and speaking to large groups remain the primary methods for teaching the next generation. The chapters in this section help readers understand these methods and establish guidelines for their effective use in ministry contexts.

Marlene LeFever's *Creative Teaching Methods: Be an Effective Christian Teacher* (Colorado Springs: David C. Cook, 1997) is a helpful resource for the many methods not covered in this section that are worth further attention.

18

Teaching the Bible So Young People Will Learn

DUFFY ROBBINS

The Smosh.com website called it "22 Ridiculous Name Misspellings That Prove Starbucks Is Just Messing with Us," and their photo gallery of Starbucks cups with customers' names horribly butchered by overly busy baristas made the headline seem entirely plausible. A quick survey showed some fairly amusing and creative renderings of common names: "Alan," spelled as "Alien"; "Oliver" spelled as "All Over"; "Whitney" as "Whiney"; and "Margaux" as "Marabcdefg." But surely one of the best was the picture of a coffee cup showing the name "Cark" scrawled with the standard Starbucks Sharpie pen and a caption explaining that the customer had given his name as "Marc with a 'c.'"

If nothing else, by this point in our text, it has surely become clear to any reader that *communication is difficult*—whether you are a coffee addict giving the barista your name or a youth worker trying to communicate to teenagers the Name above all names. Teaching the Bible to the next generations is a challenge; it's not impossible, but it is difficult. Even when one thinks it clear and obvious and the truths self-evident and "so obvious that even a child could understand," it's quite stunning how often the message is garbled and lost in translation. Creative, thoughtful youth workers, sincere and passionate Sunday school teachers, learned and articulate preachers on a regular basis offer what they believe is a clear proclamation of the name of Jesus. But what their youth groups, Sunday school classes, and young congregations hear is muddled and confused. Were there a photograph and a caption, it might well read, "Jesus, with a 'Gee, this is hard!'"

This is not a new problem, newly emerging on the youth ministry horizon, and—spoiler alert—it is unlikely that reading and carefully applying the principles of this book will make it an *old* problem that we no longer need to worry about. It's an ongoing challenge that has to be taken seriously. Many a Christian worker has launched into ministry thinking, "How hard can this be? I love young people, I love Jesus, I love the Bible, I sort of feel like I have the gift of *teaching*," only to crash back to earth when they decide, "I still love teenagers, I still love Jesus, and I still love the Bible, but my young people don't seem to have the gift of *learning*."

Reading, Writing, and Redemption

That's not to say that teaching the Bible is precisely like teaching every other random academic subject. To begin with, the last comment most Christian workers want to hear from a fifteen-year-old in the youth group is: "Wow, the way you do Bible study reminds me of how bored I get at school!" But, more important, there's a substantial difference between the types of content we teach when we're teaching God's Word and the types of content we teach when we're teaching about participles or medieval history. It's possible to live a long and happy life without knowing how to calculate the area within a trapezoid. Being ignorant or ill-informed about Jesus Christ is a neglect that misses the Source of life itself (John 4:13).[1]

When teaching the Bible to the next generations we're talking about a unique *subject matter*—Jesus, the Son of God—drawing from a unique *source*—the Bible, which is the Word of God (2 Tim. 3:16). We're talking about *goals* that are unique: the goal in teaching the Bible is not just education,

---

1. As Christians, we begin our teaching task with three critical assumptions. (1) We believe young people are creations of God, made in his likeness (Gen. 1:26), body *and* mind—not merely manipulated by bodily impulses or physical and cultural realities, but moral agents with the capacity to think, know, and will. (2) We believe that this God-given capacity has been tragically marred and damaged by sin (Rom. 1:18–32), an inherent flaw that affects both the way we learn and what we do with what we learn, especially with respect to truth about the God who made us (1 Cor. 2:14–16). (3) We believe that the great need of our students is a Spirit-transacted change that comes through a relationship with Jesus Christ (Rom. 12:1–2). For more on this, see my book, Duffy Robbins, *This Way to Youth Ministry: An Introduction to the Adventure* (Grand Rapids: Zondervan/Youth Specialties Academic, 2004), 187–89.

memorization of facts, or accumulation of truth; it's the transformation that comes in response and application of those truths (Rom. 12:2; James 1:22–25). And we're talking about a *spiritual agency* that goes beyond the teacher, the teaching space, the curricular resources, and the student, an agency that comes through the work and person of the Holy Spirit (cf. Isa. 59:21; Luke 12:12; John 16:7b–8, 13; 14:26; 1 Cor. 2:11b–14; Titus 3:5–7; 1 John 2:20).[2]

In short, what we are talking about is a strategic and critical alliance between the Christian worker and the Spirit of God. It is the teacher who teaches, but without the Spirit to "guide [our students] . . . into all the truth" (John 16:13), to convict our students of sin (John 16:8), and convince them of righteousness (John 16:13), our effort is bankrupt, no more capable of igniting the fires of passion for God than plastic logs in an electric fireplace. The lesson may look good, and it may even provide a little light, but don't expect a lot of warmth from it.[3]

John Milton Gregory was not just the president of the University of Illinois at Urbana-Champaign, he was also a Christian who showed a deep burden for effectively communicating biblical truth. Indeed, it was that burden that led him to combine his keen mind as an educator and his warm heart as an evangelist to write a book originally published in 1856 that he called *The Seven Laws of Teaching*.[4]

Good communication is good communication, and one could argue that certain principles of effective instruction are universal. In fact, it's not difficult to find clear examples of all of Gregory's Seven Laws of Teaching in the pages of Scripture. Whether it's Nathan's use of story to bring David to repentance after his adultery with Bathsheba (2 Sam. 12:1–7), God's use of the potter's house to help Jeremiah understand his dominion over Israel (Jer. 18:1–6), Jesus's use of parables and questions to provoke the minds of his audience (Matt. 10:10–13; 17:25), or Paul's appeals to the witness of his own personal lifestyle to testify to the truth of his teaching (1 Cor. 11:1; 1 Thess. 2:5–8), all of it can be vividly linked to one of the Seven Laws. While

2. Thyra Cameron and James Swezey, "Educating in the Spirit: An Examination of the Person and Role of the Holy Spirit in Christian School Education (Part One)," *Journal of the International Christian Community for Teacher Education* 10, no. 1 (2015), available at http://icctejournal.org/issues/v10i1/v10i1-cameron-swezey/.

3. The apostle Paul gives a very thorough explanation of the Spirit's essential work in our teaching ministry in 1 Cor. 2:9–14. See also his prayer in Eph. 1:18, "that the eyes of your heart may be *enlightened in order that you may know* the hope to which he has called you, the riches of his glorious inheritance in the saints" (emphasis added).

4. John Milton Gregory, *The Seven Laws of Teaching* (Boston: Congregational Sunday School and Bible Society, 1856).

it may be that effective youth workers will go beyond the Seven Laws in their Bible teaching, if they are truly wise, they had better not stop short of the Seven Laws in their Bible teaching.

Seven Laws of Learning

This chapter, then, is offered as a primer, an introduction to those seven basic principles, with some attention to practical application in the context of Bible teaching and youth ministry.

The Law of the Teacher: "The teacher must know that which he would teach." [5]

This is the first and most basic of all the laws of teaching. And, in some ways, it's the most intuitive. The first question we ask of any teacher is, *Do they know what they're talking about?*

There is a reason John begins his pastoral letter with a word of personal testimony.

> That which was from the beginning, which *we have heard*, which *we have seen* with our eyes, which *we looked upon* and have *touched with our hands*, concerning the word of life—the life was made manifest, and we have seen it, and testify to it and proclaim to you the eternal life, which was with the Father and was made manifest to us—*that which we have seen and heard* we proclaim also to you, so that you too may have fellowship with us; and indeed our fellowship is with the Father and with his Son Jesus Christ. And we are writing these things so that our joy may be complete. (1 John 1:1–4, emphasis added)

We can't teach what we don't know any more than we can give what we don't have or return from some place we've never been. We must know that which we would teach.

What does that mean in practical terms?

1. *Be authentic.* First of all, by God's grace and through the power of his Spirit, seek to practice what you teach. Our students need to believe that, in some sense, *we have heard, we have seen, we have looked at,* and *we have touched.* Ultimately, the power of the apostle Paul's ministry was not that he said, "*Listen* to me," but that he could say, "*Imitate* me" (1 Cor. 11:1).

5. Ibid., 16. Gregory summarizes his law this way: "A teacher must be one who knows the lesson or truth to be taught" (46).

That doesn't mean we have to be perfect, but it does mean we have to be in pursuit (Phil. 3:12–17).[6]

2. *Do your homework.* Do good, sound biblical exegesis so that you can speak with confidence about what the Word is teaching. Be sure you've considered some of the tough questions that might be raised by a text and are ready to address them should your students ask. Know how to pronounce names you will need to pronounce, for instance, biblical place names and proper names.

3. *Be organized.* Have a clear sense of your lesson plan. You're taking your students on a journey. If you want them to trust you as the guide, you'll need to communicate that you know where you're going. If you have media, check it in advance, and then double-check it. Make sure it works properly and that words are spelled correctly. We all make honest mistakes, but it doesn't enhance your credibility when the PowerPoint slide invites students to "Be filled with the Holy *Spit.*"

The Law of the Learner: "The learner must be interested in the truth to be learned."

The hardest part of teaching the Bible isn't *teaching* the Bible. The hardest part of teaching the Bible is getting teenagers to *listen and engage when you're teaching* the Bible. Remember the old question: If a tree falls in the forest and no one hears it, did it really make a sound? In one sense, that's the point of the second law of learning. If a youth worker leads a Bible study and no one hears it, did the youth worker *really* lead a Bible study?

Most of us are familiar with the old proverb, "You can lead a horse to water, but you can't make him drink." The Law of the Learner reminds us that even living water will be refused unless there is first of all thirst. Imagine answering a question that nobody's asking, preparing a feast for people who aren't hungry, coaching someone on the proper way to do *a* when they're perfectly happy with their *b* method, or giving the answer to the knock-knock joke without the "knock-knock" part or the question of who's there. It happens too often in congregational and youth ministry: we scratch hard where no one is itching.

One of the most basic principles of communication is that *the audience is sovereign* (1 Cor. 9:22–30).[7] We get to *lead* the Bible study; they get to

6. For more on this, see Doug Fields and Duffy Robbins, *Speaking to Teenagers* (Grand Rapids: Zondervan, 2007), chap. 4.

7. This is *not* to say the message or lesson is unimportant. It's simply to say that we can't have a very fruitful Bible study with a room full of teenagers unwilling to study the Bible.

vote whether they will *follow* our lead. And anyone who has done youth ministry for more than about twenty minutes will tell you that sometimes the vote is pretty close, and sometimes it doesn't go in our favor. When that happens, for all practical purposes, Bible study is over.

So how do we make the horses thirsty for biblical truth?

1. *Listen before you teach.* Make sure they understand that you understand. Use what they want to talk about as a bridge to bring them to what you're hoping to talk about. Use their questions to provoke interest in the Bible's answers. But don't try to manufacture easy questions or easy answers. Sometimes the most engaging element of Scripture is that it leads us into mystery and wonder.

2. *Be stubbornly committed to engagement.* Refuse to teach even a five-minute devotional without thinking through this basic question: *How am I going to engage the attention of my students?* Yes, it's hard work. But through creativity, resourcefulness, and sheer desperation, the youth ministry community has demonstrated remarkable ingenuity in answering this question. There are numerous websites and written resources that can introduce a novice Christian worker to some of these strategies, everything from movie clips to music, from art to object lessons, from case studies to dramas and melodramas, from simulation games to small groups, and from YouTube videos to stories about Starbucks name fails on Smosh.com.[8]

Resolve to never open a Bible study with these words: "Our topic for today is . . ." Not one single teenager in a youth group walks the halls of their school wondering, "What will this week's topic be in Bible study?"

3. *Become a curator of good strategies of engagement.* Not every good idea has to come from you. Effective teaching isn't about reinventing the wheel; it's about engaging students so that they'll be willing to get on board with what you wish to teach.

The Law of Language: "The language used in teaching must be common to teacher and learner."[9]

We all know the frustration: in a desire to use the new software, we consult the instruction manual, only to discover it is so poorly written that we need a second instruction manual to understand the first instruction manual! Our problem is not a lack of motivation; the horses are thirsty, and we really want

---

8. For ideas, see Helen Musick and Duffy Robbins, *Everyday Object Lessons* (Grand Rapids: Zondervan/Youth Specialties, 1998); Doug Fields, Laurie Polich, and Duffy Robbins, *Spontaneous Melodramas I and II* (Grand Rapids: Zondervan/Youth Specialties, 2000).

9. Gregory, *Seven Laws of Teaching*, 49.

to know this stuff. Nor is it a lack of credibility; we have every confidence that the author of the manual knew what he or she was talking about. No, our enterprise collapsed because, for all practical purposes, the manual was not written in a language common to both the teacher and the learner.

Youth workers, particularly those who have received formal training in seminary and Bible college, greatly benefit from learning the lexicon of the Christian tradition. Our faith is enriched by our understanding of terms like *justification*, *incarnation*, *atonement*, *ex nihilo*, and *imago Dei*. Unfortunately, when we take that vocabulary off campus, we discover that, like missionaries working in a distant culture, we are speaking a language that is unknown to the people we're trying to reach.

That doesn't mean we abandon these terms. To abandon this vocabulary would make it more difficult for us to engage in important theological conversations and rehearse valuable truths within our faith community. It would be like nuclear engineers who, in an effort to be better understood and considered less nerdy, decided to reduce themselves to conversations about how important it is to "keep that big radioactive thingy sleeping like a baby so it doesn't get all glowy." Concepts that are important and mission critical need to be maintained. But, at the same time, we need to figure out a way to translate those terms into a language that has meaning in the culture we're seeking to engage if we want them really to come to terms with the power of the gospel.[10]

Here are some practical suggestions.

1. *Be careful speaking Christianese.* Realize that most of today's adolescent population is illiterate when it comes to the Bible and to basic Christian terminology. They know little of the Bible, its customs, its geography, and its grand narrative. So, when you use these terms, translate them into a language they *do* understand. Don't assume your students speak this language. They don't.

2. *Use modern language versions of the biblical text.* It is unlikely your students speak King James English. Indeed, it's doubtful that thou dost. So stick with one of the many excellent modern translations.

If possible, provide Bibles for your students. This has the added benefit of providing each with a readable translation of the passage, and, at least as helpful, it guarantees that all eyes are seeing the same verse rendered

10. Kenda Dean discusses the difference between "inside the wall" conversations (the vocabulary we use in the church community) and "on the wall" conversations (the language we use outside the church community), and the vital importance of each. See Kenda Creasy Dean, *Almost Christian: What the Faith of Our Teenagers Is Telling the American Church* (New York: Oxford University Press, 2010), 113–14.

the same way. You can still encourage students to bring Bibles, but the reality is that many don't bring them. This just assures they *do* have a Bible to study.

For groups who are totally new to Bible study, it may be helpful to simply photocopy for each student the passage to be studied. For a fifteen-year-old teenager who isn't used to reading a Bible, it can be a big, scary book with a lot of really thin pages and a black cover that basically warns, "This book is holy, and you're not!" Sometimes that photocopied page, apart from the rest of the book, can diminish the intimidation factor. It also makes it easier for them to find the passage without wading through all sixty-six books.[11] Amplify the meaning of a verse by reading it from two or three different translations. Likewise, using a good paraphrase like Eugene Peterson's *The Message* can add color and texture to a biblical text.

3. *Invite students to paraphrase the passage.* After working through the passage in your group study, finish up by inviting students to make their own paraphrase of the passage. They can do a paraphrase in their own words, or you can assign them the task of paraphrasing in the language of a unique dialect: a computer geek, a jock, a surfer.

4. *Invite students to draw the passage.* It may help students to think more deeply about the actual words in the text if they are invited to translate the text not into words but into images.

The Law of the Lesson: "The truth to be taught must be learned through truth already known."[12]

Where are you right now as you read these words? A dorm room, a library, your bedroom at home, or maybe a coffee shop where some barista misspelled your name? Wherever it is, let's assume you're there by intention: you meant to be there. Now—and here's the important part—for you to enter that space you had to go through a sequence of steps. If you're in a dorm room, you had to enter the dorm. To enter the dorm, you had to enter the campus. To enter the campus you had to enter the town where your school is located. If you're an out-of-state student, you had to enter the state where that town is located. You get the idea: you couldn't get to location D without following the sequence of entering locations A, B, and C.

---

11. It's probably not a good long-term strategy. But we have to wade before we can dive, and wading happens at the shallow end of the pool. Additionally, college campus groups like InterVarsity and Cru use printouts that allow students to mark up the text while engaging in inductive study, or what some call "manuscript Bible study." For more, see http://manuscriptbiblestudy.com.

12. Gregory, *Seven Laws of Teaching,* 61.

The first Law of the Lesson reminds us that truth is sequential. We can't usher our students into truth C until they understand truth B, and they can't understand truth B until they understand truth A. So if we really want to teach the Bible in a way that will help our young people to learn, we have to start where they are—not where *we* are, and not where we *wish* they were. How many Bible studies and messages have missed the mark because of a lack of intention and caution in this regard! The teacher starts out with high hopes, which translates into high aim, which results in a Bible study that sails over the heads of everyone in the room. Every truth to be learned must be learned through a truth already known.

How does one give attention to this sequence in teaching the Bible?

1. *Make sure they understand truth A before you teach truth B*. One youth leader recalls completing a Bible study that explored some of the issues surrounding the gifts of the Holy Spirit (healing, tongues, prophecy, etc.). He had worked hard to explore what Scripture taught about these miraculous gifts. When the study was over and he was talking to students, one insightful sophomore girl came up and innocently commented, "That was really interesting tonight. Will you tell us what the Holy Spirit is sometime?" Don't teach on the second coming until they know about the first coming. Don't teach truth B until they understand truth A.

2. *Target your teaching*. One of the biggest mistakes we make in youth ministry programming is aiming at nothing. And we all know this: when we aim at nothing we're very likely to hit it.

Much of the language of the New Testament suggests that there are various levels of understanding and commitment (cf. Matt. 13:5–8). Consider this sampling of verses.

Jesus: "I have much more to say to you, more than you can now bear" (John 16:12 NIV).

Jesus: "As he was scattering the seed, some fell along the path, and the birds came and ate it up" (Matt. 13:4 NIV).

Paul: "I gave you milk, not solid food, for you were not yet ready for it. Indeed, you are still not ready" (1 Cor. 3:2 NIV).

The writer of Hebrews: "In fact, though by this time you ought to be teachers, you need someone to teach you the elementary truths of God's word all over again. You need milk, not solid food! Anyone who lives on milk, being still an infant, is not acquainted with the teaching about righteousness. But solid food is for the mature, who by constant use have trained themselves to distinguish good from evil" (Heb. 5:12–6:1 NIV).

Consider the following case study:

Jake showed up for Sunday night youth group prepared to lead the group in a program that consisted of a snack, a brief game or ice-breaker, worship, and a short Bible study with small-group discussion. Had all of the students in attendance been willing to buy into Jake's agenda, it might have worked out. But after only a few minutes of worship, it was clear that Heather's boyfriend, Walt, and his buddy, Marv, who were attending that night for the first time, had no intention of owning Jake's agenda. They were in the back of the room, texting each other and laughing about the messages that had been sent. As the Bible study dragged on, the disruptions and discipline problems grew worse and more disruptive.

Jake didn't want to ask these students to leave—after all, these were the students he and his team wanted to reach. On the other hand, some of his students were really eager to learn and participate in the study, and the disruptions were making that highly unlikely.

After several friendly and not-so-friendly pleas for the disinterested students to cease being disruptive, Jake reasoned that maybe he needed to change his tactics and more intentionally play to their interests. He knew that if the more committed students were bored, they would at least be bored politely. So, he decided to dumb down the study, making it shorter and more basic than he had planned. It wouldn't be as mealy as he had hoped, but what was the point of serving "meat" when several kids in the room, at least spiritually, didn't have an appetite for it? By the time he was nearing the end of the study, he decided to cut the discussion time altogether.

The evening finally ended, but it wasn't a very satisfying night. Marv and Walt left the room feeling bored and talking about never coming back. Heather went home feeling embarrassed that her boyfriend had been disruptive and that she had sort of played along. The students who really wanted to study the Word left feeling frustrated, and Jake left feeling discouraged and disheartened. He had just wasted a night trying unsuccessfully to entertain one group of students, and, in the process, he missed the opportunity to nurture another group of students. Because he hadn't targeted his programming carefully, he was playing to the lowest common spiritual denominator. He had aimed at nothing, and he had hit it dead-on.

We don't get angry at babies because they lack the ability to chew meat; we feed them milk until we can develop in them an appetite for something more. To be sure, biblical truth is an acquired taste. But spiritual growth and authentic maturity can come only with proper nutrition from the Word. A youth ministry that doesn't provide that is stunting the spiritual growth of its students. So, we need to provide both: meat for those who are willing to chew on it, and milk for those who are still in spiritual infancy.

3. *Serve in the program what you promise on the menu.* All programming, but teaching in particular, should be designed and branded (i.e., promoted on the youth group website, etc.) in such a way that both leaders and students understand the target audience. Students with scarcely an appetite for milk should know before the meeting if meat is on the menu. If the event is called Blast, and the program for the evening consists of a two-hour study of the Trinity, perhaps students could be forgiven for feeling there is a bit of a bait-and-switch in play.

However, what about the disinterested student who just shows up at Bible study with no awareness of the menu and no taste for spiritual food? As long as the disinterested student doesn't prevent others from being fed, that's fine. Targeted programming is not about the youth leader telling a student that they are *not* suited to a program or a specific teaching event. Having said that, if that student becomes disruptive, the youth leader must assume the responsibility of (a) not allowing that student to deter the growth of other students, and (b) not changing the teaching menu to cater to a junk-food spiritual appetite and dumbing down the nutrition for all the other students.

Most youth workers want to reach out to the maximum number of young people every week, so they feel compelled to do a program that appeals to some mythical, broad middle ground. The problem is still "if you aim at nothing, you'll hit it every time."

Ministries that target everybody seldom accomplish anything strategic for anybody.

The Law of the Lesson: "Excite and direct the self-activities of the learner, and tell him nothing that he can learn himself."[13]

The best way to nurture in someone a taste for Nutella is not by inviting them to come on a Sunday morning to sit in a small room so they can hear someone describe to them what it tastes like. The best way to help someone develop a taste for Nutella is by giving them a way to *taste it for themselves*. Young people are not likely to gain an appetite for Scripture by hearing other people describe it. We need to devise ways to help them taste it for themselves.

There have already been ample opportunities in this book for readers to reflect on various learning theories. We will not do that here. Suffice it to

---

13. Ibid., 83.

say that there are critics of an approach to teaching that puts the emphasis on self-discovery, an approach often described as *constructivism*.[14] But, at its best, this approach respects two essential elements of good teaching:

1. Content: the truth(s) to be taught
2. Process: the experiential element of teaching (methodology of teaching, application of the truths taught, etc.)

Jesus's charge to the Pharisees, "You are wrong, because you know neither the Scriptures [content] nor the power [process] of God" (Matt. 22:29), suggests that neither content nor process is sufficient on its own.[15] The Hebrew word for "to know" helps us understand that knowing goes deeper than mere information. The verb *to know* has a richer, wider meaning that ranges from recognizing good and evil (Gen. 3:22; 39:9; 1 Sam. 28:9), to the ability to perceive accurately (Gen. 19:33, 35; 1 Sam. 12:17), to the ability to discriminate and discern (Jon. 4:11), to growth that comes through experience (Josh. 23:14; Ps. 51:5; Isa. 59:12).

> **Young people are not likely to gain an appetite for Scripture by hearing other people describe it. We need to devise ways to help them taste it for themselves.**

So, how does one help a roomful of young people "taste and see" that the Lord is good (Ps. 34:8) in a way that respects both the nourishing truth and the truth tasted and digested? How can we teach in a way that will help them to *know*?

1. *Give them the tools, and show them where to dig.* Think of scriptural truth as treasure. The task of effective teaching is giving students direction about where to dig and then offering them tools with which to make the

---

14. It was Jerome Bruner's insights surrounding *discovery learning* that first suggested that when learners discover facts and conceptual relationships for themselves, the material is more usable and better retained than material that is merely collected and memorized. This is really the notion at the root of constructivism. Bruner strongly believed students learn best what they learn for themselves. Some critics (e.g., David Ausebel) complain that this approach wrongly supposes that learners *know* what they need to learn and that they will be *motivated* to learn what they need to learn. Others point out that such an approach is simply inappropriate for some subject areas and learning settings. Both of these criticisms have merit, but they still don't nullify the validity of Bruner's core insight. What is being proposed in this chapter is a hybrid approach that has come to be known as a *directed discovery* approach. For a fuller discussion of the learning theory behind this approach and its theoretical roots, see William R. Yount, *Created to Learn* (Nashville: Broadman & Holman, 1996), 196–205.

15. A fuller rationale is provided in my chapter, Duffy Robins, "Thinking Creatively: Beyond Schooling Perspectives in Curriculum," in *Starting Right: Thinking Theologically about Youth Ministry* (Grand Rapids: Zondervan/Youth Specialties Academic, 2001).

discovery. It's a way of making the search more engaging and the discovery more personal.

Jesus's own teaching ministry gives us vivid examples of this sort of deductive approach. He used such diverse teaching techniques as:

a. object lessons (John 4:1–42)

b. relational ministry (John 1:35–51)

c. problem solving (Mark 10:17–22)

d. conversation (Mark 10:27)

e. lecture (Matt. 5–7; John 14–16)

f. parables (John 10:1–21; 15:1–10)

g. teachable moment, teaching through experience (John 4:5–26)

h. illustrations, examples (Matt. 6:26–34)

i. simulation, symbols (John 13:1–20)

j. large and small groups (as many as five thousand, or as few as three)

k. modeling (Luke 18:15–17)[16]

Youth workers have invented and reinvented literally hundreds of other tools to help students explore and experience a biblical text: songwriting, art, drama, panel discussions, poetry (rap, limerick, etc.), case study, field trip, cartoons, graffiti, and many, many more.[17] Yes, it would be "easier," "quicker," and "more efficient" to just tell your students what they need to know. But they are more likely to value the treasure when they discover it for themselves.

2. *Vary your teaching methods.* There is still a good bit of skepticism about the value and effectiveness of addressing various learning styles in the course of a Bible study. But there is some evidence, both empirical and anecdotal (ask any youth worker), that teenagers learn in different ways. Some learn through listening, others through feeling, still others through doing, and some through thinking and reasoning.[18]

The problem is that teachers tend to teach *in the way they themselves prefer to learn.* Unfortunately, and predictably, that approach has roughly the same success rate as if we were determined to teach eagles to swim and turtles to

16. Robert Joseph Choun Jr., "Choosing and Using Creative Methods," in *The Christian Educator's Handbook on Teaching*, ed. Kenneth O. Gangel and Howard G. Hendricks (Wheaton: Victor, 1989), 166–68.

17. For more ideas, see Dan Lambert, "The World's Longest List of Teaching Methods," *Teaching That Makes a Difference* (Grand Rapids: Zondervan/Youth Specialties Academic, 2010), 147–62.

18. See chap. 8. See also Marlene LeFever, *Learning Styles: Reaching Everyone God Gave You to Teach* (Colorado Springs: David C. Cook, 2011).

fly. One size doesn't fit all. One teaching method doesn't work for every young person in the group. Wise youth workers will consider how to format their teaching so that each Bible study addresses the varied styles of learning.

Bottom line: the most memorable way to learn *not* to touch a hot stove is by touching a hot stove, not by hearing someone do a lesson on "heat and the essence of stove-ness." The second Law of the Lesson suggests that the best way to make biblical truth memorable for our students is *not* by teaching *about it* but by allowing them to touch and explore it for themselves.

Will that require guidance and instruction? Yes. This is not about throwing students in a room with a Bible and giving them instructions to "Find stuff that blesses you!" They will need a guide who knows where the treasure is buried. They will need someone who can provide for them tools with which to explore, and perhaps someone to help them recognize the treasure when they find it. They may even need someone who can make real for them the value of the search to begin with. But God has given us the treasure, and as students begin to discover it for themselves, they will hunger for more.

The Law of the Learning Process: "The learner must reproduce in his own mind the truth to be acquired."[19]

Parrots can repeat phrases: "Polly want a cracker." "Pretty boy." That doesn't mean they know who Polly is or understand the concept of a cracker, and it certainly doesn't mean they have carefully appraised the physical features of the person who cleans their cage and determined that they are, like, totally hot! This sixth Law of Teaching simply affirms that a learner hasn't really grasped a concept until he or she can articulate that concept in his or her own terms. Repetition doesn't necessarily equal recognition.

Any youth worker knows from experience that the biggest challenge in teaching the Bible is not getting young people to give the right answers; it's getting young people to translate those right answers into the real world. That's why the first Law of the Learning Process is so critical, especially in the climate of a church where there is such high value placed on learning biblical truth and passing along the faith once for all delivered to the saints. If we can't help them reproduce the ideas in their own minds, in their own words, and ultimately *in their own lives*, they will become numb to the nudging of truth. And that's a condition that soon grows into a hardened heart.

Practically speaking, how are we to flesh out this principle of learning? Here are some simple suggestions.

19. Gregory, *Seven Laws of Teaching*, 106.

1. *Ask good questions.* Stay away from yes or no questions that give clueless kids a 50 percent chance of dodging deeper discussion. Be willing to probe right answers with follow-up questions: "Why do you say that?" "Why couldn't it be this?" "How would you explain that to someone who doesn't believe in God?"

2. *Ask hard questions.* In our effort to make youth group a comfortable place, we too often ask questions with answers that are way too obvious. "What should Sally do when confronted with temptation? Pick one: (a) investigate further, (b) turn away from it, (c) click her heels together and repeat, 'There's no place like home,' or (d) ask, 'What would Taylor Swift do?'" Real life poses questions to our students that are much more difficult, and the real test of our teaching will be their ability to massage the message into the mess and muck of everyday life. While it's always kind of cool to hear students use theological words and concepts, let's force them to unpack those phrases by taking them on a trip into real-life issues.

3. *Practice the power of paraphrase.* Whether it be a principle, an idea, or a biblical passage, one of the most direct applications of this sixth law of learning is giving students an opportunity to paraphrase: "Okay, put this idea into your own words"; "Paraphrase this verse into the language of your friends"; "Turn to the person next to you and explain tonight's main lesson in your own words."

4. *Play dumb.* "Okay, suppose I had never heard of Jesus of Nazareth before. Based on what we've studied this morning in Philippians 2:5–11, how would you tell me who he is?"

We need to be alert. Just because students are using the same words we use and have memorized concepts we've taught does not mean they have learned anything. And when students don't learn and grow, they become disinterested quickly. In doing Bible study, we can heighten student interest by constantly coming back to an idea or a principle and saying in one form or another, "Now what does all this mean? *Put it in your own words.*"

> **Just because students are using the same words we use and have memorized concepts we've taught does not mean they have learned anything.**

The Law of the Learning Process: "*The completion, test, and confirmation of teaching must be made by reviews.*"[20]

Gregory emphasized the retention value of students reciting and repeating the truths they've learned. At some level, repeated words do begin to shape

20. Ibid., 119.

and form our values. Consider the way our culture's many varied and profane ways of referring to sexual intercourse have cheapened and degraded the way we think about this sacred and powerful form of human interaction.[21]

Scripture rather pointedly emphasizes that repeated phrases and words are not the ultimate goal (cf. "empty phrases" [Matt. 6:7]; and empty confessions [James 2:14–20]). The ultimate goal is transformation. So, how do we make this happen? How do we move our teaching beyond information to application? What follows are examples of strategies one could use as the closing elements of a lesson to help students examine their own lives in light of the Word:

1. Use a continuum, a line, and ask students to identify on that line where they are in terms of their obedience to a certain truth.
2. Ask students to identify something they are thankful for in this study.
3. Ask students to identify something they feel they need to confess based on this study.
4. Ask students to write down three specific actions they need to take based on what they've heard in this study.
5. Invite students to take a pledge or sign a covenant.
6. Do an "offering" in which instead of putting money on the plate, students are encouraged to write down on a piece of paper a commitment they are making as an offering to God.
7. Use a scale of one to ten to ask students to consider how they are doing in applying a certain truth.
8. Use images (faces, gears [i.e., stop, go, neutral, reverse], a light switch [i.e., off, on, dim, bright]) to help kids assess where they are in terms of obedience.
9. Ask students to write a letter from God to them, or a letter from themselves to God, based on what they've heard in this study.
10. Ask kids to identify one way their life will be different tomorrow because of a truth they've learned today.
11. Give students phrases to complete: "Because of what I have heard tonight I will _____." "If what God's Word says is true, then I need to _____." "After what I've heard here, I am thankful for _____."

21. The power of words to shape thinking has been a central theme in discussions of worldview and cultural exegesis. Cf. Brian J. Walsh and J. Richard Middleton, *The Transforming Vision: Shaping a Christian World View* (Downers Grove, IL: IVP Academic, 1984), 34; Donald Miller, *Blue Like Jazz* (Nashville: Thomas Nelson, 2002), 217.

12. Let students shape an inanimate object (paper clip, paper cup, pipe cleaner, Play-Doh, piece of paper) to allow them to verbalize their response to some truth.

13. If you are teaching a skill-oriented truth (sharing their faith, confronting a friend, etc.), let students role play how they will do it.

14. Make a list of ways students might respond to a truth, and ask them to circle two or three on the list.

15. Invite students to tell one another what decisions they've made, and invite them to pray together.

Perhaps the best way to summarize the point of this seventh Law of Teaching, and indeed the point of *all* the Seven Laws, is to reference a cartoon that shows a middle school youth leader standing in front of about a dozen bored, apathetic thirteen- to fifteen-year-olds. They are clearly disinterested. He is clearly earnest and hopeful. Holding out his Bible, he tries desperately to arouse some semblance of recognition, interest, or at least consciousness as he pleads, "So you see, young people, Levitical sacrifice really *is* a burning issue!" Actually, at the end of the day, it's not.

Surely one of the best ways to cultivate biblical truth in our lives is by building habits of application to practice doing what it teaches: not just repeated words but repeated deeds. In light of this, it's probably better to emphasize application over repetition. We teach God's Word so that our students might be formed into the likeness of Christ (2 Tim. 3:16–17).

Questions and Activities

1. If you ranked the Seven Laws, which two would be the most important ones, and why?

2. Which of the Seven Laws, are you already doing well? Which of the laws do you need to improve on?

3. Review the Seven Laws, and for each one write down the teacher that you have had who best exemplified that law in their teaching. Add a sentence as to why you picked that teacher and any effect you noticed in students' lives because of their teaching.

4. If you were to add one or two more "laws of the teacher" of your own, what would they be and why?

5. Imagine that a local church has asked you to create a two-minute video on the importance of teaching the Bible well. Based on the material

from this chapter, storyboard the scenes and script that you would use to make the video.

Further Reading

Fields, Doug, and Duffy Robbins. *Speaking to Teenagers: How to Think About, Create, and Deliver Effective Messages*. Grand Rapids: Zondervan/Youth Specialties, 2007.

Hendricks, Howard. *Teaching to Change Lives: Seven Proven Ways to Make Your Teaching Come Alive*. Colorado Springs: Multnomah, 1987.

19

The Value of Discussion

TROY W. TEMPLE

> In the midst of a generation screaming for answers, Christians are stuttering.
>
> —Howard Hendricks

When a discussion launches, it opens channels of both communication and learning. Too often, if not the majority of the time, dialogue is the target, and it's counted as a success if both parties simply talk. Maybe you remember the discussion with your parents that went something like this:

"Why?"

"Because I said so!"

Now, you won't find many who would call that a healthy discussion, but discussions like that occur every day. Students will question a teacher or youth group leader who only knows the "what" but is unable to explain the "why." Discussion is a teaching method that comes with great advantages that cannot be realized with the more common "one-way" teaching styles. A vibrant discussion is more than just talking; it opens hearts and relational lines.

Jesus used questions to stir up thoughts among his disciples. In the diverse city of Caesarea Philippi, Jesus asked his disciples who people said that he was. Jesus wasn't looking for new information; he posed the question so his disciples would think beyond the common religious laws. The disciples responded, and Jesus followed up his response with a more personal interaction. Peter's response was met with great affirmation and then a proclamation from Jesus (Matt. 16:13–19). The Gospels record numerous examples of how Jesus used questions to push the disciples to think deeply:

- Matthew 16:13—"Who do people say that the Son of Man is?"
- Matthew 22:20—"Whose likeness and inscription is this?"
- Mark 3:23—"How can Satan cast out Satan?"
- Luke 5:34—"Can you make wedding guests fast while the bridegroom is with them?"
- Luke 20:41—"How can they say that the Christ is David's son?"
- John 18:4—"Whom do you seek?"
- John 21:16–17—"Do you love me?"

The discussion method is rooted in a form of dialogue that was developed by Socrates, a Greek philosopher of the fifth century BC. He used a form of inquiry that led the student to think more critically as well as to discover new perspectives related to the line of questioning and ultimately to a personal resolution on the subject being discussed. The Socratic Method is as much, if not more, concerned about the process as with the outcome.

Discussion is an indispensable tool for those Christian leaders who want to teach well and to help their students grow in their ability to think and believe on their own. Healthy discussion includes dialogue or conversation between two or more people or groups of people that incorporates nonverbal communication as well. Consider these benefits of discussion:

1. *Discussion forces students to think and listen* to the others and weigh them against personal belief or prior convictions.
2. *Discussion helps students make application* of Scripture and theology to real-life situations or problems.
3. *Discussion builds on our desire to be known*, and a safe group discussion environment gives opportunity for various personality types to participate.
4. *Discussion invites variety*; everyone's experiences and perspectives add depth and help others see from various vantage points.
5. *Discussion serves as a learning barometer* where leaders can determine if students understand the material.

6. *Discussion helps to develop stronger community*. Shared experiences, "inside jokes," and poignant moments of caring for others create a cohesive solidarity that leads to spiritual change within a group.

Two theories from the field of psychology help us think about how to structure healthy discussions. Though there have been critiques and revisions, each informs conversations about learning processes.

Bloom's Taxonomy of Learning

Strong teaching is always guided by measurable objectives. Educational theorist Benjamin Bloom categorized cognitive learning into six levels to encourage a holistic approach to teaching and to offer a framework for setting educational goals and for prompting more complex and higher-ordered thinking. [1] His taxonomy helps us think about, create, and frame our questions to accomplish more than just rote answers. Far too often, discussion is used to lead students to regurgitate information or obvious answers while never truly weighing the value or applicability of the knowledge. The secret to productive discussion is the practice of asking good questions.

Let's take a look at how we can use Bloom's taxonomy as if we were teaching a lesson on Zacchaeus from Luke 19.

Level 1: Knowledge

The initial step in the learning process is demonstrated when students are able to recall or remember key information and ideas and foundational principles related to the topic. Before students are able to move on to higher levels of learning, they must demonstrate a grasp of the information related to the subject. If we ask students to define, identify, label, list, name, outline, or recall, we are asking a knowledge question.

Sample questions: What was Zacchaeus's occupation? In what city did the story take place? What did Zacchaeus do to get a better look at Jesus?

Level 2: Comprehension

Students should be able to demonstrate an understanding of the information through activities such as classifying, summarizing, illustrating, extending, describing, and rephrasing. If a student comprehends the material, he

---

1. Benjamin Bloom and David R. Krathwohl, *Taxonomy of Educational Objectives, Handbook 1: Cognitive Domain* (White Plains, NY: Longman, 1956), 62–200.

or she should be able to offer a basic explanation for the ideas, information, or principles involved.

Sample questions: What was Jesus's purpose for going to Zacchaeus's house? Would you consider Zacchaeus a well-liked man? Interpret Zacchaeus's response to Jesus's attention.

Level 3: Application

Students use their knowledge to solve problems and to apply to life situations. This is the first level of what Bloom categorized as the affective dimension, requiring emotional and empathetic effort on the part of the learner. Application questions ask students to choose, develop, solve, employ, identify, or plan in ways that require implementation of knowledge.

Sample questions: How would you respond to Zacchaeus? What would you highlight if you were to teach this story? What virtues from this story would you want your friends to show toward you?

Level 4: Analysis

Students should be able to break down information into parts or identify motives or causes related to people in a story. These crucial questions help students move beyond generalizations to make inferences and find evidence and support for various perspectives. Analytical questions ask students to compare, contrast, analyze, simplify, categorize, assume, and conclude.

Sample questions: What is the theme of this story? What is the relationship between Zacchaeus and the other people? Compare and contrast Zacchaeus's response with others who encountered Jesus in Luke.

Level 5: Synthesis

Students should be able to gather information and create new patterns or solutions using key action verbs such as build, create, design, invent, construct, improve, or develop.[2]

Sample questions: What would Zacchaeus's life have looked like after this scene? In what ways would he have lived differently? Develop a list of potential reasons that he wanted to see "who Jesus was." What might have happened if Zacchaeus had not climbed the tree?

2. An important revision to the taxonomy moved synthesis, or "Creating," to the highest level. For more, see Lorin W. Anderson et al., *A Taxonomy for Learning, Teaching and Assessing: A Revision of Bloom's Taxonomy of Educational Objectives* (New York: Longman, 2001).

Good discussion requires good questions, and good questions rarely happen without work. Dan Lambert identifies five types of questions.

1. *Closed questions* have definite answers, like "yes" or "no," and "true" or "false."
2. *Open questions* have more than one potential answer.
3. *Thought questions* require students to think and apply beyond the information in the lesson.
4. *Evaluation questions* push students to analyze and discover why something happened or what could have been different.
5. *Application questions* allow students to apply subject matter to their personal lives.

Dan Lambert, *Teaching That Makes a Difference* (Grand Rapids: Zondervan/ Youth Specialties Academic, 2004), 140–41.

Level 6: Evaluation

The final level concludes what Bloom labeled the psychomotor domain, where students make judgments about the information from previous levels. Some key action verbs for this level are: decide, judge, critique, justify, argue, explain, defend, evaluate, prove, and support.

Sample questions: How would someone try to defend the people's objection to Jesus's visit to Zacchaeus's house? Evaluate your own response when someone who has been mean to you comes to know Jesus and receives the gift of salvation. How are you involved in helping others see and follow Jesus? In what ways do you need to get a new perspective regarding who Jesus is?

Discussion and Maslow's Hierarchy of Personal Needs

Healthy discussion attends to the needs of those involved and connects with the motivations of those participating.[3] Though not overtly about teaching, Abraham Maslow's hierarchy offers the leader some handles to think about caring for one another during discussion, especially as it relates to discipleship purposes.[4]

3. Abraham H. Maslow, *Motivation and Personality* (New York: Harper & Row, 1954), 80–106.
4. Maslow developed this motivational theory to demonstrate what drives each person to pursue specific growth or goals. The first four levels are considered to be the basic needs that provide a foundation for healthy self-actualization, which he defined as "a person's desire for self-fulfillment, namely, to the tendency for [a person] to become actualized in what [he or she] is potentially." Abraham H. Maslow, "A Theory of Human Motivation," *Psychology Review* 50, no. 4 (1943): 382.

Shaping the Discussion

1. *Determine the objective.* It's critical to start any teaching method with the end in mind; discussion is as much about the process as it is the final conclusion.
2. *Write out your questions, putting deeper questions toward the end.* Be careful of closed questions as they tend to not promote application. Good discussions build on previous knowledge and processes.
3. *Introduce the topic, and state the discussion's goal.* This allows students to know the topic and participate more freely, since they know where it is heading.
4. *Determine the discussion starter.* Good discussions take some priming; students need to be drawn into the topic. This is an important element for a good discussion.
5. *Promote full participation.* Everyone in the discussion must be assured that they are expected to contribute and are free to add to the conversation. Discussion requires everyone to participate even if they don't consider themselves an expert on the topic.
6. *Stay on topic.* Most discussions produce tangents, but tangents can also derail a discussion, leaving it far off course from the intended outcome. Frequently, participants may suggest ideas that can be used for a later discussion. Assure group members that you will keep a list of topics for future discussion.
7. *No wrong responses.* The intention of a discussion should allow students to express thoughts or ideas related to the topic without fear of being ridiculed or rejected.
8. *Pause to reflect.* Periodically, take a minute to summarize where the discussion traveled and highlight one or two key thoughts to build on.

Physiological Needs

Maslow's first level identifies a person's basic physical needs—shelter, warmth, and food. Effective teachers understand the dramatic effect that environment can have on a good, well-intended discussion and how physiological and personal health issues affect learning.

Safety Needs

An essential element for any healthy discussion is the safety (security, structure, and stability) of the individuals who are participating. A productive discussion is realized when those involved have confidence that they will not be attacked verbally or have to act in inauthentic ways for their contribution to the dialogue. Good discussion leaders are able to monitor and ensure the safety of their groups by establishing and graciously maintaining discussion ground rules.

A nationwide research project discovered that growing youth ministries made sure their group was emotionally and socially "safe." Student leaders said they knew that each week they could be themselves, could express themselves freely, and that it wouldn't ever get "weird."[5]

Social Needs

Maslow proposes that when physical and safety needs are sufficiently met, the individual will long "for affectionate relations with people in general, namely, for a place in his group."[6] This dynamic can be observed in demographically diverse groups. A healthy discussion should seek to accentuate the commonalities and help group members develop a stronger social connection, especially across common social barriers. This "one another" aspect is a crucial litmus test for Christ-centered community (John 13:34; Eph. 4:13).

Esteem Needs

People have a desire to be confident and competent, and discussions can both develop and destroy this. The most productive discussions are discussions where each member has a healthy confidence and competence on the topic and understands how to contribute to reach the intended outcome. A poorly handled discussion can do such harm that a young person may never set foot in our ministry again for fear of future embarrassment or hurt.

People also have a desire for status within groups. This can look like someone dominating a discussion, speaking without really saying anything, or (more often) participating in order to feel valued as equally as the "popular" people in the group. When a student contributes value to a discussion, the group leader should take the opportunity to affirm and recognize the positive contribution. This builds confidence in the individual and helps him or her develop the competence needed to effectively participate in future discussions.

5. David Rahn and Terry Linhart, *Evangelism Remixed: Empowering Students for Courageous and Contagious Faith* (Grand Rapids: Zondervan/Youth Specialties, 2010).
6. Maslow, *Motivation and Personality*, 89.

Self-Actualization

In Maslow's hierarchy of needs, self-actualization is the pinnacle and refers to learners reaching a deeper awareness of who they are and who they are becoming. Good discussion allows participants to hear contrarian views, discuss these views with grace, and solidify their own views. They learn to accept themselves and others, develop openness and spontaneity, and appreciate others. People at this level have a composure that allows them to think critically, to know what to say, and to know when to say it.

Discussion within Talks

In our culture, the lecture (or "talk" or sermon) has often been considered a mundane approach to teaching and, in many cases, that reputation has been well earned. However, an effective lecture does not simply outline a topic in its entirety in an attempt to answer every possible question. Authors Stephen D. Brookfield and Stephen Preskill suggest several ways that discussion can be linked to a lecture that will add the critical elements for effective learning.[7]

Begin each session with a short set of key questions to whet the appetite of the students for more, thereby keeping them engaged. Rather than relying on the lecturer to make the first connections, students take the first steps to understand the topic.

End every lecture with a series of questions that your lecture has raised or left unanswered. Many teachers have been conditioned to offer a summary of the information covered, bringing an authoritative final word on the topic. However, many times learning would better be served by allowing students to contribute or write down questions that have yet to be answered or discussed. Failing to do so may miss the process and sabotage the opportunity for students to think critically and learn by navigating less obvious questions—leaving us to walk away with a "hope" that they learned something while we were talking.

Deliberately introduce periods of silence. Whether developing a lecture, discussion, or other method, pay attention to the moments of silence, and be sure to give students adequate time to consider the topic as a whole and particular questions or statements. Silence is not a lack of engagement; rather, it can be a more intense demonstration of engagement as the student

---

7. Stephen D. Brookfield and Stephen Preskill, *Discussion as a Way of Teaching: Tools and Techniques for Democratic Classrooms*, 2nd ed. (San Francisco: Jossey-Bass, 2005), 44.

takes time to think on the topic at hand more deeply before delivering a response. Tension is a great pedagogical tool, and silence is often tension's greatest ally.

Introduce buzz groups. Buzz groups are simply micro-discussion groups (of three or four students) used in short bursts during a lecture. These are particularly effective in involving everyone in the group.

Struggles in Using Discussion

Distractions. In small-group discussion with younger people, distractions and interruptions abound. It can be much more difficult to hide those distractions than in a large-group setting.

Overbearing group members. On any given night, "that person" can walk through the door. You know the one, the person who can talk about anything—and at great lengths. Discussions can be quickly sabotaged with one long story. When students dominate the conversation, the entire learning process can be completely lost.

Staying focused. One of the most frustrating aspects of leading a discussion is when the discussion wanders off subject for too long. Use reflective dialogue to both clarify what someone has said and refocus everyone on the topic.

The never-ending discussion. Discussion groups can sometimes seem to go on and on. When you lead a discussion, keep an eye on the time. When you have only ten to fifteen minutes left, start to draw it to a close with either a question to think about for the week or a quick summary of what you've learned.

Shy students. Astute leaders notice that often a discussion involves only about a third of their group. This doesn't mean the quiet students aren't thinking or don't have anything rich to say, but it will take intentionality to involve them. Breaking larger groups into smaller ones, using buzz groups, or making sure to ask other students to jump in will help involve more students.

Discussion is not simply a tool for effective teaching. Discussion is essential and must be a constant feature of any productive learning environment.

You can ask the buzz groups specific questions or one of the five questions that Brookfield and Preskill suggest. These work particularly well in the middle of a lecture.

- What's the touchiest statement you've heard so far?
- What's the most important point that's been made so far?
- What question would you most like to have answered regarding the topic today?
- What's the most unsupported point you've heard so far?
- Of all the ideas and points you've heard so far today, which is most obscure or ambiguous to you?

Discussion requires hard work from the teacher to keep students engaged and moving toward the chosen learning objective. If we do that, then we won't just be talking, we will be teaching.

Questions and Activities

1. How have you experienced the benefits and/or frustrations of leading group discussion?
2. Have you ever experienced a discussion where you felt unsafe to share or participate? Describe your experience.
3. What do think are the ideal environments for leading a group discussion?
4. Can discussions be truly effective without using questions? Why or why not?
5. Do discussions always need closure, or can they end with students having to consider more questions? Why or why not?

Further Reading

Brookfield, Stephen D., and Stephen Preskill. *Discussion as a Way of Teaching: Tools and Techniques for Democratic Classrooms*. 2nd ed. San Francisco: Jossey-Bass, 2005.

LeFever, Marlene. *Creative Teaching Methods: Be an Effective Christian Teacher*. Colorado Springs: David C. Cook, 1997.

Nyquist, James F., and Jack Kuhatschek. *Leading Bible Discussions*. Downers Grove, IL: InterVarsity, 1985.

20

Teaching Large Groups

JASON LANKER

No matter on which continent you observe ministry to young people, you will likely see a consistent and regular method: large-group teaching. That's because this teaching method has been prominent in church culture since the time of Jesus and the disciples.[1] This has several practical benefits. First, one sermon or talk can efficiently teach an entire group the same material. In addition, believers have found large-group teaching inspirational and valuable for their own spiritual growth. Finally, the content of a well-prepared sermon or talk serves as a gathering point for a community and informs a communal reflection afterward.

On the other hand, the actual outcomes from teaching a large group appear to be ineffective at times. That is, just because something is spoken from "up front" doesn't mean that it has been received. Also, with such regular use of technology, young people rarely spend more than seven minutes on one topic; so a thirty-minute (or more!) "talk" will definitely lose their attention.[2]

1. John Stott, *Between Two Worlds: The Challenge of Preaching Today* (Grand Rapids: Eerdmans, 1982), 15–49.

2. William W. Chaney, "Top-of-the-Hour Break Renews Attention Span," *The Teaching Professor* 19, no. 6 (2005): 1, 5.

Despite large-group teaching's long history and communal benefits, maybe it's time to find another method. Certainly, some have suggested this.[3] Although other creative forms of instruction are effective and beneficial to the development of students' faith, large-group teaching or speaking can have significant merits. For example, how many of us can recall a large-group teaching that grabbed us so deeply that our lives were changed from that moment? The question is: How did they do that? And, how can you teach like that as well?

Living the Message

First we need to realize that the book on how young people learn hasn't changed much in recent years. Youth like to learn by direct involvement and by a variety of methods. Yet the primary lens through which youth actually learn is a social one; they are watching adults who model the lessons (good or bad) in either structured or spontaneous avenues.[4] So, no matter the intended method or event, the foundation to any effective teaching is the character, demeanor, and responsiveness of the one teaching.

It follows, then, that when someone speaks in front of a large group, he or she *embodies* the message (with the potential for that to be helpful or detrimental) because "good teaching comes from the identity and integrity of the teacher."[5] If you think of Marshall McLuhan's famous quote, "The medium is the message,"[6] the example, demeanor, and character of the one speaking is part of what is being taught. Neil Postman says, "Each medium, like language itself, makes possible a unique mode of discourse by providing a new orientation for thought, for expression, for sensibility."[7] So, for instance, the passion and courage of the apostles contributed to their authority (Acts 4:13), something they had seen Jesus model in his teaching (Matt. 7:28–29). Unfortunately, personal zeal and creativity are too often lost when someone teaches a large group, and the lecture looks less like an interaction between real people and more like a banking transaction.

3. See Rick Lawrence, "The Problem with Youth Talks," *Church Leaders*, http://www.church leaders.com/youth/youth-leaders-how-tos/151657-the-problem-with-youth-talks.html.

4. Klaus Issler and Ronald Habermas, *How We Learn: A Christian Teacher's Guide to Educational Psychology* (Eugene, OR: Wipf and Stock, 2002). A group of Christian adult volunteers on a mission trip is a structured way of teaching. How they react to adversity, like a flat tire on a bus or a delay in travel due to bad weather, is more spontaneous.

5. Parker J. Palmer, *The Courage to Teach* (San Francisco: Jossey-Bass, 1998), 10.

6. Marshall McLuhan, *Understanding Media: The Extensions of Man* (Cambridge, MA: MIT Press, 1964).

7. Neil Postman, *Amusing Ourselves to Death* (New York: Penguin, 1984), 10.

Formation, Not Just Information

Historically, lecturing (a method including preaching and public speaking) was the primary way people received information until the invention of the printing press. It was the most effective means to get the same message to a community, and it remains central today even though people could get information on their own. Technological innovations like the internet and smartphones have removed the burden of information transfer from speakers. This in turn has freed teachers to focus on other benefits of lecturing. The lecture can now serve as an *affective* and *motivational* tool to arouse student interest in the subject matter. That's why lecture, or "presentation," is still a primary method for persuading others in boardrooms, auditoriums, and in online videos.

Unfortunately, we often don't give it the creative energy required to make it effective. Despite today's learners' active approach and social connectedness, large-group teaching can look like more like traditional transfer of information and less like a vital part of a vibrant community of learners. If we want to be effective, our large-group teaching times need to be times where we would, as John Stott wrote, "struggle to relate God's unchanging Word to our world . . . [and] refuse to sacrifice truth to relevance or relevance to truth; but resolve instead in equal measure to be faithful to Scripture and pertinent to today."[8]

This chapter intends to champion the role and task of preaching and teaching in large-group settings. We can't afford to shrink from the hard work required to be a good public speaker. Even if speaking in public frightens us (it's the most common fear),[9] or it's not our gift, we need to learn how to use this method and include the task of preaching (or speaking) as an essential teaching tool to help our youth to better love both God and others. Fortunately, there is renewed attention to large-group teaching in the last few years, and there are many great new resources available, some of which are listed at the end of this chapter. Most of them center on four practices that are important elements for success in teaching large groups in Christian ministries—knowing God, knowing your audience, knowing how to prepare, and knowing how to deliver.

Knowing God

As has been stated throughout this textbook, teaching is part of a larger discipleship process, a ministry of the Holy Spirit in the lives of others

---

8. Stott, *Between Two Worlds*, 144.

9. Glenn Croston, "The Thing We Fear More Than Death," *Psychology Today*, November 29, 2012, https://www.psychologytoday.com/blog/the-real-story-risk/201211/the-thing-we-fear-more-death.

(Rom. 12:6–8; 1 Cor. 12:28; Eph. 4:1–12). As Christian teachers we should have a vital relationship with God and his Word. But too often the work of ministry can take our time, energy, and interest, and there are seasons where teachers can become little more than performers—sometimes with spiritual lives in decay. Good Christian teaching flows out of a depth within where our relationship with God and our mature understanding of his Word connect deeply with our audience and their lives.

This requires biblical understanding that is adequate to the teaching task before us. In a field where various curricula are quickly reproduced for last-minute use, we can end up teaching while not having done any of the study for ourselves. This does not do us or our listeners much good. We need to start with knowing God and his Word in ways that will address the needs of the day. We need to know that "the Bible is neither that of a philosophical system nor a system of moral truths. On the contrary, the unified sum and substance of the Bible is theodramatic: it is all about God's word and God's deeds, accomplished by his 'two hands' (Son and Spirit) and about what we should say and do in response."[10]

Knowing Your Audience

It seems equally as obvious that after knowing God, we should know our audience, but it does not come as automatically as we may think. Too many teachers fail before they begin; they focus solely on the message before assessing the needs of their audience. When this happens, they end up answering questions from the text that their audience often doesn't care about. This means that the audience is uninterested in what is being said before the speaker even begins. Paying attention to both the developmental, cultural, and spiritual aspects of your audience will help you have a greater connection and greater impact.[11]

Think about a group that you lead or teach. How do the group members think? What is their culture? What concerns them? How are they doing at making moral decisions? What are their opinions of Jesus Christ, and would they say they are in a growing relationship with him? What are they learning? What are their families like? How do they describe the quality of their friendships? What are the nature and focal points of their interactions with media? What do they think about regularly when they

---

10. Kevin J. Vanhoozer, "Lost in Interpretation? Truth, Scripture, and Hermeneutics," *Journal of the Evangelical Theological Society* 48, no. 1 (2005): 101.
11. Urie Bronfenbrenner, ed., *Making Human Beings Human: Bioecological Perspectives on Human Development* (Thousand Oaks, CA: Sage, 2004).

daydream? What might they not be telling others that they really want to tell them? The best teachers regularly ask these questions and carefully listen to their youth.

Knowing How to Prepare

Once we have prayerfully selected our topic and Bible passage through listening to God and our youth, we must determine the best way to approach our audience.

There are two common approaches to preparing a large-group talk or sermon. The first is the exegetical (or "expository") approach that examines a single text of Scripture in order to properly interpret it. There are three variations of this approach:

1. A verse-by-verse approach walks through a passage verse by verse, or section by section. This is helpful because it presents a logical flow and also teaches students how to study God's Word.
2. A thematic approach emerges from the study of a biblical text but then allows the speaker to reference other passages and connect them to everyday topics.
3. A narrative approach to expository preaching "presents the biblical text in the form of story and follows that story to completion."[12] This is covered in more detail in the following chapter.

A second common approach, a topical approach, puts more emphasis on student concerns and can take many different directions. This has prompted debates on what is the best or even "right" way to preach. The topical approach is prominent in evangelistic settings and examples can also be found in the book of Acts (Acts 3:11–26; 17:22–31). One danger of this approach is that it can easily turn into talking about what we think about a topic versus what the Bible says about the topic and what conforms to Christian theology. When a topical approach is used, it's equally important to do diligent study, keep biblical texts in context, and to make sure your theme (what you say about the topic) is supported.

Though there are many models for how to prepare a large-group teaching time, there are three prominent models. The first (and most popular) is "Hook, Book, Look, Took" (from Lawrence Richards and Gary Bredfeldt

---

12. Ed Stetzer, "Four Kinds of Expository Preaching," *Lifeway*, March 1, 2006, http://www.lifeway.com/Article/Four-kinds-of-expositional-preaching.

and covered in detail by Terry Linhart in chap. 12).[13] This model allows for a variety of methods to be used:

- *Hook*—Capture your listener's attention and interest, surface a need, and set a goal for the teaching.
- *Book*—Explore the biblical text to clarify its meaning and help students to get and understand the biblical information.
- *Look*—Guide the students to discover and grasp how the topic connects to daily living.
- *Took*—Lead students to identify ways to respond, and then help them plan immediate applications.[14]

As teachers prepare for their lesson, they think through how they can accomplish each section's goal for their teaching objective. The *hook* and *took* sections are as equally crucial to teaching success as the *book* and *look*, although they are often engaged as almost an afterthought. The goal of teaching is growth in the form of transformed lives, and the information has to connect and be applied to living, not just dispensed.

Another popular model was developed by North Point Community Church pastor Andy Stanley. His outlining method is built on the relationship between the speaker and audience and is best for sermons that need a personalized or inspirational touch. It feels more like a conversation but can easily serve an exegetical study of Scripture.

Stanley's approach starts with something about the speaker ("me") and then finds common ground with listeners ("we"). Then the speaker shares what God ("God") and his Word says about the matter and then what the audience ("you") need to do about it. The closing is then a conclusion about what would happen if everyone ("we") embraced and acted on the truth.[15]

Ken Davis developed the SCORRE™ method for preparing a talk.[16] It focuses preparation around six steps—subject, central theme, objective, rationale, resources, and evaluation. The objective states what people "should" or "must" do, and the rationale explains "how" or "why" they should do it. The method asks speakers to focus on a plural noun as part of the objective,

---

13. Lawrence O. Richards and Gary J. Bredfeldt, *Creative Bible Teaching* (Chicago: Moody, 1998).

14. Ibid., 154–59.

15. Andy Stanley and Lane Jones, *Communicating for Change* (Colorado Springs: Multnomah, 2006).

16. Ken Davis, *Secrets of Dynamic Communication: Preparing and Delivering Powerful Speeches* (Grand Rapids: Zondervan, 1991).

often the most challenging part of the method. The plural noun prompts speakers to think visually and creatively while serving as the key word for the rationale that people can quickly recall days later. There are online sources that show how the method works.[17]

After getting to this point in sermon preparation, you enter into even harder work: being specific on the methods and words you plan to use to bring God's message to your students. That's because "to communicate as God communicated we need to speak not just to inform but also to transform," and "to communicate as God has communicated is to take seriously both the method and message, form and content."[18]

Knowing How to Deliver

The popularity of the TED Talk has influenced conversations about public speaking.[19] Lasting no more than eighteen minutes, these well-rehearsed, media-oriented talks have shown the power in imagery . . . and brevity. Not everything important can be shared in under eighteen minutes, but audiences are increasingly used to changing scenes (via their screens) and spending shorter amounts of time taking in information.

In fact, current research shows that students regularly check out at around thirty seconds, and then at five, seven, and nine minutes after the start of a lesson.[20] This continues in three- to four-minute intervals for the rest of the teaching time.[21] So changing our method, adding a story or effective joke, and being aware of their attention spans will help with audience engagement in large-group settings.

> Here is a final checklist for preparation.
>
> 1. Be in continual prayer and meditation on the passage.
> 2. Use more than one commentary or study Bible.
> 3. Outline your talk (see above methods).
> 4. Make sure your main theme and subpoints are clear.
> 5. Add "life" to your talk with good illustrations and examples.
> 6. Practice your talk out loud.
> 7. Make sure the application question ("So what do I do with this?") is answered.

17. John R. Meese, "SCORRE™ Outline," based on the SCORRE™ method taught by Ken Davis and Michael Hyatt of Dynamic Communicators International, https://gingkoapp.com/scorre.

18. Doug Fields and Duffy Robbins, *Speaking to Teenagers* (Grand Rapids: Zondervan/ Youth Specialties, 2007), 36–37.

19. "Ted," TED Conferences, LLC, https://www.ted.com/talks.

20. Diane M. Bunce, Elizabeth A. Flens, and Kelly Y. Neiles, "How Long Can Students Pay Attention in Class? A Study of Student Attention Decline Using Clickers," *Journal of Chemical Education* 87 (2010): 1438–43.

21. A. H. Johnstone and F. Percival, "Attention Breaks in Lectures," *Education in Chemistry* 13 (1976): 49–50.

One of the overlooked areas in speaking is that of illustrations. For each of your main points, consider the use of a story, analogy, imagery, or short video. The golden rule of illustrations is that one great example is worth three good examples. Haddon Robinson's list, which is set up by level of impact, helps in choosing which illustration you should try to use:[22]

1. The speaker's and listener's lived experience overlap.
2. The speaker's learned experience overlaps with the listener's lived experience.
3. The speaker's lived experience overlaps with the listener's learned experience.
4. The speaker's lived or learned experience does not overlap with the listener's lived or learned experience.

The final step in thinking through your talk is how you will close. The ending brings everything together in a way that helps students be unified and be challenged to put something into practice, which is one of the primary reasons that large-group teaching is encouraged. Instead of rushing the ending, make it amazing and unexpected. Have students who have already put this message or similar messages into practice share testimonies.[23] Give students the time and space to do something corporately like commitment cards, prayer at the altar, breakout groups, or "turn and share with your neighbor." Giving them a moment to engage the topic in community will help them take action on it throughout the coming week.[24]

Another important step in preparation is writing out a final full script, a practice that separates the pros from others. This may seem like overkill at this point, but if you want your students to really follow, your teaching must flow. Writing out as much of your talk as possible in advance will help. You don't have to use it when you're up front, but writing it, reading it out loud, and then thinking through nonverbal actions (smile!), gestures, illustrations, or needed voice fluctuations will help. Practicing it out loud lets your ears hear what your brain thinks it's saying and lets you catch problems in advance. Talking in front of a mirror, or recording yourself as you speak, allows you to see how you appear to others as you speak. Don't forget that 38 percent of our communication comes through the vocal intonations we

22. Haddon W. Robinson, *Expository Preaching*, 2nd ed. (Grand Rapids: Baker Academic, 2001), 156.

23. Mark Galli and Craig Brian Larson, *Preaching That Connects* (Grand Rapids: Zondervan, 1994), 136–37.

24. Jean Piaget, *The Construction of Reality in the Child* (New York: Basic Books, 1954).

use, and 55 percent comes through nonverbal elements (facial expressions, gestures, posture, etc.). The other 7 percent of our communication is the actual words.[25]

Finally, you should email the talk to others and practice the sermon out loud with a ministry volunteer or trusted friend. Their honest feedback is invaluable to refining what you want to get across. What you use when you deliver your talk can vary based on your comfort level. Some use paper notes in a Bible, some use an iPad or other tablet, some memorize it, and others use the full script (though reading manuscripts has the tendency to distance the speaker from the audience).

After reading through all the steps that an effective large-group communicator does, it's natural that you may ask, *"Really? I'm supposed to do all of that work, every time I teach?"* If you want to be as effective as you can, then *yes!* No matter your position within the ministry, your teaching is worth your best preparation and presentation. Sticking to this strenuous model of large-group teaching could be one of the most effective elements to the ministry you lead.

> In addition to your tone and body language, how fast you speak also matters. Those who study such things say that if you need to be seen as "more objective and knowledgeable," then your average rate of presentation should be around 190 words per minute, or about one double-spaced page every two minutes. On the other hand, if your goal is to be more persuasive, then you need to slow it down to about 140 words per minute, or about one page every three minutes.
>
> —Compiled from Norman Miller et al., "Speed of Speech and Persuasion," *Journal of Personality and Social Psychology* 34, no. 4 (October 1976): 615–24; Stephen M. Smith and David R. Shaffer, "Celerity and Cajolery: Rapid Speech May Promote or Inhibit Persuasion through Its Impact on Message Elaboration," *Personality and Social Psychology Bulletin* 17, no. 6 (1991): 663–69.

Questions and Activities

1. Who are your three favorite speakers and why? What approach to study, structure, and delivery do each of them take? How do they use humor?

2. Think of a large-group teaching sermon that has greatly impacted your life. What about that sermon affected you in the moment?

3. Which aspect of large-group teaching (knowing God, knowing your audience, knowing how to prepare, and knowing how to deliver) seems the most daunting? How could you grow in that aspect?

25. Albert Mehrabian, *Silent Messages: Implicit Communication of Emotion and Attitudes* (Belmont, CA: Wadsworth, 1981).

4. Watch a TED Talk, a widely viewed sermon, and a historical, inspirational speech online, then read a speech from Scripture. Pay attention to the speakers' mannerisms, their speech patterns, and the speech's structure. As an exercise, practice out loud saying some of the things they said the way they did.

5. Compile a one-page summary of this chapter's main points for you to review as you prepare, deliver, and evaluate your next sermon, speech, or talk.

Further Reading

Davis, Ken. *Secrets of Dynamic Communications: Prepare with Focus, Deliver with Clarity, Speak with Power*. Nashville: Thomas Nelson, 2013.

Fields, Doug, and Duffy Robbins. *Speaking to Teenagers: How to Think About, Create, and Deliver Effective Messages*. Grand Rapids: Zondervan/Youth Specialties, 2007.

Gallo, Carmine. *Talk like TED: The 9 Public-Speaking Tips of the World's Greatest Minds*. New York: St. Martin's, 2014.

Keller, Timothy. *Preaching: Communicating Faith in an Age of Skepticism*. New York: Viking, 2015.

Robinson, Haddon. *Biblical Preaching: The Development and Delivery of Expository Messages*. Grand Rapids: Baker Academic, 2014.

Stanley, Andy, and Lane Jones. *Communicating for Change*. Colorado Springs: Multnomah, 2006.

21

Using Narrative to Invite Others into the Story of God

JAMES K. HAMPTON

> Jesus was not a theologian. He was God who told stories.
> —Madeleine L'Engle

Once upon a time . . .

It was the best of times, it was the worst of times . . .

These well-known lines make our minds perk up and redirect our attention, and we expectantly wait as we know that there is usually a story about to be told. Whether a little child or a wizened saint, all of us look forward to hearing the story unfold and reach its climactic peak and denouement.

But there is another introductory line that also tells a story—the most important and powerful story ever told: "In the beginning, God . . ." (Gen. 1:1). For those who know the story, we can continue, automatically adding the words, "created the heavens and the earth."

We are a storied people. We frame all of our lives by the stories we hear, share, and live into. Our values, traditions, and beliefs are all passed on through stories. Narrative is one of the few human practices that is truly universal regardless of age, gender, culture, and language. Humans have a natural, instinctual need to hear a story and to know how it ends, and even more so when that story, in our case the Christian story, is one that is so central to our human condition.

This chapter will focus on narrative as a way of educating others, particularly adolescents, to help students live into the story of God.

Ask most people what first comes to mind when they hear the word *narrative*, and the vast majority of them will say "story." For many people the word *narrative* conveys fiction, a made-up story, often used to make a point. Think fairy tales (e.g., "Cinderella"), morality stories ("The Gift of the Magi"[1]), and even the parables of Jesus ("A farmer went out to sow his seed . . ." in Matt. 13:3b NIV). In its most basic aspect, narrative is tied to story. However, in the Christian and Jewish traditions, narrative is much bigger than just a story. It is about Story with a capital *S*—the Story that shapes our lives, a call to enter into a new world, a new way of thinking. For the purposes of this chapter, we will look at how narrative "focuses on the power of stories to shape the quality of human life."[2] In addition, for Christians, the Story has the power not only to shape us but to transform who we are at our core.

> Narrative is a way of doing God-talk whereby we recount the story of God and invite the listener to become a participant in that story.

The Christian narrative offers us a new world in which we are called to live, a world that is often at odds with the actual world. It differs from fictional stories because in this case it is a world that is not made up but real. In fact, it is actually the "most real" world there is. It is the world of God, sometimes referred to as the kingdom of God, that we are called to inhabit as people of faith.

To understand this, consider the three primary ways that narrative operates.[3] First, it functions constitutively. Narrative shapes the community's identity. As the members of the community read and hear the story, they are shown what it means to be the people of God. The narrative serves to point to an alternative world, the normative way by which we are called to live.

Second, narrative works descriptively. In other words, it serves as a mirror, enabling the people of God to see who we really are, warts and all. It shows us our true identity. Nothing is hidden. Narrative recognizes that before we can change, we first have to understand who we really are and thus where we fall short. It is the story of Isaiah, who first had to understand

---

1. By O. Henry, the pen name of William Sidney Porter.
2. J. H. Stone, "Narrative Theology," in *Harper's Encyclopedia of Religious Education*, ed. Iris V. Cully and Kendig Brubaker Cully (San Francisco: Harper & Row, 1990), 440.
3. I'm indebted to Dr. Tim Green of Trevecca Nazarene University for these insights passed along in a personal conversation.

who God was and who he was in relation to God before Isaiah could accept the necessity of God's cleansing (Isa. 6).

Finally, narrative functions paradigmatically. After we look in the mirror and discover who we are, narrative then helps us see how we are to act by pointing the reader toward examples of what the faith community is to be like. This is Isaiah responding to the call of God on his life with, "Here am I. Send me." When this happens, our very identity is shaped by the story, becoming what John Westerhoff calls a "story-formed community."[4]

While there are many stories that may form us, Gerard Loughlin points out, the primary narrative that guides us as Christians is Scripture. The canonical Scriptures provide the basic narratives for how the church imagines the world and itself in the world. The church imagines itself within the narrative world of the Bible, a written world into which people can be "inscribed." Rather than understand the Bible in worldly terms, the Christian understands the world in biblical ones; the Christian takes the biblical narratives (and especially the narratives of Christ) as the fundamental story by which all others are to be understood, including his or her own story.[5]

Above all, the narrative emphasizes the priority of the story of Jesus Christ. This story is what we are called to follow, to emulate, and to serve.

How Narrative Shapes Our Identity

How are we shaped as human beings? How is our identity formed? These are fundamental questions that all persons ask. And they are central to any discussion of narrative as a guiding principle. Let's examine one story from the biblical narrative that can help us better understand the answers to these questions.

At the end of the book of Genesis, we find that Joseph, who has been placed in a position of authority by Pharaoh, has settled his family in Egypt. God continues to bless them, and soon their numbers grow, continuing to fulfill the promise God had given to Abraham that his heirs would be "as numerous as the stars in the sky and as the sand on the seashore" (Gen. 22:17 NIV).

However, at the beginning of the book of Exodus, "a new king, to whom Joseph meant nothing, came to power in Egypt" (Exod. 1:8 NIV). This new pharaoh sees the Hebrew people not as Joseph's heirs but as a people who,

4. John Westerhoff, *A Pilgrim People: Learning through the Church Year* (New York: Harper & Row, 1984), 1.

5. Gerard Loughlin, *Telling God's Story: Bible, Church and Narrative Theology* (Cambridge: Cambridge University Press, 1996), 19–20.

"if war breaks out, will join our enemies, fight against us and leave the country" (Exod. 1:10b NIV). To counter this perceived threat, this new pharaoh enslaves all the Hebrews.

When Moses arrives on the scene as God's deliverer, he has a tall task ahead of him. For decades, the Hebrews have been told a number of false stories. They've been told that they are born as slaves. They've heard that they are worthless; thus it is permissible for the pharaoh to order the killing of all Hebrew male children. These false stories have been repeated so often that soon they become the very stories by which the Hebrew people live. They have adopted these stories as their identity. In one important sense, their identity has been prescribed by others, and as such, it exists outside of them. It is not an internalized identity.

However, this was not who God intended them to be. Do you remember God's promise to Abraham? "I will make you into a great nation, and I will bless you; I will make your name great, and you will be a blessing. I will bless those who bless you, and whoever curses you I will curse; and all peoples on earth will be blessed through you" (Gen. 12:2–3 NIV). God had a different plan for his people. They weren't called to be slaves but rather were called to be a great nation. They weren't called to experience death at the hands of others, but instead they were to be a blessing to the nations. God intended them to have an entirely different identity from the one they have been given. He had prescribed an identity that wasn't to exist outside them but was to be internalized, an identity that emerged as they lived into the narrative of God. Only after God uses Moses to deliver the Hebrew people are they reminded of their true identity, who they were created to be: "You will be my treasured possession. Although the whole earth is mine, you will be for me a kingdom of priests and a holy nation" (Exod. 19:5b–6a NIV).

> The grand narrative of God's story is what ultimately should shape and define our identities.

Today, many people operate in a similar manner when it comes to identity formation. All around us there are people, groups, and companies trying to tell us who we should be. These stories far too often prescribe individualism rather than community, consumerism rather than sacrifice, death rather than life. Too often, we are passive recipients of these narratives, allowing them to form us into someone different from who God intended us to be. Because of this, like the Hebrew people, we end up adopting these false stories as our own, and in so doing we adopt an identity that has been prescribed by others.

Imagine a large church that performs an Easter passion play. More than one hundred people are involved, each one wearing period costumes. Live animals are brought in, and authentic sets are built replicating the town of

Jerusalem. You sit in the audience watching the scene unfold in front of you. The actors, musicians, and even the animals all play their parts well. After the drama, you leave and think to yourself, "That was a great play to watch."

Next year, you decide to go watch the play again. You even sit in the same seat as before. You look expectantly forward, waiting for the actors to play their roles. However, this time when the drama starts, the actors come in from the back of the sanctuary. As they move toward the stage, the actors pass through the audience, interacting with you. The actors try to sell pots, bread, and fruit to the audience members. In addition, the actors stop and chat with you, talking about the events happening in Jerusalem. By the time the actors reach the stage, you aren't merely observing a story like the year before. You suddenly realize that you feel as if you are *in* the story.

Similarly, as Christians, it's not enough to just be passive bystanders, waiting for the story of God to tell us who we are. Instead, we are called to be active participants with God, joining in his story and allowing his will to become ours. It's in our participation in this story that we ultimately find our identity as children of God. We join in this drama, and we are re-created as we experience "a comprehensive truth affecting one's identity and future."[6]

Wearing Bifocals

Our identities are formed not simply by hearing the story but by living into the story. It is not about plugging God into my story (where I remain in control and decide how to follow the story). Rather, it is about submerging my life into the story of God, which, as we saw earlier, is primary.

In his insightful work, J. Louis Martyn offers a metaphor that may be helpful to us here. He suggests that Paul, in his writings, is attempting to teach his congregations how to view their everyday lives with *bifocal vision*.[7] Thus to enter into the narrative is learning to live with bifocals, wherein we see two stories—our current reality and the alternative reality God has for us. We see the identity the world wants us to adopt and the identity God has instilled in us since the beginning of time. Part of our job, then, is to find ways to help others move from the false stories that surround us to the one true story.

6. Rowan D. Williams, "Postmodern Theology and the Judgment of the World," in *Postmodern Theology: Christian Faith in a Pluralist World*, ed. Frederic B. Burnham (New York: Harper Collins, 1989), 97.

7. J. Louis Martyn, *Theological Issues in the Letters of Paul* (Nashville: Abingdon, 1997), 62–65, 280–84.

Author Leighton Ford puts it this way: "Each of us has a story—what I call a 'story with a small *s*,' the story of our own lives. At some point in our journey through life, our story collides with the Story of God—'the Story with the large *S*.' God's story calls our story into question. We must make a choice: either to reject the Story of God or to merge our story with His story."[8] Therefore, to be Christian is to live in God's narrative and allow it to become our identity.

Let me illustrate. Perhaps you've heard a pastor or youth pastor talk about the issue of priorities. Often the talk goes like this: "God should be our first priority, family our second, and our own needs should be last." So you set out to work hard that week on your priorities. You really focus on reading your Bible, spending time in prayer, going to church, and thinking about God. It's a good week, and at the end of the week, you feel good about your priorities. However, as often occurs, your next week is super busy. You wake up late, rush to classes, head to work or sports practice, study for an exam or write a paper, and tumble into bed exhausted. The next day is no easier, and soon you discover that several days have gone by and you've not spent any time reading your Bible, praying (other than at meals), or really thinking about God.

Feeling guilty, you recommit to making God your first priority. You get up earlier each morning to ensure you have time to read your Bible, pray, get to church or Bible study, and generally think about God. But again, life intervenes, and soon you find yourself swamped with assignments, your boss (or school) requires you to work extra hours, your girlfriend or boyfriend needs some attention, and again you fall into bed at midnight with things still left undone and no specific activities that made God your first priority. You begin to despair that you can ever live a life that has God as your first priority.

Let's ask the question: Who is deciding whether God is the first priority or not? Answer: You are! And that's the problem. This line of thinking still puts *us* in charge. *We* decide whether God will be first. Again, we're trying to put God into *our* lives. Instead, let me suggest that we begin to see God's story as the reality and our lives as part of that reality. Instead of boxing God into just when we read the Bible, pray, or attend church, what if we saw God as being present in all our lives because we are living in his story? What difference would it make if we understood God was with us as we walked to class, talked with fellow students, wrote our papers, served a customer, and cared for our friends? This is what it means to put

8. Leighton Ford, *The Power of Story* (Colorado Springs: NavPress, 1994), 10.

our stories in God's narrative and for it to shape us into the people he desires.

Narrative Teaching

Let's now apply this idea of narrative to the purpose of this textbook: How can it impact the way we teach? Given that stories shape our identities, culture, and traditions, it only makes sense that we begin to find ways to use story in our educational processes. As teachers, our job is to help people learn to reframe their lives in light of God's story. Through stories, songs, creeds, and sacraments, we help people come to understand God's story, bring their stories in line with God's story, and in so doing, find their true identity and character as children of God. The last part of this chapter will explore teaching strategies that are narrative in nature and can help us with this task.

Storytelling

Human beings are natural storytellers. We love both telling and hearing stories. "Stories help us organize and make sense of the experiences of a life."[9] A well-crafted story doesn't just lead to a form of escapism. Rather, its purpose is to give us the space necessary to share an experience *with* the characters of the story. It transports us into another world, shows us new possibilities for actions, attitudes, and beliefs, and relates them to our current experiences. As educator Sherelle Walker points out, "Research also shows that our brains are actually hard-wired to seek out a coherent narrative structure in the stories we hear and tell. This structure helps us absorb the information in a story, and connect it with our own experiences in the world."[10]

Because of this, stories can stand on their own without the need for interpretation; meaning is embedded in the story itself. In fact, the greatest mistake we often make is that of moralizing the story, giving *our* interpretation of the story, instead of allowing the hearer to discern what God may have to say to us through the story itself. A story-shaped identity invites one to enter into a story, stay there, ask questions from there, and roam in it. The longer one stays in the story, day in and day out, the greater the likelihood that one's identity will be shaped.

9. Herbert Anderson and Edward Foley, *Mighty Stories, Dangerous Rituals: Weaving Together the Human and the Divine* (San Francisco: Jossey-Bass, 1998), 4.

10. Sherelle Walker, "Using Stories to Teach: How Narrative Structure Helps Students Learn," *The Science of Learning Blog*, June 14, 2012, http://www.scilearn.com/blog/using-stories-to-teach.

Good stories are all around, and it doesn't take much work to incorporate them into a ministry context. Here are three quick steps to improve your storytelling:

1. Watch and learn from other good storytellers on YouTube or in person. Find a good example, and practice telling it like that person did.

2. Practice reading and telling stories out loud, learning how to convey the story through facial expressions, eye contact, and changes in your voice.

3. Have students write short parables that would help their friends understand a Bible passage or a spiritual truth.

When we hear stories, we recognize that we no longer have to have all the answers to all the questions that life presents. Because good storytelling is often left without explicit meanings, the hearers act as participants in the storytelling process by delving deeper into the open-ended story and making their own interpretations. As the hearer works through possible interpretations and arrives at a conclusion, he or she utilizes a full set of decision-making skills (i.e., imagination, intuition, language, memory, reason, and faith) that work together to help the story to both "stick" and to have greater possibility it will actually create change. Richard Osmer makes this case when he writes that "attempts to elicit a faith commitment from our students solely by appealing to their wills does not go deep enough. Their wills are directed by the narratives that shape their personal identities."[11]

Case Studies

Case studies typically involve the study and discussion of a real-life narrative that has a dilemma needing to be resolved. Most case studies will typically follow these steps: (1) identify the primary characters, (2) name the issue to be resolved, (3) carefully consider the context and background of the issue, (4) use various disciplines (biblical studies, theology, education, sociology, psychology, anthropology, etc.) to consider potential responses to the dilemma, and (5) after careful consideration, arrive at an agreed-upon solution.

Because the case study is written from one person's perspective, it allows each of the people studying the case to place himself or herself in the dilemma and look at it from that perspective. This is a narrative way of dealing with the case study. As they enter into the story, they discover how they can apply theory to practice to address the problem without having to deal with the real-world fallout of making a poor decision.

An important element of the case study is to help students understand that a situation may have *several* viable options that have to be considered.

11. Richard Osmer, *Teaching for Faith: A Guide for Teachers of Adult Classes* (Louisville: Westminster John Knox, 1992), 114.

Different groups studying the same case may arrive at differing outcomes based on each group's background, field of study, understanding of revelation, and theological tradition.

One of the values of case studies is that they "challenge our students to think, to deal with an increasing range and complexity of life experiences, and, within the Christian framework, to deal with increasing personal intentionality and responsibility."[12] This is especially important for use in Christian education because it allows students to learn how to apply their Christian faith and values to life situations. As they learn how to do this, they become more confident in doing it in real life.

> "A case study is a dramatic situation based on facts involving actual characters who are faced with actual problems that need solving."
>
> —Marlene LeFever, *Creative Teaching Methods: Be an Effective Christian Teacher* (Colorado Springs: David C. Cook, 1997), 218.

The case study then becomes an incredibly useful tool that allows learners to consider themselves in the situation, participate in the discussion, stimulate their thinking, utilize their respective knowledge base, and learn how to apply their faith to real-life situations. Good case studies don't deal with simplistic situations but provide complex issues that represent the type of life decisions all of us face. Given these benefits, it is somewhat surprising that case studies are often underutilized in educational settings in the local church.

If we want to help young people learn in ways where they can apply biblical truths to everyday life (and can develop mature thinking and social skills in the process), then narrative methods are the primary tools for that. The most important thing you will do as an educator is invite future generations to enter the story of God. When we enter the story, we quickly discover that there is nothing more exciting than helping others also find their place in the story.[13]

Questions and Activities

1. To live in a "story-formed community" means actively seeking to ask, "How does our community allow God's story to shape and form us?" How has your faith community helped you to understand and live into God's story?

12. Marlene LeFever, *Creative Teaching Methods: Be an Effective Christian Teacher* (Colorado Springs: David C. Cook, 1997), 218.
13. Special thanks to Drs. Tim Green and Dean Blevins, two friends who helped introduce me to this world of narrative and all its wonderful implications for the gospel.

2. In what ways have you tried to fit God into your story? What was the result? What difference does it make when we allow God to fit our story into his story?

3. What are some of the false stories that your generation has believed? How can God's story give your generation a new understanding of how things could be?

4. As you consider the teaching strategies discussed in this chapter, which have you experienced? How did those strategies help you understand a different way of thinking or living (an alternative worldview) than the way you previously thought or lived?

5. Take thirty minutes and read through a magazine or newspaper and find an article that would work as a source for an appropriate case study in your ministry. Would it require a few students to act it out? Write out a teaching aim for the lesson, and then write out two or three discussion questions that you would ask your group after you presented the case study.

Further Reading

Folmsbee, Chris. *Stories, Signs and Sacred Rhythms: A Narrative Approach to Youth Ministry*. Grand Rapids: Zondervan, 2010.

Loughlin, Gerard. *Telling God's Story: Bible, Church, and Narrative Theology*. Cambridge: Cambridge University Press, 1999.

Stroup, George. *The Promise of Narrative Theology*. Eugene, OR: Wipf and Stock, 1997.

Wright, John W. *Telling God's Story: Narrative Preaching for Christian Formation*. Downers Grove, IL: InterVarsity, 2005.

22

Learning through Simulations

KAREN MCKINNEY

Simulations—powerful yet underused and underappreciated teaching experiences—can be used to replicate situations where participants are presented with choices or challenges to help them understand the world through another's experiences. Simulations are frequently used in teaching about cross-cultural competency, understanding the poor, marginalized, or oppressed, and for developing counseling or similar expertise. They are common in Christian camps and conferences to provide challenging situations that require collective decision making.

Simulations work. The feedback students give affirms that experiential learning exercises like simulations and role plays are among the most effective methods we can use. Simulations are transformative when students gain depth of insight about themselves, about others, and about the world. The student reflections that simulations produce testify to the depth to which they learn . . . and unlearn.

For example, when an overseas political situation necessitated the cancellation of a mission trip, a group of leaders quickly formed a substitute leadership week at a nearby campground. During one session on morals and ethics, the staff interrupted and asked the kids to take six five-gallon jugs of water across the lake to prime a seldom-used pump. The staff claimed they were short staffed this week and needed their help.

Thus began, unbeknownst to the youth, a simulated journey of morals and ethics. They were randomly divided into three groups and given unequal amounts of resources to use to cross the lake (canoes, expensive paddles, life jackets, snacks and drinks, oarless rowboats, brooms for paddles, ragged life jackets, etc.). The last group even had to write a grant proposal to get resources.

Midway through the experience, the staff created a fake hurricane (like the ones that ravage the country where they had intended to go for the mission trip) that resulted in a third of each group being handicapped in some way—blindness, a loss of limb, or trauma-induced muteness. The groups continued the journey past a floating store selling refreshments and "miracle cures" for handicaps, which only the wealthy group could afford.

After they reached the pump and primed it with their water, it was past lunchtime. The groups were then given a cognitive challenge: in four minutes write the fifty states in alphabetical order with no spelling errors. The winning group got to pick their lunch box. Box one had an overabundance of sandwiches, fruit, veggie sticks, cookies, and drinks. Box two had the same as box one but in much smaller amounts. Box three had an onion and a jar of mustard. The group that had the least resources on the journey ended up with the wealthiest box, and the morning's wealthy group got the onion and mustard. After lunch, the debriefing session lasted two and a half hours as the students discussed the experience.

That morning's journey was a laboratory for the kids to practice nearly every moral or ethical characteristic they had brainstormed in the earlier "teaching" session. Instead of practicing compassion, they competed with one another; instead of sharing, they hoarded; and instead of being visionaries, they were blind to any perspective but their own. The "wealthy" group that had paddles had sat and waited for fifty minutes before going back to help the others who struggled to cross the lake using brooms and boards. They even forgot their blind members on shore as they pushed off, leaving them to be crowded in the poor groups' oarless rowboats. And none of the group members noticed that the seminar leaders had no food at all. These students had been trained for months for a mission experience, but the simulation exposed the limits of their knowledge at the boundaries of their character and compassion.

A simulation is *an exercise in which a mock-up of reality is recreated in order for the participants to interact in the simulated world to learn something about the real world.* Louise Sauvé, Lise Renaud, and David Kaufman have defined a simulation as having seven essential attributes: "(1) a model of a real or fictitious system that is (2) simplified and (3) dynamic, with

(4) players in (5) competition or cooperation, (6) rules, and (7) an educational [purpose]."[1] The students enter into the microcosm—the simulations—taking on whatever roles are called for.

Some practitioners speak of simulations and some speak of role plays, but the terms are often used interchangeably. The distinction between them is based on whether you ask participants to fulfill a role in the exercise or ask them to take on a role that is not themselves. *In a simulation they are not asked to be anyone other than themselves. In a role play the facilitator specifically asks participants to play a role where they are not themselves.* Participants may act out a social role as they have learned it, but simulations do not require participants to do such. Those facilitating and helping to run the simulation often play roles as well.

Simulations engage the whole person. The cognitive, affective, and behavioral domains of learners are challenged in ways lectures and discussions cannot consistently provide. Simulations are contrived, but what people experience during a simulation is real. Good simulations require the learners to think, make decisions, and take actions. Because the feelings are real, the simulations move us the way feelings authentically move us. Standing in the shoes of others, even for short periods, allows one to tap into feelings often unfelt or unexamined. Learners are allowed to be themselves during the game or exercise so their responses are authentically theirs. If they express anger or sadness after being patronized, name-called, excluded, and physically pushed, those feelings are real. If reflection after the experience moves them to sympathize and empathize with those who are treated thusly, that movement is transformative.

Simulations catch us off guard; they have the ability to let the learners hold a mirror up to themselves and look in it critically in a way matched only by immersion in real-life experience. The students in a Theology of Poverty class do not get to live with a poor family in a Mexican village. But they can feel deprivation in a poverty simulation where others have and they do not, where they are shamed for their lack and not given a voice in the society. Students may forget a lecture on Amos as prophet, but they are much less likely to forget the day they had to choose whether to literally step on their peers in order to enter the classroom—a simulation revealing what Amos meant when he said it was a sin to trample on the heads of the poor (Amos 2:7).

1. Louise Sauvé, Lise Renaud, and David Kaufman, "Games, Simulations, and Simulation Games for Learning: Definitions and Distinctions," in *Educational Gameplay and Simulation Environment: Case Studies and Lessons Learned* (Hershey, PA: Information Science Reference, 2010), 1–26.

Simulations can turn us into advocates. One simulation makes students spend an evening in a wheelchair in grease-clouded glasses, ears stuffed with cotton, wearing loose gloves. They experience what some elderly endure each day: limits to mobility, sight, hearing, and touch. They understand that someday they may have to endure these experiences. It doesn't take much for them to quickly become advocates for the elderly. Youth leaders can then help their teens to model compassion and try to maintain relationships with the elderly within their church and community. The simulation is brief, but the learning is lifelong.

Therein lies the importance of simulations; though brief, they can change lives forever. A prime example is Jane Elliott's 1968 *Blue Eyes, Brown Eyes* simulation exercise. Elliott wanted to promote awareness and change the attitudes toward racial discrimination of her third-grade class in Iowa. The simulation she created "provide[d] her white, third grade students with firsthand experience of the effects of racism."[2] Her simulation lasted the length of one school day. The long-lasting effects of her simulation exercise are documented in the PBS Frontline documentary *A Class Divided: Then and Now*.[3] In the documentary, the students testify fourteen years later to the lifelong impact of the simulation. As Christian ministers, we are about lifelong transformation of our students. Simulation is a methodology we must include in our teaching repertoire.

Simulations can be designed to teach any content; they are therefore rich sources for spiritual and faith development. Simulations are used to teach Christian morals and ethics; the value of Scripture memorization; issues pertaining to justice, gender, class, race, and poverty; lessons in leadership; the value of reconciliation; and just about anything the Bible teaches. The only limit is the imagination, and because we serve a God who is creative, that is no limitation at all.

Underlying Theory

Experiential pedagogy originates in the philosophy of John Dewey: learners are to be active. Education should value, above all, the experiences of the learner; it is to be student centered—students' needs and inquiry guide the

2. Kay Hammond, "More Than a Game: A Critical Discourse Analysis of a Racial Inequality Exercise in Japan," *TESOL Quarterly* 40 (September 2006): 545–71.

3. One of the most requested programs in *Frontline*'s history, *A Class Divided* (1995) tells the story of Jane Elliott's simulation and its impact fourteen years later. The day after Martin Luther King Jr. was murdered, she led her students through a simulation of discrimination. You can view the entire episode at http://www.pbs.org/wgbh/pages/frontline/shows/divided/.

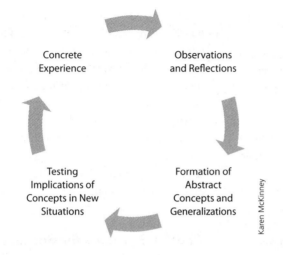

Figure 22.1 Kolb's theory of experiential learning

learning.[4] In a simulation the learner has the opportunity to experience an environment or a role that may be totally alien to them. The more isomorphic—similar in form and shape—to the real-life situation, the greater the learning possibilities are. You can therefore teach very complex, abstract concepts and systems using simulations.

For students to learn the intended outcomes of a simulation, there must be a time of reflection/debriefing following the simulated activity; this can be thought of as David Kolb's reflective stage (see fig. 22.1), a theory that was covered earlier, in the chapter on learning styles (chap. 8). It is in reflecting on the concrete experience of the simulation that the "aha's" happen.[5]

In Kolb's figure, the concrete experience is the simulation, but the leader's hope is that the participants will experience a state of *disequilibrium*. When things don't make sense, the learners must reconfigure or take in new data to make things equilibrate in their heads. The simulations and exercises cast each learner in novel situations or settings that challenge the learner's present thinking, feeling, and behavior and call for unique problem solving. Leaders/facilitators make observations throughout the simulated activity. These observations are used to guide the reflection questions raised.

When the exercise is done, "debriefing" or reflection should happen. The most common form of debriefing is as a group, but it can also be done

4. John Dewey, *Experience and Education* (Toronto: Collier-MacMillan, 1938).
5. David A. Kolb, *Experiential Learning: Experience as the Source of Learning and Development*, vol. 1 (Englewood Cliffs, NJ: Prentice-Hall, 1984).

Why simulations are effective:

- Games and simulations involve the whole student in learning.
- Participants experience the concepts they are learning about.
- Participants actually feel the concept as well as learn about the concept.
- The experiences are close to real-life situations.
- Participants develop empathy for real-life decision makers.
- Participants gain insight into the complexities of real life and develop empathy for real-world participants.

—Anita Covert and Gordon L. Thomas, *Communication Games and Simulations* (Urbana, IL: ERIC Clearinghouse on Reading and Communication Skills; Annandale, VA: Speech Communication Association, 1978).

in smaller groups, in pairs, in online discussion boards, and as written reflections. The "new knowledge/insights" gained from the reflection are what gets carried forward in Kolb's cycle and can then be applied in other situations. In a Romans Bible study simulation, students learn that many Christians sacrificed their lives for the sake of other Christians. If students generalize that lesson, they discover that Christians might willingly sacrifice their money or time for the sake of other Christians or for those in need.

Crucial Elements for Success

There are some key elements to attend to when executing a simulation.

Stay in the simulation regardless of what happens. We can never control how people will respond, no matter how much we plan. When participants in a simulation act in unforeseen ways, you as facilitator must maintain the simulation and learn to go with the flow. In one simulation on wealth and poverty, the "rich group" sent a whole box of Krispy Kreme donuts to the poor group. Usually in the simulation, the rich groups pay little to no attention to the poor; this time someone did. The leaders were stumped and didn't know what to do in the face of generous charity—and they didn't want the poor to have the donuts (for the simulation's purposes). One leader told the other leaders to take a bite from each donut, lick them, do this in plain sight of the poor group, and then give them the donuts, saying they were a taxed item. After witnessing that, the poor group did not eat the donuts, and the simulation continued.

Sometimes participants know the outcome of a simulation. At one camp, students who participated in the simulation one day told the next day's group what was going to happen. The facilitator stopped the second day's simulation and broke the continuity of the simulation, not knowing how to respond to the participants who knew how the simulation was to play out. To keep the simulation intact, the facilitator could have used a bandana to keep one of those participants from talking and/or seeing or created a distraction to draw attention away from what they were saying. By stopping

I designed a divided court simulation so students could feel what it was like to learn in the gender-segregated system of the first century. Crepe paper streamers from the ceiling created a divided room with a see-through wall. Half the students got a bandana to cover his or her head. Those with bandanas sat in the inner court. I came dressed as a first-century Jewish rabbi and taught only the "men" in the inner court. I knew the outcomes I was looking for, but when we debriefed the exercise, the students made connections that were not on my radar. They connected the restlessness and distraction of the women students in the outer court to New Testament passages we had not yet covered. They articulated understandings of Jesus's treatment of women and Paul's writings in Timothy and Corinthian passages; I had not planned for those lessons. As facilitators of simulations, we must plan well but be open to the Spirit and to students learning unplanned lessons.

the simulation because a few knew what was coming, he ruined the learning opportunity for the others that day. It is crucial to stay in the simulation even in the face of unexpected actions from participants.

Know the learning outcomes you are aiming for, but be open to lessons the Holy Spirit sends your way. When you design your simulation, know what you want the learners to learn from the exercise. Have clear cognitive, affective, and behavioral goals articulated in your lesson plan for the simulation. At the same time, know that God's Spirit works unbeknownst to us, and there may be profound learning moments that the participants help to create.

Process and debrief what happened. Use the current simulation as the springboard for students to discuss their participation, learning, and connections to real life and Scripture. It is here that connections to real life, the Bible, society, and other concepts beyond the simulation can be explored. The real skill of the facilitator is to ask the right questions so the students discover answers for themselves. Good facilitation is all about asking and rarely about telling.

No two simulations are ever the same. It is important to focus on what happened in the current simulation and to draw out the lessons experienced and learned. Facilitators lose groups' attention when they constantly refer to things that did not happen or happened in previous simulations.

The strong facilitator allows enough time to process the feelings involved. It's very important to understand that in simulations the situation is contrived, but the feelings are real. Simulations can elicit intense, volatile emotions. When emotions are high, participants are blocked from learning. It is vital to deal with emotions first when debriefing the simulation, making

1. "What?" questions are review, helping students *recall* what happened in the simulation. "What happened first?" "What were people's responses?" "What feelings came up?"

2. "So what?" questions focus on *meaning*. "Why did such and such happen that way?" "What is the significance of . . .?" "What does it mean that . . .?" "What are the parallels to real life and what does that tell us?"

3. "Now what?" questions are about *application*, asking how it *applies* to life. "What will I do differently?" "Where else do I see this dynamic at play, and with what results?" "How can I apply what I have learned here?"

sure that learners are not left feeling emotionally damaged. You may have a student who felt like you were especially difficult on her. The last thing you want is for any participants to hold long-term resentment from a simulation.

Hone your facilitation skills. The stronger the facilitator, the more likely the success of the simulation. Strong facilitators plan well with attention to detail. They train and prepare their leaders well, so they know how to respond to each situation. Strong facilitators work at observing during the simulation so they know the questions to ask during reflection and debrief times. They also give their helpers space to raise questions during reflection, knowing they themselves cannot observe everything.

Understand that the facilitator can't control everything. Often when we teach we think if we plan and organize well, we can control the outcome. In simulations, we are not in control; strong facilitators learn to live easily with this understanding. There are interruptions, things go wrong, people do the wrong thing, and weather interferes; any number of things out of one's control can disrupt the simulation—just like in real life. We must learn to let God be in control and not to stress over what we cannot control.

Simulations need to be rooted in solid understanding or you'll be merely providing students a sensation-based experience. If you were creating a simulation about a passage of Scripture and its historical context or an aspect of adolescent life, you'll need to do your research. Simulations regularly produce unanticipated questions that show that students are learning and interested. That's our teaching moment, and we can't miss it.

Designing Simulations

When designing a simulation, begin at the end: What is the overall outcome—the big picture—you desire for the students? Once you have determined the big picture outcome, step two is to plan the learning objectives. The objectives should include cognitive, affective, and behavioral ones. Depending on the context, sometimes leadership and skill development goals are also appropriate.

Once you have determined specific objectives, step three involves examining the real-life situation you want to imitate to see which elements, when duplicated, will foster the desired responses and outcomes. After these steps, figure out the time frame and outline for your simulation (step four). Once you have the bones of your simulation, step five is adding aspects that make it more real. You can design whole simulations by yourself, but working with a small group is usually more productive.

Here is an example of the five-step process using a popular cross-cultural simulation called "Squat No More," which was adapted from the "Circle of Change" simulation.[6]

A teaching colleague in the Spanish department assigned her students to read about oppression in Guatemala, but her students seemed lukewarm in their understanding and engagement. She had arrived at step one: her big picture outcome was to have students experience and critically reflect on privilege and power and the connection between economic class and the rebellion in Guatemala.

In step two, she worked with me to develop the learning objectives:

1. *Cognitive*: Students will gain insight on how social class was tied to the rebellion. Students will understand the systemic nature of oppression. Students will learn specific terms like *voice*, *privilege*, *oppression*, *power*, and *hegemony*.
2. *Affective*: Students will feel what it is like to have no voice in the system. Students will experience feelings of powerlessness or privilege and empathize with those in the texts.
3. *Behavioral*: Students will fully participate in the exercise, giving critical analysis about events in the simulation and relating them to current realities and class readings. Students will reflect on ways to expose or question oppression in their own lives. During reflection, students will develop and hone their critical thinking skills.

Step three is to examine the real-life situation you want to imitate. In this case, the context is the Guatemalan society, which is a three-tiered society with a privileged elite class, a bilingual middle class, and a lower

6. "Service Learning Project Ice Breakers," Pittsburgh Public Schools, http://www.pps.k12
.pa.us/cms/lib/PA01100449/Centricity/Domain/2018/Service_Project_Ice_Breakers.pdf.

class composed of speakers of native dialects. The rebellion sprang from the middle class, whose members spoke both Spanish and native dialects. The rebellion failed to fundamentally change the oppressive system in Guatemala, and that was the reality we re-created in the simulation.

To recreate a microcosm of this world, step four, we designed the following:

1. Four students would represent the elite class that maintains the status quo in the classroom. They would attend regular class with the teacher with the added privilege of having drinks and snacks and speaking English, if they desired, in the Spanish-only class.

2. Four students would represent the middle class. They could only stand in the classroom (a working position) and could only speak Spanish. They must take direction from the elites and can move only if so instructed.

3. Twelve students would represent the poor lower class. They would be required to sit in a squatting position, clasping their ankles with blindfolds covering their eyes. They could only speak native dialects and would have to maintain their position throughout the duration of the simulation. They would effectively be silenced since none of the elite students speak a native dialect.

4. Since the elites would be busy having class, they could instruct the middle class to maintain order (using masking tape and squirt bottles filled with water). Once the elites gave the tape and squirt bottles to the middle class to force the lower class people back into position, the middle class would have in their possession the means to turn on the elite class and start a rebellion. The stage would be set.

This simulation needed to fit into a seventy-five-minute class period. Forty-five minutes were set aside to debrief/reflect on the exercise, so this left thirty minutes to actually run the simulation. The introduction and directions would last five minutes, leaving twenty-five minutes for the simulation. Since most students couldn't squat for twenty-five minutes, this gave more than enough time for the "rebellion" to arise.

Step five (adding lifelike aspects to the simulation) required, for this simulation, creating the appropriate inequities. An adult helper would act as servant to the elite class—waiting on them, serving them food and drink, and doing their bidding. To create the difference between middle and lower class, the middle class would have the option to stand when they wanted to. Further, the middle class had to coerce the lower class to maintain their squatting positions when they became tired or expressed their pain, a parallel to what was happening in Guatemala.

The "Squat No More" simulation worked every time. Within fifteen to twenty minutes the middle class would turn the weapons (tape and squirt bottles) on the elite class, free the lower class (from their painful squatting position), and confiscate and redistribute the food. The rebellion always broke down when deciding what to do with the elite captives.

Activities

Now go create your own simulation! Is there a passage of Scripture or an aspect of the Christian faith or adolescent life that you want your students to learn through experience? Is there a historical or cultural reality that students may not understand where a simulation can help? It is hoped the "Squat No More" example shows that the possibilities are endless for teaching using simulations. Young people face all kinds of social, cultural, and missional problems that may be best addressed through a simulation. You can also simulate various stories and scenes from the Bible that will help make Scripture come alive in new ways for your students. However, what often holds us back from using this method is our own lack of initiative or our fear for how it's going to go. What's more likely, though, is that you'll soon discover that your teaching will come alive and your adult staff will enjoy creating simulations and role plays together. Use the provided design template to create your own simulation, and come to value this rich teaching methodology.

Questions and Activities

1. What is the underlying educational theory for why simulations are effective?
2. When have you been involved in a simulation? When have you been involved in a role play? What do you remember about those experiences?
3. Simulations are commonly used in teaching about cross-cultural and missional situations. What was your response to the "Squat No More" simulation? What does your response suggest about the power and effectiveness of using simulations to teach for depth of experience?

Simulation Design Template

Date:	Name:

Group description (size, gender mix, etc.):

Big picture outcome:

Biblical basis for simulation:

Cognitive objectives:

Affective objectives:

Behavioral objectives:

Spiritual formation objectives:

Leadership development goals:	Skill development goals:

Describe real-life situation to be simulated:

Time frame/outline of simulation (use separate sheet if necessary):

Aspects that make it real:	Materials needed:

Suggested reflection questions:

Evaluation:

4. Do a search online for a simulation or role play and find one that you like. List the crucial elements for success from this chapter and see if they're applicable to what you found.

5. Create your own simulation or role play using the principles and chart from this chapter.

Further Reading

Baker, Pat, and Mary-Ruth Marshall. *Simulation Games 2*. Melbourne: Joint Board of Christian Education, 1986.

Project Adventure. *Silver Bullets: A Revised Guide to Initiative Problems, Adventure Games, and Trust Activities*. 2nd ed. Dubuque, IA: Kendall Hunt, 2009.

Rohnke, Karl E. *Bottomless Bag Revival!* 2nd ed. Dubuque, IA: Kendall Hunt, 2004.

Teaching to Change Lives, Outdoors

DOUG GILMER

> It is in creation that we are able to sustain and invigorate
> our spiritual and ethical lives.
>
> —Pierre Teilhard de Chardin

We live in a society today growing increasingly distant from nature and where people spend less time outdoors. A governmental study noted that, despite the benefits of being outdoors, Americans will spend more than 87 percent of their lives indoors.[1] More than half of the world lives in urban centers, a number that will increase over the next decades.[2] Informal surveys show that more than 70 percent of American youth will rarely or never visit a state or national park and that two main obstacles to going outdoors are homework and discomfort being outside.[3] Another issue that has become

1. Neil E. Klepeis et al., "The National Human Activity Pattern Survey (NHAPS): A Resource for Assessing Exposure to Environmental Pollutants," *Journal of Exposure Analysis and Environmental Epidemiology* 11, no. 3 (May/June 2001): 231–52.

2. "World's Population Increasingly Urban with More Than Half Living in Urban Areas," United Nations Department of Economic and Social Affairs, July 10, 2014, http://www.un.org/en/development/desa/news/population/world-urbanization-prospects-2014.html.

3. Amanda Kirkpatrick, "Infographic: Kids and Nature," *Nature Rocks*, The Nature Conservancy, February 11, 2015, http://www.naturerocks.org/parents-worldwide-agree-our-kids-need-more-nature-1.xml.

more prominent is that parents keep their children playing indoors more because they are concerned about safety and security.[4]

Venturing outdoors is not only a great way to relax or spend a family vacation, it is also an effective ministry practice. Christian organizations, especially those focused on young people, have recognized this and continue to develop and implement ministry models of camping, adventure, mission trips, and others. Camping and outdoor ministry are not new concepts, but there does seem to be a resurgence of their practice in spiritual formation with increasingly busy young people.

The Role of the Outdoors in the Bible

The roots of the role of the outdoors in Christian spiritual formation are found throughout Scripture, beginning with creation. Most of us can quote Genesis 1:1, "In the beginning God created the heavens and the earth." However, few of us take the time to consider the *purpose* of God's creation. God created everything for his purpose, his glory, to communicate who he is. The King James Version says God "hast created all things, and for thy pleasure they are and were created" (Rev. 4:11). Other translations say "at his will." We don't usually think of God creating for his own pleasure, but it may be an apt explanation for why he created. If he created at his pleasure, then it was also for his pleasure to act as he chooses and be intimately involved in his creation (Col. 1:16–17). Through his creation God reveals his worthiness to take honor and glory and power (Rev. 4:11):

- "The heavens declare the glory of God; the skies proclaim the work of his hands" (Ps. 19:1 NIV).
- "And the heavens proclaim his righteousness, for he is a God of justice" (Ps. 50:6 NIV).
- "The God who made the world and everything in it is the Lord of heaven and earth and does not live in temples built by human hands" (Acts 17:24 NIV).
- "For in him all things were created: things in heaven and on earth, visible and invisible, whether thrones or powers or rulers or authorities; all things have been created through him and for him" (Col. 1:16).

Men and women were created and placed into this world by God to live in, care for, and be stewards of this creation. We were given the charge to

4. Richard Louv, *Last Child in the Woods* (Chapel Hill, NC: Algonquin, 2008), 123–32.

have dominion, or to rule responsibly, over all God made (Gen. 1:26–28; Lev. 25:23–24; Ps. 50:10; Prov. 12:10; Jer. 2:7). It is clear that nature is not to be ignored or consumed but to be stewarded as part of God's intentional creation and message.

General revelation is the knowledge of God communicated through his creation. Paul sums this up well: "For since the creation of the world God's invisible qualities—his eternal power and divine nature—have been clearly seen, being understood from what has been made, so that people are without excuse" (Rom. 1:20 NIV). Read through any of David's psalms and you'll see how deeply God's general revelation (the outdoors and all things wild) influenced and inspired him. When Job began to question all the bad things happening to him, God didn't attempt to rationalize his plan. Instead he took Job on a virtual tour of creation to reveal his majesty and sovereignty in comparison to Job's circumstances (Job 38–40). We too often forget who God is—and sometimes he uses wilderness moments to remind us.

> We don't often think of play as spiritual, and it's been a difficult topic for the church throughout history, but it may be helpful to think about the role of joy and fun as part of how we were created and as part of spiritual formation. To help, examine Psalm 96:11–12; Psalm 148; Zechariah 8:5; Mark 10:13–16; and John 10:10, and do a word study on "hallelujah" or "joy." How does enjoying nature play a role in our understanding of God and in our spiritual formation?

One of the tithes spoken of in the Old Testament was a trek God's people were to make to Jerusalem each year in order to rejoice with the Lord and thank him for his provision (Deut. 14:22–27). This outdoor festival, the Festival of *Sukkot*, was a weeklong camping expedition for the purpose of remembering one's dependence on God for all things.[5] God commanded his people to go camping together, to sleep in tents (or booths) with a view of the stars so they might never forget his faithfulness to them in the wilderness and the promise he made to Abraham.

The role of wilderness in Scripture captures an important instructional element of outdoor ministry. One of the more well-known wildernesses involved the Israelites on their journey from Egypt into Israel. The forty-year wilderness journey was not without its challenges for the Hebrews, a punishment for their grumbling at Kadesh Barnea (Num. 13–14). No outdoor adventure will be without its challenges. After its conclusion, Moses told the Israelites, "Remember how the Lord your God led you all the way in the wilderness these forty years, to humble and test you in order to know what was in your heart, whether or not you would keep

---

5. More commonly known as the Festival of Tabernacles (Lev. 23:33–44).

his commands" (Deut. 8:2 NIV). God led his chosen people for the right amount of time, in the
right environment, with purpose and intentionality, so that the true desire of their hearts might
be revealed, that their faith might be challenged
and strengthened, and that they would continue
to follow him once the wandering adventure was
over.

Wilderness played a prominent role in the New
Testament too. John the Baptist preached in the wilderness, preparing the way for the coming Messiah
(Matt. 3:3–10; John 1:23). Jesus not only resisted
Satan's temptations in the wilderness but often retreated to lonely places as part of his regular rhythm
(Mark 1:35; Luke 5:16). The apostle Paul, after his
Damascus Road conversion, retreated to the wilderness of Arabia and then Damascus before returning
to Jerusalem three years later (Gal. 1:13–18). If we look at Scripture as a
whole, we find the outdoors was used as a place of renewal—physical, emotional, mental, and spiritual healing.

> "When we lead groups of people in the wilderness, we typically live in tents for several days, and sometimes a whole week. There are practical and theological reasons for doing this, such as remembering our dependence on God in every way. . . . In the wilderness through regular times of reflection and journaling, we are often reminded of what *God has spoken to us personally* in the recent and distant past."
>
> —Ashley Denton, *Christian Outdoor Leadership: Theology, Theory, and Practice* (Fort Collins, CO: Smooth Stone, 2011), 76–77.

> Wilderness is the natural, unfallen antithesis of an unnatural civilization that has lost its soul. It is a place of freedom in which we can recover the true selves we have lost to the corrupting influences of our artificial lives. Most of all, it is the ultimate landscape of authenticity. Combining the sacred grandeur of the sublime with the primitive simplicity of the frontier, it is the place where we can see the world as it really is, and so know ourselves as we really are—or ought to be.[6]

The apostle Paul's life often seemed like one large adventure and even
misadventure. Paul knew discomfort but maintained a godly perspective.
While none of us is likely to be left adrift at sea, shipwrecked, beaten, im-
prisoned, or bitten by deadly snakes, physical and outdoor challenges and
inconveniences create environments to learn from. Blisters, minor infec-
tions, hunger, thirst, poison ivy, and being cold and wet can all be used as
teachable moments from which we can learn and communicate powerful
spiritual truths.

6. William Cronon, "The Trouble with Wilderness; or, Getting Back to the Wrong Nature" in
Uncommon Ground: Rethinking the Human Place in Nature, ed. William Cronon (New York:
W. W. Norton, 1995), 80.

What Is Outdoor Ministry?

Outdoor ministry can be defined this way: "Outdoor ministry exists to influence positive spiritual change in the lives of participants through relevant outdoor experiences specifically designed to make one more aware of and more reliant on the Creator and his creation and equipped to carry what they've learned beyond the immediate experience."[7] Outdoor ministry is about more than just having a good time and hosting fun activities. Outdoor ministry is

- purposeful—it has a stated set of educational and spiritual goals;
- intentional—the stated purposes are specific and intended to lead to positive spiritual change;
- personal—the outdoor experience is individually challenging and is focused on the people we lead and influence, not the experience itself;
- relevant—outdoor ministry can provide the right activity (or adventure) for the right person, in the right environment, at the right time, for the right outcome;
- inspired—it is focused on God and his creation; and
- applicable—participants learn lessons they can take away from the immediate experience and apply it to their lives.

People of all ages enjoy, and actually crave, adventure. A British study recently showed that people believe they get more adventurous as they grow older and are most adventurous at age forty-one.[8] Adventure reality shows continue to grow in popularity with audiences of all ages. Middle-aged adults want to watch people face challenging situations and imagine how they would act in similar situations.[9] Older adult viewers watch adventure-based television because the themes are motivating and provide an escape from reality.[10] Advances in healthcare mean people are living longer and enjoying more-active, productive lifestyles in the later years. As we live in more-urbanized, and technologically controlled, settings, the outdoors will continue to be significant places for ministry.

7. This is adapted from the Adventure Leadership and Outdoor Ministry degree program at Liberty University.

8. "We Are Most Adventurous at the Age of 41," *Daily Mail*, May 30, 2012, http://www.daily mail.co.uk/news/article-2151954/We-adventurous-age-41-money-indulge-things-wanted-29.html.

9. Rebecca Gardyn, "The Tribe Has Spoken," *Advertising Age*, September 1, 2001, http:// adage.com/article/american-demographics/tribe-spoken/43086/.

10. A. Elizabeth, "What Alaskan Reality TV Teaches Us about Market Research," *Instantly Blog*, October 11, 2012, https://www.instant.ly/blog/2012/10/what-alaskan-reality-tv-teaches-us-about -market-research.

While opportunities do exist for more-costly high-adventure activities, outdoor ministry can be done almost anywhere there is an "outdoors." Most of us, within a short drive of where we live, can access hiking or biking trails, camping areas, waterfronts, ropes courses, and other facilities. For many people today who have grown up far removed from the outdoors, a small backyard woodlot or community nature trail can seem just as wild and remote as Alaska's Tongass National Forest. Even a simple nighttime campfire is a fresh experience for many, and watching a burning pile of wood can lead to transformed lives and communities.

Spiritual Formation and Teachable Moments

Researchers studied 116 young people ages sixteen to twenty over a two-week adventure experience that combined a number of outdoor activities in a wilderness setting with relevant spiritual teaching.[11] The goal was to measure two outcomes: spiritual walk (actions) and spiritual foundations (beliefs). Students indicated they benefited from learning about perseverance, personal strengths, and talents, and from spending significant amounts of time alone with God. The action-oriented lessons were deemed by students to be more valuable than traditional teachings. The researchers concluded that spiritual growth could be best strengthened through a combination of clear spiritual teachings and outdoor experiences.

Another research project concluded, "Prolonged and challenging immersion in the outdoors, especially in relatively pristine settings, can exert a powerful physical, emotional, intellectual, and moral-spiritual influence on young people."[12] Research participants reported a far greater respect, affinity, appreciation, and sense of humility and spiritual connection with the natural world as a consequence of their outdoor experience. "A child who experiences the sense of wonder in the face of creation is learning, not only about nature, but about the glory of God. Children and adults who have no contact with the outdoor world are robbed of devotional knowledge, not just of natural interests."[13]

Another study examined the effects of wilderness and spirituality on the mental health of students and found that spirituality was an intrinsic

11. Cay Anderson-Hanley, "Adventure Programming and Spirituality: Integration Models, Methods and Research," *Journal of Experiential Education* 20, no. 2 (1997): 102–7.

12. Stephen R. Kellert, "A National Study of Outdoor Wilderness Experience" (New Haven: Yale University Press, 1998), 169.

13. Albert J. Mohler, "Avoiding 'Nature Deficit Disorder'—It's about Theology, Not Therapy," *Albert Mohler*, June 5, 2007, http://www.albertmohler.com/2007/06/05/avoiding-nature-deficit -disorder-its-about-theology-not-therapy/.

aspect of wilderness experience. Staff reported that students who attended the wilderness retreat with religious backgrounds grew deeper in their faith, and many of those with no or limited religious or spiritual upbringing began a personal quest seeking spiritual growth. The study concluded that wilderness experiences foster spiritual growth and interest among its participants and create environments for therapeutic success.[14]

The Outdoor Environment Is Perfect for Teaching

Critical to outdoor learning is the pace or tempo at which events occur. Time seems to slow down in an outdoor setting, and life is left behind. When free of life's demands, we are provided an opportunity to relax, listen, reflect, and be more attentive. Waking up to a sunrise over a fog-covered lake, witnessing the northern lights dance in the sky, watching wildlife up close, and successfully crossing a rugged landscape all have a way giving us pause and perspective. Mark Batterson provides the equation, "Change of pace + change of place = change of perspective."[15]

The outdoors also provides an environment in which we can move people out of their comfort zones through intentional exercises. A dictionary definition of *adventure* is any activity in which the outcome is not predetermined or controlled by us. Adventure involves uncertainty and an element of risk. Outdoor adventures, such as high ropes courses, camping trips, and backcountry adventures, create tension and challenge by design.

Risk is essential to the outdoor learning experience and the concept of adventure, though not at the expense of safety. By definition, risk is the potential to lose something of value. In this case, risk reminds people of their limits and even their own mortality. Inherent risks are present and inescapable anytime we venture outdoors. Actual risk is associated with the specific activity or element we are undertaking. Perceived risk is our goal, but we do not scare or manipulate people. Our goal is to create teachable moments while not

> Author Benedict Carey gives five keys to effective learning that are naturally present in outdoor teaching.
>
> 1. Pace activities appropriately.
> 2. Switch locations of the normal learning environment.
> 3. Mix up the methods we use.
> 4. Get outside.
> 5. Challenge yourself.
>
> —Benedict Carey, *How We Learn: The Surprising Truth about When, Where, and Why It Happens* (New York: Random House, 2014), 3.

---

14. Lauren Rothwell, "Wilderness Therapy and Spirituality," *Journal of Therapeutic Camping* 8, no. 1 (2009).
15. Mark Batterson, *Wild Goose Chase* (Colorado Springs: Multnomah, 2008), 40.

putting anyone in needless danger. We want to introduce students to stress in the form of managed risk.

What Does the Outdoors Teach Us?

1. Outdoor ministry teaches us about our limitations, reminding us of our need for others and for God. We learn very quickly in the outdoors, especially in extreme adventures, that we cannot do things on our own.
2. Outdoor ministry allows us to see the very nature of God and learn about his provision and faithfulness. We are humbled when we see just how big God is and how small we and our problems are. Richard Louv says nature introduces us to the idea of knowing we are not alone.[16]
3. Outdoor ministry helps us develop a more missional worldview and see the needs of the world in new ways. Participating in outdoor experiences is critical to understanding the life-sustaining role of nature and the environment on humanity. To be less than conscious of this is to risk producing environmentally irresponsible behavior.[17]
4. Outdoor ministry creates an atmosphere for us to see ourselves as God sees us. Spending time in an outdoor environment has the tendency to break down walls and facades, which tend to hide our true nature.

Being unplugged, distraction free, with little or no attention to personal appearance, having access to only basic hygiene care, and being at the mercy of the elements, we are able to view our true identity, our spiritual state before God, and the possibilities of our future. The world sends so many different messages about who and what we should be, that only when we distance ourselves from that influence can we often see ourselves for who we really are in the eyes of God.

Leading Outdoor Ministry

Becoming an effective outdoor leader doesn't happen by accident. It takes practice. No matter how many books you read or episodes of Bear Grylls you watch, if you haven't spent much time outdoors, your ability to effectively lead and teach others will be lacking. Surprisingly, while the ability to light a fire without a match, find water, build an emergency shelter, and

16. Louv, *Last Child in the Woods*, 296.
17. Cronon, "Trouble with Wilderness," 87.

How Outdoor Experience Teaches

Research on short-term missions has helped us understand how people learn and are spiritually formed through experience. One of the most helpful theories is that of Laura Joplin. Joplin developed a timeline that illustrates how experiences are effectively structured for learning. The illustration also helps teachers to identify problems if something breaks down in the experience. Terry Linhart adjusted the model based on his short-term mission research.

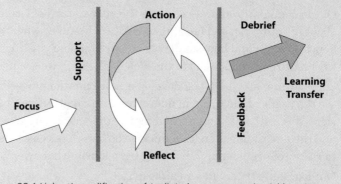

Figure 23.1 Linhart's modification of Joplin's theory on experiential learning

Laura Joplin, "On Defining Experiential Education," in *The Theory of Experiential Education*, ed. Karen Warren, Mitchell Sakofs, and Jasper S. Hunt Jr. (Dubuque, IA: Kendall Hunt, 1995), 15–22; Terence D. Linhart, "How We Learn from Short-Term Mission Experiences: A Grounded Theory Modification of the Joplin Model," *Christian Education Journal* 7, no. 1 (Spring 2010): 172–85.

get yourself (and others) out of risky outdoor situations is important, these hard skills are not the skills you will you use the most. The soft skills—empathy, sensitivity, compassion, and especially communication—are far more important. With these comes the ability to recognize and communicate teachable moments in the outdoor context.

What can you do to prepare yourself for outdoor leadership? First, spend time alone in the outdoors. There is no substitute for experience, and some of the most intimate and spiritually enlightening moments come from spending time alone outdoors. You don't have to go camping or on an extreme backcountry adventure. Go for a walk on a local nature trail or a day hike in a well-known area. Sit outside at night, listen to the sounds, and watch the stars.

Second, spend time learning outdoor skills. Find someone to take you outside and teach you skills if you are unsure of what to do. You can also sign up for mini outdoor adventure trips through local stores: REI, L.L. Bean,

Linhart's Version of Joplin's Model

Focus—Before the experience(s), the participant focuses on the task, and attention is given to the challenges ahead.

Support—The first "boundary" of the experience, support comes from adults, organizations, logistics, and other members of the experience that support and define the edges of the experience and keep participants acting effectively.

Action—Participants step into the situation or activity, using new skills and knowledge to solve problems, forcing them to act on what they know.

Reflect—As the participant acts, he or she reacts, deciphers, and reflects on the meaning of his or her actions.

Feedback—The other edge of the experience, feedback usually comes from the teacher/facilitator in providing needed direction, encouragement, and other forms of support and clarification.

Debrief—After the experience, this is the initial process where the learning is recognized, discussed, and evaluated either individually or through structured experiences like group discussions or journals.

Learning transfer—Often overlooked but perhaps the most important, this is the long-term effect of learning recognition. How and what from the experience was transferred into the lives of participants after the experience?

Cabela's, Bass Pro, or other outdoor retailers. Some are free, others are cheap. Spending time learning under the teaching of someone who knows what they are doing will help you become competent in skills such as using a map and compass, practicing outdoor survival basics, climbing, paddling, and so on. With competence comes confidence. If you have both, your participants will notice and afford you greater respect; and thus you'll be more effective in reaching your ministry goals.

Finally, keep an outdoor journal chronicling what you experience and learn and what spiritual and personal application there might be. This exercise helps identify the teachable moments and prepares you to teach these ideas effectively within the context of a biblical worldview.

Once you are ready to lead your first experience, here are some practical considerations to think through.

1. *Know your audience.* What ages are the people you're leading? What are their needs spiritually, emotionally, socially, and physically? What are their physical limits and capacities? You lead others into the

outdoors not for yourself but rather to effect change in the lives of the participants.

2. *Determine the purpose of the activity from the beginning.* Though you can never be certain of the final outcome, what do you hope to have happen in the lives of your participants? Is the purpose team building? Leadership development? Evangelism? Spiritual growth? How does (or doesn't) that goal connect to your intended experience?

3. *Assemble a team of leaders who share your vision.* This team may include not only other adult leaders but also respected student leaders if you are leading a group of young people. Don't underestimate the influence of respected student leaders to begin laying the foundation and generating enthusiasm for your planned activity. Ensuring everyone shares the same vision up front sets expectations, provides accountability, and helps ensure you have appropriate leadership in case you, as the trip leader, get hurt or are otherwise unable to complete the event.

4. *Determine what resources you have available.* Think through the time, finances, equipment, transportation, and logistics involved in your program. Have a trusted veteran leader look over your event planning and give you feedback. Think through contingencies for injury, weather, transportation problems, and other potential challenges.

5. *Be realistic about your limitations.* People get into trouble when they attempt activities in the outdoors far outside their levels of experience and competence. It is perfectly appropriate and often helpful to hire an experienced guide who can help mitigate risk, respond to contingencies, and provide you with additional leadership.

6. *Prepare your participants.* Make sure everyone knows in advance what they are signing up for. Don't hold back. Be honest. The last thing you want is to tear down the trust you have established by not telling them everything in advance. You also want to make sure everyone knows what is expected of them and the outcomes you hope to achieve. Make sure you have signed permission forms with insurance information.

7. *Write a trip plan.* Everyone—leaders, participants, families, supervisors—will appreciate this. And all should have a copy. Address the basics: what you are doing, who is going, why you are doing it, when you are going and returning, where you are going, how you are getting there, and especially the "what if"—detailed plans for contingencies such as medical emergencies and dangerous weather.

There are always risks to outdoor adventures, but there are also ways to mitigate those risks and prepare for them in advance. Here are my "T.E.A.M. C.A.R.E." ways you can be prepared for teaching outdoors:

T—Training: Be competent and confident in your skill sets.

E—Emergency plan: Know what you are going to do in the event of emergencies.

A—Access to medical care: Know where you'll get it before you need to use it.

M—Manage risk: Don't take unnecessary risks no matter what, despite your confidence in yourself or your team's ability. Don't let ego get in the way of safety.

C—Communicate: Everyone should know what to expect, and others should always know where you are, your route, and when you'll return.

A—Accountability: You are accountable as a leader to yourself, your team, and God. Don't place yourself in a situation with a student or an adult that could cause harm to your ministry.

R—Remember who is in charge: You are! There is a reason you are the leader. At the end of the day, you have to make the tough calls, and those who follow you should respect your decisions.

E—Environment: Know it and respect it. Plan for it. Lightning, rain, snow, cold, dangerous storms, and water issues are constants. Environmental conditions claim more lives than any others, and often it's due to groups and leaders taking unnecessary risks.

Questions and Activities

1. What were the best and worst outdoor learning experiences that you've had? What made them so?

2. What role does nature (general revelation) have in revealing who God is?

3. Make a list in a column of all of the outdoor experiences you can remember. Next to each one write down what you learned from the experience—personally, spiritually, and socially. How do those outcomes compare to the main themes of this chapter?

4. A part of being outdoors is having fun, yet we don't talk about that much in Christian circles. What role does *play* have, if any, in the Christian life? Why do you think that is?

5. Imagine that you're assigned the task of training a group of student leaders to lead small groups. Design the training using each stage of Linhart's adaptation of Joplin's theory.

Further Reading

Crabtree, Jack. *Better Safe Than Sued: Keeping Your Students and Ministry Alive*. Grand Rapids: Zondervan/Youth Specialties, 2008.

Denton, Ashley. *Christian Outdoor Leadership: Theology, Theory, and Practice*. Fort Collins, CO: Smooth Stone, 2011.

Gorman, Julie A. *Community That Is Christian*. Grand Rapids: Baker Books, 2002.

Leyda, Richard. "The Ministry of Christian Camping." In *Introducing Christian Education*, edited by Michael J. Anthony, 262–68. Grand Rapids: Baker Academic, 2001.

SECTION FIVE

MANAGING TEACHING FOR MAXIMUM IMPACT

Too often discussions of teaching and learning are limited to curriculum, the teacher-student relationship, and the delivery. However, teaching is greatly affected by the environment and systems beyond the classroom experience. This section focuses on three of the most critical areas of teaching effectiveness—evaluating, equipping others, and using technology.

Without evaluation our teaching may completely miss our audience and have limited effectiveness. Effective Christian leaders consistently evaluate their ministry and teaching. In the same way that an orchard keeper has to come close to the tree to inspect the fruit, effective teachers regularly inspect the fruitfulness of their teaching.

Jesus's command for us to make disciples has implications that we are to be developing other adults to participate in the teaching ministry. Additionally, if adolescents learn as much or more from watching adults than from hearing them, then we need a strategic approach to developing other adults to be capable and exemplary teachers. This takes time and focus, but it's energy well worth investing.

Finally, we talk often about technology, but its use is typically limited to videos, presentation software, and a few smartphone apps. There are numerous technologies that can give strong support to our teaching and discipling efforts. The final chapter prompts us to think deeply about a myriad of educational technology opportunities for Christian teaching and discipleship.

24

The Importance of Evaluation

KERRY LOESCHER

By Chris's[1] fifteenth birthday, his dad had walked out, his mom was addicted to drugs and in jail, he lived involuntarily with his widowed grandmother, and he was arrested for "joyriding" in a stolen car. The judge sentenced Chris to community service, hoping this would give Chris both a wake-up call and new direction in life. His grandmother called a church to see if there were some "odd jobs" he could do to fulfill his community service hours.

Chris started out helping the set up/clean up crew for Sunday morning services; the set up and tear down for these services were weekly parts of the church's rhythm. Before long, people discovered that Chris naturally excelled at getting the sound equipment to work. He could get all the pieces working well and have them set up in near record time. Chris not only found something he was good at, but he connected relationally with the other adults and youth on the tech team.

During this time, the church launched a capital campaign to build a new facility. On the big launch Sunday, the equipment started malfunctioning shortly after the worship music began. Chris and the rest of the team jumped into action trying to solve the problem. At about this time, one of the church pastors arrived with a group of affluent, older members from the congregation on a tour for potential donors to see the needs and hear the vision for the proposed new facilities.

1. Chris is not his real name, but this is his real story.

The tour's timing could not have been more perfect . . . or more awful. The group entered the back of the room right next to the tech booth where Chris and others worked frantically to get the equipment back online. The group had a front-row seat when the soundboard's lid slammed shut on Chris's hand, eliciting some colorful language in response.

Reflecting on this event, would one call the youth ministry a success or a failure? From whose perspective is Chris's progress evaluated? How would the youth ministry's effectiveness be evaluated? Unfortunately, healthy and productive evaluation is not common in Christian ministry settings. In fact, in many contexts there is no formal assessment at all. The reasons for this are beyond the scope of this chapter; but the result is that too many problems are left uncorrected, and things that should be recognized go uncelebrated.

Reality #1: Evaluation Happens All the Time

Despite the lack of formal evaluation, informal assessments happen all the time. Parents, learners, leaders, teachers, other team members, silver-haired grandmothers, the pastoral team, trustees, and other people all have thoughts about how and what the ministry is doing. They voice their opinions in the hall, on social media, in committee meetings, and in the parking lot. People talk, and everyone has an opinion.

The downside to informal assessment is that it can feel (and get) personal. Leaders invest time, energy, and heart into loving and leading the next generation and their families. Real, effective ministry requires a serious personal investment. Thus, how can assessment *not* be personal? When done well, formal assessment brings leaders face to face with the strengths and weaknesses in their character, stylistic choices, programming/teaching endeavors, communication abilities, and much more.

However, authentic assessment produces widely varied emotions, ranging from insecurity and defensiveness to excitement and anticipation. Why? Assessment dares to look objectively at the *personal* investments made, evaluating what has and has not been effective. When complete, assessment requires change, and change is work—and sometimes can be threatening.

Reality #2: Evaluation Is a Biblical Expectation

The law of the farm dictates that if farmers plant wheat, then barring any sort of freak weather event, they will harvest wheat. If farmers plant corn, they harvest corn. At harvest time, they expect a crop. Jesus expressed this principle to his disciples when he cursed the fig tree in Matthew 21:18–22. Hungry, Jesus saw a fig tree with luscious leaves and no fruit. Jesus cursed the fig tree, and it withered. Jesus expected fruit.

Transformed lives and communities represent the true fruit of the gospel at work. Scripture declares that Christ followers will be "transformed" into the Lord's likeness (2 Cor. 3:18). In fact, "if anyone is in Christ, he is a new creation. The old has passed away; behold, the new has come" (2 Cor. 5:17). This transformation of the very human soul *is* the good news!

Matthew 25:14–30 recounts Jesus's parable of the talents, a story about opportunity and expected fruit. Going on a journey, a man entrusted his property to three servants to act as stewards while he was gone. Expecting fruitfulness while he was gone, he wanted them to manage the resources in the same way he would. When the master returned to settle accounts, two servants had worked hard on the master's behalf, doubling what they were given. The third simply buried the talents he received in the ground. The master rewarded, commended, and celebrated the fruitful servants and denounced the unfruitful servant. The unfruitful servant failed to meet the master's expectation for fruitfulness.

> To what extent does the church and next-generation ministry effectively fulfill the Great Commission? What examples of transformed lives can be found demonstrating the ministry's true fruitfulness?

Jesus's command to his disciples that the Father has given all authority in heaven and on earth to him and that they are to go out and make disciples is an expectation of fruitful work. Jesus expects his disciples to be fruitful in their proclamation and demonstration of the gospel to every nation. They are to baptize new believers, teaching each one everything that Jesus commanded. Jesus has given them authority, he promises his presence, and he tells them exactly what fruit he expects. The mandate and the expectation remain the same, providing ministry's first and most important area of assessment.

Reality #3: The Faithfulness vs. Fruitfulness Tension

Faithfulness and fruitfulness are not antithetical but complementary. God clearly expects both—meaning, they exist in a needed dynamic tension. The need for faithfulness informs the call to fruitfulness. Believers faithfully persevere in their efforts to see fruitfulness occur until it actually happens. The need for fruitfulness forces evaluation of the ministry's efforts to ensure the church works faithfully on what is considered fruitful. Faithfulness without fruitfulness wastes time and resources. Fruitfulness without faithfulness may quit prematurely while more harvest remains.

Assessment's Challenge

One could argue that much about discipleship is more caught than taught, or at least that its components are both taught *and* caught. Here are four primary questions each ministry will have to answer as they implement effective assessment:

1. How can the fruit of what is caught be captured and measured accurately for evaluation?
2. How can the fruit of relational ministry be measured when it is often less formalized?
3. How can the depth of discipleship happening in the life of an individual and a group over time be assessed?
4. What role will numbers (i.e., amount of participants, money, and budgets) play in regular evaluation?

As leadership teams meet to determine how progress is to be measured, they will have to decide what benchmarks will be used to indicate growth. They will need to choose indicators that validate the progress as genuine, meaningful, and healthy. Sadly, behavior modification to fit in with the "Christian club" does not describe the desired fruit of discipleship, nor does it justify the investment of resources. Only transformation of the disciple's heart by the Holy Spirit and his or her submission to Jesus in increasingly broader ways qualify as legitimate indicators of fruit.

Assessment's Value

Assessment serves as a valuable guide to best practices. Knowing what worked, why it worked, and for whom it worked are critical elements in choosing effective methods and how best to execute these strategically. Assessments can confirm or invalidate the leader/mentor's "hunches" about effectiveness. Formalized evaluation also provides greater accountability benchmarks for those doing the ministry. The benchmarks give leaders and learners specific areas for growth, reasons to adjust or stay the course, and opportunities to celebrate!

Though evaluation of the teacher/mentor should occur, it is secondary to *learner* outcomes. For content to truly be learned, measurable assessment should take place in four categories:

- *Cognitive:* Can the disciples demonstrate a solid grasp and understanding of the content and concepts presented? What fruit is seen?

  Can the disciples demonstrate a basic understanding of who, what, when, where, why, and how (if relevant)? Can the learners restate the basic content in their own words? Can they demonstrate an understanding of the lesson's or experience's main point?

- *Affective:* What attitudes and core values can be found that line up with those of a disciple? What fruit is seen?

  What opinions have they formulated about the content or experience? How concretely are they comparing the challenges of the new material with their previously held beliefs and expressing agreement or conflict with these ideas in productive ways? (Often emotions provide the first clue in this assessment category.)

- *Psycho-motor:* How have the skills and abilities for implementation and application of the change been concretely exhibited? What specific fruit is seen? (This includes skills and choices made to preserve positive habits.)

  To what extent are they owning their choices and taking responsibility for the results of those choices? Do they demonstrate an ability to avoid negative peer pressure or to help create positive peer pressure? To what lengths can they "walk the talk" even when there is no one around to encourage or challenge them?

- *Outcome:* What long-term effects are the disciples having on the community with whom they have influence? What specific fruit can be seen?

  In what specific ways do the learners demonstrate transformed lives that cause transformation in the lives of those around them? Can outsiders tell the difference? If so, in what specific ways? (Christ-centered choices over time will change the dynamics of every relationship in a community.)

These four assessment categories apply whether the content involves basic budgeting skills, changing a flat tire, or theological training. Discipleship always seeks to affect the head, heart, hands, and lives of people, but this quest raises two questions. (1) What does a true disciple look like?

(2) What does growth toward maturity look like in concrete and measurable terms?

Assessment Benchmarks

All successful endeavors begin with some form of this principle: begin with the end in mind.[2] Jesus's mandate to make disciples requires disciple makers to step back and determine what a disciple actually looks like in some concrete and measurable terms. Without such a picture, how can effectiveness be measured with any level of accuracy?

Josh Hunt in his text *Disciple-Making Teachers* lists nine traits, or assets, of true disciples in the form of an acrostic, along with accompanying benchmarks that depict each asset when lived out on a daily basis.[3] The benchmarks identified offer just a sampling of those that are possible.

D—Disciplined Daily Life

This characteristic generally supports the other characteristics, and if it falls apart, the other areas do as well.

- Driven by a deep and profound love for God, they discipline themselves to make time for God devotionally and live for him obediently.
- Their actions are motivated by biblical core values and a scriptural worldview, not a legalistic adherence to a list of Bible-based "shoulds" and "should nots."
- Their schedules reflect the priorities of the Christian life.

I—Intimate Friendships

These friends are ones where "the real me connects with the real you."

- They pursue intimacy through honesty and authenticity.
- They make themselves accountable to a selected few.
- They exhibit healthy conflict resolution and walk in forgiveness.
- They live in community, serving others and doing life together with them.
- They honor and prefer others above themselves.

2. Steven Covey made this idea famous.
3. Josh Hunt, *Disciple-Making Teachers*, with Larry Mays (Loveland, CO: Group, 2009), sec. 1.

S—Self-Esteem

People rarely rise above the level of their self-esteem, and here Hunt and Mays speak not in psychological terms but in terms of their new identity in Christ.

- They learn the implications of being new creations in Christ (2 Cor. 5:17; dead to sin, Rom. 6:11; alive to God in Christ, Rom. 6:11; sitting with Christ at God's right hand, Eph. 2:6; marked by the Holy Spirit, Eph. 1:13; etc.), causing them to overcome temptation more consistently.
- Disciples discover their worth before God in terms of who they are onto-logically, not in relation only to their works (beloved, 1 Thess. 1:4; saints, Eph. 3:17b–18; children of God, Eph. 2:8–9; temple of God, 1 Cor. 3:17; etc.). Insecurities diminish and become less of an influence on their lives.
- Likewise, they discover their mission in this world via other biblical word pictures (a royal priesthood, 1 Pet. 2:9; witnesses, Acts 1:8; sol-diers of Christ, 2 Tim. 2:3; etc.) and begin to act in accordance with those word pictures.

C—Corporate Worship

This involves disciples learning to worship God with other believers in a corporate setting.

- Disciples understand this differs from their personal quiet time, and this provides an opportunity for them to participate with other believ-ers in one spirit, mind, and purpose to bring glory to God.
- They find delight in praying and worship with other Christ followers.
- They learn that focusing on God in worship and ministering to him is more important than what they get out of worship personally, impact-ing the way they worship.

I—Intimate Family Life

The home is the first arena for truth to be applied and can be the most important and difficult arena to live out the truth.

- They pursue family intimacy through honesty, authenticity, and good listening.
- Disciples demonstrate a growing aptitude for healthy conflict resolu-tion and the ability to forgive.

- They look for ways to love their family members like Christ loved the church (Eph. 5:25), serving them selflessly.
- They find ways to be unified even when they do not agree on everything, because they are committed to one another through the good and the bad.

P—Passion for God

Love for God and his presence grows as the primary motivating factor in believers' lives.

- Deeper passions overcome lesser passions, enabling disciples to overcome sin and temptation more easily.
- Disciples have a love for God that is tested and trusted over time, with or without the "goose bumps." The passion has been tried and fortified through many life challenges.
- They view themselves as part of God's team and mission more than seeing God as an add-on part of their lives.
- Passion for God becomes the central focal point around which their entire lives revolve.

L—Lay Ministry Involvement

Freely they received God's grace and mercy, now freely they want to share that same grace and mercy with others. Christ's love compels them (2 Cor. 5:10).

- Disciples find ways to serve others in the church and in the community in order to fulfill God's command to love others.
- Disciples discover their God-given passions, temperaments, and spiritual gifts and find ways to minister that are commensurate with their unique wiring.
- They serve as spiritual mothers and fathers to those young in the faith, helping spiritual novices to progress in their spiritual journey in Christ.

E—Evangelistic Involvement

Called to be "salt," "light," and "witnesses," believers must be empowered and mobilized to engage actively in the Great Commission.

- Growing disciples look for ways to participate in passing faith in God on to younger generations by acting as disciplers and mentors themselves.
- They make the most of every opportunity to share the gospel with and make disciples of their peers.
- They pray and intercede for the unsaved.
- These disciples reflect more compassion than judgment toward those outside the faith.

S—Sacrificial Giving

Rather than giving when it is comfortable, this trait describes disciples who choose to give sacrificially, beyond their comfort zones.

- Believing that 100 percent of what they own belongs to God, these believers hold onto all they "own" loosely, releasing and giving whatever God asks as needed.
- They practice the principle of giving the first fruits of their work as an indicator that God is their source and provider.
- Rather than hoarding, these Christ followers constantly look for ways to give a greater percentage of their income for the advancement of God's kingdom.

Once again, assessing whether the above assets and accompanying benchmarks reflect lives deeply transformed by the power of the Holy Spirit or reflect the habits of people who have conformed to the expected norms remains a challenge. In the context of meaningful relationships with disciplers and mentors, the genuineness of these benchmarks can be evaluated more effectively. Observing disciples' participation in short-term mission trips, local service projects, and local church ministry can provide further indicators of their progress. Listening to their testimonies about God's work in their lives reveals much about the authenticity of their transformation. The next section proposes an intentional framework for helping young people grow spiritually.

Methodology: Developmental Relationships and Asset-Building Communities

The Search Institute conducted extensive research to discover necessary developmental assets that help young people grow to be healthy, caring,

The Developmental Relationships Framework

Express CARE Show that you like me and want the best for me.	• **Be Present**—Pay attention when you are with me. • **Be Warm**—Let me know that you like being with me and express positive feelings toward me. • **Invest**—Commit time and energy to doing things for and with me. • **Show Interest**—Make it a priority to understand who I am and what I care about. • **Be Dependable**—Be someone I can count on and trust.
CHALLENGE Growth Insist that I try to continuously improve.	• **Inspire**—Help me see future possibilities for myself. • **Expect**—Make it clear that you want me to live up to my potential. • **Stretch**—Recognize my thoughts and abilities while also pushing me to strengthen them. • **Limit**—Hold me accountable for appropriate boundaries and rules.
Provide SUPPORT Help me complete tasks and achieve goals.	• **Encourage**—Praise my efforts and achievements. • **Guide**—Provide practical assistance and feedback to help me learn. • **Model**—Be an example I can learn from and admire. • **Advocate**—Stand up for me when I need it.
Share POWER Hear my voice, and let me share in making decisions.	• **Respect**—Take me seriously and treat me fairly. • **Give Voice**—Ask for and listen to my opinions and consider them when you make decisions. • **Respond**—Understand and adjust to my needs, interests, and abilities. • **Collaborate**—Work with me to accomplish goals and solve problems.
Expand POSSIBILITIES Expand my horizons, and connect me to opportunities.	• **Explore**—Expose me to new ideas, experiences, and places. • **Connect**—Introduce me to people who can help me grow. • **Navigate**—Help me work through barriers that could stop me from achieving my goals.

Copyright © 2014 by Search Institute, http://www.search-institute.org.

Figure 24.1 Search Institute's developmental relationships framework, http://www.search-institute.org/downloadable/Dev-Relationships-Framework-Sept2014.pdf

and responsible adults.[4] They resolved to identify which core characteristics young people need to make a successful transition from their developmental years into adulthood, calling them "developmental assets." Similarly, church leaders/mentors can develop a list of biblical "developmental assets" that characterize growing disciples, much like those listed in the D.I.S.C.I.P.L.E.S. acrostic proposed by Hunt and Mays. Without such a list, any intentionality would be vague, and discipleship effectiveness could not be evaluated.

Second, the research revealed a significant trend. The young people who were most likely to have the necessary developmental assets had (and

4. In 1993, Peter L. Benson, PhD, and the Search Institute released their findings concerning a significant study into what causes some adolescents to be resilient and others to fail at entering a healthy adulthood. They concluded there were forty key traits, *developmental assets*, in the lives of these resilient young people (http://www.search-institute.org/about/history).

The Journey . . .

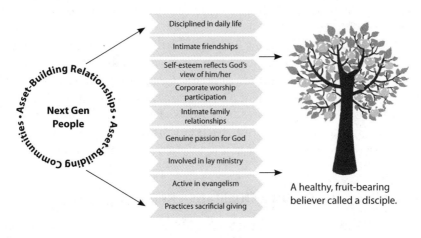

Figure 24.2 The journey

This image is the combination of ideas presented by the Search Institute (especially concerning asset-building relationships and communities), Josh Hunt's habits of a disciple, and Kerry Loescher's application for ministry.

needed) caring, intentional adults present in their lives. Raising a young person truly takes a village! This finding birthed what they call "The Developmental Relationships Framework," which outlines five key tasks for these developmental relationships (see fig. 24.1).

The Search Institute argues that the best learning happens in the context of "developmental relationships." In the context of church ministry, leaders/mentors strategically involve other believers in the disciples' lives relationally to help facilitate growth and development. They evaluate these relationships based on established criteria to ensure that discipleship, not just "hanging out," happens. With grace *and* intentionality, these "developmental relationships" provide support, express care, and challenge disciples toward progress (as seen in fig. 24.1).

As extensions of the asset-making developmental relationships, asset-building communities form support networks around young people where everyone (church, school, neighborhoods, towns, etc.) works toward their success.[5] These asset-building communities reach across traditional organizational lines of race, age, family ties, structure, and the like with one goal in mind—making sure the next generation becomes successful, responsible, healthy members of the community. For church ministry contexts,

5. "Developmental Communities: The Missing Link," Search Institute, http://www.search-institute.org/what-we-study/communities.

asset-building communities offer support and encouragement, helping individuals become Christlike disciples and participating, relationally connected members of the body of Christ.

Figure 24.2 illustrates how developmental assets (discipleship traits), developmental relationships (with leaders and mentors), and asset-building communities (local church bodies) relate to one another in the process of Christian spiritual development. The diagram helps leaders/mentors visualize the process so that they can be strategic and intentional. Additionally, the diagram gives leaders/mentors a visual way to evaluate where breakdowns in the process may be occurring.

Examining the Results: Qualitative Reporting

Changed lives and transformed communities create powerful testimonies and a valuable means for qualitative examination of discipleship results (1 Pet. 3:15; Rev. 12:11). Disciplers listen for these testimonies and encourage disciples to share them in venues where these qualitative expressions of fruitfulness can be trumpeted. Each testimony's "guts" include the same components: "I was . . . ," "Jesus did . . . ," and "Now I am. . . ." Testimonies of transformation provide some of the best qualitative data available.

So how can these stories be collected?

- For perhaps the most revealing and authentic data, engage in one-on-one conversations with the disciples, asking them to describe their own growth in one or more of the nine disciple assets. Developmental relationships exist for this purpose.
- Create public opportunities for them to share their stories. Have participants write out what they want to say first and practice their testimonies with trusted leaders.
- Incorporate "cardboard testimonies" where participants write on one side of a piece of cardboard a completion to the phrase "I said . . . ," and on the backside a completion to the phrase "God says. . . ."
- Use video testimonies of participants during milestones like baptism or graduation.
- Create "God Sighting" banners for special events like mission trips, retreats, camps, or conferences. Display the logo from the event, and then encourage disciples and leaders to write on the banner moments when they saw God at work. Hang these banners in a prominent place after the event, creating a "wall of faith."

- At key times of transition or during significant events, have students fill out a "My Story" card. After documenting their names, date, and the event, they answer questions like,

    "Where are you now in your journey with Christ?"

    "What areas would you like to grow in?"

    "What are you willing to do to grow?"

    "What are you most proud of so far?"

    "What do you think God is speaking to you about?"

    "What would you like to have God give you clear direction on?"

Answers to these questions help leaders/mentors learn where disciples are in their journeys with Christ, enabling them to think strategically about next steps. These cards provide quality "mini testimonies" for use in newsletters, committee reports, training meetings, and more. By gathering this information in a comprehensive format, growth in the lives of leaders, mentors, team members, and parents can also be evaluated.

Examining the Results: Quantitative Reporting

For those who prefer "hard data," a personalized survey could be created. Hunt's *Disciple-Making Teachers* provides a list of discipling assets that can be looked for in growing Christ followers. Those engaged in developmental relationships with disciples would be best able to evaluate and quantify the growth happening in those areas. They could do this by completing a discipleship developmental asset growth survey on a quarterly or semi-annual basis. These surveys act as quantitative evaluations, rating disciples on each of the nine assets and their accompanying benchmarks using a simple numeric scale (like one to ten). Starting below zero may be helpful for assessing disciples who do not begin at "zero" but at a deficit. Over time, a collection of these surveys provides a beneficial picture of a disciple's growth or lack of growth.

The Charge

For fruitful fulfillment of the Great Commission, leaders/mentors need three vital elements.

1. A clear picture of what a disciple looks like (where the developmental assets of a disciple are identified and defined)

2. An intentional process for making disciples (including asset building, developmental relationships, and asset-building communities)

3. An intentional process for assessing discipleship effectiveness (both qualitatively through testimonies and quantitatively through surveys)

Regular assessment enables leaders/mentors to ensure that they are using time, money, and human resources in the most effective ways possible. Done wisely and well, evaluation leads to creative innovation, moments of celebration, and renewed anticipation for further spiritual growth.

Evaluate. Celebrate. Innovate. Anticipate. Do all for the glory of God.

Questions and Activities

1. Thinking through the D.I.S.C.I.P.L.E.S. acrostic for the qualities of a growing believer, what areas are you going strong in? What areas need additional growth?

2. Consider the qualities of a developmental relationship as described in the chapter. Who fulfilled these in your life? How did they make a difference for you?

3. How is the local church uniquely equipped and called to be a developmental community?

4. What are the hindrances to doing healthy evaluation? What are practical solutions to these challenges? (Be specific and realistic.)

5. What are your next steps to become someone who values and uses effective evaluation?

Further Reading

Boulmetis, John, and Phyllis Dutwin. *The ABCs of Evaluation*. 3rd ed. San Francisco: Jossey-Bass, 2011.

Branson, Mark Lau. *Memories, Hopes, and Conversations*. Lanham, MD: Rowman & Littlefield, 2004.

English, Leona. "Evaluation in Christian Education." *Christian Education Journal* 6NS, no. 1 (Spring 2002): 25–34.

25

Equipping Others to Teach

ROBERT BRANDT

Jesus invested three years of ministry leadership training in a small group of leaders and then released them to use their gifts. The exponential impact of that investment has been manifested in countless lives over the last two thousand years. Developing other ministry leaders is part of this Christian heritage of teaching and multiplication. Jesus propagated the kingdom of God by the recruitment of followers for his leadership team. He initiated a teaching process when he recruited the Twelve (Matt. 10:2–4; Mark 3:16–19; Luke 6:14–16) and developed them as servant leaders who would catalyze the multiplication of disciples in successive generations.

Those in ministry are directed to empower others for ministry by helping them to use their spiritual gifts in service to others (Rom. 12:3–8; 1 Cor. 12; Eph. 4:11–16). In fact, David Chow contends, "One of your main jobs as a team leader is empowering team members to discover, develop, and deploy their spiritual gifts for God's kingdom."[1] Too often, volunteer adult leaders are seen and used as merely helpers, as if their primary function is to serve the ministry leader. When a ministry leader fails to equip other believers to use their gifts in service, he or she obstructs the personal and leadership development of adult volunteers, hinders their own leadership influence, and severely limits ministry multiplication and health.

1. David Chow, *No More Lone Rangers: How to Build a Team-Centered Youth Ministry* (Loveland, CO: Group, 2003), 121.

Success at developing, training, and retaining volunteers does not happen without intentional support. Here are the critical areas necessary.

1. A clear organizational infrastructure must be established and communicated.
2. The leader of volunteers must be able to manage that structure with clear, near-perfect communication to the volunteers who serve.
3. Appreciation is foundational. As volunteers serve they need to be shown consistent, personal, and sincere appreciation for their service.
4. Nurture is also foundational. This involves structured and consistent training that includes orientation of overall ministry vision, purpose, values, roles of volunteers, guidelines, and expectations.
5. There is feedback from volunteers to the leader on all ministry matters that is well received and valued.

—Susan Phillips, Brian R. Little, and Laura Goodine, "Recruiting, Retaining, and Rewarding Volunteers: What Volunteers Have to Say," Canadian Centre for Philanthropy, 2002, http://www.volunteernanaimo.ca/PDFs/Recruiting%20Retaining%20and%20Rewarding%20Volunteers.pdf.

The development of other adults to lead, minister, and teach is a critical component of an effective discipleship-focused ministry that has a significant level of growth and impact beyond the influence of the primary leader. This is such a truism that youth ministry experts Jim Burns and Mark DeVries say, "Beyond your programs—and even beyond the students themselves—your most precious commodity is your volunteer team."[2]

The most skilled Christian worker cannot develop and maintain a fruitful ministry alone. Even the most gifted teacher needs to have others leading and teaching alongside him or her. The development and equipping of a team of volunteers who can teach is an essential and ongoing practice for ministries that want to be as fruitful as possible.

Recruit Adults to a Ministry Role

In ministry, this personal aspect of motivation need not be considered as selfish but instead may be intrinsically connected to a volunteer's unique desire (and design) to make a greater difference through volunteering in ministry. Barbara Houle, Brad Sagarin, and Martin Kaplan studied the preferences and motives of volunteers in various organizations. They found "that individuals choose tasks which best satisfy their personal motives

2. Jim Burns and Mike DeVries, *The Youth Builder: Today's Resource for Relational Ministry* (Ventura, CA: Gospel Light, 2001), 156.

... [and] that individuals may have more positive volunteer experiences when allowed to choose volunteer tasks that will meet their motives."[3] Bo Boshers echoed similar guidance when he advised that the "What's in It for Me?" principle highlights the reality that though potential ministry volunteers want to serve, they also want to grow and use their individual gifts and talents.[4]

People want to serve where they are valued and where they have a moderate level of freedom. If ministries provide a wide range of opportunities, they will recruit a wider range of highly committed individuals and will avoid losing volunteers over time because volunteer roles lack meaning or purpose. If leaders offer opportunities and latitude to volunteers, they will have a great chance to recruit and retain volunteers, because people do not hesitate to get involved in what is meaningful and purposeful in their lives.

The other critical element for the effective use of volunteers is time, for both the leader and the volunteer. If people get involved in what is meaningful, they stay involved because their volunteered time is well used. They want to know that their gifts, talents, and abilities are valued. If this value is in place, then recruitment is easier because volunteers will know in advance that their service will be valued. If it's difficult to find and recruit volunteers, then it's likely that people aren't confident that they will be valued and able to help in ways that are meaningful to them.

When thinking about how time is to be spent, keep in mind that the best use of time is at the beginning of the volunteer recruitment process. Investing time and effort early, when recruiting, screening, and placing a volunteer, will provide benefits for many years. When the process is rushed and a volunteer is not placed well, or there aren't clear and well-communicated expectations, various problems and conflicts can arise that are difficult to address or undo.

Ministries who recruit well do two things. First, they usually have a clear outline of steps they take for recruiting, screening, and involving adults as volunteers—and this process is regularly reviewed by leaders and volunteers for possible improvement. Second, they have a probationary period that is clearly communicated up front to the volunteer. For a designated length of time (six months is common), the new volunteer is observed and given limited chances to be involved. Although the volunteer is not officially on

3. Barbara J. Houle, Brad J. Sagarin, and Martin F. Kaplan, "A Functional Approach to Volunteerism: Do Volunteer Motives Predict Task Preference?," *Basic & Applied Social Psychology* 27, no. 4 (2005): 343.

4. Bo Boshers, *Student Ministry for the 21st Century* (Grand Rapids: Zondervan, 1997).

the ministry team, how well he or she gets along with students and with other adults will become clear. Is there evidence of spiritual maturity, and is he or she comfortable in the ministry setting? Each context is different, but thinking through the process and timing of how someone joins the volunteer team is the first step before you begin considering putting the individual in teaching roles.

Definition before Delegation

The goal for empowering other adult leaders is to let them have influence in the lives of students and serve as pastors and shepherds as well. Some volunteers can be given strategic roles in the direct oversight of other adult volunteers who lead and direct other volunteers in their ministry with students. Secure leaders will seek to spiritually reproduce and multiply their leadership impact (2 Tim. 2:2). When adults are utilized in ministry based on their gifts, passions, and personality, new avenues of ministry will be created that were previously ignored, unexplored, or impossible. Ministry leadership is transformed when a leader becomes a leader of leaders and invites volunteers into an environment where they are empowered to lead other volunteers and ministry teams and where they can also recruit and develop other volunteers.

As you think about how to create a team of teachers from your volunteers, it's important to prayerfully look for those who have the gifting and aptitude to teach well. Not all good teachers are extroverts, and not all who say they want to teach should automatically get to teach. Teaching positions and responsibilities should be clearly delineated so that the teaching purposes and goals of the ministry or event may be fulfilled. It is helpful to develop a job description that lists expectations and responsibilities for those who teach. Keeping in mind why people volunteer, "these descriptions clearly define the boundaries so that a leader can understand the responsibilities of the role and the goals that need to be met. Leaders want to know how success is defined and what is expected of them."[5]

Intentionally developing others who can teach in your ministry is important because leadership training is *always* about multiplication and exponential impact! Your ministry development may be part of the plans that God has for the adults who serve in your ministry, and those may reach far beyond the confines of their present role of service. Their current youth ministry involvement may actually be part of God's process to foster and

5. Ibid., 156.

prepare them for his yet unannounced purposes. Be a catalytic ministry leader who does not limit the volunteers around himself or herself by relegating them to secondary roles and limited involvement but rather spurs them on to fully fulfill God's destiny for their lives, even if that means they move on from your ministry. This sensitivity to the Holy Spirit's work should be modeled for, and reproduced in, other ministry leaders so that they invest in the same manner in other developing leaders and students, and in those who have yet to be identified as leaders.

The organizational leadership structure must be proactively modified to prepare for and facilitate growth. Do not strive to oversee all aspects of ministry leadership with a micromanaging approach. A leader's capacity to oversee, coach, and nurture volunteers has limits. Once that personal limit is exceeded, the ministry operates from an insufficient leadership structure that is incapable of adequately teaching an increasing number of volunteers to provide the spiritual influence to impact students. Chow says, "*True leadership* isn't about hoarding authority; it's about giving it away to others."[6]

Training the Teaching Team

Though there are many materials on working with volunteers, there are few that deal with how to empower them as fellow teachers. To facilitate the development of a diversified group of teaching volunteers into a healthy team that is unified and prepared for ministry leadership requires intentional training. Though ministry is often learned on the job, formal training of volunteers is necessary, especially when it comes to helping them fit in and feel equipped for the demands. An effective teacher training program has three components: (1) initial training, (2) ongoing training, and (3) specialized training.

Initial Training

When prepared well, new leaders will begin their ministry with a level of confidence and self-efficacy about their ability to teach. The first time teaching in front of a group of young people can quickly chip away the confidence and present a reality check. A volunteer's enthusiasm to teach must be met with a parallel commitment of the ministry leader to provide all the resources needed for them to be successful.

6. Chow, *No More Lone Rangers*, 124.

Too often teacher training takes place in a classroom and is mildly engaging. The best training takes place "in the field." The first-time step in developing teachers is to have them watch you teach. This is the old "I do it—you watch" level of training. Follow up with discussion on various teaching elements—lesson aim, outline, biblical focus, interaction with audience, variety of methods, use of illustrations, and conclusion. The goal is to hear the volunteer's thinking about teaching.

> Some ministries are blessed with volunteers who have many years of experience in ministry or school teaching. They are to be treasured! Each volunteer situation is different, and sometimes young Christian workers don't recognize the experience levels of the volunteers. The recommendations in this section are focused on developing more-inexperienced volunteers.

The second level of training is to have them co-teach alongside you. Bring them in alongside to help study, plan, create, and deliver a lesson. They get a chance to then experience what is involved in teaching. Be sure to allow adequate time for questions and reflection on the process. By doing this in a fun, creative, and yet professional way, you establish the level of excellence expected in preparation and teaching. This tandem teaching can take place for quite some time before you move to the next level.

The third level of training puts the volunteer up front and teaching, but with the leader watching at every step. This is a critical step in leadership development because it will become clear where the strengths and weaknesses are. The leader's feedback, affirmation, and evaluation are necessary for the growth of teaching skills. In some ministries, this is a part of a year-long apprenticeship with new staff. The same kind of attention can be given to motivated and gifted adult volunteers.

It may seem like a lot of work. Well, it is! But, the teaching aspect of any ministry is the most visible, the most scrutinized, and amazingly often underserved. We just assume people can teach, or we settle for mediocrity in our nurture of other adult staff members. If we implement what's found in these last chapters of this book (evaluating, training, praying, practicing, and growing others' proficiencies) to create a broad culture of teaching excellence among our staff members, we will help those around us grow in their own ministry versus just "using" volunteers. Their best is worth your best.

Ongoing Training

Though ministry brings fulfillment and personal satisfaction to volunteers, they are sacrificing and investing long-term; therefore they need consistent encouragement as they minister to students. Each context has its own rhythm for how often encouragement should happen, but there should be some form of regular training and appreciation. When that training involves meeting together, those meetings need to be well planned, purposeful, and scheduled so as to respect your adult volunteers and their other commitments. Be sure to maintain a unified spirit focused on Christ and shepherd your people well (1 Pet. 5:1–3). Ministry team unity can quickly dissipate and negatively impact the ministry and the spiritual lives of young people and volunteers.

Ongoing training meetings should include the following:[7]

- Worship—Rather than a mini-church service, create a time where volunteers are given space to connect with God. Provide Scripture, various prayer exercises, and opportunities to share about God's work in their lives.

- Celebration in community—Select specific leaders to share stories of success, challenges, and struggle. This creates team solidarity and a realization that each volunteer is not alone working toward the spiritual formation of adolescents.

- Topical training—Address topics and issues from which all team members can benefit in community. Training volunteers about youth ministry skills and practices can occur individually (through articles, videos, books, etc.) and within specific ministry teams, outside the monthly meetings.

- Encouragement—Team members must be reminded how their involvement plays an important role in the larger purpose of the youth ministry. Encourage the team with the good news, and let them know they are making a difference.

- Character development—It's important to remind volunteers every time that who they are as examples is often the primary way that teens learn and is often stronger than what they teach. All ministry skills and competencies must always be built on, and proceed from, the foundation of godly character.[8] Character is foundational to ministry leadership (Acts 6:3; 1 Tim. 3:1–13; Titus 1:5–9; 1 Pet. 5:1–4).

- Communication—Clear communication conveys that the team is valued and critical to the success of the ministry. Volunteers are more likely to stay if clear instruction is given about what is precisely expected of them.

---

7. Some material comes from Duffy Robbins, *This Way to Youth Ministry: An Introduction to the Adventure* (Grand Rapids: Zondervan/Youth Specialties Academic, 2004).

8. James Estep Jr., "Leadership Strategies," in *Management Essentials for Christian Ministries*, ed. Michael J. Anthony and James Estep Jr. (Nashville: Broadman & Holman, 2005), 349.

- External resources—Bring in experts to train on a particular topic (i.e., CPR, basic counseling skills, technology), or take your group of volunteers to regional and national training events.

Specialized Training: The Personal Element

The organizational structure for training will have to be consistently adapted in order to sustain and potentially increase the number of leaders involved. Leadership multiplication must be part of the DNA of your organizational culture and common in the teaching of leaders for ministry involvement. One of the often understated and forgotten elements to working with volunteers is the personal connection. Adults will be as interested in working alongside you and your team as in the task of ministry. Do you have a reputation of knowing well the adults that have committed themselves to the ministry and to you? After you have formed your team, it's important to have regular times to connect individually with each leader—take them out for a meal or coffee, and make sure to send birthday or anniversary cards when appropriate. When you're with them, think about what you may not know about them, and allow them to share their life and personal experiences. An effective and healthy team of volunteers is one where each person is valued and known versus being used for their service or skills.

The personal investment into the development of volunteers doesn't always require being physically present. Passing along a blog post article, sending out a group email, or even talking on the phone can help. You can create a private group page on Facebook to foster the collective identity and community that will help give your volunteer leaders a wide variety of personal, spiritual, leadership, and ministry development tools.

How to Keep Volunteers

The research by Susan Phillips and colleagues focused on recruiting, retaining, and rewarding volunteers and found there were three key factors to improve the retention of volunteers. First, show appreciation and respect for volunteers. Be generous and consistent with specific affirmation and appreciation. Notice volunteers' unheralded service, and specifically tell them why they are valued and appreciated. Consistent affirmation is more important than extravagant yearly celebrations.

Second, provide meaningful and varied volunteer experiences. This includes providing the freedom for volunteers to try out different things within the organization in order to find their niche, offering new and varied experiences and responsibilities that involve testing different skills and learning new things, providing training and other means of personal development, establishing clear expectations at the outset, and checking in on these from time to time.

Third, communicate with and be responsive to volunteers. The practice to communicate with and be responsive to volunteers "ranges from providing information through newsletters to involving volunteers in program and activity planning."[9]

Evaluation Is an Essential Part of Appreciation

One of the underdeveloped areas in most Christian ministries is evaluation. Christians don't like to hurt others' feelings, and those who love to do evaluation often like it so much they're not fun to be around. However, whatever is valued is evaluated. Boshers uses the process of evaluation to train leaders and maintains that "strong leaders want to know if they are hitting the mark and ways they need to improve performance. We need to let our leaders know if they are doing well, fair, or poorly."[10]

Evaluation can actually be a positive time of encouragement. Les Christie says, "Our job is to give volunteers confidence that God is working in and through them. Remember these are ordinary people in the hands of an extraordinary God."[11] Formal evaluation should occur on a yearly basis (scheduled at the end of the school year) so the volunteer understands areas of success and areas that need improvement. Informal evaluation (after an event, over a lunch meeting) should occur throughout the year so that leaders see progress, receive affirmation, and also are gently made aware of areas of performance that could be improved on.

Staying Motivated

Dawne Clark and Rena Shimoni conducted research that involved volunteers in long-term social change initiatives where tangible change was not

9. Susan Phillips, Brian R. Little, and Laura Goodine, "Recruiting, Retaining, and Rewarding Volunteers: What Volunteers Have to Say," Canadian Centre for Philanthropy, 2002, http://www .volunteernanaimo.ca/PDFs/Recruiting%20Retaining%20and%20Rewarding%20Volunteers.pdf.
10. Boshers, *Student Ministry for the 21st Century*, 165.
11. Les Christie, *How to Recruit and Train Volunteer Youth Workers* (Grand Rapids: Zondervan, 1992), 141.

expected to be demonstrated for years. Four of their directive insights about retention and support have been adapted and applied for leaders who work with volunteers in ministry contexts:

1. The process of discipleship as a lifelong endeavor should be stressed. Volunteers participate in building the foundation on which adolescents experience spiritual development over a lifetime, not just expedient evidence in the present.

2. Affirm realistic, short-term goals for the volunteers in their ministry with students. Spiritual growth typically occurs in small increments. Understanding the long-term, big picture of spiritual development will give volunteers added confidence about their role in youth ministry.

3. Celebrate volunteers' successful efforts. Monthly training events can include volunteers' success stories and encouraging moments so that fellow volunteers may be inspired in their own efforts.[12]

4. Be aggressive encouragers for your volunteers. Leaders must share with volunteers encouraging stories, cards, emails, and conversations about the impact of the youth ministry on students. Veteran volunteers can attest, especially to new volunteers, the impact over time that volunteers have in youth ministry.[13]

The application of these practical insights by ministry leaders can serve to keep volunteers motivated and excited about their work in youth ministry, even when tangible results are not directly seen. Volunteers will be motivated and encouraged that their investment of time and energy into young people is making a difference.

When volunteers are motivated through active participation, training, and ownership, they will be stimulated to seek to enlist others to serve and help the organization accomplish its mission. There is a reciprocal relationship between the recruiting and training process of volunteers. In order for ministry leaders to recruit volunteers, these volunteers must grasp the reality that they will be adequately cared for. The implementation of this care requires a well-planned, successful, and consistent training program that consequently aids in the continued volunteer recruitment process. If

12. Doug Fields, *Purpose Driven Youth Ministry* (Grand Rapids: Zondervan, 1998).
13. Dawne Clark and Rena Shimoni, "Recruiting, Retaining, Supporting Volunteers for Long-Term Social Change," Canadian Centre for Philanthropy, 2002, http://sectorsource.ca/sites/default/files/resources/files/Clark_FS_E_Web.pdf.

the training is beneficial, meaningful, and appropriate, volunteers feel that they belong, are valued, and share in the ownership of the ministry endeavor. They become more satisfied, motivated, and empowered; they desire to remain in service; and they seek to involve others in their ministry endeavor. A healthy reciprocal relationship is experienced between teaching and the growth of a ministry team. In short, "health breeds health."[14]

Questions and Activities

1. What have been your experiences as a volunteer? What made them positive for you? What were some of the struggles you experienced?

2. What are the major points the author makes about developing a volunteer team? Which of those were especially helpful to how you think about leading others?

3. Sometimes how we lead is as important as the "what" of our leadership. Review this chapter and consider ways that a young leader could implement all these practices and yet do so in a style or manner that fails to create team unity or high trust levels. Consider ways that implementing the steps in this chapter in a Christlike manner could contribute to the spiritual formation of adult volunteers.

4. Contact two or three adults you know who are currently volunteers, and ask them what volunteering is like for them. What do they enjoy? What do they struggle with? What are their dreams for their work?

5. Find a person who leads a volunteer team, and set up an interview. Ask this person what he or she does to recruit, train, support, retain, and evaluate volunteers. What are common problems they face regarding volunteers?

Further Reading

Kageler, Len. *The Youth Ministry Survival Guide: How to Thrive and Last for the Long Haul*. Grand Rapids: Zondervan, 2008.

Poppino, Gene. "Building a Staff Team." In *Impact: Student Ministry That Will Transform a Generation*, edited by Steven Patty and Steve Keels, 211–19. Nashville: Broadman & Holman, 2005.

14. Chap Clark, "Leadership in Youth and Family Ministry," lecture presented at Denver Seminary, Littleton, CO, January 20, 1997.

St. Clair, Barry. "How Can We Find and Support Volunteers?" In *Reaching a Generation for Christ*, edited by Richard R. Dunn and Mark H. Senter, 261–82. Chicago: Moody, 1997.

Strommen, Merton, Karen E. Jones, and David Rahn. *Youth Ministry That Transforms*. Grand Rapids: Zondervan, 2001.

Technological Tools for Dynamic Christian Teaching

FREDDY CARDOZA

Technology changed everything. Since the dawn of the new millennium there has been an exponential increase in the connections between technology and learning. From online degrees, educational apps, and streaming video to open access,[1] the two fields have become inseparably linked. These realities present both enormous possibilities and significant challenges for Christian teachers. Not every resource or type of resource will meet the needs of every teacher or interest every learner. Some technology tools will be practical for some educational settings and impractical for others. Even so, the sheer number of educational technologies now available represents game-changing learning opportunities for both classrooms and discipleship.

For the Christian teacher, educational technology can be defined as *the effective use of electronic or digital resources to enhance the teaching-learning process with the transformation of the learner as its goal*. The skillful teaching of God's truth using digital learning can provide the next generations the meaning and methods they crave while outfitting them with the knowledge,

---

1. Diana G. Oblinger, ed., *Game Changers: Education and Information Technologies* (Lawrence, KS: Allen, 2012), 85–87. Open access refers to educational research freely and openly available to anyone able to electronically access these materials.

convictions, and character needed to live as dual citizens in the kingdom of earth and the kingdom of God.

Effective Christian teaching involves several important factors. Most important is the illuminating teaching ministry of the Holy Spirit (John 14:26). Next is the cultivation and skillful use of the spiritual gift of teaching (Rom. 12:6–8). Also central are the careful study and accurate interpretation of the Word of God (2 Tim. 2:15). Then there is the integration of truth with the human experience and its application to our lives (2 Tim. 3:16–17). These are aided by the winsome communication of God's Word and its delivery in various settings using different teaching methods and educational technologies.[2]

The delivery and application of the content by the teacher is the decisive moment. In real time, our teaching makes its mark as truth is heard, understood, and applied—or not. Good teachers want to leverage every available resource at their disposal. The effective use of technology is one of the keys that can connect learners with the relevance of God's Word.[3] Because the world now speaks the digital language, it is the vernacular of choice for today's generations—one that engages students' learning styles and imagination.[4]

A Technology Teaching Mind-Set

Despite the opportunities of the digital age, Christian workers can feel unprepared to integrate educational technology into their teaching. Too often, equipping in these areas is not a part of classes or training programs.[5] The speed of change has occurred at a velocity and with a force that few expected. Even so, good teachers are internally motivated to excel in effectiveness and are willing to make the adjustments needed to reach the goal of digital fluency.

Realism about Technology

One helpful perspective is to reject outright pessimism about technology as well as naive optimism.[6] For this reason, a middle way of realism provides

2. Kenneth Gangel, "Thinking about Teaching Methods," Bible.org, March 10, 2005, https://bible.org/seriespage/1-thinking-about-teaching-methods.

3. David Bourgeois, *Ministry in the Digital Age* (Downers Grove, IL: InterVarsity, 2013), 18–23.

4. Wilbert J. McKeachie, *McKeachie's Teaching Tips: Strategies, Research, and Theory for College and University Teachers* (Boston: Houghton Mifflin, 2002), 210–13.

5. Susan L. Peterson, *Teachers and Technology* (Lanham, MD: International Scholars, 1999), 4–13.

6. Mark Gura and Bernard Percy, *Recapturing Technology for Education: Keeping Tomorrow in Today's Classrooms* (Lanham, MD: Rowman & Littlefield, 2005), 95–108.

TECHNOLOGY

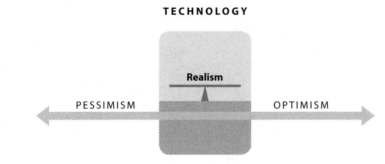

Figure 26.1 Realism about technology

the proper balance that will keep teachers from the dangerous extremities of the imbalance caused by an either-or perspective (see fig. 26.1).[7]

Christian teachers ought to avoid the emotional extremes of fear of and fascination with educational technology. Some who fail to embrace a realistic view of technology gravitate toward an unhealthy infatuation or obsession with it.[8] This imbalance might be called *technolatry*—where technology becomes their deity. Others move in the opposite direction and develop irrational caution and unnecessary fears about technology that could be termed *technophobia*.

A more thoughtful approach seems to be one in which the strengths, weaknesses, opportunities, and threats of educational technology are all acknowledged. Then teachers can begin to avoid the abuse of technology, begin to use technology properly, and indeed grow in their digital competencies until they are able to exploit the amazing opportunities of digital learning without falling victim to it (see fig. 26.2).

A Theology of Technology

A final mind-set helpful for Christian teachers to embrace is a proper theological view of technology. Technology is, in essence, the application of science. Science, from the Latin *scientia*, is rooted in "knowledge." As such, technology has to do with the practical application of scientific knowledge in our world. The Bible has much to say about knowledge, particularly that it is foundational to wisdom and that it should be submitted to God's authority (Prov. 9:10).

7. Aaron Smith, "U.S. Views of Technology and the Future," Pew Research Center, April 17, 2014, http://www.pewinternet.org/2014/04/17/us-views-of-technology-and-the-future.

8. Allan Collins and Richard Halverson, *Rethinking Education in the Age of Technology: The Digital Revolution and Schooling in America* (New York: Teacher College Press, 2009), 9–37.

Freddy Cardoza

TECHNOLOGY

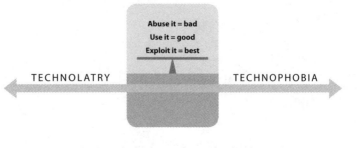

Figure 26.2 The fear or favor of technology

Freddy Cardoza

Technology is not new; it was applied as early as Genesis 4:17 when Cain built a city for his son Enoch. People then, like now, built things and named them to reflect glory for themselves.

When technology moves from the principles of utility and progress for human betterment and becomes an expression of self-worship or rebellion, as seen in the construction of Babel, its purposes become perverted. In such instances, technology is hijacked and becomes a means of creating new ways of doing evil. That is the essence of what occurred in Babel. It caused God to grieve, saying, "This is only the beginning of what they will do. And nothing that they propose to do will now be impossible for them" (Gen. 11:6). That typifies much technology in our world today.

There are, of course, good and benevolent uses of technology. Scripture provides examples of advances in technology that include the fashioning of musical instruments (Gen. 4:21), the development of bronze (an alloy representing sophisticated technology), the building of seaworthy ships (e.g., Gen. 6), and other forms of art such as implements used in the construction of the tabernacle (Exod. 31:3–5), among others.[9] These all show the use of technology for the common good and for the glory of God.

At last, technology proves itself to be essentially amoral in nature. It can be used for great good or woeful evil. A biblical view of technology affirms its responsible use and application. This includes obvious enhancements to benefit human life and things that enhance our love and devotion to God. Among these should be the savvy and even shrewd employment of technology in media. Media is, by definition, a medium for communication between persons. Christian educators hoping to be effective in teaching the next

9. Jeffrey L. Nyhoff and Steven H. VanderLeest, "What Does God Tell Us about Technology?," Calvin College, 2005, https://www.calvin.edu/academic/rit/webBook/chapter1/lesson2/bible.htm.

generations should use but not abuse media to powerfully communicate truth through its many applications, particularly in the ministry of teaching.

Thinking theologically about technology will govern teachers in effective biblical instruction and guide learners in effective Christian living. The outcome should be the avoidance of pathologies in our personal lives while working toward the health, wholeness, and holiness that is possible when technology finds its proper place.

Educational Technology Tools for Next-Generation Teaching

Because resources are constantly emerging, educational technologies are best understood when placed into categories by type. This helps teachers locate the kinds of help they need rather than being overwhelmed by the sheer number and names of available options. The following are categories from a collaboration of over one thousand global educational technology leaders with the Centre for Learning and Performance Technologies,[10] each with brief descriptions of how they might be effectively used in various teaching ministry settings. Becoming conversant in these resources and their capabilities will better facilitate learning through the use of educational technology.[11]

Digital instructional tools are designed for teachers who want to create a more formal learning environment. These resources allow students to interact with other learners through a variety of online programs while also giving teachers enhanced means of delivering content, facilitating educational experiences, and holding students accountable for their participation. While much of these are school-oriented, the potential for use in ministry settings for all ages is vast and untapped.

There are at least three types of instructional tools. *Course authoring tools* help teachers design web-based e-learning (electronic learning) experiences for learners by building the environments necessary for online learning. *Evaluation tools* include dozens of ways to build e-flashcards for memorization, quizzes and tests for evaluation, and other means of assessing learning.[12] *Simulation and gamification tools* allow learners to engage in

10. Jane Hart, "Directory of Learning and Performance Tools and Services," Centre for Learning and Performance Technologies, http://c4lpt.co.uk/directory-of-learning-performance-tools.

11. Darrell M. West, *Digital Schools: How Technology Can Reform Education* (Washington, DC: Brookings Institution Press, 2012), 105–19.

12. Lawrence Tomei, *Teaching Digitally: A Guide for Integrating Technology into the Classroom* (Norwood, MA: Christopher-Gordon, 2001), 229–75.

immersive virtual experiences.[13] These devices simulate or augment reality through role play and educational game play. In doing so, they facilitate the teaching of knowledge, attitudes, behaviors, or skills.

Social collaboration tools gained nearly immediate acceptance in church ministries and include popular *social networks* that involved microblogging, image sharing, and other creative social communications. Some provide learners with the opportunity to gather in online small-group interactions for building community, group identity, and class cohesion. There are at least three types of resources provided through this technology category. The most obvious are *social networks*, which allow personal interaction, including sharing one's location, activities, thoughts and ideas, surveys, and other information. *Group collaboration platforms* allow teams of learners to brainstorm, track projects, do teamwork and task management, upload and share documents, and produce materials for group work. *Social classroom tools* are interactive online platforms where students can receive messages, collectively share assignments and events, and partner in group blogging, wikis, social bookmarking, and class forums.

> How might developing a virtual learning environment be received by children? Youth? Young adults? What would be the benefits? Drawbacks?

Web conferencing and virtual world tools bridge the simulated and physical worlds through internet-based technology. It includes programs that allow learners, depending on the capabilities of their devices, to connect by real-time audio or audio-video through computers, tablets, mobiles, and even some wearables. These also enable participation in computer-based simulated environments through massive multiplayer online worlds (MMOW). Each of these has applications for teaching in either creative academic or ministry-based settings. *Webconferencing tools* provide different means of conducting live personal or group meetings with people near and far. They can include web classroom environments using special resources for teachers, or they can be online conferences and webinars. *Screen-sharing tools* allow remote desktop sharing, where others allow a guest user control over their personal computer. Some of these resources also provide screen-sharing possibilities, where others are granted the ability to view a live or recorded version of another user's screen for collaborative interaction. *Webcasting tools* provide the ability to conduct web-based broadcasts or targeted narrowcasts to audiences using bandwidth-saving, one-way, noninteractive presentations. *Virtual world tools* are an exciting frontier of learning where

13. Douglas Thomas and John S. Brown, *A New Culture of Learning: Cultivating the Imagination for a World of Constant Change* (Seattle: CreateSpace, 2011), 90–105.

2-D and 3-D simulated environments (virtual worlds) allow multiple users to participate in learning games, alternate realities, and immersive learning experiences. These are made possible through photo-realistic worlds, video characters, and avatars (a computer icon representing a person). Some of these experiences, once considered niche hobbies, have produced rich possibilities for teaching and learning.

Office-related suite tools include products capable of creating, editing, displaying, and sharing documents, presentations, and spreadsheets. *Document creation tools* allow the creation and hosting of written content through word processing. Teachers and learners can author, share, collaborate, and view creative, practical, and theological content through written prose. *Presentation creation tools* allow the creation and sharing of professional and attractive multimedia that uses linear or dynamic content presentation styles.

Blogging, website, and wiki tools are capable of dynamic learning experiences. These include two-way, give-and-take, interactive (Web 2.0) learning as well as interactive learning that adds the additional component of responsive social collaboration (Web 3.0) experiences.[14] Whereas some electronic tools are based on learners "consuming" content, Web 3.0 experiences focus on learners becoming actively engaged in *content creation*.

> One of the telling markers between Web 2.0 and 3.0 experiences is *participation*. Technology today offers opportunity to engage students throughout the week. If, however, it's just a more sophisticated bullhorn in a one-way conversation, interaction and interest will be low.

Blogging tools include resources capable of helping teachers and learners author their own weblogs (blogs) that serve as a web publishing tool to reach large audiences with student-produced content by sharing information that includes uploaded audio, images, videos, and written text. *Wikis* are tools that help learners create and share information through individual or collaborative websites. *Wiki* is the Polynesian word for "quick," signifying the ease and speed of building these sites to display and share information in very versatile formats. *Website tools* are similar to blogging and wiki tools except for their sophistication. Website-building tools provide the opportunity to build very powerful customized internet destinations limited only by the creativity and ability of the author. *Form and survey tools* enhance learning through the creation of online or printed forms that include questionnaires, surveys, and polls that can help generate research for teaching. *RSS feed tools* refer to "real simple syndication," which makes it possible for anyone with a message to

14. Sharon Smaldino, Deborah Lowther, and James Russell, *Instructional Technology and Media for Learning*, 10th ed. (Boston, MA: Pearson, 2012), 124–43.

share to be able to distribute it at little or no cost. Several services like these exist, and they are helpful for disseminating teaching to large audiences.

Image, audio, and video tools are increasingly available because of increased bandwidth speeds and the ability to harness the power of fast microprocessors. These have the ability to produce and edit images of all types, in addition to doing postproduction on audio files for podcasts and video files for instructing, equipping, and training.[15] *Image tools* are capable of editing photographs, computer-generated illustrations, and electronic drawings. They can also capture and manipulate images on screens and webpages. This includes photos produced from personal computers, webcams, tablets, and other smart devices. Other programs provide portfolios to show and share these images in online galleries, which can all be used in teaching visuals when video projectors are available. *Audio tools* are capable of capturing, converting, and producing edited versions of spoken teaching content. Some can provide voice-overs, captioning, and revoicing in foreign languages. Other tools can provide metadata information, then prepare the teaching content in different formats for online sharing as audio files or host them in syndicated podcasts.[16] Beyond these, there are programs that allow teachers to set up live interactive audio discussions or voice message boards for their students. *Video tools* allow for video creation and editing, live computer screencasting, and webcam and recording use. Some resources allow for the creation of time-stamped discussions about posted videos that have been viewed and the ability to conduct video chats. Teachers can also create and host presentation or training videos and tutorials and use Chroma key (green screen or blue screen) technology for creative instruction, information, and inspiration.

Communication tools allow for live (synchronous) communication that is especially helpful when learners are able to participate in the discussion in real time. Many tools also provide for those who cannot communicate at the same time (asynchronous) due to personal schedules. *Text tools* include the ability to send brief short-character-count SMS (Short Message Service) messages by mobile devices. *Live chat tools* allow teachers to embed live discussion boards into their websites, blogs, and social network profiles, all while monitoring them for security. Some have online whiteboards for sharing drawings and other creations with virtual classroom participants.

Collaborative sharing tools are resources that help people work together to increase learning or to produce something superior to what could be

15. Ibid., 187–253.

16. Douglas McConatha et al., *Mobile Pedagogy and Perspectives on Teaching and Learning* (Hershey, PA: IGI Global, 2014), 41–57.

produced working alone. Though much learning and work in the Western Hemisphere has traditionally been primarily individualistic, the influx of people from cultures that value the development of collaboration and learning communities has greatly influenced American thinking. *Collaborative research tools* have similarities to social bookmarking sites but focus on helping groups of people study together in order to share, organize, and discuss scholarly references with others.

Content curation services allow groups of people to gather and universally share videos, blogs, webpages, and other information with others. As they curate content, the services compile it by creating attractive and well-organized portfolios with media streams of content. This aids learning by giving people access to large amounts of curated material while saving them great amounts of time.[17] Collaborative tools are indispensable to facilitating different types of interaction and learning.[18]

Learning portfolios (also called *e-portfolios)* are another widely used resource whose popularity is increasing. These allow users to create self-styled formatting for sharing one's ideas with others. Digital portfolios are a tremendous way for teachers, ministry students, and other learners to promote the things they have learned from various events or seasons.[19]

Public learning resources account for a large and growing category of web destinations that provide learners with information or instruction about a wide range of subjects, often for free.[20] These include sites that provide individual lessons, series, and entire courses of study in addition to various types of research databases that can aid in personal study that can support or supplement Christian teaching. Two primary types of public learning resources are especially useful for the purpose of Christian education. The Open Education movement makes available nearly every type of content imaginable, including an increasing amount of biblical and theological content. *Electronic research databases* are another important type of public learning resource helpful to those in Christian education. The movement of many journals and other research materials from print to digital has rapidly expanded what is already available in search engines and scholarly databases. Examples of these include digitally searchable articles, collected essays, research reports,

17. To find available collaborative tools, perform online searches for shareable digital notebooks, group organizers, mindmapping tools, or digital bulletin boards.

18. James M. Hudson, *Chatting to Learn: The Changing Psychology and Evolving Pedagogy of Online Learning* (Youngstown, NY: Cambria, 2007), 1–7.

19. Gordon Lewis, *Bringing Technology into the Classroom* (Oxford: Oxford University Press, 2009), 72–74.

20. Hart, "Directory of Learning and Performance Tools and Services."

periodicals, and even dissertations or theses.[21] These resources can help equip students in ministry-based programs by enriching their knowledge, ultimately making them better prepared for a life of Christian service.

Digital Christian Teaching Resources

The quality and volume of digital Christian teaching resources have greatly accelerated in recent years. This enormous investment on the part of Christian entrepreneurs has radically improved the creative digital resources available for students and professionals in ministry. At least four types of important developments exist in this category.

Bible software has entered a type of golden age as many fresh and robust tools continue to be offered by organizations with tremendous vision of how to share truth with the world. This software is available at a variety of price points, including for free, and they offer an array of features. These include study and teaching materials on the original languages, primary ancient and modern literature, lexicons, visual tools, semantic tools, comprehensive libraries, and much more.

Bible lesson software programs are available from many providers. Available options include the ability to create customized Bible studies and curriculum for various age groups using powerful time-saving technology. Each lesson-planning software program offers specific features for different types of needs, such as those of age-group ministers, including those with or without theological training.

Digital ministry equipping services represent a newer but expanding type of educational technology tool filling a niche. Increasingly, the best legacy material available from key leaders across Christendom is being captured on video and audio as an equipping resource. Well-produced media of significant leaders in Bible, theology, ministry, curriculum, and teaching are available in streamed video or audio format, allowing today's Christian teachers and their students to be instructed by top leaders of this and the last generation.

Christian teaching ministry websites provide a significant educational resource for today's Christian teachers. The number, quality, and content offered by various ministers and professors continue to expand, offering an inexhaustible body of materials to enrich one's teaching in any context or setting.

21. A list of searchable destinations can be found at "Books: Monographs and Collected Essays," Taylor University Library, http://library.taylor.edu/dotAsset/4726c833-e1be-4e3a-baa9-6848e7a44670.pdf.

Ministry's Challenge to Engage Educational Technology

Educational technology is here to stay, and though it does not replace teachers, it can enhance our teaching. Though philosophical and practical issues must be considered about its effective use, ample evidence points to its value and utility.[22] Some early and middle adopters have already embraced these educational tools while others have hesitated for various reasons.

The time has come for Christian teachers to embrace a more radical brand of incarnational teaching. It is one that enters the world of today's digital native and seeks to become digitally fluent in educational technology. To do this, teachers need to feel comfortable with technology, to have skills motivating students to learn with technology, and to implement educational technology at various student ability levels. Doing so will help increase the educational effectiveness of today's teachers as we learn to speak the language of the next generations.

Questions and Activities

1. Based on your reading, how would you define and/or describe "educational technology"?
2. What are the major elements of effective Christian teaching, and how does educational technology relate to them?
3. What are some strengths, weaknesses, opportunities, or threats you learned from this chapter about the possibilities of educational technology for teaching the next generations?
4. What three categories of educational technology were new to you? Do a search for what's available, and create two potential ways you could integrate them into a ministry or Bible study setting.
5. How might people in ministry work stay up to date with new technology and continue educating themselves on new resources and the new lingo of their students?

Further Reading

Miller, Matt. *Ditch That Textbook*. San Diego: Dave Burgess Consulting, 2015. Though geared toward schoolteachers, this is a rich resource for various technologies and their role in teaching and learning.

22. John Gresham, "The Divine Pedagogy as a Model for Online Education," *Teaching Theology and Religion* 9, no. 1 (2006): 24–28.

Contributors

Ron Belsterling (PhD, Talbot School of Theology) is ordained in the Christian and Missionary Alliance and is professor of youth ministry at Lancaster Bible College. He has been working in church and parachurch youth ministries in the Northeast United States for more than thirty years. Ron has extensive pastoral and clinical counseling experience and speaks regularly at youth, family, and marriage retreats and camps. Ron and his wife, Julie, have been happily married for thirty years.

Robert Brandt (PhD, Talbot School of Theology) is assistant professor of youth ministry and adolescent studies at Bethel College in Indiana. Prior to that, Robert was involved for fifteen years in full-time youth ministry in churches in California and Colorado in both associate and senior pastor positions. Robert has been married to his wonderful wife, Melody, for more than twenty-three years, and they have seven children.

Mark Cannister (EdD, University of Pittsburgh) serves as professor of Christian ministries at Gordon College and executive administrator of the Association of Youth Ministry Educators. He is the author of *Teenagers Matter: Making Student Ministry a Priority in the Church* (Baker Academic, 2013). He has served as president of the Society of Professors in Christian Education and the Association of Youth Ministry Educators and as senior editor of the *Journal of Youth Ministry*. Mark has also served in a variety of leadership capacities at Grace Chapel in Lexington, Massachusetts.

Freddy Cardoza (PhD, Southern Baptist Theological Seminary) is chair of the department of Christian education at Talbot School of Theology and Biola University in greater Los Angeles. Freddy's leadership and research primarily center on the areas of teaching, educational technology, leadership, and higher education administration. Freddy serves as the executive director of the Society of Professors in Christian Education. His website is www.freddycardoza.com.

Ken Castor (DMin, Trinity Western University) is assistant professor of youth ministry at Crown College, St. Bonifacius, Minnesota. He has authored, coauthored, and edited several student discipleship resources, including *Grow Down: How to Build a Jesus-Centered Life* (Group, 2014), and has pastored next generations to follow Jesus for twenty-five years in the United States and Canada. He enjoys drinking coffee and exploring the world with his wife, Kathy, and their three kids.

Amanda Drury (PhD, Indiana Wesleyan University) is assistant professor of practical theology at Indiana Wesleyan University and is ordained in the Wesleyan Church. She teaches, speaks, and writes on youth ministry, and her passion is to see teenagers empowered to express their faith in words and actions. She is the author of *Saying Is Believing: The Necessity of Testimony in Adolescent Spiritual Development* (InterVarsity, 2015). She resides in Marion, Indiana, with her husband and three children.

Doug Gilmer (MNR, Virginia Tech) is the founder of the Camping & Outdoor Adventure Leadership (COAL) academic program at Liberty University in Lynchburg, Virginia. Drawing on his years of outdoor experience and high adventure, he specializes in making the theoretical practical and turning seemingly routine outdoor moments into teachable moments from a biblical worldview. His outdoor cooking skills, whether over open flame or with Dutch ovens, are well known among Liberty students and much anticipated each year.

James K. Hampton (PhD, University of Kansas) is an author, speaker, and professor of youth ministry at Asbury Theological Seminary in Wilmore, Kentucky. He has written several books for both youth workers and teenagers and serves as the cofounder of Barefoot Ministries (www.barefootministries.com). An ordained elder in the Church of the Nazarene, Jim is married to the lovely Carolyn and has two great kids.

Mark Hayse (PhD, Trinity Evangelical Divinity School) is professor of Christian education, director of the undergraduate honors program, and codirector of the Center for Games and Learning (www.mnu.edu/games) at MidAmerica Nazarene University in Olathe, Kansas. He researches, writes, and consults on matters of digital and nondigital games, curriculum design, educational studies, and religious studies. His academic work is informed by twenty years of youth work in congregational and missional settings.

Allen Jackson (PhD, New Orleans Baptist Theological Seminary) is senior pastor of Dunwoody Baptist Church in Dunwoody, Georgia. Previously, Allen was professor of youth and collegiate ministry at New Orleans Baptist Theological Seminary in New Orleans, Louisiana. He has written nine books, contributed numerous chapters to books like this one, and written extensively in other youth publications. He regularly speaks for youth training events and consulting visits with churches.

Karen Jones (PhD, Southwestern Baptist Theological Seminary) is professor of ministry and missions and heads that department at Huntington University in Huntington, Indiana. She spent more than fifteen years working with youth and continues to give leadership to student mission projects each year. Jones has served on the boards of the Society of Professors in Christian Education, the International Association for the Study of Youth Ministry, and the executive board of the Association of Youth Ministry Educators.

Sharon Galgay Ketcham (PhD, Boston College) is associate professor of theology and Christian ministries at Gordon College in Wenham, Massachusetts. Sharon equips students and churches to engage in theological reflection and join God's movement in the world. She envisions a new generation of churches in which teenagers actively contribute to churches' missions, and she writes about the values churches should hold in order to accomplish this.

Jeff Keuss (PhD, University of Glasgow) is professor of ministry, theology, and culture, as well as director of the University Scholars Program, at Seattle Pacific University. He is the North American editor of *Literature and Theology* (Oxford University Press) and the author of *Blur: A New Paradigm for Understanding Youth Culture* (Zondervan, 2014); *Your Neighbor's Hymnal: What Popular Music Teaches Us about Faith, Hope and Love* (Cascade, 2013); and *Freedom of the Self: Kenosis, Cultural Identity and Mission at the Crossroads* (Pickwick, 2010).

Jason Lanker (PhD, Talbot School of Theology) is associate professor of ministry at John Brown University in Siloam Springs, Arkansas. He has written multiple articles and is a frequent speaker on the topic of youth mentoring and spiritual formation. In addition, he is a founding elder and regular speaker at New Heights, a congregation committed to the integration of youth in the life and service of the body.

Terry Linhart (PhD, Purdue University) is professor of Christian ministries at Bethel College in Indiana, where he also serves as chair of the department of religion and philosophy. He has authored numerous books on youth ministry and Christian leadership. He regularly speaks and teaches in seminars and consults with churches and international organizations on numerous research projects with the Arbor Research Group. He and his wife, Kelly, have three adult children, and they both serve as volunteer youth workers in their local church. His website is www.terrylinhart.net.

Kerry Loescher (MA, Oral Roberts University) is instructor of practical ministry in the undergraduate College of Theology at Oral Roberts University in Tulsa, Oklahoma. With more than twenty years of professional youth work experience, Kerry's passion is training leaders to help young people and their families connect the dots between Jesus and their everyday lives. She and her husband, Randy, are the proud parents of five kids, and they have three dogs.

Bob MacRae (DMin, Bethel Theological Seminary) is professor of youth ministry and also marriage and family at Moody Bible Institute in Chicago, Illinois. A veteran of more than forty years in youth ministry, Bob continues to speak to middle school and high school groups. Bob's passion is to see students become fully devoted disciples of Jesus who seek to reproduce themselves among their peers and the next generation.

Scottie May (PhD, Trinity Evangelical Divinity School) is associate professor of Christian education and ministry at Wheaton College in Wheaton, Illinois. She is coauthor with Catherine Stonehouse of *Listening to Children on the Spiritual Journey* (Baker Academic, 2010) and *Children Matter* with Beth Posterski, Catherine Stonehouse, and Linda Cannell (Eerdmans, 2005). She also contributed to *Perspectives on Children's Spiritual Formation: Four Views*, edited by Michael Anthony (B&H, 2006). Scottie's research focus is on the spiritual formation of children.

Karen McKinney (EdD, University of St. Thomas) is associate professor of biblical studies, and she teaches in the missional ministries program at Bethel University in St. Paul, Minnesota. A native Minnesotan, she is a Bush Fellow. In her varied career, she has been a youth pastor, youth leadership training specialist, youth chaplain, training consultant, and adult trainer.

Barrett McRay (PsyD, Wheaton College) is associate professor and chair of the Christian formation and ministry department at Wheaton College. He is a coauthor of *Modern Psychopathologies: A Comprehensive Christian Appraisal* (InterVarsity, 2005), a book that explores problems of mental health from a Christian perspective. He also serves as clinical director for Alliance Clinical

Associates, a multidisciplinary mental health practice.

Ginny Olson (MA, Wheaton College) is the director of youth ministry for the Northwest Conference of the Covenant Church, as well as an adjunct professor at North Park University in Chicago, consultant, writer, speaker, and trainer. She has been involved in youth ministry on a variety of levels: youth pastor, youth speaker, and a youth ministry professor at both the college and seminary levels.

David Rahn (PhD, Purdue University) is currently senior vice president for Youth for Christ USA and has taught youth ministry at Huntington University for thirty years. He has considerable research and writing credits, and his most recent book is *Symmetry: Fixing Broken Patterns for Kids in Crisis* (Youth for Christ, 2014 e-book).

Duffy Robbins (DMin, Fuller Theological Seminary), professor of youth ministry at Eastern University in St. Davids, Pennsylvania, is a respected youth ministry veteran with more than forty years of experience in the field. He speaks around the world to teenagers and people who care about teenagers. Duffy also serves as a teaching pastor at Faithbridge Church in Spring, Texas.

Andrew Root (PhD, Princeton Theological Seminary) is the Carrie Olson Baalson associate professor of youth and family ministry at Luther Seminary. He is most recently the author of *Christopraxis: A Practical Theology of the Cross* (Fortress, 2014) and *Bonhoeffer as Youth Worker* (Baker, 2014). He is also the principal leader of a John Templeton Foundation project called Science for Youth Ministry: The Plausibility of Transcendence.

Brenda A. Snailum (EdD, Talbot School of Theology) is associated faculty at Denver Seminary in Littleton, Colorado. She has more than twenty-five years of youth and family ministry experience, is author of several articles on intergenerational ministry, and is a contributor to *The Encyclopedia of Christian Education* (Rowman & Littlefield, 2015). Brenda currently serves as president of the Association of Youth Ministry Educators and is a member of the Society of Professors in Christian Education.

Troy W. Temple (PhD, Southern Baptist Theological Seminary) serves as the associate dean for graduate programs for Liberty University's School of Divinity. He has taught at Liberty University, the Southern Baptist Theological Seminary, and various schools internationally for twenty years in the fields of local church leadership, discipleship, and teaching as well as theology and family ministry. He and his wife of twenty-five years live in Virginia with their two beautiful daughters.

Scripture Index

Old Testament

Genesis
1:1 249, 273
1:26 212n1
1:26–28 274
3:15 189
3:22 222
4:17 316
4:21 316
9 190
11:6 316
12:2–3 252
17:7 189n7
19:33 222
19:35 222
22 190n8
22:12 30n15
22:17 251
39:9 222

Exodus
1:8 251
1:10b 252
3:15 189n7
4:11–12 168
9:14 30n15
19:5b–6a 252
31:3–5 316
33:13 26

Leviticus
23:33–44 274n5
23:43 30n15
25:23–24 274

Numbers
13–14 274
16:28 30n15

Deuteronomy
1:38 190n8
3:28 190n8
4:10 26
4:39 30n15
5:1–3 190n8
6 16
6:1 30
6:4–7 14
6:4–9 189n7
6:6–7 179
6:6–9 25
7:9 189n7
8:2 275
12:11 30n15
14:22–27 274
16:11 180
16:14 180
31:4 190n8
31:12 26
32–33 33
32:44 190n8
34:9 190n8

Joshua
3:10 30
4:24 30n15
23:14 222

Judges
6:10 30n15

1 Samuel
12:17 222
16:13 190n8
17 197
17:15 188
17:20 188
17:46 30n15
28:9 222

2 Samuel
7:20 30n15
12:1–7 213

1 Kings
8:60 30n15
19:19 190n8

2 Kings
17:26 30n15
19:19 26

1 Chronicles
5:18 26n2
28:9 30n15

2 Chronicles
13:5 30n15

Ezra
7:9–10 35

Job
9:5 30n15
38–40 274

Psalms
1 158
1:1–2 80
1:1–3 x
19:1 273
20:7 26
22 190
22:30–31 190n10
23 158
25:4 29
34:8 222
45:17 190n10
46:10 30n15
50:6 273
50:10 274
51 29
51:5 222
51:13 29
67:73 33
71 190
71:18 190n10
78 189
79:13 190n10
89:1 190n10
96:11–12 274
102 190
102:18 190n10
119 33
119:11 25
119:13 27
119:15–16 25
119:38 27
119:42–43 27
119:43–44 26
119:46 27

119:105 25, 28
119:130 28
119:136 28
119:151 30
119:160 30
119:165 30
119:174 30
139:14–16 87
139:23 29
145 33
145:3–7 190n10
145:4 190
148 274

Proverbs

1:7 26
1:8 25
2 190
4:1 25
4:13 26
4:23 82
9:10 315
12:10 274
18:2 31
19:3 31
21:31 141
22:6 26
23:9 31

Ecclesiastes

3:14 30n15

Isaiah

6 251
28:9 29
41:20 153
43:10 30n15
53:10–12 189n7
59:12 222
59:21 213
60:1 28

Jeremiah

2:7 274
2:19 30n15
18:1–6 213
18:18a 15

Ezekiel

20:20 30n15

Daniel

12:3 28

Hosea

13:4 30n15

Joel

1 190
2:27 30n15

Amos

2:7 261
9:15 30n15

Jonah

4:11 222

Micah

6:8 29, 30n15

Zephaniah

3:17 30n15

Zechariah

6:15 30n15
8:5 274

Malachi

2:16 30n15

New Testament

Matthew

3:3–10 275
5–7 223
5:14–16 28
5:15 153
5:19 27
5:43–48 x
5:44–45 37
6:7 226
6:26–34 223
6:27–29 153
7:3–5 29
7:28–29 240
8:19 5
10:2–3 301
10:10–13 213

10:27 32
13:3b 250
13:4 219
13:5–8 219
16:13 230
16:13–15 6
16:13–19 230
17:25 213
19:16–22 10
20:25–28 118
21:18–22 289
22:20 230
22:29 222
23 42
25:14–30 141, 289
28 27
28:16–20 153
28:18–20 xi
28:19 133
28:19–20 34–35,
   190

Mark

1:27 6
1:35 275
3:14 118
3:16–19 301
3:23 230
3:33–35 119
9:38–39 5n5
10:13–16 274
10:17–22 153, 223
10:27 223
12:13–17 153
16:15–18 153

Luke

2:41–52 26
4:16–22 26
5:1–11 114, 153
5:16 275
5:34 230
6:14–16 301
6:40 35
6:40–41 5
7:40–41 5n5
9:23–24 12
9:51 12
9:57 12
9:59 12
10:25–28 7

10:27 x
10:29 116
10:36–37 116
12:11–12 27
12:12 213
14:25–33 10
15 42
18:15–17 223
19 231
20:41 230
23 33

John

1:23 275
1:35–51 223
3:2 5n5
3:8 168
3:16 27
3:34 x
4:1–42 223
4:5–26 223
4:7–30 121
4:13 212
6:60–69 6
8:46 7
10:1–21 223
10:10 274
13 7
13:1–20 223
13:13 5
13:34 235
13:34–35 37, 190
14–16 223
14:15–23 x
14:26 27, 28, 213,
   314
15 33
15:1–8 35
15:1–10 223
15:5 29
15:12 7
16:7b–8 213
16:8 213
16:12 219
16:13 213
17:1 153
18:4 230
21:16–41 230

Acts

1:8 190, 293
2 127

2:41–47 191n17
3:11–26 243
4:13 240
4:32 11
6:3 307
6:7 11
9:26 11
11:26 10, 11
17 144
17:22–31 243
17:24 273
17:24–31 29n14

Romans

1:18–32 212n1
1:20 274
2:21 27
3:23 27
6:11 293
10:9–10 x
12 30n19
12:1–2 xi, 212n1
12:2 ix, 213
12:3–8 301
12:6–8 242, 314
12:7 27
12:9–21 xin4
13:8–14 xin4
15:6 153
16 191

1 Corinthians

2:9–14 213n3
2:11b–14 213
2:14–16 212n1
3:2 219
3:9 141
3:17 293
4:16 9
9:22–30 215
11:1 191, 213, 214
11:14 27
12 301
12:11 196
12:28 242
13 158
13:1–3 120
13:12 29

14:20 x
15:14 xi

2 Corinthians

3:18 29, 289
4:6 28
5:10 294
5:17 xi, 289, 293
7:5–6 39

Galatians

1:13–18 275
3:28 127
3:29 106
5:22–25 xi
6:1 29

Ephesians

1:5 106
1:13 293
1:18 213n3
2:6 293
2:8–9 293
3:17b–18 293
4:1–12 191n17,
   242
4:11–13 141, 175
4:11–14 x
4:11–16 301
4:13 235
4:25–5:10 xin4
5:25 294
6 25

Philippians

1:18 40
2:5–11 225
2:6–8 118
3:10 x
3:12–17 215
3:14 141
3:17 9
4:1 70
4:9 9, 70, 191

Colossians

1:9–10 xi
1:15 273

1:16–17 273
1:28 142
1:28–29 7, 147
3:1–17 xin4
3:10 45
4 191

1 Thessalonians

1:4 293
2 9
2:5–8 213
5:12–22 xin4

2 Thessalonians

2:15 28
3:7–9 9

1 Timothy

2:1–13 307
3:2 28
3:13–4:4 xin4
4:6 28
4:11 28
4:12 168, 191
6:1–2 28
6:3–5 28

2 Timothy

2:2 9, 28, 304
2:3 293
2:14–15 28
2:15 314
2:24 28
2:25 120
3:10 36
3:12 36
3:14–17 12
3:16 212
3:16–17 28, 227,
   314
4:3 28, 32

Titus

1:2 29
1:5–9 307
2:1–6 191
2:1–8 191n17
2:7 9

2:10 154
3:5–7 213

Hebrews

5:12 29
5:12–14 x–xi
5:12–6:1 219
6:1 xi
11 22
13:3 130

James

1:22–25 213
1:23–25 29
2:10 29
2:14–20 226
2:18 79
3:1 83

1 Peter

2:9 293
2:12 153
3:15 298
5:1–3 307
5:1–4 307

2 Peter

1:5–7 xin4
3:18 ix

1 John

1 27
1–2 28
1:1–4 214
1:9 27
2:5 x
2:7–14 191n17
2:20 213

Revelation

4:11 273
7:9 124, 127
12:11 298

Subject Index

accommodation, 74
accommodative learning style, 96–97
activate (curriculum design), 162
active learning, 80, 105, 262–63
activities as the curriculum, 138–39
adaptation, 73
adolescents
    diversity among, 125
    identity formation of, 179
adult learning, 164–75
adventure, 278
affective dimension of learning, 73, 80–81
affective domain, 7
    in simulations, 261, 267
affective learning outcomes, 291
age-segregated ministry, 182, 183
AIM (acronym), 143
Ambrose, 84
analysis, 232
analytic learning, 89–91
anchor identity, 177
andragogy, 167–68
Angelou, Maya, 124
antifoundationalism, 61
application, 227, 232
application questions, 233

appreciation for volunteers, 308–9
approachability of teachers, 40–42
appropriation, 105n15
Aristotle, 17
asking questions, 8, 225
assessment, 288, 290. *See also* evaluation
asset-building communities, 298
assimilation learning style, 96–97, 105n15
Attention Deficit Hyperactivity Disorder (ADHD), 79
audience, 242–43
    for outdoor learning, 281
    sovereignty of, 215–16
audio tools, 320
auditory learning, 91
authenticity in teaching, 214
authoritarian teaching, 6
autism spectrum disorders, 76
awareness, 78
awe and wonder, power of, 152, 157

Babel, 316
"backward design" approach (curriculum), 146

Batterson, Mark, 278
Baym, Nancy K., 206–7
becoming, learning as, 107–9
behavioral dimension of learning, 73, 78–80
behavioral domain, in simulations, 261, 267
behavioral objectives, 52–53, 202
belonging, learning as, 106–7
Benson, Peter L., 296n4
Bible
    as basis for teaching, 25–33
    modern English versions of, 217–18
    paraphrasing of, 218, 225
    on role of outdoors, 273–75
    on technology, 315–17
    unique subject matter of, 212
Bible software, 322
bidirectional reciprocity, 179–80
bifocal vision, 253–54
blogging, 319
Bloom, Benjamin, 82, 231–33
bodily/kinesthetic intelligence, 93
Bonhoeffer, Dietrich, 18

book (curriculum), 144, 244
books, 138
boredom, 174
Boshers, Bo, 303, 309
brain, 71–72, 79, 88–89
Bredfeldt, Gary, 32, 144, 243
Bridges, Ruby, 167
Brown, Scott, 182
Brueggemann, Walter, 15, 22
Bruner, Jerome, 222n14
Brunner, Emil, 18
Buechner, Frederick, 18
buzz groups, 237

Calvin, John, 23
canon and community, 22–23
cardinal virtues, 31
Carr, Nicholas, 205
case studies, 256–57
character development, 307
children, teaching of, 152–63
Chow, David, 301
Christianese, 217
Christian life, certitude, disruption, and mystery in, 15
Christie, Les, 309
Christlikeness, 4
church
    as family, 180, 184–86
    losing its young adults, xi–xii
Churchill, Winston, 207
church system, 131–32
clan, 180
Clark, Dawne, 309
clergy-laity distinction, 11
closed questions, 233
cognitive domain, 7
    in simulations, 261, 267
cognitive equilibrium, 74
cognitive learning, 70, 73–78, 231–33, 291
cognitivism, 46–47
collaborative learning, 152, 158

collaborative sharing tools, 320
collateral learning, 201
comfort zones, 87
communication, 211, 213, 280, 307
communication tools, 320
community, 19–20, 66, 103, 307
    and canon, 22–23
    in digital world, 207
    formation of, 107
    shaped by narrative, 250–51
compassion, 260, 280
comprehension, 231–32
concepts vs. words, 8
conditioning theories, 69–70
conjunctive faith, 166
consequences, 69–70
constructivism, 71, 222
consumerism, 252
content curation services, 321
contribution, 110
conventional morality, 75
convergent learning style, 96–97
conversion and discipleship, 11
cooperative learning strategies, 119–20
core curriculum, 149
corporate worship, 293
Crabb, Larry, 39
"creating a space," 16–17
creation, 273–74
creative methods, 32
critical appropriation, 105–6
critical realism, 62–64
critical thinking skills, 71
cue associations, 69–70
cultural awareness, 125, 126–27
curriculum, 135, 137–39
    checklist for evaluating, 150
    choice of, 161–62
    creating, 142–43
    evaluating, 147–50

theories and practice, 140–41
    types of, 50–52

daily life, discipline in, 292
Davis, Ken, 244–45
Dean, Kenda, 217n10
debriefing, 263, 265
delayed gratification, 156
delivery, 245–47
Denton, Ashley, 275
Denton, Melinda, 140
developmental assets, 298
developmentalism, 48–49
developmental process, 65
developmental relationships, 296, 298
Dewey, John, 49, 76, 116, 201, 262
digital teaching resources, 199, 317, 322–23
disciples
    as committed believers, 10
    as learners, 10
    as ministers, 10–11
    as students of the Word, 35
discipleship, xi, 9, 191, 291–92, 299–300, 310
    with children, 161
    models of, 10–12
    not separated from salvation, 11
    and teaching, 3–13
discovery learning, 77, 222n14
discussion, 229–38
disequilibrium, 74, 263
dispositional dimension of learning, 73, 81–82
distractions, 237
divergent learning style, 96–97
diversity, 124–33
divorce, 181
doing, learning as, 102–4
Downs, Perry G., x, 4, 33
Dunn, Kenneth and Rita, 94
Dykstra, Craig, 104

economic system, 129
"educated atheists," 174
education and social reform, 49
educational objectives, 52–54
educational philosophy, 44–55
educational psychology, 65, 68–69
educational system, 130–31
educational technology, 199–208, 317–23
effective teaching, 32
Eisner, Elliot, 51, 52
elaborate (curriculum design), 162
e-learning, 317
electronic research databases, 321
Elliott, Jane, 262
Elmer, Duane, 125, 127
embodied community, 207
embodied understanding, 17–18
emotional intelligence, 84
emotional support, in small groups, 109
emotions, 80–81, 94
empathy, 280
encouragement, 194, 197, 307, 309
engaging students, 216
Enlightenment, 58
epistemology, 59, 61, 62–63
e-portfolios, 321
equipping, 8
equipping teachers, 301–11
Erikson, Erik, 115, 165n1
Estep, Karen Lynn, 139
evaluation, 233, 285, 287–300
    of volunteers, 309
evaluation questions, 233
evangelism, 294–95
exegetical (expository) approach, 243
experiential learning, 95–98, 104–5, 152, 156–57, 262–63

explicit curriculum, 50, 199–200
expressive objectives, 54
eye contact, 127
Ezra, consistency of study and behavior, 35

face-to-face intimacy, 207
facilitation skills, 266
faith, practice of, 110
faith formation
    and community, 103–4
    as messy process, 46
    in ministry setting, 109
faithfulness, 289–90
faith journey, cycles in, 15
family
    church attendance of, 180
    and faith formation, 176–78, 179–80
    fragmentation of, 181
    functional view of, 176–77
    structural view of, 176–77
family-based youth ministry, 184
family-equipping approach to ministry, 183–84
family-integrated approach to ministry, 182–83
family life, 293–94
Farley, Edward, 16
fathers, spiritual influence of, 182
field trips, 54, 156
Finkel, Donald, 75
focus, 237
following Jesus, 12
Ford, Leighton, 254
formal assessment, 288
formation, 241
foundationalism, 58–61
4MAT learning style model, 97, 145–46
Fowler, James, 166–67
Frankena, William K., 154
Franklin, Benjamin, 91
Freire, Paulo, 46–47, 48, 83

friendship, 292
fruitfulness, 289–92
fruit of the Spirit, 31
fun, 174

Gangel, Kenneth, 27
Gardner, Howard, 92–93, 145
gender, and technology, 206
generational interaction, 195
generation gap, 181
generative empowerment, 189–98
genetics, 177
gifting, 196, 304
global learners, 89–91
God
    desires to be known, 29–30
    narrative of, 254–55
Gorman, Julie A., 6
Great Commission, 27, 34 35, 133
Greene, Maxine, 201
Gregory, John Milton, 213–26
Gregory the Great, 67
Groome, Thomas, 103–4, 105–6
group collaboration platforms, 318

Habermas, Ronald, 69, 73, 81
hanak, 26
Hauerwas, Stanley, 103
Hayes, Edward, 28
heart, 23, 82
Hendricks, Howard, 229
hermeneutic, 142
hidden curriculum, 50–51
hierarchy of needs, 115, 233–36
Hipps, Shane, 204
holistic formation, 7, 104
Holt, John, 47, 156
Holy Spirit
    application by, 213
    change through, 212n1

illumination of, 28
teaching ministry of, 27
homework of teacher, 215
hook (curriculum), 144,
    244
Houle, Barbara, 302
household, 180
humanism, 47–48
humility, 39–40, 66
Hunter, George, III, 187
Hunt, Josh, 292, 293, 296

iceberg metaphor (cul-
    ture), 128
identification, 105n14
identity formation, 251–53
Ihde, Don, 205
illuminate (curriculum de-
    sign), 162
illumination, 28
illustrations, 246
image of God, 86
image tools, 320
implicit curriculum, 50–
    51, 200, 201
individualism, 58, 181,
    185, 252
individuation, 179
individuative-reflective
    faith, 166
indoctrination, 50
industrialization, 181
informal assessment, 288
informal interactions, 4
information, 231, 241
information processing
    theories, 70
innovation, 206
instructional objectives, 52
instrumental use of knowl-
    edge, 49
integrate (curriculum de-
    sign), 162
intellectual disabilities, 76
intentionality, 193
intergenerational commu-
    nity, 184
intergenerational ministry,
    185
interpretation creates
    community, 107

intimacy, 172–73
intimate family life,
    293–94
intimate friendships, 292
intrapersonal intelligence,
    93
intuitive-projective faith,
    166
Issler, Klaus, 73, 81

Jackson, Philip, 201
Jesus-centered character,
    192–93
Jesus Christ
    asked questions, 6–7,
        229–30
    discipling ministry of,
        5–6, 9–10
    "exampling" approach to
        teaching, 7
    expected fruit, 289
    love of, 7, 118
    parables of, 6–7, 116
    as a person, 63
    respecting cultural diver-
        sity, 127
    teaching ministry of, 6,
        118–19, 153, 223
job descriptions, 110
Jobs, Steve, 203
Jones, Karen, 145
Jones, Timothy Paul, 182
Joplin, Laura, 280, 281
Jung, Carl, 95
justice system, 129–30

Kaplan, Martin, 302
Kapp, Alexander, 167n3
Kaufman, David, 260–61
kinesthetic learning,
    91–92
kingdom of God, 7, 250
Kinnaman, David, xi–xii
Knight, George, 45
knowing God, 26, 29–30,
    241–42
knowledge, 62, 231
Knowles, Malcolm, 167–
    68, 171
Kohlberg, Lawrence,
    74–75, 165n1

Kolb, David, 263–64
Krathwohl, David, 82

lamad, 26
Lambert, Dan, 233
Lane, Patty, 128
Langland, William, 14–15
language of teaching,
    216–18
large groups, 239–48
Larson, Scott, 113
Lawrence, Rick, 192, 194
lay ministry, 294
leadership, shared, 190
leadership training, 304–5
learner, interest of, 215–16
"learner-based" approach,
    197
learners' perspective on
    curriculum, 148
learning
    as active engagement,
        105
    as becoming, 107–9
    as belonging, 106–7
    dimensions of, 72–83
    as doing, 102–4
    as experiencing, 104–5
    with others, 71, 105
    as transformative, 32
"learning by association,"
    69
"learning by example," 70
"learning by mental pro-
    cessing," 70
learning disabilities, 76
learning outcomes, 265,
    291
learning portfolios, 321
learning preferences,
    88–89
learning process, 104,
    224–27
learning styles, 94–97,
    145, 156
learning theories, 69–72
"learning through collabo-
    ration," 71
LeBar, Lois, 80
lecturing, 76, 241
LeFever, Marlene, 257

L'Engle, Madeleine, 249
Lewis, C. S., 31, 86
"life to lesson" approach,
   71
light, Word as, 28
likeness of Christ, 227
likeness of God, 212n1
listening, 83, 216
live chat tools, 320
locate (curriculum design),
   162
logical/mathematical intelligence, 93
look (curriculum), 144–45,
   244
Loughlin, Gerard, 251
love, 29, 36–37
Luther, Martin, 19

Martyn, J. Louis, 253
Masia, Bertram, 82
Maslow, Abraham, 115,
   233–36
maturity, x–xi, 4, 7, 31
Mayer, John, 94
Mays, Larry, 293, 296
McCarthy, Bernice, 97, 145
McLuhan, Marshall, 204–
   5, 207, 240
McTighe, Jay, 146
mechanistic approach to
   teaching, 65
memory, 200
mentoring, 70, 193
mirror, Word as, 29
mission, 18
missional mind-set, 195
mission trips, 54
mobility, 181
modernity, 58–61, 62
Montessori education, 140
moralism in curriculum,
   147
motivation
   of students, 66, 112–22
   of teachers, 302–3,
     310–11
multicultural teaching
   ministry, 132–33
multiple intelligences,
   92–93, 145

musical/rhythmic intelli-
   gence, 93
mythical-literal faith, 166

narrative, 243, 249–58
   as mirror, 250–51
   as pragmatic, 251
   shapes identity, 251–53
naturalist intelligence, 93
nature and nurture, 177
neurological disorders, 76
neuroscience, 71, 88–89
neurotheology, 71–72
new scholasticism, 45
next generation as focus of
   God's mission, 189–90
Nouwen, Henri, 16–17,
   19, 83
nuclear families, 184–85
null curriculum, 51–52,
   149, 200

objective culture, 128
O'Donnell, Peter, 115
Old Testament, family in,
   180
ontology, 63
open questions, 233
open source, 206
opportunity to lead, 195
organization of teacher,
   215
organizing principle of curriculum, 143
outdoor ministry, 272–84
overbearing group mem-
   bers, 237

pace-setting, 133
Palmer, Parker, 16, 79, 168
paradigmatic challenges,
   196–97
paraphrasing Scripture,
   218, 225
parenting style, 179
parents, equipping of, 185
participation, 110, 132
passion for God, 294
Pattison, Stephen, 16
Paul
   as discipler, 9
   on Holy Spirit, 213n3

Mars Hill discourse, 144
   teaching of, 27–28
   and Timothy, 36, 120
Pazmiño, Robert, 68
pedagogical objectives and
   methods of curriculum,
   147
performance objectives, 52
personality types, 95
Peterson, Eugene, 20
Phillips, Susan, 308
philosophy of education,
   44–55
physiological needs, 234
Piaget, Jean, 73–75, 77–78
Pineda-Madrid, Nancy, 107
planning for outdoor
   teaching, 281–83
Plueddemann, Jim, 118–
   19, 126
pluralism, 60
political system, 129
population, 132
possessive leadership, 196
postconventional moral-
   ity, 75
postfoundational critical
   realism, 62–64
postmodernity, 59–61
power, 132
practice, 18–19, 103, 110
practices of ministry, 63
practicing delivery, 246
pragmatism in curriculum,
   148
preaching, 241
preconventional moral-
   ity, 74
preparation for large
   group talk, 243–45
priesthood of all believers,
   169
primal or undifferentiated
   faith, 166
problem-solving objectives,
   53
psychology, 68–69
psychomotor domain, 7
psycho-motor learning outcomes, 291
public education, 181

public learning resources, 321
public speaking, 241
Puentedura, Ruben R., 205–6
purpose, 152, 153–55
purposeful narrative, 133

qualitative reporting, 298–99
quantitative reporting, 299
questions, types of, 233
quietness in teaching children, 157

racism, 131, 262
rationalism, 45, 59
reason, 58
reconstructionism, 49–50
Renaud, Lise, 260–61
Renfro, Paul, 182
repetition, 149, 224, 227
revelation of God as foundation of Christian education, 141–42
Richards, Lawrence, 32, 144, 243
right brain/left brain theory, 88–89
risk as essential to outdoor learning, 278
Robinson, Haddon, 246
role-playing, 261
Root, Andrew, 9
Rosenstock-Huessy, Eugen, 167n3
Rousseau, Jean-Jacques, 48
Ryken, Leland, 36, 40–41, 67–68

sacrificial giving, 295
safety needs, 234–35
Sagarin, Brad, 302
Salovey, Peter, 94
Samaritan woman, 121, 126
SAMR (model for educational technology), 205–6
sanctification, 107

Sankofa Experience (North Park University), 131
Santos, Jason, 177
Sauvé, Louise, 260–61
science, 315
scope and sequence in curriculum, 148–49
SCORRE™, 244–45
"scratch an itch," 169–71
Scripture, memorization of, 52–53
Search Institute, 295–97
secondary socialization, 177–78
self, 108
self-actualization, 233n4, 236
self-discovery, 221–24
self-esteem, 292
sensitivity, 280
sensory impairment, 76
sensory learning, 91–92
Setran, David, 193
setting and curriculum, 139
seven laws of teaching, 213–26
"shared praxis," 105–6
shema, 189
Shimoni, Rena, 309
short-term missions, 280
shy students, 237
silence, moments of, 236–37
simulations, 259–71, 317
sin, 212n1
skills, 53
  in outdoor ministry, 280
Skinner, B. F., 202
slowness in teaching children, 157
small groups, 109
Smith, Christian, 140
Smith, Efrem, 133
social collaboration tools, 318
social construction, 61, 62
social environments, 65
social learning theories, 70, 101–9

social media, 203–4
social needs, 235
social networks, 318
social participation, 152, 158
social reform, 49
Socratic method, 230
specialized training, 308
spiritual formation, 3, 104
spiritual growth, x–xi, 3
stages of faith (Fowler), 166–67
stage theory, 165–67
Stanley, Andy, 244
STEM fields, 206
stimuli and responses, 69
story, 22–23, 249–50
storytelling, 255–56
Stott, John, 241
students and curriculum, 139
subjective culture, 128
Sukkot, 274
synthesis, 232
synthetic-conventional faith, 166

talents, parable of, 141
target programming, 221
teachable moments, in outdoor activities, 277–78
teacher
  as approachable, 40–42
  character of, 31–32
  as the curriculum, 138
  as discipler, 34–35
  embodies message, 240
  as exemplary, 35–36
  as humble, 39–40
  knowledge of, 214
  as loving, 36–37
  metaphors for, 118–19
  as transparent, 38–39
teacher training
  initial, 305–8
  ongoing, 306–8
teaching
  for change, 171–72
  as co-learning, 168–69
  context for, 21–22, 139, 149

268

L·7559.38

difficulty of, 211
and discipleship, 3–13
involves listening, 83
for learning, 211–28
and life, 153
as preparing, 8
toward fun, 174
toward intimacy, 172–73
teaching methods, 209, 223
teaching outdoors, 272–84
technique, 168
technolatry, 315
"technological" approach to
teaching, 202
technology, 199–208, 241,
286, 314–17
technophobia, 315
techno-utopianism, 204
TED Talk, 245
teenagers as teachable,
140–41
Teilhard de Chardin,
Pierre, 272
telling, 75–76
Ten Commandments, 52
testimony, 63
text tools, 320
thematic approach, 243
theological basis of cur-
riculum, 147
theological education by
extension, 116
theological virtues, 31
theology of education,
14–24
Timothy, 27, 36
took (curriculum), 145, 244
topical training, 307
traditioning, 107

training, 195
transformation
from the Bible, 213
learning as, 32, 170, 226
transmissive education,
45–46, 48
transparency in teaching,
38–39
tribe, 180
truth as sequential,
218–19
Turkle, Sherry, 207
Tyler, Ralph, 202

understanding, 78
universalizing faith, 167

Vella, Jane, 80, 83
verbal/linguistic intelligence, 93
verse-by-verse approach,
243
video tools, 320
virtual world tools, 318
virtues, 31
visual learning, 91–92
visual/spatial intelligence,
93
Volf, Miroslav, 106
volunteers
motivating, 302–3,
310–11
recruiting, 302–5
retaining, 308–9
training, 305–8
Vygotsky, Lev, 77–78, 171

Ward, Ted, 116–18
Watters, Audrey, 206

ways of knowing, 92
webcasting, 318
web conferencing, 318
websites, 319, 322
Wenger, Etienne, 101–2,
106–8, 110
Wesley, John, 107, 109, 174
Westerhoff, John, 103, 174,
251
Wiggins, Grant, 146
wiki tools, 319
wilderness, 274–75,
277–78
Wilhoit, James, 36, 40–41,
67–68
Wilkins, Michael, 10–12
Willard, Dallas, 3, 82, 104
wisdom, 78
Witkin, Herman, 89
Wolterstorff, Nicholas, 73
Woodward, James, 16
worldview, 128, 226n21
worship, 307
Wright, N. T., 21
Wuthnow, Robert, 109

Yount, Rick, 8
youth ministry, 63, 176,
181, 182, 184
humble vision for, 185
modernist approach to,
59
postmodern approach,
60–61

"Zone of Proximal Devel-
opment" (ZPD), 77,
171–72

3 4711 00228 0214